Neo-Confucianism

We dedicate this book to our families

Neo-Confucianism

A Philosophical Introduction

Stephen C. Angle and
Justin Tiwald

Polity

First published in 2017 by Polity Press

Polity Press
65 Bridge Street
Cambridge CB2 1UR, UK

Polity Press
350 Main Street
Malden, MA 02148, USA

ISBN-13: 978-0-7456-6248-0
ISBN-13: 978-0-7456-6249-7(pb)

A catalogue record for this book is available from the British Library.

Library of Congress Cataloging-in-Publication Data

Names: Angle, Stephen C., 1964- author. | Tiwald, Justin, author.
Title: Neo-Confucianism : a philosophical introduction / Stephen C. Angle, Justin Tiwald.
Description: Malden, MA : Polity, 2017. | Includes bibliographical references and index.
Identifiers: LCCN 2016038448| ISBN 9780745662480 (hardback) | ISBN 9780745662497 (pbk.)
Subjects: LCSH: Neo-Confucianism.
Classification: LCC B127.N4 A538 2017 | DDC 181/.112–dc23 LC record available at https://lccn.loc.gov/2016038448

Typeset in 10.5 on 12 pt Sabon by Toppan Best-set Premedia Limited

Contents

Preface

The first ideas that there should be a book like this came gradually to the two of us as we each, independently, began our studies of Neo-Confucianism. Carsun Chang's two-volume *The Development of Neo-Confucian Thought*, published in the late 1950s, was still valuable but long out of date. Much of the best scholarship published in the decades since then focused on intellectual biography or the history of ideas, which we found useful but not entirely satisfactory. We were confident that Neo-Confucian ideas had the depth and sophistication to be engaged with as philosophy, but – with the exception of our teachers, Donald J. Munro and Philip J. Ivanhoe – few philosophers were paying attention to Neo-Confucianism.

A second stage in the book's emergence occurred in 2011, when Tiwald wrote a review of Angle's book *Sagehood: The Contemporary Significance of Neo-Confucian Philosophy*. Tiwald was enthusiastic but also critical, and the journal's editor asked Angle to write a reply, and subsequently invited Tiwald to write a follow-up response. Happily, this exchange resulted not in pointless sparring but in what we felt was a genuine process of mutual learning. We valued one another's perspectives and came to see that, with further conversation, we might be able to arrive at that rarest of treasures within philosophy: agreement.

When Polity's Emma Hutchinson proposed to Angle that he write an introductory book on Neo-Confucianism, therefore, he immediately thought of Tiwald and proposed that we write the book together. The conversations and debates that have ensued surpassed either of our expectations. This book is a joint product, written over a period of five years. Evernote has allowed us to share many hundreds of notes and text snippets, on the basis of which – and with the help of Dropbox – we drafted and redrafted the chapters of this book.

Early on we decided that in order to most effectively highlight the philosophical questions and debates of Neo-Confucianism, we would organize the book topically instead of chronologically – a choice that we discuss in both the introduction and in the appendix on using the book in the classroom. Over the course of the writing process, we also developed several conventions to help us organize the massive amount of information that we synthesize here. Original texts from the Neo-Confucian era and before are available in many editions. We reference these texts in our notes with acronyms (for example, YL for ZHU Xi's *Yulei*) which are all listed and explained in the appendix listing abbreviations of primary sources. Modern editions themselves, as well as modern secondary scholarship, we reference using the author-date system. We take responsibility for all translations, but have consulted existing translations whenever possible, and the notes use "cf." to refer readers to these other translations.

In our efforts to recapture the historical thinkers featured in this book we have incurred debts to many of our contemporaries. To begin with, we owe a special debt to our teachers and mentors in Neo-Confucianism, Donald J. Munro and Philip J. Ivanhoe.

We have also presented portions of this book at forums far and wide and benefited from feedback of many audiences. These include the participants in the Buddhist Roots of Neo-Confucianism group, who were John Makeham, John Jorgensen, Dan Lusthaus, and Brook Ziporyn. We thank the scholars at Academia Sinica for their valuable insights, as well as participants in two workshops at the Center for East Asian and Comparative Philosophy, City University of Hong Kong. The book has also benefited from feedback given by audiences at Seoul National University, the Third Annual Northeast Conference on Chinese Thought at Connecticut State University, the Connecticut Philosophy Reading Group, the London School of Economics, the Harvard International Interdisciplinary Conference on Middle Period China, Chengchi University in Taiwan, the International Conference on Mind and Nature in Chinese Philosophy at Tunghai University in Taiwan, Columbia University, the International Conference on Nature and Value in Chinese and Western Philosophy at Rutgers University, and audiences at the 2016 meeting of the Pacific Division of the American Philosophical Association. Among the many generous participants in these events were Ari Borrell, LEE Ming-huei 李明輝, Fabien Heubel, KIM Youngmin, Katalin Balog, Eirik Harris, KIM Sungmoon, Leah Zuo, Weimin SUN 孫衛民, SHEN Hsiang-min

沈享民, and Mathew Foust. We are particularly grateful for feedback on an early iteration of the complete manuscript from David Wong, Bryan Van Norden, JeeLoo LIU 劉紀璐, Brook Ziporyn, Kai Marchal, and PENG Guoxiang 彭國翔.

We wish to express our thanks to the Australian Research Council for funding that has, in part, supported aspects of the research underpinning this publication. Research funding from Wesleyan University was also instrumental in allowing us to meet face to face on several occasions. We have also benefited enormously from the electronic textual resources maintained by the Hong Kong Society of Humanities and by Ctext.org.

We also thank the students who joined the classes in which we presented drafts of these chapters in progress, especially including Jennifer Kanyuk, Brett Rysula, and Lisa Wilcut at SFSU, and Holt Akers-Campbell, Dylan Awalt-Conley, and Rachel Savage at Wesleyan. We are indebted to Maxwell Fong, our talented research assistant, for helping with citations and his many other contributions.

At Polity, in addition to Emma Hutchinson who initiated the project, Pascal Porcheron has been a supportive and thoughtful editor, and we are also grateful to Ellen MacDonald-Kramer and the rest of the staff.

Finally, we owe our deepest gratitude to our families for their patience and support, and love.

1

Introduction

This is a book for anyone who would like an introduction to Neo-Confucian philosophy. Most of our readers will have little or no background in Neo-Confucianism or in the last millennium of Chinese history; many will also be unfamiliar with the sources from which Neo-Confucianism emerged, such as classical-era Confucianism, Chinese Buddhism, and the great social transformation of China around the year 1000 CE. Do not worry. This Introduction is designed to help all readers get oriented, and the eight topical chapters that follow assume only that you have a basic familiarity with this Introduction. In writing the book as we have, we have of course made a series of decisions about its scope and approach, and the purpose of section 1 of the Introduction is to explain our thinking. The three key terms in our book's title help to organize what we discuss. In section 2, we turn to the background needed to make sense of the rest of the book.

1 This book

"Neo-Confucianism"

"Neo-Confucianism" is not a translation of any word that the individuals we are calling Neo-Confucians ever used to refer to themselves. We use "Neo-Confucianism" to capture the broad renaissance of Confucian thinking that emerges in the Song dynasty (960–1279) and which becomes central to Chinese and much of East Asian culture over the following eight centuries. The central reason for eschewing a native term to label this phenomenon is that no single Chinese term corresponds to the whole sweep of intellectual activity that we discuss in this book. Admittedly, we will have to be careful that the vagueness of "Neo-Confucianism" does not lead us into historical inaccuracies or the sense that all "Neo-Confucians" agreed with one another.[1] In a work such as this, which spans multiple centuries and dynasties, it remains the case that native terms are inadequate to call attention to all the continuities and also the differences that we believe are important.

Within Neo-Confucianism, we also recognize a narrower, though still quite diverse, category that we call "Daoxue" – a native term that can be translated as "Learning of the Way." This term emerges early in the Song to refer to an emphasis on the moral Way instead of on literary attainments and soon becomes a label used by the brothers CHENG Hao and CHENG Yi and the many subsequent philosophers who saw themselves as developing the Cheng brothers' ideas.[2] The scope of the movement and of the label narrows in the thirteenth and later centuries, though, such that many Ming dynasty thinkers who share a great deal with earlier Daoxue come to reject the label.[3] In this book, we use "Daoxue" in essentially the way that twelfth-century Chinese used it, except that we extend their inclusive sense of Daoxue ideas forward into later centuries, instead of restricting it to a narrow kind of orthodoxy centered on the teachings of ZHU Xi, as happened historically.[4] We are therefore comfortable referring to many Ming dynasty Confucians as Daoxue thinkers who themselves would have rejected such a label. Importantly, though, throughout our era there are individuals who count as Neo-Confucians but not as adherents of Daoxue. These critics of Daoxue orientations – people like SU Shi, WANG Tingxiang, and DAI Zhen – form important parts of Neo-Confucian discourse.

As we will emphasize throughout the book, Daoxue thinkers often disagreed with one another. We find the ways in which these differences have been marked in the past, such as different scholarly genealogies, regional identities, and ideas of "orthodoxy," to be of limited use for our purposes. This is important data for intellectual historians, and can often help us understand particular texts or statements, but is less central to the idea-driven approach that we take here.[5] Most scholarship on Neo-Confucianism from the twentieth century to the present divides what we call Daoxue up into two "schools," generally referred to as Cheng–Zhu Pattern learning (*lixue*) and Lu–Wang heartmind learning (*xinxue*).[6] Each school is named after the two figures putatively at its core – CHENG Yi and ZHU Xi, and LU Xiangshan and WANG Yangming, respectively – and are sometimes also distinguished as "rationalism" and "idealism." For three reasons, we find the division of Daoxue into these two schools to be problematic. First, it does not correspond with historical reality. Certainly, there is truth to an explicitly recognized "Cheng–Zhu" configuration, but there was no corresponding Lu–Wang grouping, so seeing Neo-Confucianism as structured by two competing schools is misleading.[7] Second, dichotomizing Daoxue into two schools both overemphasizes the differences among many ideas and thinkers, and it leaves no place for thinkers clearly within the Cheng–Zhu lineage who demonstrate key philosophical emphases that supposedly are the purview of "Lu–Wang." We will see that there are a range of issues that crosscut the supposed Cheng–Zhu/Lu–Wang divide. Third, the association of the two schools with "rationalism" and "idealism" is greatly misleading, no matter how those terms are understood. So we will avoid this talk of "schools." Still, we do acknowledge that there is some truth lying behind such locutions, and we think that readers find it helpful to have rough categories into which they can place Neo-Confucian thinkers. Therefore, we talk about three general areas of emphasis within Daoxue: vital stuff, nature, and heartmind. This is graphically expressed in Table 1.1 (and in the fuller version of the same table included as appendix 2 at the back of the book). These central categories (vital stuff, nature, and heartmind) are introduced in the first three topical chapters. All these thinkers are discussed at some length in the book (and still more will receive brief mention), with the four individuals marked by shaded boxes featuring most prominently.

To sum up, our book is concerned with Neo-Confucianism in quite a broad sense, ranging from the eleventh through the eighteenth centuries. Our main attention is directed at developments in China but, since Neo-Confucian thinking extended to the rest of East Asia, we will sometimes be able to point out philosophically significant innovations outside China.

"Philosophical"

The second key term in the book's title is "philosophical." As was the case with "Neo-Confucianism," neither "philosophy" nor its translation into Chinese (*zhexue* 哲學) was used by the thinkers whom we study here. A term corresponding to the English word "philosophy," like those for "religion," "politics," and many others, did not exist in Chinese prior to the nineteenth century.[8] And it was only in the early twentieth century that Chinese and foreign scholars began explicitly to refer to "Chinese philosophy" (*zhongguo zhexue*).[9] These facts have allowed for much debate, both within China and without, over

Table 1.1 Prominent Neo-Confucians			
Dynasty	Vital stuff emphasis or Other	Nature emphasis	Heartmind emphasis
Northern Song (960–1127)	ZHOU Dunyi 周敦頤 (1017–1073)		
	ZHANG Zai 張載 (1020–1077)		
	CHENG Hao 程顥 (1032–1085)		
			CHENG Yi 程頤 (1033–1107)
Southern Song (1127–1279)			ZHANG Jiucheng 張九成 (1092–1159)
		ZHU Xi 朱熹 (1130–1200)	
			LU Xiangshan 陸象山 (1139–1193)
Ming (1368–1644)	LUO Qinshun 羅欽順 (1465–1547)		
			WANG Yangming 王陽明 (1472–1529)
	WANG Tingxiang 王廷相 (1474–1544)		
Qing (1644–1911)			HUANG Zongxi 黃宗羲 (1610–1695)
	DAI Zhen 戴震 (1724–1777)		

whether it is in fact appropriate to analyze China's traditions of learning as philosophy. Many pioneering scholars of "Chinese philosophy," especially in China, took their major categories of analysis from existing approaches to western philosophy and sought ways to fit Chinese traditions into these frameworks. This meant identifying Chinese thinkers as "rationalists" or "empiricists," "materialists" or "idealists," or as advocates of "heteronomy" or "autonomy." Such work is often based on meticulous readings of the texts and can be helpful if used carefully, and we ourselves sometimes find it convenient to use terms like "metaphysics" or "epistemology" in loose senses, but we are sympathetic with the many critics who argue that whenever one tries to fit Chinese traditions into pre-existing categories, there is a danger of misunderstanding the source material.[10] At the same time, we resist the extreme conclusion of some of these critics, which is to reject the idea that traditional Chinese scholars can be thought of as engaged in philosophy. So long as "philosophy" is understood in an appropriately broad sense, we believe that it is obvious that Neo-Confucians (and Chinese thinkers of other eras) were engaged in philosophy, and that it is fruitful to view them this way.

Philosophy is systematic reflection on our existence, seeking to answer questions like "What is our place in the cosmos?" or "How should we best live our lives?" For many philosophers – very much including the Greeks who stood at the beginnings of western philosophy – the asking and answering of such questions was part of a philosophical way of life: that is, philosophy is not confined to abstract, intellectual pursuits but is implemented in one's daily life.[11] We think that even cursory examination of the Neo-Confucian thinkers we cover in this book makes it clear that they were centrally committed to philosophy in precisely this sense. They discoursed about issues from the structure of the cosmos, to the proper organization of human society, to the best means of personal improvement; and they sought to implement their ideas in their state, society, schools, and families. As with any other philosophers, they of course had multiple motives for what they did. At various times they sought status, political influence, wealth; they debated not just because they cared about living the best possible life, but also because they sought greater influence within the Neo-Confucian community. These various motives are critical to the intellectual, social, and political histories of their era, and they sometimes lie in the background of our own interpretations of Neo-Confucian philosophy. For the most part, though, our focus is on the ideas.

One difference between our approach and many previous discussions of Neo-Confucian philosophy, we have said, is that we will not try to fit Neo-Confucianism into pre-existing western categories. We let the Neo-Confucians speak in their own terms. Another, equally important difference is that we strive to do this in a way that is maximally accessible to our modern, English-speaking readers. Accessibility does not just mean that we seek to write as clearly as possible; more importantly, it means that we want our readers to be able to make sense of Neo-Confucian categories and arguments. It is not enough that one learns that ZHU XI holds that Pattern is identical to nature. One has to know what this means, have a grasp of the key concepts, be able to deploy them in new ways, and see their point. We want our readers to learn to see and engage with the world in Neo-Confucian terms to the extent that this is possible. Only then can they begin to critically engage with Neo-Confucian ideas in the manner that philosophy demands. Let us be clear: our project here is not full-fledged, constructive, comparative philosophy. In the book's conclusion, we discuss some of the ways that today's scholars (from East and West) have sought to put Neo-Confucianism into critical dialogue with other ideas in ways that may lead all sides to learn and change. But this sort of philosophical construction is a possible outcome of books like this, not the goal of our book itself. Even though a history of philosophy like this one does not engage in open-ended philosophical construction, it still must make it possible for us to reflect on the Neo-Confucians' ideas, and not just learn to parrot back the Neo-Confucians' words.

In keeping with our recognition that Neo-Confucian thinkers have multiple motives for teaching and arguing as they did, we also understand that there can be various different "points" to making a given theoretical assertion, including gaining adherents or influence at court. Our focus here, though, is on what is at stake philosophically, and this goal of making the philosophy accessible informs the structure of our book in two major ways. First, the book is organized topically rather than chronologically or biographically. Second, within each chapter, we emphasize philosophical disputes (both within Daoxue, and between Daoxue thinkers and other Neo-Confucians). We have made these choices because within each chapter we can then focus on those thinkers or texts who make the most interesting philosophical contributions on a given topic, while also bringing out ideas that are shared by many individuals, without too much repetition. We feel that when we examine different solutions to shared philosophical problems – even when these solutions are separated in time, and perhaps not directly responsive to one another – we can more readily see what is at stake in the problems with which the Neo-Confucians grappled.

Our decisions about what topics to cover have mainly been guided by our judgment of what concepts and topics are central to Neo-Confucian philosophy. Many chapters are loosely organized around one or two key concepts, such as "nature," "heartmind," or "knowing." Following the model of an influential twelfth-century anthology of Neo-Confucian writings, we arrange these topics in a progression from most general and abstract at the beginning to most concrete and practical toward the end. As we emphasize throughout the book, though, these concepts are all interrelated, and for all Neo-Confucians, the abstract and general issues are intimately related to concrete goals of personal development and social harmony. So while the chapters do not necessarily have to be read in order, they do build on one another. For the most part, we expect that the topics we have chosen would not surprise a Song or Ming dynasty Neo-Confucian, should one be reborn today. One exception might be the degree to which we have emphasized issues of women and gender in chapter 8. As we explain there in more detail, such issues were indeed discussed by men – and occasionally women – during the Neo-Confucian era, but with few exceptions they were hardly matters of central concern. We have chosen to highlight these discussions because we know that what to make of the Neo-Confucians' default, usually unreflective assumption of a gender hierarchy, can be an obstacle to many moderns taking Neo-Confucianism seriously. We do not write as apologists for Neo-Confucianism so we face its shortcomings directly. Still, we do hope to show that Neo-Confucianism, like so many other patriarchal philosophical and religious traditions, need not be as exclusivist as its adherents and practitioners assumed. In the same vein, we have chosen to translate certain terms in gender-neutral ways. Although these translations (for example, "people" instead of "men" for *ren* 人; "superior person" instead of "gentleman" for *junzi* 君子) are semantically appropriate, they might be thought to conceal the fact that the "people" about whom the Neo-Confucians were writing were often only men. Again, our intention is not to hide anything but rather to open these writings up to understanding as best we can. Finally, let us note here that contemporary Euro-American philosophers might be surprised at certain absences: for example, there is no chapter here on philosophy of language. We hope our readers will come to see these disparities not as evidence that Neo-Confucians were not philosophers, but rather as evidence of the historically contingent ways in which different philosophical traditions around the world have developed.[12]

The book's topical organization foregrounds ideas rather than historical context. We nonetheless recognize the importance of understanding ideas and thinkers as existing in history and have accounted for this in several ways. Most basically, while our presentation of the ideas focuses on philosophical reasoning, we take our interpretations of the ideas to be accountable to the full context and have referenced historical scholarship in our notes when it is especially relevant. This Introduction also contains a survey of the history of Neo-Confucianism (and of the societies and institutions that produced it) that, while concise, is based on the most current scholarship available. This history is regularly referenced and supplemented by information in specific topical chapters.

If Neo-Confucianism can be fruitfully studied as philosophy, what does this say about its relation to that western category with which philosophy is often contrasted, namely, religion? The first thing to realize is that, while various explicit distinctions between "philosophy" and "religion" have been with us in the West at least since the Greeks, this type of differentiation does not map onto any of the ways in which Neo-Confucians or their predecessors divided up the world. Rituals associated with the followers of Confucius were undertaken at individual, family, and state levels, including the enshrinement of major Neo-Confucian figures in state-run temples.[13] The canonical "classics," many of which were believed to have been edited if not authored by Confucius, were memorized, recited, and exhaustively studied, enough so that at least some modern scholars believe they belong in the category of "scripture."[14] One broad distinction that was commonly employed in the Neo-Confucian era is between a focus on "culture" (*wen* 文), which means texts, poetry, and commentary, and on the "Way" (*dao* 道), which means both personal and social transformation. But this distinction does not help us with placing Neo-Confucianism into either "philosophy" or "religion," since both religion and philosophy have elements that fit into "culture" and "Way."

A second and important point is that just because a tradition is a religion, it doesn't necessarily rule out the possibility that it is a philosophy as well. Western philosophy in the medieval and early modern periods was almost entirely both, and the philosophical views of Aquinas and Descartes are at least as difficult to extricate from their religious commitments as are the works of CHENG Yi and WANG Yangming. Arguably, this is even truer of Aquinas and Descartes than of any of the major Neo-Confucian philosophers. If we adopt a broad understanding of religion, such as Frederick Streng's widely cited view that religion is any "means of ultimate transformation," then there should be little doubt that Neo-Confucianism is religious in this sense, so long as we keep in mind that, for Neo-Confucians, the "transformation" in question is a this-worldly affair.[15] As we will see, beginning in chapter 2, Neo-Confucian ideals like "supreme void," "Pattern," and "supreme pivot" qualify as "ultimate" standards, but they are not wholly disconnected from the world of our everyday experience. This is not yet the time to go into details, so suffice it to say that, even though there is some talk by Neo-Confucians about spirits, and undoubtedly a reverential attitude toward a cosmos that they take to be meaningful and full of value, "nevertheless, the chief significance of spirit and spirituality in Neo-Confucianism is not a transcendence of the natural order but a continuity with it....Spirit, or spirituality, is the perfection of human understanding – *ordinary* human understanding."[16]

In addition, it will become clear as the book proceeds that we take seriously the sustained engagement among Neo-Confucianism, Buddhism, and Daoism. This is not a matter of a "philosophy" reacting against two "religions" but rather the complex interactions among three multifaceted traditions of theory and practice. Quite regularly, the dividing lines between the three are blurred, with texts, terminology, and practices appropriated in multiple directions. Nonetheless, it is clear that many Neo-Confucians took there to be a significant difference between their views and those of the Daoists and (especially) Buddhists. While sometimes this was more an issue of sectarian politics than philosophical dispute, we will show that often enough there were important philosophical issues underlying such arguments.

"Introduction"

The final word in our title is "Introduction," and we take a few moments here to address the distinctive features of our approach. We are writing for (at least) four different audiences: instructors who use this book as part of their courses; students in their classes; non-specialists who read the book independently of a course; and fellow specialists in Neo-Confucianism. Since we have done our best to present a synthetic account that reflects the best, state-of-the-art secondary scholarship, as well as offering our own, novel interpretations whenever needed, we hope that specialists will find our account of use. We feel that all readers will benefit from our effort to make the philosophical concerns of the Neo-Confucians accessible to contemporary readers in English. Both authors have considerable experience teaching Neo-Confucianism, including using draft versions of this book in our classes. One of our favorite anecdotes about teaching these ideas occurred some years ago in the midst of Angle's first-ever course on Neo-Confucianism, when a student noted that what she liked so much about the class was how "relevant" she found it. She had grown up without explicit moral or religious instruction, and so this turned out to be the first time she had been exposed to a rigorous, systematic way of talking about our place in the world and our responsibilities to one another. She was encountering Neo-Confucianism not simply as historical facts but as provocative, intelligible concepts – even if, in the end, they may rely on assumptions about the cosmos that she could not personally accept. We hope that many readers find themselves similarly engaged by the Neo-Confucians' ideas.

Our aim has been to make sure that everything that a newcomer to Neo-Confucianism needs to understand our subject is present on the pages of our main text, whereas references, further details, and justifications of interpretive choices we have made are all found in the endnotes. In addition to the main text and the endnotes, we provide four other types of support. First, bearing in mind that most existing courses on Neo-Confucianism are organized chronologically, we offer an appendix that explains how courses can be successfully designed following the topical approach of our book. Second, at the end of each of the topical chapters we append suggested primary source readings that match well with the themes of the chapter, along with several questions that should prompt readers to think critically about the ideas in the chapter. Third, at the back of the book we include a complete listing of dates and philosophical emphases for all Neo-Confucians covered in the book, as well as an index listing key technical terms. Finally, at the book's associated website (http://www.neo-confucianism.com) we document the original Chinese text corresponding to every quotation in the book; make available sample syllabi for different ways in which the book can be used; and maintain a blog where we discuss new scholarship, translations, and teaching ideas.

2 Background

Chinese language, Chinese names, and translation

The language in which Neo-Confucians wrote the texts on which this book is based is Literary Chinese, a language that played a role in China somewhat akin to the function of Latin in Europe. We translate all texts we quote or paraphrase and all the Neo-Confucians' technical terms. In some cases, though, it is useful to be able to refer directly to the Chinese word (for example, when discussing different possible translations), and so sometimes we employ romanized Chinese: that is, using roman letters to spell out the pronunciation of the Chinese characters. Various systems of romanizing Chinese have been invented; we use the pinyin system, which is now the most common. English speakers can readily guess the correct pronunciation of most pinyin letters, but there are a few that cause problems. Table 1.2 sums up the more difficult cases.

Since we translate technical terms, readers will most often encounter pinyin in the form of people's names. We know that unfamiliar

Table 1.2 Pinyin

Pinyin	Pronounced as	Example(s)
qi	chee	qi (vital stuff), Qing (dynasty)
shi	sure	Su Shi (critic of Daoxue)
xin	hsin	xin (heartmind), xing (nature)
zhang	jǎng	Zhang Zai (philosopher)
zhi	jr	zhi (knowing)
zi	dz	Xunzi (Master Xun, classical Confucian)

Chinese names are difficult to remember, and we do our best to keep names to a minimum, but some names just have to be learned. A potential stumbling block with names is that the Chinese custom is the opposite of most European customs: family names come first, followed by an individual's given name. To help readers keep this straight, we use SMALL CAPS to indicate the family name whenever needed; however, in cases where we only refer to an individual by a family name, we dispense with the small caps. So, Wang is the family name of WANG Yangming; Zhu is the family name of ZHU Xi, and so on. A second challenge is that Chinese literati typically use more than one given name: they have pen names, honorary names, and so on. In this book we consistently use a single name for each thinker we discuss.

We take responsibility for all translations but have consulted existing translations, sometimes following them quite closely, and reference them in the notes (usually by appending "cf." and a citation to the translation). As mentioned above, the original Chinese texts for all passages that we translate here are available on the book's website. Our translations are guided by four principles:

1. Always translate the same term in the same way, except in cases where a given term has two very different meanings.
2. Translated sentences should be clean, clear, relatively literal renderings of the original; they should neither be too alien-seeming nor too familiar.
3. Translations of technical terms should express, as concisely as possible and as well as possible, the meaning of the term.
4. To avoid confusion when readers consult existing translations or other secondary scholarship, we will follow existing standard translations to the extent possible.

We regularly encounter some tension between principles 3 and 4. Sometimes longstanding translations are simply too problematic, and we have chosen new alternatives. To help curtail any resulting confusion, the index at the back of the book lists alternative translations, directing readers to our preferred translations.

Classical Confucianism and classical sources

The Neo-Confucians saw themselves as carrying on the teachings of the Confucian tradition's founding figures in what we now call China's classical period, more than a millennium before the emergence of Neo-Confucianism. Because the Neo-Confucians often expressed themselves in relation to these earlier figures and texts, a brief introduction to them is important. "Confucius" is the Latinized name that Jesuit missionaries assigned to KONG Qiu, who lived from 551 BCE to 479 BCE and is a central figure in the tradition of thought and practice that we now call "Confucianism." Confucius saw himself not as the founder of anything, but rather as a teacher and scholar trying to transmit values that he believed were held by earlier kings and culture heroes of Chinese civilization. In fact, though, the way that Confucius reframed these values, coupled with the enormous social and political changes that China underwent starting around the time of Confucius' life, meant that Confucius' teachings came to be seen as vital touchstones for the growing class of restive, reflective thinkers who sought to improve their society and their own lives. The era of "classical Confucianism" thus begins with Confucius and the *Analects*, a text composed largely by generations of students to present their understandings of the Master's ideas. Politically, this period is marked by increasingly violent rivalry among regional rulers as the power of the king of the Zhou dynasty waned. Soon enough, ambitious nobles declared themselves "kings" of their own realms and sought to unify the entire Sinitic world under their rule; from this point on, the period is traditionally dubbed the "Warring States" era. It ended in 221 BCE when the king of Qin succeeded in conquering his final opponent, declared himself "emperor," and founded the Qin dynasty, inaugurating China's long imperial era.

The *Analects* is far from the only significant classical-era text. Later scholars would eventually settle on a listing of Thirteen Classics, which range from compendia of speeches and stories, to ritual manuals, to early histories and commentaries, to more theoretical teachings. Some of the Thirteen were themselves made up of multiple, distinct texts, among which certain treatises received more attention than others. A partial listing of the classical texts that matter for the Neo-Confucians includes:

- The *Book of Changes*. Originally a divination manual, the *Changes* becomes a major source for thinking about the nature of the cosmos; we discuss it in chapter 2.
- The *Book of Documents*. Tells the stories of early sages like Yao and Shun who established the basic parameters for Chinese culture.
- The *Book of Rites*, among which two chapters are especially influential:
  - *Greater Learning*. This short text connects individual self-cultivation to widespread social harmony.
  - *Centrality and Commonality*. Sometimes translated as "Doctrine of the Mean," an abstract treatise that inspires many important Neo-Confucian ideas.
- The *Spring and Autumn Annals*. A very compressed, year-by-year history of the state of Lu; later authors used this text as a framework for commenting on political theories.
- The *Analects*. Sets the stage for subsequent Confucian thinking with its emphasis on the need for people to strive to realize humaneness (*ren* 仁) and ritual propriety (*li* 禮) in order to become superior people (*junzi* 君子).
- The *Mencius*. Perhaps the most influential of all early texts on the Neo-Confucians. The text is named for its author, Mencius (or Mengzi), who argued that human nature is fundamentally good, containing moral drives toward compassion and wisdom, in addition to more neutral feelings like hunger and thirst.

In addition to these texts that were designated as classics, one other important early text to which we will need to refer is the *Xunzi*, a sophisticated philosophical work by the late-Warring States Confucian thinker Xunzi. Xunzi's view that human nature is basically bad was anathema to most Neo-Confucians, but they nonetheless drew on him in other ways.

Neo-Confucianism is a revivalist movement. A key dimension of Neo-Confucianism is its insistence that important classical texts have been neglected or misunderstood. As we will see throughout this book, therefore, passages from these classical texts are hotly debated, reinterpreted (sometimes radically), and put forward as evidence for controversial claims. It is not that Confucius and the other early authors were seen as infallible or the recipients of revelation;

they were simply people, and from time to time a Neo-Confucian will (respectfully) suggest that one of the early texts may have been mistaken in some way. But there are two widespread beliefs that help to ground the Neo-Confucians' confidence in these early texts: first, that certain ancient eras – though certainly not the Warring States period – were harmonious utopias, and so worthy of emulation; and, second, that some of the people whose words are contained in the classics had attained sagehood. Although sages are people, they are people who have managed, by birth or effort, to perfect their characters so that they respond aptly to whatever situation they encounter. Their insights into political organization, cosmic order, or personal cultivation are thus of the first importance.

Buddhism and Daoism

The tradition that we are calling classical Confucianism ended when Warring States China was united under the first emperor of the Qin dynasty (221 BCE), thereby commencing what is known as the imperial era in Chinese history. In the subsequent nine centuries, the fortunes of Confucian thought both rose and declined. The first dynasty after the short-lived Qin, the Han dynasty (206 BCE–220 CE), made Confucianism its state ideology, thereby providing it with tremendous authority. Following the Han, though, was another period of instability and disunity, the Six Dynasties (220–589 CE). It was in this period that Daoism and Buddhism took hold as the two religio-philosophical traditions that were to become Confucianism's dominant and enduring rivals. Neo-Confucians regularly contrast their teachings with those of Daoism and Buddhism, though modern scholarship has revealed that all three traditions influence one another as they develop over time.[17]

The texts most often associated with Daoist thought are the *Daodejing* (also known as the *Laozi*) and the *Zhuangzi*, both of which were written in the classical period. It was not until well after the authors of these texts lived that people began to characterize them as belonging to a single school, but by the Six Dynasties era they were widely regarded as offering a relatively consistent and comprehensive vision of life and cosmological order. The *Daodejing* and, to a lesser extent, the *Zhuangzi* both used the term *Dao*, or "Way," to describe forces closely associated with the natural, cyclical changes evident in the world. Both texts promoted ways of life that were in various respects close to the Way, stressing the acceptance of the inevitability of change, ways of thinking that either pre-dated or transcended popular social conventions, and ways of life that drew on the same, spontaneous forces that moved heaven and earth. Because the major Daoist texts were frequently cryptic or admitted of a wide range of interpretations, later Daoists came to read them in diverse and sometimes surprising ways, perhaps most notably as esoteric manuals providing the alchemical secrets to long life. But even Daoists of this kind continued to share in the core vision described above. Most notable are the Daoist emphases on paring down the desires to the most natural and basic ones, and on a certain form of activity known as *wuwei* ("non-action" or "effortless action"), conceived as spontaneous, unselfconscious behavior that is modeled on or draws directly on the Way.

Buddhism was founded in India at around the same time that Confucius lived. Most historians believe Buddhism arrived in China during the Han dynasty, but it was in the Six Dynasties period that it began to have broad appeal. It was also in this era that rulers started to support and grant privileges to Buddhist leaders and sects, making it the chief rival to Confucianism for state patronage in the post-classical period. Over time, it began to develop distinctively Chinese forms, perhaps most evident in the school known as Chan (pronounced "Zen" in Japanese), which promoted forms of life that arguably came closer to Daoism than to the Buddhism of ancient India, particularly in its idealization of non-action and spontaneity. Despite these developments, however, many Chinese continued to regard Buddhism as a foreign religion.

At the heart of Buddhist thought are a specific understanding of the causes of human suffering, a vision of religious salvation, and a set of ideas about the fundamental nature of reality. Buddhists in China's imperial era believe suffering to be a product of human desire, which in turn is caused by attachment. They also uphold a doctrine of transmigration or rebirth, so that death alone does not allow people to escape this predicament. Trapped in the cycle of life and death, the only solution is to adopt practices that enable individuals to achieve non-attachment from all things, including, most controversially, from one's family. At some stage in a Buddhist's spiritual development (a process that stretches across many lives), the Buddhist must leave his or her family and become a monk or nun, and it is this requirement that most shocks the consciences of many Chinese in the imperial era. Leaving one's family is a dramatic departure from a way of life that most see as inextricable from Chinese culture and also as the core of Confucian views about moral development and the proper expression of virtue.

Buddhist views about the fundamental nature of reality are similarly dramatic. Probably the most widely shared formulation of the view among Buddhists is that all things are illusory in the following sense: they lack their own independent identity and existence. Things like wealth, health, and vision would not have the particular features that they do without other things to confer that identity upon them. In the language of Buddhism, all things are "co-dependent," "empty" of "essence" or "self-nature." But the nature of this dependence and the broader implications of the doctrine vary greatly across different Buddhist schools. One way of understanding emptiness is that the existence and nature of things comes instead from the mind or consciousness. This view is central to the Yogācāra, or "consciousness-only," school of Buddhism, one of the schools whose ideas come most directly from the Buddhism of India. However, Chinese Buddhists develop their own distinctive interpretations of the doctrine of emptiness. Some stress the interdependence of things, both on one another and on the larger whole to which they belong, as a rafter gets identity from the part it plays in supporting a house. Others propose that emptiness is characterized by a fundamental openness and receptivity called Buddha nature, understood as the underlying ground for all things, shared by all and representing the potential for Buddhahood. The concept of Buddha nature may or may not have its origins in Indian Buddhism, but in China it comes to take on a life of its own, becoming, as we will see, a major inspiration not just for Chinese Buddhists but, indirectly, for Neo-Confucians as well.

Historical overview

The new forms of Confucian thought and practice that we call Neo-Confucianism emerge over a period of centuries, and play central – albeit changing – roles in Chinese society for nearly a millennium. Our goals in this section are twofold: to offer a succinct explanation of the emergence, development, and decline of Neo-Confucianism, and at the same time to provide an historical framework into which readers can place the thinkers with whom we will be dealing in the chapters to come. The best general structure for such a narrative is the series of dynasties that make up Chinese political history (see Table 1.3).

We begin our story with the Tang, which is in many ways the culmination of the early imperial period and yet lays the seeds for the growth of the quite different political and intellectual trends to come. Neo-Confucianism is most vital during two subsequent dynasties: the Song (which is divided into two phases, northern and southern) and the Ming. Philosophical brilliance in the Qing dynasty is mostly generated by critics of Daoxue, and the whole Neo-Confucian era

Table 1.3 Chinese Dynasties from Tang to Qing

Dates (all CE)	Dynasty	Brief Description
618–907	Tang	Culturally pluralistic; dominated by great aristocratic families
960–1127	Northern Song	Rise of the literati; experiments with political reform
1127–1279	Southern Song	Song dynasty loses the north to Jurchens, who found the Jin dynasty
1271–1368	Yuan	Mongols conquer all of China
1368–1644	Ming	Powerful emperors seek to coopt Daoxue
1644–1911	Qing	Manchus conquer all of China

then comes to an end as new currents of thought – and eventually, dramatically new approaches to Confucianism – emerge in the nineteenth and twentieth centuries.

For our purposes, it is important to understand two things about the Tang era: the nature of its intellectual-social-political synthesis, and the ways in which challenges to this order are harbingers of Neo-Confucianism. At the height of the Tang – say, around 725 CE – it was possible to envision a unified, hierarchical, universal order, centered on the Tang emperor (or "Son of Heaven"). The great clans of the hereditary aristocracy staffed the empire's bureaucracy; Tang armies ensured that tribal peoples surrounding the cultural and political heartland recognized the emperor as the ultimate authority. The imperial state had elaborate means of control over commerce and local society. Scholarship and intellectual life were dominated by two things: studies of the canonical ancient classics, and an ever-growing industry of translating and commenting on Buddhist scriptures, much of which took place in the great, state-sponsored monasteries of the day.[18] Many of the key challenges to this order begin soon after the mid-eighth century rebellion of General AN Lushan, which came close to overthrowing the dynasty. In the unsettled times thereafter, intellectuals sought deeper answers than those provided by the then dominant textual approach to the classical tradition. Instead of focusing on literature and culture (or *wen*), scholars paid more attention to seeking underlying answers about the "Way" (or *dao*) that the world functioned. Buddhist and Daoist texts were helpful here, but so were certain classical texts associated with Confucius and his followers

– texts like the *Mencius, Centrality and Commonality,* and *Greater Learning.* Thinkers from a range of backgrounds drew on these texts and contributed to a shared Confucian-Daoist-Buddhist discourse about the Way, even while they often exhibited at least some sectarian leanings. In the ninth century, two of the most famous forerunners of Neo-Confucianism, LI Ao and HAN Yu, produced essays about philosophical topics that both anticipate key subjects of concern for later thinkers and (especially in the case of HAN Yu) insist on the need for a distinctively Confucian approach.[19]

Despite some similarities between late-Tang philosophers and those of the Northern Song, we agree with the scholarly mainstream in seeing the range of new, self-consciously Confucian philosophical voices that we call Neo-Confucianism as fully emerging only in the Northern Song. A combination of social and political changes created fertile ground for new theorizing. The key marker of social status in the Tang had been one's pedigree, and the society was organized around something close to a state-sponsored aristocracy. Seeking its own legitimacy, the leaders of the new Song dynasty settled on a partnership with a transformed elite class, now based more in education and claims of merit than in ancestry. Instead of official families, the elite become a "community of the educated"; Song society is far more literate and published than its Tang predecessor. We refer to this elite as the "literati."[20] In this fertile soil, the idea that literati should reflect on the Way and seek to influence their society took root and grew. With hindsight, it is possible to divide these literati voices into several groups. First is the "conventional Confucians," whose scholarship and writing continues to follow Tang models.[21] For other literati, Buddhist or Daoist texts and practices were their main sources of inspiration, though many of them also drew on and wrote about the classical Chinese tradition. The final group is the Neo-Confucians: those literati who articulated novel approaches to understanding society and cosmos, explicitly identifying themselves with the tradition of Confucius. Though they also drew on the shared Confucian-Daoist-Buddhist discourse about the Way that had emerged in the Tang, they emphasized the distinctiveness of Confucianism and often were critical of Buddhists and Daoists. Early on, one of the most influential was WANG Anshi (1021–1086), a scholar, political philosopher, and politician who twice served as prime minister. Wang promoted a vision of a unified state and society actively harmonized by top-down state activity, called the New Policies. Wang's philosophy and his policies were vigorously opposed by other Neo-Confucians, including many who would coalesce into the Daoxue movement. The most important of these was CHENG Yi (1033–1107), though we will see that there was quite a bit of diversity even among Daoxue thinkers. Beyond his theoretical innovations, Cheng was known as a strict moralist quick to criticize the failings of others; this probably contributed to the emergence in popular culture of a caricatured "Mr Daoxue."[22]

For all its commercial and cultural flourishing, the Song dynasty was continually threatened by increasingly settled, organized, and powerful groups to its north and west. In 1127, the Jurchens captured the Song capital of Kaifeng, executed the reigning emperor, and declared themselves the Jin dynasty. Enough of the Song royal family escaped south, though, to re-found the dynasty – now called the Southern Song – in Hangzhou. Confucian theorizing continues in the north under the Jin, but the center of intellectual gravity even under the Northern Song had been moving southward, and we will focus there.[23] Two major concerns of southern literati were diagnosing the reasons for the loss of the north and, at least on the part of the "War Party," advocating for its recapture. The era's philosophizing thus took place against the background of profound ethnic and cultural humiliation, and it is no accident that this was a period in which the Neo-Confucians were most concerned about purging their tradition of foreign (especially Buddhist) elements.

Like their predecessors, Southern Song literati thought of government as their vocation, but they also increasingly recognized that, despite their educational attainments, many of their number would not find a position in the state system. Combined with the growth of China's population and economy, these trends (which had already begun in the Northern Song, but accelerated now) led to members of literati families seeing an ever-higher percentage of their opportunities for playing constructive roles in their societies to be located in local, non-governmental capacities. It has been common to portray this as an "inward turn" in Neo-Confucian thinking, but more recent scholarship makes clear that while there is certainly considerable attention to personal moral cultivation, this often goes hand in hand with outward attention to society, governance, and institutions. Indeed, for some philosophers at this time, political and institutional issues take pride of place in their thinking. During the Southern Song, the Daoxue fellowship solidifies into an explicit movement that is sometimes at odds with – even proscribed by – the imperial court. In the twelfth century, Daoxue is defined by no one set of ideas or individual, though ZHU Xi (1130–1200) is gradually able to solidify a position as the movement's leader.[24] In part as a result of Zhu's efforts, the scope of the movement begins to narrow, though (as discussed above) we will use "Daoxue" here in a broader sense than it took on in the thirteenth and later centuries. Late in the Southern Song, the state also reverses course and embraces Daoxue, enshrining a number of its leaders in the Confucian Temple.[25]

Mongol clan leader Kublai Khan established the Yuan dynasty in northern China in 1271, and by 1279 had dealt the Song their final defeat. The Mongol rulers relied heavily on Chinese bureaucrats and advisers, which enabled supporters of the Daoxue movement to exert significant influence at court.[26] When the civil service examination system was reinstituted in 1313, ZHU Xi's commentaries on the classics were declared to be their officially approved basis, and when in the following years government scholars compiled the *History of the Song Dynasty*, it included a special section containing biographies of leading Daoxue figures.[27] Some of the more innovative thinking during the Yuan came from efforts of local-level activists to reform their localities; the lessons they took from their experiences subsequently informed thinkers who exerted significant influence at the beginning of the Ming dynasty.[28]

When he defeated the Mongols in 1368, the founder of the Ming dynasty ushered in an era of prosperity and cultural flourishing. The Ming sent great fleets as far as the east coast of Africa, before choosing to focus on regional challenges, in part by constructing the stone-faced Great Wall – much of which still stands today – in an effort to contain restive peoples to their north. The Ming founder drew on a range of intellectual and religious resources in crafting his moral and legal vision of empire, among which the narrow, orthodox version of Daoxue that prevailed during the Yuan played a significant role. Daoxue as a social movement at least partly independent of the state faced great challenges during the reigns of the Ming's first three emperors, however. Both the first and, especially, the third emperor worked to crush independent sources of authority and to co-opt Daoxue for the imperial court; these emperors declared themselves to be sage-kings and commissioned new compendia of Daoxue teachings as a way of broadly declaring their own moral and cultural authority.[29] Nonetheless, the spirit of Daoxue as an independent philosophical and social movement was not so easily destroyed. By the mid-Ming, thinkers proliferated who were critical of what they saw as the "vulgar" and superficial learning associated with those who simply memorized and regurgitated the imperially sanctioned curriculum. Many of these philosophers fit within our broad category of Daoxue, even if they were critical of what Daoxue had become in their own day; chief among these was WANG Yangming (1472–1529), whose distinctive formulations of Daoxue ideas shaped much of the later-Ming philosophical discourse. The Ming also had its share of philosophers who rejected core Daoxue premises; thinkers like WANG Tingxiang (1474–1544) play an important role in our book, as they help us to see a broader range of possibilities within Neo-Confucian thought.

This is a good moment to note that, while our focus throughout the book is on Chinese Neo-Confucianism, various strands of Daoxue and other Neo-Confucian teachings spread throughout the East Asian region, especially around the time of the Ming dynasty. To varying degrees, Confucian texts, practices, and institutions can be found in Korea, Japan, and Vietnam from earlier on, but it is only in the fourteenth century and thereafter that Neo-Confucian teachings make major inroads. And these influences are often profound. The establishment of Korea's Chosŏn dynasty in 1392 has been described as "history's only Neo-Confucian revolution," and Korean philosophers subsequently develop Daoxue thinking on many topics to an extremely highly level of sophistication.[30] Neo-Confucianism's role in Japan's Tokugawa era, which began in 1600, is also significant. Ideas of ZHU Xi and others had been known since the early thirteenth century but were taught mainly in Zen monasteries as supplements to other forms of Zen theory and practice. In the Tokugawa, this changes as new influences both from Chinese and from Korean Neo-Confucianism are injected into a very different intellectual and social order.[31] Neo-Confucianism plays less of a role in Vietnam, where classical Confucian ideas continue to have more sway (together with various Buddhist and other teachings), though there is still much to learn about to what degree and why Confucianism developed as it did in Vietnam's distinctive political and social context.[32]

In some ways, the Qing dynasty, founded by Manchu conquerors in 1644, reprises the relationship between state and Daoxue that we saw in the early Ming. Powerful emperors seek to establish themselves as sage-kings, and do so in less bloodthirsty (and thus less self-defeating) ways than their Ming forebears.[33] The result is that, while one can find standard-bearers for Daoxue in the Qing, the majority of innovative and influential philosophical work tended to be produced by thinkers who stood outside of Daoxue.[34] Overall, we see two trends. On the one hand, there is an important movement away from philosophical speculation toward more empirical textual scholarship; one dimension of this is the gradual de-canonization of the classics. On the other hand, we see fascinating novelty from non-Daoxue Neo-Confucian thinkers, even though they are often in critical dialogue with Daoxue ideas and terminology. The best example is DAI Zhen (1724–1777): he still has enough in common with the philosophical currents we have been tracking to count as a

Neo-Confucian, but he is unstinting in his arguments against much of Daoxue. Such figures are harder to find in the nineteenth century. There is still Confucian philosophizing, to be sure, but it has less continuity with Neo-Confucianism. By the twentieth century and the fall of the Qing in 1911, Confucianism has had to confront a whole new set of issues and ideas. Many modern Confucians look back to Neo-Confucianism for inspiration, but there is little question that the Confucian tradition has entered a new era.

For further study

Discussion questions

1. Is Neo-Confucianism philosophy? Is it religion?
2. How does Neo-Confucianism differ from classical Confucianism?
3. How does the transition from the Tang to the Song dynasty set the stage for the emergence of Neo-Confucianism?
4. What is Daoxue?
5. How does Daoxue's relationship to the Chinese state change over time?

2

Pattern and Vital Stuff

---

1 Introduction and background

When Neo-Confucians offer systematic presentations of their views, they often begin with the most fundamental categories in terms of which they understand the cosmos to be organized. We do the same here, bearing in mind Neo-Confucians take these abstract issues to be important mainly insofar as they support the goals of moral cultivation and political harmony to which we will turn later in the book. In this chapter, we focus our attention on two primary concepts. The first is *qi* 氣 ("chee"), a word whose roots go back to the idea of "breath," but which long before the time of the Neo-Confucians had broadened to mean the basic stuff of the world, including what we would call energy, matter, and psychological phenomena. In order to highlight its dynamic quality, we will translate it as "vital stuff."[1] The second key concept is *li* 理, which we will translate as Pattern.[2] To put things very roughly for now, Pattern accounts for the structure, order, and thus value of things, which themselves are composed of vital stuff. Exactly how Pattern does this, and how it is related to vital stuff – for example, whether they signify two different levels of reality – are among the questions that this chapter explores. We borrow a term from the history of western philosophy and loosely refer to these topics as "metaphysical" questions.

To set the stage for exploring Neo-Confucian metaphysics, we begin with two key dimensions of the textual and conceptual background from which Neo-Confucianism emerged. First of all, from the early days of Chinese civilization, it has been very common to think about our world as made up of changing processes. Rather than speculate about unchanging essences of discrete things, Chinese thinkers have tended to postulate regular patterns of change. Two well-known terms are frequently used to discuss these changes: *yin* 陰, which originally referred to the shady side of a hill; and *yang* 陽, which originally referred to the hill's sunny side. Imagine the sun moving through the sky: *yin* and *yang* will gradually change. Another common pattern is the changing seasons, something especially relevant in an agricultural society like China. Think of *yin* as cold and dark, while *yang* is associated with warmth and light. Over the course of a year, the balance between the two shifts back and forth, but neither ever disappears completely; even the coldest and darkest day still has some *yang*, and indeed the very coldest day marks a turning point, leading eventually back to the warmth of summer and the height of *yang*.

For some thinkers in some eras, *yin* and *yang* were elements of a quasi-scientific theory explaining the world. Many premodern Chinese thinkers also put considerable stock in divinatory practices that involved talk of *yin* and *yang*. Our primary concern here, though, is with the more abstract use of *yin* and *yang* to articulate the idea of patterned change. All three of these uses of *yin* and *yang* can be found in the ancient *Book of Changes*. The earliest part of this text consists of a series of 64 hexagrams, each one made up of six solid or broken lines. The 64 hexagrams represent every possible permutation of these two types of line; the solid lines signify *yang*, and the broken lines signify *yin* (see Figure 2.1 for an example). The hexagrams have names and explanatory texts associated with them, and the interpretation of these texts was central to the divinatory use of the *Changes*. More important for our purposes, though, was a philosophical essay that was attached to the text, called the *Great Commentary*. This was where early thinkers reflected on the cosmological, ethical, and other sorts of significance that they found in the idea that our cosmos was continually changing through complex patterns that we could, in principle, understand. Phrases and categories

Figure 2.1 The Meng Hexagram

introduced in the *Great Commentary* are used again anc
Neo-Confucian discussions of metaphysics. For example, ι
Commentary offers definitions like these:

> The alternation of *yin* and *yang* is called "the Way."
> Life-giving generativity is called "change."
> That which is formless is called "the Way." That which is within form
> are called "concrete objects."[3]

Texts like the *Book of Changes* tend not to be interested in the
origin or creation of the cosmos, much less in its creator; their vision
is of ongoing processes of change which themselves are generative
of life.[4] As we can see, the text implies that there is an abstract
("formless," or more literally "above form") "Way" that we should
follow, which is somehow connected to the patterns of changing
objects.[5] All of this will be grist to the mill of Neo-Confucian
theorizing.

The second key bit of background is the tendency within certain
strands of Chinese thought to intuit or infer the existence of some
kind of deep, unchanging reality. Basically, everyone agreed on the
existence of patterned change, but while some thinkers believed that
patterned change was all there is – or at least showed no philosophical interest in the question of whether there was some deeper layer of
reality – other thinkers argued for one or another type of underlying
constancy that somehow explained the changing phenomena that
we more readily perceive. There might be a hint of this view in the
Great Commentary's distinction between "formless" and "within
form," but other, later, texts develop such ideas more explicitly, frequently borrowing the term "formless" to designate what they have
in mind. It is useful to think of the idea of deep, unchanging reality
as developing through several stages. Stage one, of which the *Great
Commentary* is a good example, contains provocative statements
that might suggest an underlying reality, but they do not develop the
idea into a full-blown theory.[6] Stage two is the explicit theorization
of distinct levels of reality in early-medieval Chinese thinkers; these
are complex matters, but the details are not particularly important
for present purposes.[7] One thing to keep in mind, though, is that
stage two mediates the way that the texts from stage one are subsequently understood: that is, under the influence of stage two, stage
one texts come to be seen by many as unambiguously endorsing
two levels of reality. Stage three focuses on changes within Chinese
Buddhism. To summarize: some centuries after Indic Buddhism first
reached China, distinctively Chinese schools of Buddhism, along with

Buddhist texts composed in China, began to emerge and eventually to dominate Buddhism in China. These Chinese schools placed much greater emphasis on ways of talking about an underlying level of reality like the "one heartmind" or the "Buddha nature" than did Indic Buddhism. The details are again complex, but suffice it to say that stage two thinkers certainly influenced the Buddhist philosophers responsible for stage three developments.[8] Stage four, finally, denotes the way in which the idea of two levels of reality becomes a default assumption for most intellectuals in the Tang and Song dynasties; this is one of the key aspects of what in our introduction we called the "Confucian-Daoist-Buddhist shared discourse." In this chapter, we explain many of the ways in which the ideas of patterned change and a polarity between *yin* and *yang*, on the one hand, and the distinction between levels of reality, on the other, interact in Neo-Confucian discussions of vital stuff and Pattern.

2 Vital stuff

As introduced above, vital stuff is an ancient term.[9] An early meaning is "breath," but it gets extended in many different directions. One context is cosmic origins: an early imperial-era text speaks of the differentiation of vital stuff into heavy and light varieties, which in turn leads to the creation of the heavens (*tian* 天) and the earth.[10] Another context is medical texts, in which the circulation and regulation of vital stuff play a central role.[11] By the Song dynasty, one could talk about one-and-the-same vital stuff as encompassing both of these contexts: vital stuff was pervasive, fluid, and made up everything. Its prominence within Neo-Confucian theorizing, though, is owed in significant part to the novel ideas of the great early Song thinker ZHANG Zai, on whose understanding of vital stuff we focus in this section.

Like many in his day, ZHANG Zai is attracted to the idea that there is some kind of deep reality that is difficult or impossible to perceive. Zhang is worried, though, by what he takes to be the Buddhist approach to this topic, according to which our apparent experiences are in fact illusory, and the deep "reality" is simply emptiness. Zhang feels that continuous change (the brief experience of an emotion, or the gradual wearing away of a mountain) does not make things unreal. To his way of thinking, there is nothing more real than the vital stuff whose patterned transformations make up the cosmos. What is missing, though, is an explanation for how it is that such change is possible. How can vital stuff change from one state to another, expand and contract, solidify and then disperse?

Zhang's answer is to posit something he calls the "supreme void" (*tai xu* 太虛).[12] It might be tempting to think of this as a physically empty location that somehow creates vital stuff, but that is not what Zhang has in mind.[13] Rather, he means that all reality is characterized by voidness at the same time as it has (varying degrees of) substantiality. He writes: "The supreme void is without form. It is the inherent reality (*ti*) of vital stuff. Its condensation and its dispersal are the temporary forms taken on through change and transformation,"[14] and "The supreme void cannot be without vital stuff; vital stuff cannot but condense and be the myriad things; the myriad things cannot but disperse and be the supreme void."[15] There is a necessary pattern of change. Sometimes vital stuff is maximally tenuous and dispersed; in this state, we might say that it is close to just being the void. Even when vital stuff is maximally condensed, its "inherent reality" is still the void. So we always have both, vital stuff and void. Zhang explains: "The condensation and dispersal of vital stuff with respect to the supreme void is like the freezing and melting of ice with respect to water, thus we know that the supreme void is vital stuff and there is no nothingness."[16] In short, there is a sense in which void is vital stuff, just as water can be ice. But there is still a difference. In Zhang's metaphor, water represents the underlying potentiality – the "inherent reality," a term we will explore in more detail later – while a given form of ice is always temporary. What is permanent, in other words, is instability or the potential for change. That is what void is really about: not nothingness, not emptiness, but changeability.

But not random changeability. Zhang insists that voidness enables things to be responsive to one another such that they can fit together into a harmonious unity. Indeed, when he first mentions the idea of voidness, he actually calls it "supreme harmony" instead of "supreme void."[17] As he subsequently puts it: "That which has nothing to which it is not receptive (*gan* 感) is voidness. This receptivity is precisely joining together. ... Because all things are inherently a unity, this unity can join together the different; because it can join together the different, it is called receptivity. If there is no difference, there can be no joining together."[18] So voidness enables receptivity, which in turn allows for harmonious joining together. It might be helpful to think of the indents (the voids) in Lego building blocks, which enable them to fit together with one another in countless ways. Void functions in something like this way, except that it is not fixed and physical: it is rather the ability of things to change and respond to one another. We can think of this patterned flexibility in terms of polarity (that is, a tendency in opposite directions), both between substance and void and between *yin* and *yang*. Zhang actually writes that "Because of these two poles, there can be receptivity; because they are originally a unity, there can be joining."[19] It is important to add, finally, that these harmonious joinings are then productive. Think, again, of the productive cycle of seasons, or the productive joining of male and female. There is decline and death (winter, old age), but there is also renewal and birth. And so he makes repeated reference to the line from the *Great Commentary* that we quoted earlier: "Life-giving generativity is called 'change.'" Built into ZHANG Zai's understanding of vital stuff, in short, is the idea of dynamic, generative polarity.[20]

Vital stuff serves one other critical role for Neo-Confucian theorists, including for ZHANG Zai: it helps to explain recalcitrance, failures of harmony, stupidity, and even wrongdoing. The idea that vital stuff can play such a role has early antecedents. The *Mencius* has a famous passage stating that if one is not focused, vital stuff can lead one astray, and early medical texts diagnose disorders as imbalances of vital stuff.[21] As we have already seen, it is central to the idea of vital stuff that it has different states (for example, *yin* and *yang*). For the most part, ZHANG Zai does not present any member of the many pairs of possible vital stuff-states as better than its polar opposite. Instead, both are necessary for harmony. For example: "The supreme void is clear; when clear, there are no obstructions; without obstructions, there is spirit (*shen* 神). The reversal of clarity is muddiness; when muddy, there are obstacles; when there are obstacles, there is form."[22] Clear and muddy are opposites, but both are needed: without muddiness, there would be no form – no actual people, emotions, or world. "Spirit" is much like "void," and describes the capacity for change; note that it is opposed in the quotation to "form." Although there are places in which Zhang might be read to suggest that muddiness is connected to badness, on the whole this does not seem to be Zhang's view. Instead, badness comes from an imbalance of vital stuff – just as Chinese medical specialists had been saying about the cause of disease for many centuries.[23]

ZHANG Zai's understanding of the origins of badness was not shared by his nephew and principal founder of Daoxue Neo-Confucianism, CHENG Yi. As we will explain in more detail in the next chapter, Cheng argued that all things have two different kinds of natures: a formless, inherent nature, which is in fact the same in everyone, and a physical nature, which he also calls our "endowment" (*cai* 才). The formless nature is identical to Pattern (on which, see the next section). Here, we are concerned with the physical nature or endowment. CHENG Yi holds that the endowment is made up of vital stuff, not Pattern, and it is the endowment that explains why some people are good while others are bad. What makes a given endowment of vital stuff bad? Cheng says: "When one's vital stuff is clear then one's endowment is good; when one's vital stuff is muddy then one's endowment is bad. Those endowed with maximally clear vital stuff are sages, and those endowed with maximally muddy vital stuff are ignorant."[24] In contrast to ZHANG Zai, for whom muddy vital stuff is useful insofar as it helps forms to congeal, for CHENG Yi muddy vital stuff is bad – and the muddier, the worse.

For subsequent Neo-Confucians, Zhang's use of vital stuff as a central category, especially as slightly revised by CHENG Yi, becomes common property.[25] The idea of "Supreme void" proves controversial and is not as influential; as we will shortly see, in some ways "Pattern" comes to take its place, which in turn generates further controversies about the relation between vital stuff and Pattern. To all of this we now turn.

3 Pattern

Two meanings

All interpreters agree that *li*, which we translate as "Pattern," is the most important and probably the most disputed concept within Neo-Confucianism. As contemporary scholar Brook Ziporyn explains, the term

> has a strange history. It came into prominence as the central metaphysical category rather gradually, seemingly only through the intervention of Buddhist uses, taking on its decisive role only in the thought of the Cheng brothers and further developed by ZHU Xi, read back into the pre-Buddhist tradition, although its actual appearance in the early texts is sparse and problematic.[26]

Li appears occasionally in early texts. Some of its first uses are clearly verbal: "dividing [land into cultivatable fields]" and "dressing [jade, in keeping with its veins]."[27] In these cases, patterning something involves finding a way to cut or divide some aspect of the world, in keeping with its objective nature (such as the veins in the jade), so that it fits our needs. A bit later, *li* is sometimes used to mean an "order" that we find in the world.[28] We can connect these two early senses of *li* by noting that, in general, we humans need to find order and structure in the world that we live in; living a good, meaningful, or valuable life depends on our success in this important task. This includes finding order in our own needs, desires, or emotions: as some early thinkers understood very clearly, we can shape ourselves (through ritual and habituation) to fit together harmoniously with other people and with our (constrained) natural environment.

So one basic meaning of *li* is a coherent pattern whereby we can order ourselves harmoniously – coherent both because it involves things fitting together and because it makes sense to us.[29] As Ziporyn emphasizes, it is not yet particularly central to the way philosophers are conceptualizing things, but it is a recognizable concept. It is natural to see it as related to the deep concern with patterned change that we identified at the outset of this chapter.

Over time, a second understanding of *li* emerges in parallel with the idea of a deeper reality that we also discussed above. On this reading, in describing a thing's *li*, you are describing what it truly is, its ultimate nature, which is characteristically contrasted with how it appears or how it is conventionally understood. For example, we tend to think of a thing like a cart as being something that remains relatively stable over time, but it is quite arguable that the cart is, in fact, undergoing a constant process of change. Similarly, we might be tempted to characterize carts in terms of their tangible properties – e.g., that they have wheels and some sort of flat surface – but many would hasten to add that we haven't grasped its true nature until we know how to use it.

This way of thinking about *li* was made a centerpiece of Chinese Buddhist thinking. Many Buddhists found it a convenient term with which to articulate the doctrine of emptiness: the view that all things are ultimately empty, which is to say that their true nature is complete interdependence with other things. When Buddhists use *li* in this way, modern scholars often translate it as "absolute" to emphasize that it refers to reality, independent of points of view or perspectives.[30] The opposite of *li* in these contexts would be "phenomenon" (*shi* 事), referring to the aspect of things more readily available to ordinary human experience.[31]

By the time the Neo-Confucians rose to prominence in the Song dynasty, Buddhist frameworks thoroughly pervaded metaphysical discourse, and the distinction between *li* and more tangible phenomena was chief among them. Many Neo-Confucians (especially Daoxue thinkers) shared the view that *li* is profound, difficult to articulate, and not reducible to its tangible qualities. But they still took a less radical stance than the Buddhists, arguing that while *li* is sometimes hard to articulate and not reducible to vital stuff, many aspects or manifestations of *li* are nevertheless readily available to ordinary experience. For example, ZHU Xi uses boats, chairs, and fans as instances of things whose *li* are intangible and yet in a certain sense readily available. The *li* of a fan, for example, prominently includes its being appropriately used in particular ways, such as for cooling oneself in the heat rather than for serving soup. (For more on how such a distinction can be justified, see the section "Normativity and value" below.) Such features of *li* are not so far removed from ordinary experience, and yet Zhu maintains we cannot fully explain something like a fan by appealing only to its tangible makeup. Thus the *li* of these ordinary objects is "formless."[32] For ZHU XI, a key marker of being formless is that it cannot be directly grasped through the senses, though it can be inferred from direct experience, as when one infers from the clarity of flowing water that water is inherently clear.[33]

In effect, thinkers like Zhu sought to further combine the two senses of *li* that we have noted, both the coherent pattern idea and the ultimate nature idea. We will call this general approach to *li* the "core Neo-Confucian account," not because all Neo-Confucians shared it, but because it came to be the center of their discourse – even if they disagreed with it – much as medieval and early modern European philosophers understood the omnipotent and omni-benevolent conception of God to be at the center of theirs. To signal this distinctive approach to *li*, we translate it here as "Pattern," with a capital P. The capital P indicates that Pattern is not just any old pattern that one happens to find; it is a deep truth, and (at least according to some thinkers) an independent ontological category, as we will discuss further below.

One and many

On the core account of Pattern, then, the ultimate nature of a thing is a coherent pattern. What can this mean? To make matters even more difficult, Neo-Confucians who support the core account regularly talk about the Pattern of this thing (a cart) as opposed to the Pattern of that thing (a boat), but they also say that Pattern is ultimately one – and indeed, one and the same Pattern is in all things. They often rely on analogies to try to convey this point. For example, ZHU XI says, "The Buddhists say, 'The one moon is commonly reflected in all pools of water; in all pools the moon is the same moon.' Herein the Buddhists have glimpsed the Pattern of the Way."[34] To begin to get a handle on this, let us suppose we had instead said that the ultimate nature of a thing is the set of all natural laws. It makes sense to say that all natural laws are present in, or at least apply to, every thing. After all, there are no things that are exempt from a particular law, so they must be the same in everything, just as the moon is the same moon in each of the pools of water. Admittedly, there are questions about the sense in which natural laws "exist" or are "present in" things; in section 4 below, we will look into a corresponding series of questions that Neo-Confucians debate concerning the relation between Pattern and vital stuff. For now, let us ask whether the ubiquitous presence of Pattern might be understood in the same way as the ubiquitous applicability of natural laws.

Answering this depends in part on how narrowly we mean "natural law." Just the laws of physics? Or do the "laws" of biology, economics, sociology, and even ethics count as well? A capacious understanding of law fits better with Pattern: the Neo-Confucians were aiming to make sense of the entire cosmos – very much including human society – rather than just modeling physical reactions. Pattern is the vast network of interdependencies that structure our world and thus can be parsed at different levels with equal correctness. We again draw on ZHU Xi here: "Someone asked, 'There is the single Pattern, yet also the Five Norms; how is this?' Master Zhu replied, 'You can call it the single Pattern and you can also call it five Patterns. When covering everything, we speak of one; when distinguishing, we speak of five.'"[35] The Five Norms are the five standards for a virtuous life, discussed in chapter 8. And Pattern is even more flexible: Zhu also says, "There is only this Pattern; we can distinguish it in four sections, or into eight sections, or even make still finer distinctions."[36] Finally, when asked if the Way must be understood in terms of the Five Norms, Zhu replies, "There is just one Pattern of the Way. Divided up, one can speak of it in terms of seasons, in which case there are spring, summer, fall, and winter; ... or one can speak of it in terms of a day, in which case there are dawn, daylight, twilight, and night."[37] The idea is that depending on our perspective, there are any number of ways we can distinguish the one Pattern into many.

This aspect of the core account of Pattern is typically referred to with a slogan first stated by CHENG Yi: "Pattern is one and its particularizations are many."[38] Things are distinct from one another because of their distict configurations of vital stuff, and thus what is most salient about Pattern as applied to a given thing will differ, but Pattern in its entirety is equally real and present in each and every thing. In fact, it is the unity of Pattern that provides the determinacy to any given aspect of Pattern, which we can think of as a sub-pattern. Think of the contrast between a boat and a cup. Both float and both hold water, but given how they fit into a cosmos in which the boat- and cup-users are human-sized, we say that the Pattern of a boat is to float across rivers, whereas the Pattern of a cup is to hold tea. When Neo-Confucians want to refer explicitly to the whole of the single, unified Pattern, they often call it cosmic Pattern (*tianli* 天理).

Modern physicists are often concerned about how their various theories and laws can fit together into a single, unified theory. Social scientists typically say that their generalizations are true only "if all else is equal," which at least implicitly suggests that, from a more all-encompassing perspective, perhaps we could combine different social scientific theories and remove these qualifications. Still, we moderns lack a concept with the ambition of ZHU Xi's idea of Pattern (and ZHU Xi is, in this respect, quite representative of the core account). Pattern thus has more in common with earlier western ideas of God-given natural law that included political and moral content, although even here two important differences remain.[39] First, as we will see below in section 4, for Neo-Confucians, there is no lawgiver outside of the system; Pattern is *sui generis* rather than stipulated. Second, as we have just seen, Pattern is constituted by an interdependent network, not a set of specific laws or principles. In part for this reason, it is not codifiable into a set of statements but has to be discovered and understood in a different way, as chapter 7 will explain. Still, like earlier European ideas of natural law, Pattern has definite content to it, which we will now examine.

The contents of Pattern

Buddhists – at least on the Neo-Confucian understanding – deny that any real structure can be found in nature: all that nature reveals is a process of continuous change or "impermanence," where all things fade or end with the passage of time. Any claim that there is some identifiable Pattern, on this view, is actually just superimposing specific content on Pattern (the "Absolute") that isn't to be found in Pattern itself. To use Buddhist terminology, the Pattern of a thing is "empty" (*kong* 空), and thus open to change and differences of interpretation across time and perspectives.[40] By contrast, the Neo-Confucians argued that the Pattern in individual things does have specific, "substantial" (*shi* 實) content, so that the kind of order we will find and should aim to instantiate is fixed across time and perspectives.[41]

Attributing substantiality (though not form) to Pattern was important to the Neo-Confucians for many reasons. As we will see in later chapters, one is the powerful idea that standards of order shouldn't be "up to us." Another reason is that the main virtues and ethical practices remain the same across time, even if details about how they are manifested can change. Things like filial piety and seeing to the basic needs of one's subjects will always have fundamental ethical value. Most relevant for our purposes here is the idea that even where

everything appears to be in constant change, there will be regularities
that suggest some sort of underlying, permanent structure or source.
One of the Cheng brothers makes the case against the Buddhists as
follows:

> Students of Chan say: "The life of plants, trees, birds and beasts is all
> illusion." I say: "You consider them illusory because they live in the
> spring and summer and then decay when autumn and winter come,
> and you similarly conclude that human life is also an illusion. Why
> not give this answer: things are born and die, are completed and
> decay, there is this Pattern naturally; how can they be considered an
> illusion?"[42]

When observing the ongoing, patterned process of change that leads
to birth and death, growth and reproduction, Cheng connects this
to a ubiquitous, underlying Pattern. In their search for some sort of
classical authority to establish the link between Pattern and life, Neo-
Confucians found their clearest candidate in the *Great Commentary*.
As noted above, the commentary characterizes the dynamic manifestations of the cosmic Way as "life-giving generativity" (*sheng sheng*
生生).[43] Most Neo-Confucians took the message of the *Book of
Changes* to be that the cosmos is organized so that life and growth
give rise to further life and growth in some orderly manner.[44] They
also thought that the cosmos functions in this way naturally or
effortlessly, so that (unlike for most human exertions) its productive
activity can go on "unceasingly" (*bu xi* 不息).[45] Another frequently
quoted expression comes from the *Book of Odes:* "The hawk flies
up to the heavens; the fish bounce and bob in the deep waters."[46]
Noticing that this line was quoted again in another early Confucian
classic (*Centrality and Commonality*), some Neo-Confucians took
this line to be the ancients' way of conveying that the life-generative
processes were tangible and all encompassing, stretching from the
bottom of the oceans to the upper reaches of the heavens.[47]

Although the idea that our cosmos is coherently unifiable into a
harmonious, all-encompassing whole was very widespread in the
China of the Neo-Confucians, some thinkers did dissent. WANG
Tingxiang from the Ming dynasty is a particularly good example. In
the words of a contemporary scholar:

> Wang did not believe that there existed an overarching unified struc-
> ture to the universe. Wang says, "The myriad things have the myriad
> *li*. Each of them possesses its own distinctiveness." Wang's denial of
> the unity (of *li*) of the world does not mean that he denied any order
> in the world. What he denied was the idea of an overarching unity

that penetrated (the myriad *li* of) the whole world. In other words, Wang repudiated the totalizing aspiration contained in [Daoxue's] notion of *li*.[48]

Even among critics of Daoxue, Wang is an outlier. The eighteenth-century philosopher DAI Zhen rejects may features of the core account of Pattern, but still embraces the idea that a coherent, all-encompassing harmony is attainable.[49]

Normativity and value

Scholars trained in the western philosophical tradition who encounter the core Neo-Confucian understanding of Pattern (which, recall, is that the ultimate nature of things is a coherent pattern) sometimes complain that it illegitimately combines description – "boats float" – and prescription – "children should respect their parents."[50] The mistake that these interpreters make is to think that Pattern is ever merely descriptive. Let us review what we have learned in the last two sections. First, although we can speak of some limited dimension of Pattern as applying to a particular thing or event, as when we say that "it is the Pattern of a boat to float," the whole of Pattern is always present. This means that the reason why "it is the Pattern of a boat to float" is because of the way that this sub-pattern fits into the whole, vast array of patterns that make up Pattern. However, one might say, boats also sink! Surely this is also recognized in Pattern somehow? (Recall our analogy to natural laws: there are certainly such laws that explain that boats can and do sink.) So how can we be sure that "it is the Pattern of a boat to float"?

The first thing to say here is that the language of Pattern can be employed to distinguish between possibility and impossibility. If something is impossible, "there is no Pattern" for it. In this sense, there is in fact a Pattern for boats sinking. Next, we must recognize that interdependent systems can take on different meanings, depending on which aspects of the systems have priority. Even if in a healthy, peaceful society we want boats to float, from the perspective of an assassin whose job it is to scuttle boats, boats' tendency to float is an obstacle to be overcome, rather than anything prescriptive about the way the world should be. Brook Ziporyn has explored this feature of holistic systems and shows that, for such systems to have consistent meaning and value, there must be some one point that acts as a "center" in reference to which the rest of the system attains its significance.[51] So we can talk about Pattern centered on the assassin, in terms of which at least some boats "should" sink. But this is where we turn to Neo-Confucian claims about the content or substantiality of Pattern. Considered impartially, Pattern has a "center": it is life-giving generativity. As we will see below, ZHU Xi emphasizes this feature of Pattern by calling it (in some contexts) the "supreme pivot." On the core Neo-Confucian account, at least, Pattern is the underlying aspect of reality, which ensures that all the various aspects of our cosmos, taken together, are able to facilitate life-giving generativity. For many Neo-Confucians, Pattern also ensures that we – individual human agents – can discover that we cannot avoid valuing our life-giving cosmos; this will be the major topic of the next chapter.

In other words, most Neo-Confucians hold that Pattern is always prescriptive: being based around life-giving generativity, even seemingly descriptive statements have prescriptivity built in. "It is the Pattern of a boat to float" and "it is the Pattern of a child to be respectful to his or her parents" are both aspects of Pattern, which we can abbreviate as "boats should float" and "children should be respectful."[52] In both cases, what justifies or explains them is the way that they fit into the broadest, cosmic Pattern, as centered on life-giving generativity. To be sure, we might want to challenge the Neo-Confucian core account, asking them either how we know that Pattern is centered on generativity or how we know that a generativity-centered Pattern requires that boats float or that children are respectful. Even if one accepts the general framework, that is, it is still possible to question whether it requires the detailed values and practices that Neo-Confucians endorsed.

4 Debates over Pattern's relation to vital stuff

So far we have focused on facets of Pattern that unite most Neo-Confucians and distinguish them (at least in their own minds) from the Daoists and Buddhists. It is equally important to attend to conceptual territory that is heavily disputed within Neo-Confucianism, which concerns the metaphysics of Pattern and its role in moral agency. While all Neo-Confucians think that Pattern exists in some sense or another, some think it exists in ways reducible to the ordinary stuff of the world, while others take Pattern to have a more robustly independent mode of existence. We will explore these disputes here.

Li as the inner Pattern of vital stuff

The disagreement that launches Neo-Confucian debate about vital stuff and Pattern takes place between ZHANG Zai and his nephew

CHENG Yi. As we have already seen, Zhang puts vital stuff at the center of his analysis, viewing it as the stuff of the universe, the patterned changes of which generate life. Zhang often uses the word Pattern (*li*) to bring out the patterned nature of vital stuff; in one edition of his collected works, the term appears 472 times. He uses it to speak about the patterns of interaction between vital stuff and human intention and also the patterns of natural phenomena; sometimes, by indicating there is not such a Pattern, he in effect denies that certain things are possible. When we recall that Zhang believes that the life-giving nature of the cosmos derives from harmonious patterns of change, it will be no surprise to learn that he often says we should strive to match or follow this Pattern. With hindsight, though, we can also notice two things that Zhang does not say about Pattern. First, he does not refer to Pattern as one ultimate Pattern that encompasses the entire cosmos. The closest he comes is in passages like this: "As the *yin* and *yang* vital stuff revolve through their cycle of alternation, they react upon one another through integration and disintegration. ... They include and determine one another. ... There being no agent which causes this, what can it be called other than the Pattern of nature and decree?"[53] Zhang is saying that there are broad patterns that can only be referred to as the "patterns of nature and decree," but this still falls short of the idea we will see CHENG Yi advocate (namely, that there is one universal Pattern in everything). Secondly, the idea that these patterns are not caused by an agent external to the system is very important. Nowhere does Zhang suggest that Pattern has some special ontological status or causal role. In the words of a contemporary scholar, Pattern is the "internal logic" of the transformations of vital stuff.[54]

CHENG Yi disagreed. One easy way to see this is in his dispute with Zhang over how to understand the line "The alternation of *yin* and *yang* is called 'the Way'" from the *Great Commentary*. As we saw above, Zhang holds that vital stuff cycles in and out of form: things come to be and then disperse. Even when tenuous, dispersed, and thus without form, though, this is still vital stuff. Therefore, relying on the fact that the *Great Commentary* defines the Way as formless, Zhang explains the line about the alternation of *yin* and *yang* by saying, "Because the alternation of *yin* and *yang* cannot be restricted to formed, concrete objects, it is called the Way."[55] The Way includes both formed and formless; it is the changing pattern of all vital stuff. For CHENG Yi, in contrast, the Way is not the literal transformations of vital stuff, but rather "that by which there is *yin* and *yang*."[56] This is a momentous difference. Cheng makes a sharp distinction between all vital stuff, which he views as "within form," and concepts like the

Way or Pattern, which are "formless." Cheng repeatedly argues that Patterns are the "that by which" things are as they are or change as they change. It is not just the pattern of movement, but something that explains this movement. While ZHANG Zai would agree with this to some extent – recall the idea that, for Zhang, Pattern represents the internal logic of vital stuff – Cheng's insistence that the Way and Pattern exist in a different fashion than vital stuff is where they part company. In Cheng's hands, "formless" no longer means tenuous and dispersed vital stuff, but something qualitatively different.

The question of how to characterize the existence of Pattern (and the Way) becomes a key fault line within Neo-Confucianism. ZHU Xi's development of CHENG Yi's position is extremely influential, and we will examine it in a moment. Throughout the era, though, there are thinkers who dissent from the idea that vital stuff and Pattern are so sharply distinct. CHENG Yi's older brother, CHENG Hao, seems to have been less committed to a clear distinction between the concepts than was his sibling.[57] LUO Qinshun in the mid-Ming dynasty, WANG Fuzhi at the transition from Ming to Qing, and the eighteenth-century philosopher DAI Zhen are the best-known later Neo-Confucians to argue explicitly against the idea that Pattern has a distinct kind of existence. For example, Luo writes that "Pattern is only the pattern of vital stuff" and denies that there is "a single entity that acts as a controlling power" amidst the transformations of vital stuff.[58] WANG Fuzhi distinguishes between the Way and Pattern: the Way is comprehensive, universal, and normative, whereas he tends to attribute Pattern to particular things as a description of the ways that things transform.[59] Similarly, DAI Zhen argues that we discover the unity of the "human Way," but this unity does not emerge from a pre-existing, unified Pattern. Rather, Pattern is just the patterns of things, very much like for WANG Fuzhi. Dai explicitly criticizes ZHU Xi for having held that Pattern is like a "thing" that is somehow distinct from the vital stuff of the cosmos.[60] As we will shortly see, it is not at all clear that Zhu actually held this view, but there is no question that he thinks of Pattern as having at least a quasi-independent existence.

ZHU Xi and asymmetrical co-dependence

ZHU Xi is adamant that Pattern and vital stuff cannot exist apart from one another. There has to be a Pattern for things like birds, fans, and writing brushes in order for any bird, fan, or writing brush to exist. At the same time, Pattern cannot exist without some vital stuff. Here, Zhu tends to use a variety of metaphors to explain the relationship: Pattern must have some place in which to "drop" or "settle," some place on which to "stand," or something to which to "adhere" or "attach."[61] Whatever the language, we can call Zhu's thesis the "ontological co-dependence" of Pattern and vital stuff: neither Pattern nor vital stuff can exist without the other. Zhu is also clear that vital stuff does certain kinds of work that Pattern simply cannot do: for one thing, the distinction between different types of things (e.g., carts, goats, human beings) is made possible by the fact that there are different configurations of vital stuff. Snakes have configurations of *yang* vital stuff which make them venomous and distinguish them from non-venomous things; human beings have more clear vital stuff than any other creatures, and a capacity to further purify their vital stuff. Vital stuff also explains how there can be numerically distinct individuals within each kind: Jiang is constituted by one batch of vital stuff and Joan by another.[62]

To further spell out Zhu's views on the relation between Pattern and vital stuff, we will focus on two controversial topics, both of which emphasize that, despite their co-dependence, Pattern and vital stuff are asymmetrical: first, the type of priority that Pattern has with respect to vital stuff, and second, the sense in which Pattern is the "master" of vital stuff. The issue of priority arises because of some ambiguous remarks that Zhu makes when asked whether Pattern is prior to vital stuff. In Zhu's response, he seems to want to have it both ways. He says that "basically one cannot speak of Pattern and vital stuff in terms of which is first and which is after." But then Zhu adds, mysteriously, "But when we proceed in making inferences, it seems as if Pattern comes first and vital stuff comes after."[63] In another recorded lesson, Zhu reiterates that one cannot speak of either Pattern or vital stuff as prior but then adds, "But if one needs to draw inferences about where they come from, it must be said th this Pattern comes first."[64]

These remarks suggest that Zhu is considering at least t of "priority," one in which Pattern *is* prior to vital stu which it is not. Most commentators and interprete that when Zhu denies that Pattern comes first, v what we could call "temporal priority." Zhu before vital stuff, or at least that specif exist before the vital stuff to which taken to be an implication of or cannot exist without vital stuff expect that either one will preced

There is less scholarly consensu *is* prior to vital stuff.[65] A close look though, suggests that Pattern's priority h we go about making inferences about the world. In the first of the quoted passages in which Zhu concedes Pattern's priority, he says Pattern seems to be prior "when we proceed in making inferences." In the second of these passages, he said Pattern is prior when "one needs to draw inferences about where Pattern and vital stuff come from." To illustrate what Zhu has in mind, consider the way that he explains the value and importance of parental love (*ci* 慈) by highlighting similarities between parental love and the nurturing of plants in the spring. Zhu emphasizes that both consist in recognizing the life-generating impulse in nascent organisms, which stimulates a natural sense of compassion for them. This in turn contributes to an orderly process of life-generation more broadly, where each of the fundamental virtues play roles analogous to the four seasons. And doing this, finally, shows that parental love has an important place in the order of things.[66]

So what sense of priority is at play here? Zhu's idea is that it cannot be a coincidence that things fit together as they do. We see the analogy between parental love and springtime nurturance because the cosmos is structured in a coherent, life-affirming fashion. It is not just that we happen to find it to be coherent: we discover that the diverse aspects of the world (including our own feelings) fit together. This would be the remotest of coincidences if vital stuff were randomly structured and interacted in chaotic ways: instead, we see that an explanation of our cosmos requires that it be structured, through and through, by Pattern. We will see in a moment that Zhu characterizes this "structuring" role of Pattern as a kind of "mastery." The present point is that, in order to understand our world, we must see that it is Pattern structuring vital stuff, rather than the other way around. Pattern and vital stuff may be dependent on one another, but it is an asymmetrical dependence in which Pattern has explanatory priority.[67]

This explanation of the priority of Pattern, though, just pushes us toward a second and still more vexed question: whether (and how) Pattern can intervene in worldly affairs, such that it actually alters the course of things and events constituted by vital stuff. This issue contentious because Zhu takes pains to say that Pattern doesn't ually direct or act upon vital stuff, suggesting that Pattern cannot as a causal agent in space and time (as, say, a deity might step enforce a divinely ordained mandate or law). Yet much of language seems to suggest otherwise. He sometimes describes as "manifesting" (*fa* 發) certain virtuous moral reactions and He also says that Pattern "pervasively circulates" (*liuxing* rhaps his most striking language is that Pattern is some- heartmind (*xin* 心) which can act as master (*zhuzai* 主宰)

over the world.[69] He even compares the relation of vital stuff and Pattern to that between a horse and its rider.[70] All of this has led to major debates in later Neo-Confucianism, but here we will simply unpack Zhu's meaning, as we understand it.[71]

How, then, should we understand the powers of control that Pattern exercises in its role as "master"? First of all, as we noted above, there are certain similarities between Pattern and the set of natural laws. So, Zhu says, in a passage that a modern physicist might appreciate, "This Pattern exists, and so this heaven-and-earth exists; if it were not for this Pattern, there would be no heaven-and-earth, no people, no things."[72] Pattern is the set of background conditions that make our cosmos possible. But, again as explained earlier, it is not limited to the spare background laws of the physicist. It is much more inclusive: it is the complete network of interdependencies that makes possible not just our physical world, but also a fully flourishing, harmonious cosmos. It is thus more vast, but also weaker than, physical law. Also, recall from above that in distinction from "law," Pattern is not a set of specific laws or principles, and it is not codifiable into a set of statements. Rather, it holistically limns what can and should happen for all things to fit together, and it orients us in this direction (see chapter 4), but it cannot insist that it is followed. The "mastery" of Pattern over vital stuff is thus limited and indirect (see chapter 3 for the role that the heartmind plays in exercising more direct causal power). In fact, one of Zhu's slogans is that "Vital stuff is strong; Pattern is weak," as seen here:

> Although Pattern produces vital stuff, once it has been produced Pattern is no longer able to control it. Once a Pattern comes to reside in some vital stuff, then how it is deployed in daily affairs depends on this vital stuff: vital stuff is strong while Pattern is weak. ... It is like the relationship between fathers and sons. If the sons are worthless characters then their fathers are not able to control them. The reason that the sages established their teachings is precisely because they wanted to save these sorts of sons.[73]

Pattern lays down the rules of the game and the means of success, but it does not make us play well.

Sons with worthless characters, perhaps overly irascible or insufficiently empathetic, will undermine harmony rather than promote it, taking us further from realizing cosmic Pattern. Because Pattern is our nature – in a sense which we explore in the next chapter – however, the cosmos has a tendency to nudge us back in the right direction.[74] Think now of Zhu's analogy to a horse and its rider: what are the ways that horse and rider can fit together? A wild horse (representing bad or imbalanced vital stuff) might try to buck a rider off of its back, or even ignore the rider and rub against a tree to scratch an itch. A well-trained horse (now representing good or balanced vital stuff) will do none of these things but will carry the rider swiftly and safely. A danger of this analogy is that it tempts us to think Pattern controls vital stuff in the way that a rider might guide the horse via spurs and reins. But Zhu never says anything that requires such a reading. Instead, Pattern is something that is natural to follow, not an order that must be obeyed.[75]

5 The many faces of Pattern

Pattern is a hard-working concept in Neo-Confucian metaphysics. Consequently, readers will frequently come across moments in which some relatively abstract or philosophically weighty notion is explained rather laconically as Pattern or an aspect of Pattern. Thus we find Neo-Confucians saying that the cosmic decree is Pattern, the cosmos itself is Pattern, the Way is Pattern, and in some cases that even human nature or the heartmind is Pattern. It can easily appear that the Neo-Confucians are being deliberately mysterious, but this is not their intention. Rather, the point is to emphasize that many concepts that people are inclined to treat as independent from one another are in fact closely interdependent and should be seen as ways of emphasizing different aspects of Pattern. For example, Neo-Confucians regularly say that characterizing something as the "cosmic decree" highlights the functions and implications of Pattern that are beyond our control, and that "the Way" stresses Pattern's role in determining general trajectories or goals (what paths things follow and what roads we should follow, so to speak). We will expand on these and other notions identified with Pattern in the rest of this section. Since it is primarily the Daoxue philosophers that identify these notions with Pattern, we focus on these thinkers, although we mention points of departure by non-Daoxue thinkers where they are most significant.

Cosmic decree (*tianming* 天命)

The term that we are translating as "cosmic decree" (*tianming*) is made up of two words: *tian*, which we translate as "cosmos" or "cosmic," but has often been rendered as "Heaven"; and *ming*, which can be "decree" or "mandate."[76] The most basic meaning of *tian* is the sky. In ancient China, for a period of time, it referred to a sky deity worshipped during an early dynasty. This combination of sky and religion led early translators to interpret it as "Heaven." Such a translation has two major problems, however. First, it inevitably suggests to readers familiar with Christianity a series of associations that are highly misleading. This is especially true because, second, already by China's classical era, the religious and normative content of *tian* had been significantly attenuated, with some early Confucians understanding *tian* as simply "nature." For Neo-Confucians, *tian* generally means something like the all-encompassing cosmos outside of our control. As we discuss here, though, this cosmos still has a normative and religious significance, which relates in part to its early religious meaning and which Daoxue Confucians, at least, explain via its connection to Pattern. In addition, when *tian* is used in certain contexts, it still refers to the sky or to the heavens above us, and in these places we will translate it as "heaven."[77]

The cosmic decree refers to those aspects of Pattern that are not entirely within our control, so we might say that this is the Neo-Confucian version of fate. Our choices and actions can cut short our lives or improve our chances of living longer, but in some sense our lifespans are still fated, for they aren't completely up to us. Disease, accidents, and human hostility can intrude, no matter how careful we are, and the fact that we must die is itself unchangeable. The Neo-Confucians do not assume that things are intentionally fated, as though by a deliberative and purposeful agent. Daoxue Neo-Confucians sometimes find it useful to think of fate as something ordered or commanded by a superior, but they also say this is to be understood metaphorically, as the superior in question – *tian* – doesn't give orders so much as leave certain capabilities and limitations embedded in the nature of things, built in at birth, as it were.[78] Finally, the Pattern-imbued structure of the cosmos is such that benevolent, life-nurturing behavior is often rewarded and reciprocated, at least when social structures are in good order. Generous people are generally rewarded with the loyalty and appreciation of those they are generous to, for example. But in apportioning cosmic justice, *tian* is not a micro-manager. The built-in mechanisms and limitations don't guarantee that every good person is rewarded and every bad one punished, much less rewarded or punished according to some carefully calibrated assessment of her merits.[79] If there's any consolation in knowing that something is decreed by the cosmos, it is not in thinking that it is a just reward or punishment, but rather in knowing that it fits into a unified whole of mutual life-generation to which we belong and in accepting that we cannot control it.[80]

Sometimes the Daoxue thinkers make a distinction between "decree" and "cosmic decree." The former refers to decrees that can be analyzed in terms of one's allotment of vital stuff; the latter, to the decree that is defined as Pattern, either making it explicit or just assuming that their students will recognize which sense is being used. When they invoke "cosmic decree" in the sense defined simply as Pattern, they mean to stress the fact that the Pattern-based norms we live by are not of our own making or choosing.[81] We inherit the moral demand to develop and embody the right combination of faculties and dispositions to make ourselves proper (virtuous) participants in the cosmic system, which is made possible by the instantiation of Pattern in our individual natures. A reverential, grateful attitude toward the cosmos that is arranged in this way is a core part of Neo-Confucian religiosity. When referring to the sort of decree that can be analyzed in terms of vital stuff, they have in mind the specific endowment of vital stuff that we have at birth, and the roles and positions that we find ourselves born into, particularly those that bear on the quality of life that we will lead (e.g., daughter or son, older or younger sibling, royal family or peasant family). We will discuss this type of allotment or endowment at more length in the next chapter.[82]

Supreme pivot (*Taiji* 太極)

In the introductory section to this chapter, we discussed the idea shared by all Neo-Confucians that patterned change – comprehensible via the categories of *yin* and *yang* – was basic to reality. As noted there, much of the Neo-Confucians' vocabulary for understanding and debating the nature of reality comes from the *Book of Changes*, and especially its *Great Commentary*, including the term with which we are concerned here, "supreme pivot."[83] This term was employed by the early Neo-Confucian ZHOU Dunyi in a brief, controversial text and associated diagram, called *Explaining the Diagram of the Supreme Pivot*, which proved to be the flashpoint for many subsequent debates. Let us begin with Zhou's diagram (see Figure 2.2) and the first portion of the text:

> Nondual and yet the supreme pivot! The supreme pivot in activity generates *yang*; yet at the limit of activity it is still. In stillness it generates *yin*; yet at the limit of stillness it is also active. Activity and stillness alternate; each is the root of the other. In distinguishing *yin* and *yang*, the Two Modes are thereby established. The alternation and combination of *yin* and *yang* generate water, fire, wood, metal, and earth. With these five phases of vital stuff harmoniously arranged, the Four Seasons proceed through them. The Five Phases are unified in *yin* and *yang*; *yin* and *yang* are unified in the supreme pivot; the supreme pivot is inherently nondual. Yet in the generation of the Five Phases, each

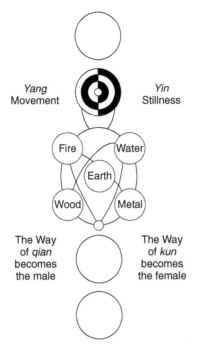

Figure 2.2 The Diagram of the Supreme Pivot

one has its nature. The reality of the nondual and the essence of the Two Modes and the Five Phases mysteriously combine and coalesce. "The Way of *Qian* becomes the male; the Way of *Kun* becomes the female"; the two types of vital stuff stimulate each other, transforming and generating the myriad things. The myriad things generate and regenerate, alternating and transforming without end.[84]

To unpack all of this, let us begin with Zhou's understanding of the diagram.[85] The diagram reads from the top down: the top, empty circle represents nonduality; the small, white circle at the very middle of the second large circle is the supreme pivot, around which are layered *yang*/movement and *yin*/stillness. Zhou sees this as a cosmogony: that is, an accounting for the emergence of our cosmos, starting with the nondual and supreme pivot and ending with a cosmos populated by the myriad things (which include people).

Now, what does this all mean? There are two key issues to understand: (1) the meaning of nonduality and its relation to the supreme pivot; and (2) the significance of the supreme pivot itself, and how it accounts for the rest of the cosmogony. Let us deal with the second issue first. Perhaps it will help to think of the way that what you see on a computer screen is the result of complex interactions among the specific terms of a computer language, which in turn are made up of strings of hexadecimal characters, which in turn are made up of ones and zeroes. The pattern of ones and zeroes ultimately generates the "myriad things" that we see on our computers. And what makes the ones and zeroes possible? That is where the supreme pivot comes in. It is dynamic (i.e., changeable) creativity itself. Note its location in the diagram: the pure circle at the center, around which *yin* and *yang* revolve. It is a "pivot" because it is what causes change: it causes *yang* to change to *yin*, and vice versa. Everything else ramifies from there.[86] As for the first issue – namely, what to make of the nondual – we follow Joseph Adler's interpretation, according to which even though the supreme pivot creates a polarity or duality (*yin* and *yang*), the pivot itself, and indeed the whole system, is ultimately one – that is, nondual.[87] The cosmos is unified, rather than composed of two irreducibly different things, so it is unlike a Manichean (light and dark) or Cartesian (mind and matter) dualism.

There are two final issues to examine: ZHU Xi's influential reinterpretation, and a quick look at what some critics of Zhu, or of Daoxue more generally, made of the "supreme pivot." Zhu's key move is to assert that the supreme pivot is no more and no less than Pattern itself.[88] It is not a uniquely formless or tenuous kind of vital stuff which then produces the more substantial *yin* and *yang* vital stuffs, but instead is the Pattern which governs and is co-present with all vital stuff, all the time. This also changes the diagram from being a cosmogony to a timeless ontology: that is, an abstract representation of what exists.[89] Supreme pivot, as Pattern, and all the rest of the categories, as vital stuff, are simply different aspects of reality. With this one change to the diagram, Zhu was able to unify two different strands of Northern Song Neo-Confucianism: the discourse of *yin* and *yang*, supreme pivot, and life-giving generativity from the *Book of Changes*, on the one hand, and distinction between vital stuff and Pattern (especially as developed by CHENG Yi), on the other. This, in turn, allows him to explain somewhat more clearly what Pattern is: it is like a center, a pivot, in terms of which the changing configurations of vital stuff are able to coexist and, indeed, flourish. At the same time, there is no question that his identification of supreme pivot and Pattern led to new controversies. Many critics suggest (correctly) that the term "supreme pivot" came primarily from Daoist cosmology, and thus should be rejected by a self-respecting Confucian. WANG Tingxiang in the Ming dynasty maintains that "supreme pivot" refers to the transformative but unknowable qualities of vital stuff.[90] In the Qing dynasty, DAI Zhen argues that the supreme pivot is better understood as a heuristic or interpretive device for representing the alternations of *yin* and *yang*.[91] Nonetheless, after ZHU Xi it became commonplace among Daoxue philosophers to think of the supreme pivot as another face of Pattern, used primarily when one wants to stress the dynamics between the polar opposites of *yin* and *yang*.

Inherent reality (*benti* 本體) and function (*yong* 用)

A final face often worn by Pattern is "inherent reality," an idea that is sometimes expressed with the binome *benti* (inherent + reality) and sometimes just with the single word *ti*.[92] Both versions mean the same thing: what a thing is in itself, "unconditioned" (as Buddhists would say) by its particular context. Very often Neo-Confucians will speak of a thing's "inherent reality" together with its "function," which is the way it actually, perceivably behaves in a particular context. Functions can change from moment to moment, context to context, while the inherent reality remains the same. For example, ZHU Xi often uses the handheld fan as an illustration: waving the fan is its function but, just because it is being waved does not mean that it has changed in substance or identity: it is a fan, whether it is being waved or not. Or as ZHANG Zai puts the point, inherent reality refers to "that which is never absent" in the midst of the processes of things' life, growth, and death.[93]

Two things stand out about Neo-Confucian uses of the inherent reality–function pair. The first is that while there is a sense in which they agree with Buddhists that inherent reality is unconditioned – that is, not influenced by any particular pattern of causal events – they nonetheless strongly dissent from the Buddhist claim that inherent reality is "empty" and that conditioned reality (or "function") is therefore illusory. According to most Neo-Confucians, inherent reality has a structure to it, making some "functions" (but not others) natural, life-promoting, and good. This structure is, of course, Pattern. It is natural to ask how we can know this. While we deal with Neo-Confucian theories of knowing extensively in chapter 6, what we want to emphasize here – this is the second point mentioned above – is the role of "function" in knowing the "inherent reality." Because one-and-the-same inherent reality can function in many ways, we must be cautious here: it is not the case that any given functioning can equally well reveal the inherent reality. When a particular pattern of behavior happens reliably and spontaneously, though, that is a sign that we can fairly confidently read the inherent reality (the Pattern) off from the function. We discuss this idea in more detail in chapter 3.

This concludes our initial introduction to vital stuff, Pattern, and related concepts, but many of these ideas resurface repeatedly in the coming chapters. These new contexts – such as Pattern's relation to our "nature," "heartmind," and "emotions," the featured topics of the next three chapters – help to further flesh out the concepts we have already introduced, though they also spark new debates. Ultimately, as we will see, Neo-Confucians tend to agree that the most important role for abstract ideas like vital stuff and Pattern lies in the ways they enable us to live better lives in more harmonious communities.

For further study

Selected primary sources

1. ZHANG Zai (CHANG Tsai), selections from *Correcting Youthful Ignorance* and *Additional Selections from the Works of Chang Tsai*, in Chan 1963: 500–7 and 514–17.
2. ZHU Xi, selections from *Classified Conversations*, in Tiwald and Van Norden 2014: #32, 168–77.
3. LUO Qinshun, selections from *Knowledge Painfully Acquired*, §§1–15, in Luo (1997: 49–67).
4. DAI Zhen, selections from *An Evidential Commentary on the Meaning of Terms in the Mengzi*, §1, §2, and §4, in Tiwald and Van Norden 2014: #51: 318–25.
5. ZHOU Dunyi, "Explanation of the Diagram of the Great Ultimate" (n.b. "Great Ultimate" is an alternate translation for supreme pivot [taiji 太極]), in Tiwald and Van Norden 2014: #24.

Discussion questions

1. What does ZHANG Zai mean by saying that vital stuff is characterized by voidness?
2. Explain what is at stake in the disagreement between ZHANG Zai and CHENG Yi over the meaning of the sentence "The alternation of *yin* and *yang* is called 'the Way.'"
3. Does ZHU Xi actually hold the "asymmetrical co-dependence" doctrine? Is such a doctrine coherent and defensible?

4. How different is ZHU Xi's view from the way other philosophers like LUO Qinshun have understood the relationship between Pattern and vital stuff?
5. Look at the diagram on p. 45. What is represented by the empty circle at the center of the second large circle from the top?

3

Nature

---

1 Introduction and background

In chapter 2's discussion of Pattern, we began an account of why there is value in the world, but gave short shrift to a crucial question: How do humans fit into this picture? Much of the Neo-Confucian engagement with Pattern is ultimately in the service of explaining why and how we humans can be good – and, indeed, why we should be good. For Daoxue Neo-Confucians, at least, the basic answer to these questions is "because that is what we truly are." We are inherently good, even though we do not always act this way. Too often, we are confused or mistaken, misperceiving our world and ourselves. Sometimes our emotions guide us well, but many times we overreact or fail to be moved when we should. The theoretical challenge which the Neo-Confucians shoulder is explaining how it could be that unreliable creatures like ourselves really are good, deep down, and also have the capacity to realize this goodness in a much more consistent and even spontaneous way.

Neo-Confucians build their explanations of our goodness on three main conceptual foundations. Together, the concepts of nature (*xing* 性), heartmind (*xin* 心), and emotions (*qing* 情) enable them to construct theories that bridge the gap between metaphysical accounts of the cosmos and explanations of our individual psychological realities. This chapter focuses on the parameters of "nature." As we suggested in the introduction to this volume, Neo-Confucians can be roughly divided into three categories, depending on whether their theoretical emphasis is on vital stuff, nature, or the heartmind. A "nature-focus" indicates that a proper understanding of nature is at the center of clearing up the confusions by which people are afflicted. Nature-focused Neo-Confucians hold that our nature is the source of our goodness. Even those thinkers who focus on vital stuff or heartmind still discuss nature, although some of them question whether nature itself can be called good. Altogether, then, this chapter looks at the following questions: (1) How is nature able to guide us? (2) Is nature itself actually good? (3) How should we account for moral failure – that is, why are most of us predisposed to do bad things? To round out the chapter, we conclude by turning to a later Neo-Confucian who was often critical of Daoxue views, DAI Zhen, and consider his alternative understanding of nature.

Already, in chapters 1 and 2, we have indicated that the intellectual landscape inhabited by all Neo-Confucians was shaped by several interrelated forces. Here, we will concentrate on two of them: the philosophical and spiritual agendas of Chinese Buddhism, and a renewed emphasis on certain classical-era Confucian texts. Let us first look at the Confucian sources. As we discussed in chapter 1, a new emphasis on the *Mencius* is one of the key elements of the intellectual ferment out of which Neo-Confucianism emerges, and the *Mencius* is indeed a key text in the present context, for Mencius famously argued that human nature is good. For instance: "The goodness of human nature is like water's tendency to flow downhill. Every person is good; all water flows downhill."[1] Mencius is well aware that water can be forced upwards and that people do not always act properly. His point is that we have some spontaneous inclinations toward the good, an idea that he substantiates elsewhere in the text, for example by arguing that anyone, upon suddenly seeing a child about to fall into a well, would feel "alarm and commiseration."[2] Mencius also acknowledges that humans have other sorts of spontaneous inclinations that are more neutral, such as the way our mouths are disposed toward delicious flavors. But it is the good spontaneous inclinations that grow when human beings are brought up under conditions conducive to their natural growth. Human nature is good in this sense.

Two other points are worth making before moving on. First, both in the *Mencius* and in *Centrality and Commonality*, human "nature" is connected to the cosmos (*tian*). Mencius says, "To fully fathom one's heartmind is to understand one's nature. To understand one's nature is to understand the cosmos. To preserve one's heartmind and nourish one's nature is the way to serve the cosmos."[3] As we have already seen, the Neo-Confucians sometimes use "the cosmos" (and especially "cosmic Pattern") to refer to that which brings order and coherence to everything – to the cosmos as a whole – and so they saw

Mencius as here indicating an intimate tie between our own natures and that of all things (whatever exactly Mencius himself may have had in mind).

The second thing to note here is that Mencius's view did not go unchallenged. In the *Mencius* itself, we read about a rival who believed that "nature" properly referred only to the physical processes of growth and procreation with which we are born.[4] Other thinkers argue that our natures are mixed (some good aspects, some bad), variable (some having good natures, others bad), or simply bad (because if untutored they lead us toward boundless desires).[5] It is clear that Mencius would reject all these alternatives because he fears they would leave human ethics without an adequate grounding. Even though their understanding of nature is certainly different from that of Mencius, the Neo-Confucians were drawn to him in large part because they agreed on the necessity of an adequate grounding for ethical value. If there is to be a viable way of accounting for ethical value, most thought, it would have to appeal to human nature.

The second crucial influence on Neo-Confucian ideas of nature is Chinese Buddhism, within which the idea of "Buddha nature" had, in the centuries prior to the Song dynasty, taken on enormous significance. We cannot here delve too deeply into the complex details of Buddha nature doctrines, but a few points will be important to our subsequent analyses. To begin with, at least in careful, philosophical treatments, Buddha nature was not seen as a straightforward endowment of valuable emotions or dispositions. To simply say that compassion, for instance, is part of the "nature" that we all share with the Buddha would run headlong against central Buddhist teachings. Buddhists argue for the emptiness of all seemingly existent things and events, as well as for the even more basic idea that attachment to anything, even one's seemingly good nature, is a source of suffering. This view draws on the tenet – widespread in Buddhism – that all phenomenal things are causally "conditioned": everything that seems to exist is causally dependent on (or "conditioned" by) everything else, so that there are no independent, self-subsisting things. Nothing truly "exists" on its own. This idea is called "conditioned origination."

But already well before the time that Neo-Confucian philosophy began to get a grip on the Northern Song dynasty, influential strains of Chinese Buddhism had jettisoned the idea of conditioned origination, replacing it with the view that the source of each thing's existence is a special, profound nature that inheres in itself, the aforementioned Buddha nature.[6] It was often glossed as our "inherent" (*ben* 本) nature: "inherent" not in the sense of biologically innate, but rather unconditioned by interactions with anything. Thus these latter

Buddhists replaced the doctrine of conditioned origination with what they called "nature origination." This idea of Buddha nature was explained in indirect and abstract terms, rather than being ascribed any clear content, but some Buddhists still saw it as able to provide a grounding for ethics. The important ninth-century Buddhist thinker Zongmi, for example, was worried about the nihilistic implications of radical strands of Chan Buddhism that were emerging in his day. Zongmi emphasized doctrines related to "Buddha nature" because, in a modern scholar's words, they "provided a firm ontological ground for Buddhist practice."[7] The notion of "inherent nature" had played little role in earlier Chinese debates about nature but would come to be critical to the Neo-Confucians.

As we discussed in chapter 1, the various elements that will, in the Song dynasty, coalesce into Neo-Confucianism are already starting to interact and to catalyze new ideas in the latter part of the Tang. Some of the writings in which these developments occur are explicitly Buddhist and some are more overtly Confucian, though they share much of the vocabulary and some of the arguments that later Neo-Confucians will deploy. One revealing example is an essay called "On the Nature" by HAN Yu (768–824), an avid promoter of Confucianism and influential prose stylist.[8] The somewhat confused argument of this tract, which both claimed that humans' natures can be distinguished into three different grades and yet that common people and sages share the same nature, suggests that some philosophical work still needed to be done before Buddhist-inspired ideas of inherent nature could be fully integrated into a Confucian worldview.

2 Nature as ground of morality

We turn now to the Neo-Confucians themselves and to the central issues concerning nature on which they spent so much of their intellectual effort. In the early Song Dynasty, "nature" is important for ZHANG Zai and is repeatedly discussed by ZHOU Dunyi, even though both arguably focus on vital stuff more than they do on nature. Nature lies at the heart of some of the most famous writings by both Cheng brothers, and it continues to be critical for subsequent generations, including for ZHU Xi. Why was it so significant? From a philosophical perspective, the answer is that a robust conception of nature offers a way of accounting for the differences between right and wrong ways to live. If it turns out that it is good to accord with or develop one's nature, then that gives us something other than our own arbitrary inclinations on which to ground distinctions between good and bad ways of being. This is all the more true if it turns out that we have reasons to think our nature is in tune with the needs and interests of the larger world. For the Cheng brothers and their followers, at least, such a conception of nature also gives their view a major advantage over Buddhism, which they believe treats people's arbitrary inclinations as the basis for right and wrong ways of being.

In order to understand the implicit structure of our nature, many Daoxue Neo-Confucians present their readers with a serious conceptual challenge. On the one hand, they say that nature represents a kind of open-ended equilibrium prior to the arousal of emotions. On the other hand, they are clear that there is some pre-existing structure in our nature, and this is what they take to distinguish their account of nature from the Buddhist one: our true, inherent nature is so structured as to make us essentially moral beings. Not only that, but it is structured to make us moral beings of the very sort that the Confucian texts have long praised: filial children, loyal subjects, respectful juniors, loving or benevolent parents and superiors, and so on. So it seems that the Daoxue Confucians want to have it both ways: they want to say our nature is essentially open-ended and not yet predisposed to make us act in one way rather than another, but they also want to say – perhaps in another sense – that it *does* predispose us to act as virtuous Confucians. The conceptual challenge is to understand and appreciate how nature can be constituted in both of these ways simultaneously.

A good place to begin is with this famous passage from the classical-era *Centrality and Commonality*:

> What the cosmos decrees is called "the nature"; complying with nature is called "the Way"; cultivating the Way is called "teaching." ... When joy and anger, sorrow and happiness are not yet manifest (*weifa*), call it "the center." When they are already manifest (*yifa*), and yet all are hitting the proper measure, call it "harmony." Being in "the center" is the great foundation of the world; being in "harmony" is the all-pervading Way of the world. By reaching "the center" and "harmony," heaven and earth occupy their positions and the ten thousand things are brought forth.[9]

In his commentary to this passage, ZHU Xi explicitly says that "nature" is characterized by the state in which the emotions (joy and anger, sorrow and happiness) are not yet manifest; in other places, he makes the same point by saying that our nature is "inherent."[10] To understand what is going on, we need to further investigate two aspects of the passage: what it means to speak of the nature (or the "not yet manifest") as "the center," and what sort of relation to the nature is manifest when emotions attain "harmony."

Let us begin with nature itself, the "not yet manifest." From some of the metaphors that Zhu uses to elucidate the nature, we find evidence that he believes a core feature of nature is what might be described as a kind of open-ended potential to act or respond in a wide variety of ways. For example, he repeatedly says that nature is like a fire or like light, which would shine forth except for the degree to which it is blocked.[11] But while nature's potential is open-ended, it also has a sense of direction – that is, a sense of what general direction is proper for it. Consider Zhu's suggestion that nature is like the responsibility a minister has to his ruler: insofar as one understands oneself as a minister, one thereby has a sense of direction.[12] In both cases, the idea is that to have a "nature" is just to have a combination of two things: first, an ability to respond in a great variety of different ways; second, a sense of the right direction to take.[13]

The language of being centered takes advantage of these notions. When we are in the center of an open area – say, a room – we have each direction as a possible way to go and so can respond in a great variety of different ways, moving in whatever direction we want. But this does not imply that any direction will be as good as any other. The room will be structured in such a way that some directions will be better than others. There is little to be gained by moving toward a wall when trying to avoid something dangerous. So although one *can* move in a number of different directions, a wise person has some sense of which ones are preferable. For this reason, one also needs a sense of directionality, an awareness of which directions are the better ones given the situation one is in. ZHU Xi makes these points when explaining what it means to say that emotions in their not-yet-manifest state are "centered"[14]:

> The not-yet-manifest joy and anger, sorrow and happiness can be compared to being in the center of a room, not yet having determined on setting out to the north, south, east, or west; this is what is called "being centered." With respect to their manifesting, this is like having left through a door – if to the east, then there is no need to also exit west. ... When each exiting is in accord with the circumstance without contrariness, that is called "harmony."[15]

So part of what makes our natural emotional capacities so powerful is that they, like a person at the center of some open area, are positioned to respond in a great variety of different ways. But Zhu takes pains to add that this does not give them free rein to do whatever they want.

The *place* in which one is centered will make some ways of moving more sensible than others; where the windows and doorways are located make some directions the better ones by which to leave, for example. Zhu explains this in connection with the not-yet-manifest emotions which are seen as starting points for virtue: "When the Four Beginnings [i.e., the moral emotions of alarm and commiseration, disdain, deference, and approval and disapproval] are not yet manifest, although [one's heartmind is] silent and unmoving, yet its center, on its own, has ramifying Pattern (*tiaoli* 條理)[16]; on its own, has structure [literally, rooms and house-frame]; it is not homogenous with nothing in it at all."[17] An obvious question to ask, then, is about the kind of structure in which our nature is centered – what is the arrangement of rooms and house-frame that would make some movements better than others, and thus give the centered person a sense of which directions are better than others, so to speak?

When Neo-Confucians ask what value orientation structures our nature – that is, defines the space in which it is centered – they say that it is the "life-giving generativity" (*sheng sheng*) which is manifest in the productive alternation of *yin* and *yang*, as we saw in the last chapter. In that metaphysical context, the point was that cosmic Pattern itself is structured by life-giving generativity. Now, we want to highlight that the same is true of our nature: for Daoxue thinkers like Zhu, this means that "life" specifies the center and directionality that our nature endows in us.[18] How do we know this? Zhu suggests that we ask what normatively infused responses we find unavoidable. Strip away ulterior motives and the perceptual blinders caused by selfishness, and look to our spontaneous reactions. This can be hard to do, and the Neo-Confucians have a great deal to say about how to cultivate one's ability to reliably respond in this way. But they are sure that what such thought-experiments and personal investigation reveal is a caring for life. In particular, Zhu builds on Mencius's famous example of encountering a child about to fall into a well. According to Mencius,

> anyone in such a situation would have a feeling of alarm and commiseration – not because one sought to get in good with the child's parents, not because one wanted fame among one's neighbors and friends, and not because one would dislike the sounds of the child's cries. From this we can see that if one is without the feeling of alarm and commiseration, one is not human.[19]

Mencius goes on to say that three other emotions are equally deeply rooted in us, and then adds that each of these four are "beginnings" (*duan* 端) of four corresponding virtues; for alarm and commiseration, that virtue is humaneness (*ren* 仁). Zhu argues that these "beginnings" are "clues" (*xu* 緒, literally the tip of a thread) to the not-yet-manifest nature within us.[20] After all, Zhu says, "If we did not have this Pattern within us inherently, how could there be this 'beginning' on the outside? Since we have this beginning on the outside of us, we know for sure that we have this Pattern within us, without possibility of deception."[21] Not all Neo-Confucians relied on this kind of inference; others, as we will see below, felt that one could directly experience one's not-yet-manifest nature.

There is one final issue before moving on. We know from chapter 2 that Daoxue Confucians tended to hold that every thing and event has its own Pattern, even though all Patterns are ultimately one; and that all Patterns are in some sense possessed by every thing and event. Our question now is: when we are told that "nature is Pattern," does this mean that every Pattern is actually, simultaneously, present in our nature, or are they merely implied? Since it is through our heartminds that we possess our natures (as we will see more fully in the next chapter), we could reformulate this question as follows: when ZHU Xi says that our heartminds "possess the myriad Patterns,"[22] do we possess each of them individually? Although some scholarly interpretations use examples or metaphors that suggest that ZHU Xi conceptualized the nature as a vast set of pre-existing items of knowledge, we believe that the evidence points toward a different picture.[23,24] The same letter we quoted from above (saying that nature has an internal structure) continues as follows:

> When there is a stimulus from outside, the inside then responds, as when, upon encountering the stimulus of a child about to fall into a well, the Pattern of humaneness responds, and the emotion of alarm and commiseration takes form; or when, upon encountering the stimulus of passing a temple, the Pattern of propriety responds, and the emotion of respect takes form. From within, where the myriad Patterns are all integrally and indivisibly possessed, individual Patterns become distinctly manifest.[25]

The Pattern that is our nature is an interdependent whole that cannot be fully captured in words,[26] but at the same time it is possessed of a complex structuring that results in reliable responses to any of a wide variety of external stimuli. As we saw in chapter 2, it can be distinguished at different levels, or divided in different ways, depending on the need and context. Zhu says that the reason Mencius focuses on the Four Beginnings is to show students that Pattern reliably ramifies in these ways, and so we can conclude that our nature is good. In short, Zhu wants us to see that nature is not empty but possessed of a complex and interdependent structuring – possessed of the myriad Patterns, which is just to say Pattern – that can guide us to be good.[27]

3 Beyond good and bad?

We have now seen the most important strand of Neo-Confucian discourse concerning the nature: the inherent nature that we share with all the cosmos, centered on life-giving generativity, serves as a grounding for human ethics. As such, it is fundamentally good. In the section that follows this one, we will turn to the relation between this good nature and our actual, psycho-physical makeup (which clearly can lead us to do bad things, at least some of the time). Here, we examine views denying that our nature is inherently good.

Worries about relativism

We mentioned above that Mencius's view of nature, which sought to ground morality in our tendencies toward goodness, was only one of a number of competing positions. Most of the possibilities explored in the classical period also found adherents in the late Tang and Song dynasties. HAN Yu developed a view with roots in the *Analects'* brief discussion of "nature," according to which human nature comes in three different grades – good, intermediate, and bad – only the middle of which can change. However, this position does a better job explaining why many people are not good than at providing a solid ground for ethics.[28] For their part, some early Song thinkers argued that nature was a mixture of good and bad, capable of development in either direction.[29] Others stressed the human role in establishing morality.[30] Such potential relativism worried those in the emerging Daoxue movement; for example, SHAO Yong opined that "using things to contemplate things is nature. Using self to contemplate things is emotions. Nature is impartial and clear; emotions are partial and murky."[31] While Shao's view on the "emotions" was not shared by all Daoxue thinkers – see chapter 5 – his view that nature is objective was common ground within Daoxue.

Exactly how to characterize the objective nature, though, generated a key dispute. Was the nature, after all, "good"? Or was it beyond the reaches of human good and bad, resistant to description in human categories? As early as the classical Daoist text *Daode Jing,* the Way was described as beyond language, and that text seems to suggest that human values are our own invention.[32] The *Book of Changes* can also be taken to suggest that the Way is prior to goodness, though the status and meaning of "nature" in that text is more ambiguous.[33] Because of the problem that arises from fixating on any value or direction, no matter how seemingly good, influential Buddhist texts also assert that the Buddha nature is "neither good nor not good."[34] A Song dynasty Buddhist scholar-monk suggests a different route to the same conclusion: "Good and bad are emotions, not the nature. Why is it that emotions have good and bad but the nature does not? Because the nature is tranquil while the emotions are active. The manifest shape of good and bad becomes apparent in activity."[35] Even though it would be artificial to reduce these various sources to each making a single point, we can nonetheless see three different kinds of reason to conclude that nature is not appropriately characterized as good: (1) metaphysical – since there simply is no goodness (or badness) in nature itself; (2) ethical – since it would lead us astray to objectively fix anything as good (or bad); and (3) epistemic – since we have no access to the characteristics of the "tranquil" nature.

Daoxue debates

Among the several Daoxue approaches to nature's being beyond good or bad, two are particularly interesting and will suffice to give us a flavor of the issues at stake, especially if we pay close attention to the ways their reasons relate to the Daoist and Buddhist reasoning we just saw. First is HU Hong, an individual who served as a crucial intermediary between the main Northern Song developers of Daoxue and the major thinkers of the Southern Song. According to Hu, nature "is a mystery of heaven, earth, ghosts, and spirits. 'Good' is not adequate to speak of it." Hu adds that he learned from his father that "when Mencius said that the nature was good, he used the word only as an exclamation of praise, not with a meaning opposite to 'bad.' "[36] It might be thought from this that Hu believed goodness and the norms of human ethics to be human creations, founded only on the basis of our emotions, and indeed, this is how ZHU Xi did react to Hu's statement.[37] Zhu also claims that Hu's father learned this idea from a Chan Buddhist monk.[38] Before we conclude that HU Hong is offering versions of the metaphysical or epistemic reasons mentioned above, though, we need to consider two things. First, HU Hong's main work, *Understanding of Words*, is filled with statements critical of Buddhists for being contented in tranquilly "viewing the nature." Hu says that it is easy to find such quiet reflection enjoyable; the hard thing – which he associates with the cardinal Confucian virtue of humaneness – is to find joy in proper activity.[39] Thinking that nature on its own is "good," it seems, risks a kind of amoral inertness. So Hu's criticism is an ethical one, but not the Buddhist criticism mentioned above. Furthermore, there is evidence that HU HONG also believes that nature grounds ethics by providing direction, although we have to read between the lines a bit. He says that "Pattern is the great inherent reality of all-under-heaven"; that both nature and Pattern can be equated to the "cosmic decree," and thus to one another; and that rightness and order are the nature of sentient creatures.[40] ZHU XI would agree with all of this. In short, HU HONG has a reason for insisting that one has to play an active role in the world to merit "goodness," but his general view fits comfortably in mainstream Daoxue.

The other Daoxue philosopher most famous for holding that nature is in some sense beyond good and bad is WANG Yangming. The central text to consider is often referred to as the Doctrine in Four Axioms, which Wang pronounced rather late in his life:

> In the inherent reality of heartmind, there is no distinction between good and bad;
> When intentions are activated, there is distinction between good and bad;
> Good knowing is that which knows good and bad;
> Getting a handle on things does good and removes bad.[41]

In what became known as the Colloquy at the Tianquan Bridge, Wang discusses these four lines with two of his senior students. One student – the radical WANG Ji, about whom we will hear more later – embraced the idea that there should be no distinction between good and bad, arguing that if there is no such distinction in the heartmind's inherent reality, then neither should there be a genuine distinction in one's intentions, knowing, or in things. The other student disagreed, maintaining that because our actual heartmind is dominated by habits, the good–bad distinction runs throughout our actual psychology. If this were not the case, he asks, why would the effort of self-cultivation be necessary? In response, WANG Yangming somewhat unhelpfully says that both of the students are right: one student's approach is apt for teaching those of "sharp intelligence," while the other's is for the more common type of person.[42]

What does WANG Yangming mean by the distinction in his original four axioms between the heartmind's inherent reality being without good and bad, and the other three all registering good and bad? First of all, it is important to note that Wang makes clear in several places that the inherent reality of the heartmind is "completely good."[43] Saying that the heartmind's inherent reality is "without good and bad," therefore, does not mean that it is morally neutral or inert. Instead, what Wang means is that external, rigid standards of good and bad have no place in the heartmind's inherent reality. The heartmind's natural responses (which he also calls "good knowing," *liangzhi* 良知) spontaneously establish the proper norm for each given situation, without following any guidelines that apply across all cases. "When the seven emotions follow their spontaneous courses of operation, they are all instances of good knowing, and cannot be separated into good and bad." At the same time, though, "There is but one good knowing, and good and bad are thereby distinguished; what other good and bad is there to think about?" The functioning of our heartminds cannot be pre-separated into good and bad precisely because its responses – at least, when they are natural, spontaneous, and not biased by selfishness – create the explicit norms of good and bad on the spot.[44] There are certainly questions we might ask about how one can know when one's emotional reactions are natural and thus norm-instantiating; we will deal with these issues in chapters 5 and 6. For now, the key point is that the reason that WANG Yangming insists that the inherent reality of the heartmind (alone) is beyond good and bad is because he denies that there are rules of right and wrong action that apply across all contexts. Wang is not denying the grounding or objectivity of morality. He thus describes the ancient sage Shun's decision to marry without getting permission from his nasty parents in this way:

> Was there someone before him who did the same thing and served as an example for him, which he could find out by looking into certain records and asking certain people, after which he did as he did? Or did he seek the genuine knowing in an instant of his heartmind's thinking, thereby weighing all factors as to what was proper, after which he could not help doing what he did?[45]

Wang's subsequent discussion makes it clear that the answer is the latter, and that Shun's proper ("good") reaction establishes no rule (an external, rigid "good") that can now be followed ever after. Good and bad emerge, that is, from the functioning of the heartmind which itself is prior to our external determinations of good and bad.[46]

4 Individuality and badness

For the many Confucians over the centuries who have held that people's natures are mixed, different, unreliable, or even bad, it has been simple to explain why people do bad things. Most Chinese Buddhists, on the other hand, believe that we all share the same inherent "Buddha nature," and even if they typically do not say that this nature is "good," they are still faced with explaining our actual, mixed behavior. At the core of Buddhist explanations lies the idea of delusion. Our most basic beliefs and desires are mistaken; only when we awaken to their "emptiness" can we realize our nature. In chapter 5, we will see this put in terms of whether or not we can generally trust our "emotions" (*qing*): for Buddhists, the answer tends to be no, and even early Neo-Confucians (including some early Daoxue philosophers) are also suspicious of the emotions. As we have seen, Daoxue Confucians share with Buddhists the idea of an inherent nature, and for the Daoxue thinkers our inherent nature provides the direction that grounds human ethics – whether or not it is correct to call nature "good." These Confucians therefore reject the Buddhist idea of delusion or emptiness, insisting instead that nature and Pattern are "substantial" (*shi*) and that at least some of our actual reactions are reliable. In other words, Daoxue Confucians neither claim that our natures are to blame for our bad behavior, nor that delusion is the problem. What, then, explains that our actual characters and behavior are a mix of good and bad?

Faced with this challenge, early Neo-Confucian philosophers like ZHANG Zai, CHENG Hao, and CHENG Yi developed related answers on which most subsequent Neo-Confucians would draw. Their core idea is that the vital stuff out of which we are made is often imbalanced or even flawed in some way, and thus imperfectly expresses our inherent nature. This one sentence contains some complex and controversial ideas, and we will devote the balance of this section to exploring its implications.

Nature as vital stuff

Zhang and the two Chengs use several different terms to speak about an individual's particular configuration of vital stuff, the most important of which is *qizhi* 氣質.[47] The second of these terms, *zhi*, means material or substrate. In the context of "*qizhi*," *zhi* can be understood as a kind of material substrate that generates the more immaterial (though still physically present) *qi*, or vital stuff; together, the interaction of *qi* and *zhi* constitute us.[48] (In the more basic sense of vital stuff emphasized in chapter 2, all this can be said to be vital stuff, possessing some kind of form.) *Qizhi* has two aspects, the endowment (or substrate) and the more readily changeable dimension, but it is ultimately one thing, just as a living and changing plant is one dynamic thing. This idea that *qi* and *zhi*, representing less and more stable aspects of our physical reality, interact and change over time, is actually quite intuitive. Think of an individual with an irascible disposition. There are various obviously physical aspects to this, from underlying brain structures to the ways that one's heartbeat accelerates under stress; and also aspects that we might be tempted to categorize as mental, like angry thoughts and emotions. On the *qizhi* model, both the more fixed and the more ephemeral aspects of these phenomena all count as vital stuff in its basic sense, so the ways in which they interact with one another – *zhi* generating *qi* (in its narrower sense), and *qi* influencing *zhi* – are not mysterious, unlike in more dualist models of mind–body relations. Becoming less irascible will require changing some aspects of the substrate, which in turn will affect the particular emotions we experience moment by moment. One contemporary scholar describes *qizhi* as being one's "contingent constitution," which nicely expresses the idea that with work the *qizhi* can be changed, but for good or ill, it reflects our current dispositions and is thus an important constituent of us.[49]

This general idea – that our contingent constitution, typically expressed via the term *qizhi*, explains our badness – becomes common property of Daoxue after the Cheng brothers. ZHU Xi not only uses the term repeatedly, but also echoes the analysis of it that we have just given when he says, "That through which Pattern is realized in practice necessarily follows vital stuff that has been made into substrate (*zhi*)."[50] There are complex metaphysical issues here, concerning the relation of Pattern and vital stuff, which we discussed in chapter 2. Here, we want to note two further aspects of the contingent constitution. First, in addition to explaining badness, it in fact explains all of the ways in which we differ from one another. As we have seen, our natures are identical (and all-encompassing), but the interaction of the vital stuff and its substrate with which one is endowed at birth, encompassing both the physical and emotional dimensions of all the situations that one has so far encountered, shapes the contingent constitution that one finds oneself with at a given point in time. One's height is a matter of one's contingent constitution, as are any quirks or dispositions that might be related to one's history of encountering the world as a person of above-average height (or below-average, or what have you). Second, it is striking that most Daoxue philosophers believe non-human animals to have just the same inherent nature that humans do, but to be dramatically less able than humans at transforming, straightening, or purifying their contingent constitution so as to be more consistently ethical. We can see clues in bees, wolves, and other social animals that suggest the same kind of directionality

in their natures as in us.[51] However, there are some important differences between human and non-human constitutions. It may be
that something about non-human vital stuff simply renders them less
amenable to change, though this idea is not made very explicit. What
is clear is that the constitution of the human heartmind enables a kind
of learning that non-humans cannot undergo, and thus, while non-
humans may be able to respond perfectly to narrowly constrained
aspects of their experience, they will never have the broad, flexible,
flawless capacity of a human sage.

One nature or two?

In addition to the terminology introduced in the last section to talk
about our contingent constitutions, the Cheng brothers use one other
means of making a similar point, but it turns out to be problematic.
The Chengs were faced with a twofold challenge to their claim that
nature is identical with Pattern and is the same in all of us: on the
one hand, there is the intuitive sense that we are different from one
another, and not all good; on the other hand, there are classical passages that seem to discuss actual differences between people's constitutions in terms of their "natures" (*xing*). The former issue could be
addressed in the ways we have just seen, by reference to ideas like the
contingent constitution. The latter problem, though, seems to require
a different approach. The only substantial mention of "nature" in the
Analects goes as follows: "The Master said: By nature near together,
by practice far apart."[52] While the point Confucius is making seems
quite plausible – people's differences mainly come about as a result
of their different experiences and efforts – it fits poorly with the
understanding of a single nature that the Chengs are advocating.
Similarly, the *Mencius* contains a famous passage that begins by
quoting one of Mencius's rivals, Gaozi, saying "Life is what is meant
by 'nature.'"[53] This is challenging to the Chengs in much the same
way as the *Analects* passage because the Chengs do not take nature
to be identical to the actual functioning of our life processes, which
is what Gaozi and Mencius here seem to have in mind.

CHENG Yi's solution is explicit and ingenious: argue that the term
"nature" can be used in two different senses, either referring to our
inherent nature (which he labels with another classic-derived phrase,
"the cosmic decree is what is meant by 'nature'") or to our actual
life-nature:

> Someone asked: Are "life is what is meant by 'nature'" and "the
> cosmic decree is what is meant by 'nature'" the same?

CHENG Yi replied: The word "nature" is not to be explained always in the same way. "Life is what is meant by 'nature'" only refers to that with which one is endowed (*bing shou*), while "the cosmic decree is what is meant by 'nature'" speaks of the Pattern of the nature. When people speak of someone's cosmic nature (*tianxing*) as soft and lax, or hard and energetic, it is one's endowment that is meant, because in common speech any quality that goes back to birth is ascribed to the cosmos. As for the Pattern of nature, it is entirely good. In this latter context, reference to "the cosmos" refers to spontaneous Pattern.[54]

The only problem with CHENG Yi's "two natures" solution is that it leaves it unclear how the two different senses of nature relate to one another; as we will soon see, this difficulty is clear to his later critics, who therefore advocate a somewhat different answer.

CHENG Yi's older brother, CHENG Hao, also grapples with these same issues, though in his best-known treatment of the matter he struggles somewhat to articulate his viewpoint, which has resulted in considerable debate about what, exactly, he means. Here is the key passage:

"Life is what is meant by 'nature'": here, nature is vital stuff and vital stuff is nature; they refer to life. In accord with Pattern, the endowment of vital stuff that one receives at birth has both good and bad, but it is not that within our nature there are originally two contrasting things with which we are then born. Some are good from infancy and some are bad; this is due to the endowment of vital stuff. The good is of course nature, but the bad must also be called nature. Now with respect to what comes before the "life that is what is meant by 'nature'" and "the tranquility of humans at birth,"[55] we cannot speak; as soon as we have spoken of nature, that already is not the nature. Whenever people speak about the nature, they are only talking about "following the Way, which is good"; Mencius's statement that nature is good is such a case.[56] "Following the Way, which is good" is like water's tendency to flow downward.[57] It is all water. Some of it flows all the way to the ocean without ever a touch of pollution; is any human effort needed in such a case? Some of it will inevitably get progressively dirtier before it goes far; and some of it gets dirty only after a long distance. Some has plenty of dirt, and some only a little; cleanliness and dirtiness are different, yet we cannot say that the dirty water is not water. This being so, people must accept the responsibility for cleaning and regulating it. The water will be cleaned quickly if efforts are prompt and bold, more slowly if efforts are careless, but when it is clean, it is still only the original water. It is not that clean water was fetched to replace the dirty, nor that the dirty has been taken away and placed to the side. The cleanliness of the water corresponds to the goodness of nature. Thus it is not that goodness and badness are two contrasting things in the nature which each emerge separately.[58]

Unlike his brother, CHENG Hao does not clearly distinguish two different senses of "nature" here, but the most plausible reading of this passage in fact relies on just such a distinction. CHENG Hao begins with one sense, our actual life-nature, which is the same as our endowment of vital stuff. It is clear, though, that he also has another sense of nature in mind, even though it is difficult to speak about because we do not directly experience it. This is what he is referring to when he says "as soon as we have spoken about the nature, that already is not the nature." So even Mencius's famous statements about the nature are really about the actual flow of vital stuff, which is different from the metaphysical fact that our vital stuff has an inherent directionality (as water has a tendency to flow downwards).

There is a lesson in all this: taking the phrase "life is what is meant by 'nature'" seriously as a definition of "nature" gets one into trouble. Both Chengs are sometimes criticized by later Daoxue adherents for their views about nature.[59] For his part, ZHU Xi chooses not to emphasize life-nature in the manner of the Chengs, but instead uses the term "contingent constitution" (*qizhi*) and, more controversially, "the nature of contingent constitution" (*qizhi zhi xing*). A natural question to ask is: isn't "the nature of the contingent constitution" just as likely to get Zhu into trouble as is the Chengs' "life-nature"?

ZHU Xi credits both CHENG Yi and ZHANG Zai with the term "nature of the contingent constitution," though it does not appear in the major modern collection of the Chengs' works. For that matter, in the very few times that ZHANG Zai uses "nature of the contingent constitution," he simply means the general characteristics (or nature) of one's contingent constitution: for example, that one has desires. For Zhang, it is the contingent constitution itself that is doing the philosophical work, not these general characteristics. Indeed, he emphasizes that superior people do not think of this as a kind of "nature" at all.[60] Turning now to ZHU Xi, we make three observations. First, "nature of the contingent constitution" plays an important theoretical role for him and he uses it often. Second, he is quite explicit that there is really only one "nature" – and for him, this is the inherent, completely good nature that we discussed above. Therefore, third, his use of "nature of the contingent constitution" is either inconsistent or subtle. We will argue that it is the latter.

Zhu is very clear that there is only one nature: "The contingent constitution is the result of *yin* and *yang* and the five phases; nature is the complete inherent reality of the supreme pivot. When speaking specifically of the nature of the contingent constitution, this is simply the complete inherent reality descended into the midst of contingent constitution, and not another, distinct nature."[61] ZHU Xi has a very similar two-aspect understanding of contingent constitution to that we described earlier: he even distinguishes vital stuff from substrate by associating the former with more ethereal "heaven," and the latter with more material "earth."[62] The nature of the contingent constitution, though, is not just a generalization about the contingent constitution itself: it is the actual formless nature as instantiated ("descended into") in a specific entity. Given the way that ZHU Xi uses "*qizhi zhi xing*," therefore, a better translation would be "embodied nature" rather than "nature of the contingent constitution." As he says, "Nature is just Pattern. Without the heavenly vital stuff and earthly substrate, though, this Pattern would have nowhere to reside. … Thus when speaking of nature, it is necessary to simultaneously speak of contingent constitution (*qizhi*) in order to be complete."[63] Similarly, he elsewhere says "Discussing 'the nature of heaven and earth' is only to refer to Pattern, but discussing 'the embodied nature' is to speak of Pattern and vital stuff mixed together."[64] So it seems clear that he avoids the "two-nature" problem. Of course, there remains the large question of what, exactly, it means for nature to "descend into" vital stuff; for Zhu's answer to that question, we refer readers back to chapter 2's discussion of the asymmetrical co-dependence between Pattern and vital stuff in Zhu's thought.

5 Debating DAI Zhen's alternative picture

The Daoxue Confucians share a common understanding of the inherent nature as being not just good but good in a way that is fully formed, so that all of the dispositions necessary to understand, feel, and behave virtuously are already present in some sense. As we have seen, they do not conclude from this that we are necessarily good from birth, as most of us are endowed with vital stuff that interferes with the natural functioning of the inherent nature. Still, the Neo-Confucian tradition includes outspoken skeptical voices that challenge the idea of a fully formed nature (as they understand it). In this final section, we examine one of the most influential skeptics, the mid-Qing philosopher DAI Zhen. But, first, we will make note of a crucial dispute in the interpretation of the Confucian tradition, a dispute that drives much of Dai's criticisms of Daoxue and helps to launch his own alternative.

In several ways, it is quite appealing to hold the view that our nature is fully formed and good. It helps to explain how sincere and wholehearted virtue is possible for flawed creatures such as our-selves, and it also makes clear how the human heartmind can come to accord so thoroughly with the demands of morality, as we will see in chapters 4 and 8. However, philosophical attractiveness is not the only issue at stake. Neo-Confucians are also concerned that their views align with those expressed in classical texts. DAI Zhen argues that Daoxue interpretations of Mencius's understanding of human nature are seriously mistaken, and like many contemporary schol-ars, we believe that Dai is largely correct. While Mencius explicitly endorses the view that human nature is good, by this he does not mean that the dispositions to understand, feel, and behave virtuously are already fully formed. Rather, he seems to mean that it is in our nature to *become* good, and in fact it is part of the natural course of human development to become a sage, but only if brought up in a healthy environment. Mencius famously insists that we have some moral capacities in us from the start, which are evident, for example, in a young child's love of his or her parents and our natural sense of alarm and commiseration for a child on the verge of falling into a well.[65] But these moral capacities are nascent, being both weak and also covering a relatively narrow range of moral actions.[66] A thing's nature tracks the outcomes of its healthy process of development, not its innate qualities or substance.

DAI Zhen's view comes much closer to Mencius in this regard than do any of the Daoxue interpretations. As Dai understands it, the nature of something describes not the innate material that it has right from the start but rather the salient features of its mature and healthy form. Dai motivates this point by noting how one distinguishes the natures of peaches and apricots – both very similar in seed-form but quite different when allowed to flourish.[67] So when one claims that a thing's nature is good, one need not go so far as to say that it has all of the material necessary for virtue innately. It could be that one has enough of the material that, given the proper nurturance and environ-ment, one could become fully good. Dai thinks that the thesis that human nature is good is much easier to defend on this conception, for we can show that people do have certain nascent moral emotions that tend to grow with experience and education. He highlights in particu-lar the natural capacity for empathy or sympathetic understanding (*shu* 恕), which he takes to be the best way of identifying and taking into account the desires that help to support birth, growth, and life fulfillment more generally.[68]

A related development in Dai's thought is to argue that human nature is constituted entirely of vital stuff rather than Pattern, which makes him a good example of a vital stuff-focused philosopher. Here again, he appeals to common ways of thinking about a thing's nature. Imagine, he says, that one wants to know how to cultivate a certain kind of plant or tree, or heal someone using medicine. These are the sorts of practices that normally require some understanding of the nature of the thing to be cultivated or healed, but if that is the case then citing a thing's Pattern is of little help because what determines how a thing should be cultivated or healed is the configuration of its vital stuff (e.g., the nature of its skin, the fluids by which it circulates nutrients, the concrete and organic features of its mental faculties). In fact, Dai suggests, it is really what helps us distinguish between methods of cultivation and treatment that give us the most salient information about a thing's nature whereas, by the Daoxue Confucians' own admission, Pattern is the same in all.[69]

Dai was perhaps the most explicit Neo-Confucian about this error in Daoxue ways of rendering the Mencian thesis that human nature was good, but he was by no means the only Neo-Confucian philosopher to return to the more developmental account of human goodness that Dai articulated. He was preceded in the seventeenth century by several like-minded philosophers, all of whom insisted on reducing human nature to vital stuff, rather than treating Pattern as an independent explanatory principle. These included WANG Fuzhi and HUANG Zongxi.[70] Contrary to first impressions, the idea of a fully formed good nature was hardly taken for granted in the Neo-Confucian tradition.

For further study

Selected primary sources

1. ZHU Xi, "First Letter to the Gentlemen of Hunan on Equilibrium and Harmony," in Chan 1963: 600–2.
2. CHENG Hao, "Letter on Calming the Nature," in Tiwald and Van Norden 2014: #26,
3. CHENG Hao, Selected Sayings, passages 1–5, in Tiwald and Van Norden 2014: #27, 143–6.
4. CHENG Yi, Selected Sayings, passages 27–8, in Tiwald and Van Norden 2014: #31, 163.
5. WANG Yangming, "Questions on the Great Learning," §3, in Tiwald and Van Norden 2014: #38.

6. DAI Zhen, "Evidential Commentary on the Meaning of the Terms in *Mengzi*," §21, in Tiwald and Van Norden 2014: #51.

Discussion questions

1. What is the problem with CHENG Yi's idea that we have two natures?
2. Does CHENG Hao solve the problem? Does ZHU Xi?
3. In saying that, in some sense, nature is beyond good and bad, is WANG Yangming committing himself to nihilism (that there are no values)?
4. Read very carefully the passage quoted from *Centrality and Commonality* on p. 54. How does "nature" relate to the "not yet manifest" and then the "already manifest"? How, in turn, are those two ("not yet manifest" and "already manifest") connected?
5. Are you convinced that nature, on Zhu's conception, can be both non-empirical ("above form") and yet direct us?

4

Heartmind

---

1 Background: the accordance problem for Neo-Confucians and their predecessors

A major focus of the prior two chapters has been on the "form-less" dimensions of Neo-Confucian thought, especially its notions of Pattern and nature. Although the Neo-Confucians think these concepts are fundamental and that it is important to get them right, they do not engage in metaphysical speculation for its own sake. Their ultimate concern in getting an accurate account of Pattern and nature is to justify their specific visions of goodness and virtue and to specify the means by which they can be achieved. Thus the Neo-Confucians paid close attention to the connections between their metaphysics and their views on moral understanding, good character, and moral cultivation. One crucial way of making these connections is by clarifying how the subjective cognitions, emotions, and inclinations of people can be made accurately to reflect and express Pattern, especially the cosmic Pattern (*tianli*) that gives value to the entire whole. In order to account for this alignment, they take a great deal of interest in the seat of mental and emotional phenomena which is called, in Chinese, *xin* 心, a term that is variously translated as "mind," "heart," or some combination of the two. In the most basic sense of the term, *xin* refers to the organ that we today call the heart but, like virtually all Chinese thinkers, Neo-Confucians take this organ to be the locus of both conation (emotions, inclinations) and cognition (understanding, beliefs). "Heartmind" expresses this unity well and is the translation we adopt in this volume. In this chapter, we focus on how the heartmind connects up with Pattern and nature. In subsequent chapters, we will discuss its relations to the emotions and examine the ways that it enables us properly to know and respond to our world.

To begin with, let us look a little more closely at one of the issues that motivates Neo-Confucians to take a philosophical interest in the heartmind. On their view, one thing that distinguishes Confucianism from rival schools of thought is that Confucian ethics and methods of moral cultivation help to create a heartmind that is responsive to Pattern rather than to contingent and subjective whims and inclinations. Daoxue philosophers like CHENG Yi and ZHU Xi identify this as a major point of departure from Buddhism, and a mark of Confucianism's commitment to the greater good.[1] To show how we can develop heartminds that accord with Pattern, however, we need to know something about the nature and function of the heartmind as such: how it comes to have intentions and emotions that do or do not track the larger world and its underlying structure. Let us call this set of issues the "accordance problem."

Simplifying somewhat, we could put most answers somewhere along a spectrum. At one end is the view that the heartmind's primary role consists in adjusting itself to fit norms that are independent of it, much as we may revise our beliefs or feelings in light of new evidence. But this is not the only way to bring moral norms and the heartmind into accordance. At the other end of the spectrum, some instead say that the heartmind is itself a source or basis of the norms, so that the norms are, in some sense and to some degree, already aligned with the heartmind just by their nature. For example, a young person might be required to treat an elder with respect because respect for elders is part of the deep structure of her thinking and emotions. Perhaps the very status of the other person as an elder, or even as a person, is a product of her heartmind. For ease of reference, we will say that the first sort of answer makes it the heartmind's task to *adapt* to externally given norms, and the second sort of answer makes the heartmind a *source* of those norms. To preview where some of the philosophers we discuss in this chapter fit on such a spectrum, see Figure 4.1.

Even at this general level of description, we can begin to see why both sorts of answers might be problematic. If we want to solve the accordance problem by saying that the heartmind is a source of moral norms, then we will have trouble justifying corrections to the emotions, desires, and thoughts that our heartminds are already predisposed to have. If we think there is something wrong with a father's inclination to abandon his young children and elderly parents, we would need some way of explaining why this inclination is wrong.

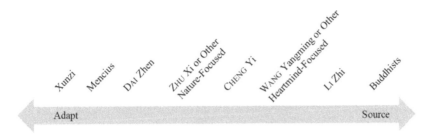

Figure 4.1 Solutions to the Accordance Problem

Let us call this the problem of finding an independent standard of assessment. If one thinks that a given heartmind's reactions (i.e., emotions, desires, or thoughts) are incorrect, on what basis can they be criticized? If the only standard of assessment is the heartmind's reactions themselves, this seems too subjective, without any independence whatsoever. As we will see, there are possible responses to this challenge, some of which are adopted by the Neo-Confucians themselves, but it represents a worry that looms large in Neo-Confucian discourse.

Appeals to the adaptability of the heartmind may also be problematic. Most obvious is that the heartmind seems to be riddled with powerful emotions, attachments, and cognitive predispositions that set barriers – perhaps insurmountable ones – to its powers of adaptation. For example, no matter how much we may aspire to love everyone equally, it seems nearly impossible to avoid loving members of our own family more than people completely unknown to us. Another limitation is more subtle. Let us say that virtuous people are more wholeheartedly invested in their thinking and behavior than are people who merely follow the rules. A virtuous youth does not just respect her elders because it is required; she respects them because she has powerful aversions to seeing her elders treated with disdain, because she takes joy in seeing them treated respectfully, and because she understands at a deep level how respect for elders maintains a kind of social harmony and, ultimately, contributes to ongoing life-generativity. Without wholeheartedness, furthermore, she may have only a thin and fragmentary understanding of how to show proper respect, and consequently she may experience uncomfortable doubts about her actions. Perhaps the heartmind's powers of adaptation might be stretched to fulfill everything demanded of it, but it is hard to see how it could have the strong, thoroughgoing cognitive grasp and emotional investment in this way of life if these demands are completely detached from its own internal constitution.

Neo-Confucians are particularly concerned about this latter limitation, which we can call the problem of wholeheartedness. To sum up, then, the accordance problem has two basic types of answers (setting aside for now efforts to stake out middle positions): *adapt* the heartmind to norms, which then faces worries about wholeheartedness, or understand the heartmind as the *source* of norms, which then faces worries about independent standards of assessment.

Both sorts of answers had precedents in Chinese philosophy before Neo-Confucianism, and the Neo-Confucians gave voice to all of the above criticisms and concerns about these sorts of answers. Probably the most notable defender of the adaptation view was Xunzi, the classical Confucian who proposed that the heartmind in its original state is largely bad, but nevertheless can be brought to "approve" (*ke* 可) practices that it perceives as in accordance with the Way, a process which can over time reshape one's emotions and desires.[2] Thus, on Xunzi's view, the heartmind is not itself a source of norms but is expected to adjust to and reflect them.[3] With some exceptions in the Qing dynasty, most Neo-Confucians considered Xunzi an outlier to the Confucian tradition,[4] and they objected to him in part because they thought it impossible for us to develop virtues that are wholehearted, sincere, and have the requisite degree of self-confidence unless our heartminds have an underlying deep structure and source of control that is good to start with.[5] Many Neo-Confucians also thought that there were certain insurmountable limits to the sort of emotions and desires a heartmind might express. For example, all people form special attachments that resemble in crucial ways one's attachments to parents and siblings, so that even monks who aspire to leave family relationships behind entirely nevertheless develop ersatz parents and siblings in their monastic communities.[6]

Some forms of Chinese Buddhism offer answers to the accordance problem that look to be at the far end of the "source" side of the spectrum, proposing that the heartmind is a source not only of norms but also, in some sense, of the world itself.[7] This position – or perhaps just an uncharitable misreading of it – becomes a kind of *reductio ad absurdum* for many Neo-Confucians. One of the most widely invoked criticisms of Buddhism is thus to suggest that it treats certain matters of fundamental importance as based merely on the contingencies of one's own psychology, suggesting that whether one should or should not serve and care for one's parents depends on whether one happens to feel like it, or even on whether one happens to have the relevant desires and emotions. For many Neo-Confucians, this view was not just dangerous but based on a mistaken understanding of the nature of ethics, for (they thought) the Buddhist view countenances emotions and behaviors that pay little heed of more objective considerations like the ethical value of care, the needs of one's parents, and so on. In contrast with the radical subjectivism that they find in Buddhism, the Neo-Confucians tend to highlight the fact that ethics is properly grounded in the cosmos (*tian* 天), emphasizing that the cosmos is by its very nature something that is not up to us or open to the whims of personal interpretation.

The early Daoxue thinker CHENG Yi declares that Confucian "sages base themselves on the cosmos, while the Buddhists base themselves on the heartmind."[8] As is apparent to Cheng's contemporaries and students, this is another way of saying that the Confucians stand for objectivism against Buddhist subjectivism, seeking beyond the emotions and perceptions that our heartminds happen to have for a deeper basis for standards and norms. That is, it is a way of saying that Confucians, unlike Buddhists, offer an independent standard of assessment, and that standard closely tracks the larger, objective world (the cosmos). A student of CHENG Yi's makes much the same point when he argues that "What the Buddhists call 'nature' is what the sages call 'heartmind'; what the Buddhists call 'heartmind' is what the sages call 'intention.'"[9] On this view, Buddhists lack a genuinely objective notion like the Confucian understanding of "nature." The Buddhist version of nature, on this account, is really only what the Confucians view as the heartmind – something that is less objective than nature, but more objective than mere occurrent "intentions" (*yi*).

To be sure, answers to the accordance problem that propose to treat heartmind as a source will vary a great deal, admitting of different types and different degrees. The most extreme version of this would be to identify Pattern itself with our actual, current motivational set (and our actual set of emotional reactions): this is a kind of ethical subjectivism since ethical norms are identical to one's own subjective reactions. In fact, we saw in chapter 3 that influential Chan Buddhists took a position that resembles this radical view, or at least the monk Zongmi worried about it and criticized such a tendency among his peers. Those Neo-Confucians tempted by a "source" view usually take a less extreme position, suggesting that Pattern is identical to the heartmind in a certain fundamental phase or state, usually labeled the "inherent" (*ben*) state independent of or prior to stimulation and distortion by external things. A third option is to suggest that norms arise not from the heartmind in any phase or state presently available to it, but rather to the heartmind as it would naturally develop if given a healthy environment in which to grow. So, for example, it might be that we should respect our elders not because we currently have heartminds that predispose us to respect them (in some more fundamental phase or state) but because our heartminds *would* feel respect for elders if allowed to develop naturally, much as a peach pit would eventually be able to produce other peaches if allowed to develop naturally.[10] This sort of view, although more qualified, still treats the heartmind as a source of norms, and in fact it lines up rather neatly with a view held by the classical Confucian philosopher Mencius.[11]

2 Identifying heartmind with Pattern

Generally speaking, most Neo-Confucians rejected Xunzi's extreme version of the view that it is the heartmind's function to adapt to norms given to it externally. But as noted above, they also were worried about Buddhist views that turned heartmind into a source of norms, a view that appeared to them to verge on pernicious subjectivism. For many Daoxue Confucians, an appealing way to avoid both of these unhappy alternatives was to maintain that norms were in some important sense internal to the heartmind, and yet not merely dependent on the contingent and subjectively variant psychological phenomena that people happen to have. They could do this by proposing that, in some sense, the heartmind is identical to Pattern. This move is characteristic of what we call a heartmind focus. On this view, the heartmind is not fully a source of norms because it is not more fundamental than Pattern, but it nevertheless has norms internally rather than externally. In this section, we will canvass the Daoxue theories that attempt to explain this relation between heartmind and Pattern, beginning with the somewhat ambiguous stance of CHENG Yi and then moving on to three thinkers who strongly identify heartmind and Pattern.

CHENG Yi's view depends on using "heartmind" in two different ways. On the one hand, there is our physical heartmind, which has "form," can be mistaken or biased and is limited in its scope. On the other hand, CHENG Yi also uses heartmind in a formless sense, closely identified with Pattern, which is unlimited in capacity and necessarily good. Consider the following:

> Someone asked: "The human form is limited; is the heartmind similarly limited?" CHENG Yi replied: "If you are speaking of the heartmind's form, how could it not have limits?" "Is the marvelous functioning of the heartmind also limited?" CHENG Yi replied: "From the perspective of one's being human, there are limits. Limited form and limited vital

stuff mean that functions cannot connect to everything. With respect to the Way, then, how could there not be limits? Mencius said, 'To fully fathom one's heartmind is to understand one's nature.' Heartmind just is nature. With respect to the cosmos, it is the decree; with respect to humans, it is nature; when speaking of its ability to be master, it is heartmind; but these are all a single Way. If one can connect them all with the Way, then what limits are there?"[12]

Elsewhere, Cheng also says that "Pattern and heartmind are one; it is just that people cannot understand that they are one."[13] If heartmind is the same as nature (as in the first passage) or Pattern (as in the second), though, why do we need the notion of heartmind at all? A possible answer lies in the first passage's reference to mastery. Somehow the heartmind explains how we humans, unlike other aspects of the cosmos (animals, plants, and other things), are able to transform ourselves to become the flawless moral agent that is a sage. Thus by talking about the heartmind in the formless and unlimited sense, we refer not just to the underlying source of order and value for things in general (Pattern or cosmic Pattern), but more specifically to the power of that source to win control over unruly intentions and emotions – in a word, mastery.

If we are to understand our capacity for mastery and agency, though, we need to understand the connection between the limited, physical heartmind that we experience, and the heartmind that is equivalent to nature and to Pattern. Does speaking of these two different senses of heartmind help to explain our ability to transform? CHENG Yi attempts to address this question by invoking what had been an obscure passage from the *Book of Documents*. The original passage reads: "The human heartmind is precarious; the Way heartmind is subtle. Be discriminating and undivided, that you may hold fast to the center."[14] In one of his comments on this text, CHENG Yi associates the "human heartmind" with "selfish desires" and thus with danger, and the "Way heartmind" with cosmic Pattern, and thus with subtlety and profundity. He adds: "Eliminate selfish desires and cosmic Pattern will shine forth."[15] One might wonder, though, where the "control" aspect of the heartmind figures in this explanation. The "human heartmind" seems to be simply problematic, while the "Way heartmind" seems to function automatically, once the human heartmind has been removed, suppressed, or otherwise brought in accord with the Way heartmind. Is there room for agency here? Perhaps control is exercised in the very process of eliminating selfish desires, but what is it that exercises such control? It is tempting to reply that it is the heartmind, but which one, or which aspect? As we will see in a later chapter, CHENG Yi has influential teachings about how we are to change ourselves, but he has very little to say about how our heartmind, under some description, can be imperfect, improvable, and yet contribute positively to its own improvement. We will see later in this chapter, though, that ZHU Xi may have a more satisfactory explanation for the nature of and relation between human and Way heartminds.

In order to understand the range of things that Neo-Confucians mean when they equate the heartmind and Pattern, let us spend a moment here on the idea of "inherent heartmind" (*benxin*). This term is used only a few times in the classical era, including once in the *Mencius*, when he criticizes those who have "lost" their *benxin*. The meaning of the word *ben*, which we translate as "inherent," also includes the idea of "root," and *benxin* in the *Mencius* is often translated as "original" heartmind. This is definitely not apt for the many Buddhist and Neo-Confucian appropriations of the term, however. The problem with "original" is its implication that the heartmind was a certain way, and now it is not. When Buddhists talk about the inherent heartmind, they refer to something about the heartmind that is never lost: it is an aspect of the heartmind, or a perspective on the heartmind, that is always with us, even if we do not see it. When Neo-Confucians begin to pick up the term, the same general point applies to them as well: "inherent heartmind" refers to the enduring, inherent capacity of one's heartmind to function in normatively positive ways.[16]

Understanding the idea of inherent heartmind is important because it allows us to see one way in which thinkers who say that "heartmind is Pattern" are still striving to achieve a kind of independent standard of assessment, while at the same time believing they have answered worries about wholeheartedness. Given the close ties between heartmind and Pattern in CHENG Yi's writings (as well as in those of his brother CHENG Hao[17]), it should be no surprise that many of his students and their students also develop similar themes to an even greater degree.[18] The best example is probably ZHANG Jiucheng. He explicitly asserts that "heartmind is Pattern, and Pattern is heartmind"; even more strikingly, Zhang also equates the heartmind and cosmos.[19] Now the idea that there is an interdependence between humans and the cosmos is certainly not new, but Zhang's assertion that the heartmind is the key fulcrum to the interdependence has few precedents in Confucian writings, and erases the distinction between cosmos and heartmind that CHENG Yi was struggling to draw.[20] Zhang is not claiming that there is no actual cosmos – that somehow the cosmos just exists in our heartminds – but rather that there is no meaning or value in the cosmos independent from the inherent heartmind, which is in some sense shared throughout the cosmos. This

commonality of the inherent heartmind is what prov
tivity and thus for an independent standard of asses
is not identical with just any set of responses one h
but with the eternally existing inherent heartmind. Of course, —
may raise as many questions as it answers: for instance, where and
what is this inherent heartmind, and how do we access it? Without
some answers, we are no better off than we were with CHENG Yi's
distinction between human heartmind and Way heartmind. Here, too,
ZHANG Jiucheng has a provocative response. Recall from chapter
3 the distinction between "not yet manifest" and "already manifest." Zhang believes that true meaning and value are grounded in
our "not-yet-manifest" heartmind, which is our inherent heartmind.
Zhang is therefore one of the key advocates of an approach to self-
cultivation according to which one focuses attention on this "unseen
and unheard" state within oneself. That is, one tries to grasp this
purity and then retain it as one moves into activity, which might
provide for the needed sense of wholeheartedness, as we discuss in
detail in chapter 7. For now, what is important is that Zhang's answer
to the question "what is the inherent heartmind?" is as follows: it is
the not-yet-manifest heartmind in its pure tranquillity.

Like Zhang, LU Xiangshan effectively collapses CHENG Yi's distinction between cosmos and heartmind (though he uses the term
"universe" instead of "cosmos"), asserting that "the universe is my
heartmind; my heartmind is the universe."[21] He also objects to CHENG
Yi's distinction between the "human heartmind" and the "Way heartmind"; for LU Xiangshan, this distinction led one to downplay the
importance of one's very own heartmind, with precisely the negative
consequences that we earlier identified as following upon a lack of
wholeheartedness. First, one looks to external standards of value
(such as the classics) which themselves are only murky traces of the
early sages' own heartminds, instead of the pure source and standard
that exists within oneself. Second, the possibility that one can become
a sage, in complete harmony with the cosmos, is lessened to the extent
that self-cultivation becomes a process of gradually trying to piece
together ideas and values from outside oneself.[22] So far, Lu's account
of heartmind closely approximates Zhang's, but we see a significant
departure from Zhang on another important issue. Unlike Zhang, Lu
does not insist that we identify Pattern with heartmind only in its
tranquil, not-yet-manifest phase. On the contrary, according to Lu,
Pattern is to be found in activity as well:

> to claim that tranquility alone is cosmic nature – does this imply
> that movement is not an expression of cosmic nature? The *Book*

of Documents says, 'The human heartmind is precarious. The Way heartmind is subtle.' Many commentators understand the 'human heartmind' to mean human desires and the 'Way heartmind' to mean cosmic Pattern. But this is wrong. There is only one heartmind. How could humans have two heartminds?[23]

If there is only one heartmind, though, then what can the "inherent heartmind" refer to? As we understand it, Lu's position is this: the inherent heartmind, which is always with us, is simply the (one) heartmind insofar as it is responding perfectly spontaneously, perfectly impartially, to a particular stimulus in the actual world. How to get oneself to respond spontaneously and impartially is a matter for discussion in chapter 7. Here, the key is to see how Lu might think that equating Pattern with the inherent heartmind will lead to wholeheartedness: the impartial deliverances of one's own heartmind are perfectly concrete and clear, shaped precisely to deal with the particular nuances of whatever situation one is encountering. This brings us to one final feature of Lu's view: namely, he, like WANG Yangming, holds that standards of right and wrong, or good and bad, vary according to context, so that no standards apply across all contexts. While Lu does not entirely reject the value of texts and teachers, he emphasizes that any past attempt to crystalize Pattern in writing refers to that particular situation and cannot be inflexibly applied to any new situation.[24]

The best-known advocate of identifying heartmind and Pattern is WANG Yangming, the dominant figure of Ming dynasty Neo-Confucianism. Wang adds some important nuances to the arguments we have just seen, and several of Wang's key teachings that we discuss in other chapters – such as the role of "good knowing" (chapter 5) and the "unity of knowing and acting" (chapter 6) – are undergirded by his argument that there is no Pattern apart from the heartmind. When one of his students suggests that, in our interactions with others, there are various Patterns that it would behoove us to investigate, Wang replies:

> In the matter of serving one's parents, it will not do to seek a Pattern of filial piety in one's parents, and in the matter of serving one's ruler, it will not do to seek a Pattern of devotion in one's ruler. ... They are all in this heartmind; heartmind is Pattern. When the heartmind is free from all obscuration by selfish desires, it just is cosmic Pattern, which requires not an iota added from the outside.[25]

It should be clear why, when Wang discovered the writings of LU Xiangshan rather late in Wang's life, he felt that he had discovered a kindred spirit. Recall our discussion in chapter 3 of Wang's rejection of the view that there are ethical rules that apply across all contexts. In the context of explaining why he holds that the inherent reality of the heartmind is "beyond good and bad," we mentioned Wang's discussion of the sage Shun's decision about whether to marry. Wang argues that Shun's proper ("good") reaction establishes no rule (which would be an external, rigid "good") that can now be followed ever after. Similarly, in the passage about serving one's parents cited above, we should not look for a Pattern outside us, but rather attend to how our heartmind guides us. Good and bad emerge, that is, from the functionings of the heartmind, which itself is prior to our external determinations of good and bad. Wang takes the implication of this identification of heartmind and Pattern very seriously. A student asks him what he makes of CHENG Yi's statement that "What is in a thing is Pattern." Wang replies: "The word 'heartmind' should be added, so that it reads: 'When heartmind is engaged in a thing, there is Pattern.' For example, when this heartmind is engaged in serving one's parent, there is filial piety."[26] In other words, a thing in itself, disconnected from any heartmind, would be Patternless.

Indeed, the tight relationship between the heartmind's engagement with things and the existence of Pattern has led some interpreters to read Wang as an idealist – that is, as believing that the world depends for its existence on the activity or functioning of the heartmind, and thus is in some sense a creation of our consciousness or subjectivity. The passage most often cited in support of this reading runs as follows:

> What emanates from the heartmind is the intention. The inherent reality of intention is knowing, and wherever the intention is directed is a thing. For example, when one's intention is directed toward serving one's parents, then serving one's parents is a 'thing.' When one's intention is directed toward serving one's ruler, then serving one's ruler is a 'thing.' ... Therefore I say that there are neither things nor Patterns outside of the heartmind.[27]

If we take it out of context, "there are neither things nor Patterns outside of the heartmind" certainly sounds like idealism. But here Wang seems to be talking about "things" in a technical sense, understood as objects of consciousness. In a separate dialogue, one of Wang's friends presses him to clarify his view. His response suggests that he readily acknowledges the heartmind-independence of things in the more ordinary sense, although he seems little interested in their heartmind-independent state:

The master was strolling in the mountains of Nan Zhen when a friend pointed to the flowering tress on a nearby cliff and said, "If in all the world, there is no Pattern outside the heartmind, what do you say about these flowering trees, which blossom and drop their flowers on their own, deep in the mountains? What have they to do with my heartmind?"

The master said, "Before you looked at these flowers they along with your heartmind had reverted to a state of silence and solitude (*ji* 寂). When you came and looked upon these flowers, their colors became clear. This shows that these flowers are not outside your heartmind."[28]

As we see here, Wang acknowledges that there is a sense in which the flowers exist on their own, independently of the heartmind; this is the flowers in a state of "silence and solitude." But Wang's concern is to correctly grasp not the flowers themselves but rather the Pattern of the flowers, which he indicates by speaking of how the colors of those flowers become clear. This is the point at which the flowers acquire meaning and value for us, and the meaning and value of the flowers do not lie in the flowers alone but only in the interaction between the flowers and one's heartmind.[29]

One problem that we have been tracking throughout this chapter is that of identifying an independent standard of assessment, one that would put us in a position to criticize and revise the intentions and emotions that we happen to have. Do the several versions of the view that "heartmind is Pattern" that we have just examined have satisfactory responses to this problem? If Pattern is related to heartmind in the way that Wang proposes, on what basis could we assess, for example, a father's seemingly natural inclination to abandon his children? How can he show that such an inclination is only a contingent and personal feature of the father's heartmind, rather than an inclination warranted by considerations of Pattern? Here, we can point to two lines of response available to WANG Yangming. The first line of response is that the father in question is too selfish. He sees himself as standing outside of the larger whole and has an exaggerated sense of his own importance and too little sense of the importance of his children. Wang readily acknowledges that many of our psychological reactions can go awry, and he blames selfish desires (*si yu* 私欲) and selfish intentions (*si yi* 私意) for this problem.[30] The second response is that even extended work at removing selfishness is no guarantee that one will respond correctly, but, as we will see in the next chapter, Wang deploys an idea he terms "good knowing" to explain how objective Pattern insistently calls itself to our attention.

3 ZHU Xi on nature, emotions, and the heartmind

We turn now to ZHU Xi, whose account of the heartmind is explicitly designed to avoid two sorts of extremes: those that insist too strongly on heartmind as the "source" of Pattern and those that identify heartmind too closely with vital stuff (which often goes hand in hand with an emphasis on the need to "adapt" the heartmind). On the one hand, he holds that views like those who collapse the distinction between heartmind and Pattern – and here he names LU Xiangshan and ZHANG Jiucheng – seem to eliminate the possibility of actual psychological guidance from our heartminds. He also worries that it might lead to a Buddhist subjectivism, according to which nature, Pattern, and the whole cosmos lose their objectivity, becoming simply inventions of our subjective heartminds. He insists that "heaven and earth are inherently existing things; they are not created by our heartminds."[31] On the other hand, Zhu is also not happy to think of the heartmind as simply the physical organ or the contingent emotions that it happens to have at a given time. He regularly uses the term "inherent heartmind" and also emphasizes the "Way heartmind" (recall that CHENG Yi had earlier called attention to this idea, as discussed above), thus ascribing to the heartmind a certain independence from the contingent state of one's vital stuff.

Zhu defends a middle position which, in his view, avoids the hazards of each of the two extremes, and to express this position he borrows a phrase from the earlier Neo-Confucian ZHANG Zai: "the heartmind unites nature and emotion."[32] Zhu means that the heartmind is the crucial nexus that brings together our formless nature and our contingent, empirical emotions, but how does it do this? What sort of "uniting" (*tong* 统) does Zhu have in mind? There is considerable scholarly controversy here, with some influential voices claiming that Zhu understands the heartmind as simply vital stuff: that is, as an empirical entity capable of grasping empirical truths. However, in light of both specific statements that Zhu makes to the contrary, and our overall understanding of Zhu's philosophical position, we believe that Zhu cannot hold that the heartmind is simply vital stuff.[33] Instead, we find the recent interpretation of Michiaki FUJI – which builds on the work of a range of other scholars – to be compelling.[34] Fuji argues that Zhu's view is that the nature and the emotions mutually constitute one another, and that this process of mutual constitution is the heartmind. So heartmind is neither Pattern nor vital stuff alone.

Let us explain. Recall from above the distinction between the not yet manifest – the realm of nature, centeredness, Pattern – and the already manifest, where we find emotion. Zhu says that the "heartmind is not placed between the already manifest and the not yet manifest; it is both, through-and-through."[35] How, then, do we interpret Zhu's statements that the "heartmind possesses (*ju* 具) Pattern," "heartmind includes (*bao* 包) nature," and "Pattern is just in the midst of heartmind"? As Fuji emphasizes, the answer is not to envision an actual space inside of the heartmind where Pattern/nature is located, even though Zhu does on rare occasion say things that might suggest this.[36] Instead, it helps to think in terms of processes rather than spaces. The ongoing process of the not yet manifest becoming manifest – which we just saw Zhu identify with the heartmind – can also be understood as the process of emotions emerging from nature. As we explained in chapter 3, nature is a kind of directionality or centeredness. It is present throughout the process of our emotions being manifested in response to a given stimulus, even when our response is ultimately inapt or off-center (i.e., bad). Putting this all together, we can say that the heartmind is really a process: it is the emotions continuously emerging under the (often partial) direction of nature. Fuji suggests that the heartmind can be understood diagrammatically as follows:

$$[\text{nature} \to \text{emotion}] = \text{heartmind}.[37]$$

This conception of the heartmind is made explicit by ZHU Xi's student CHEN Chun, who says that only when Pattern (nature) and *qi* (emotions) come together do we have heartmind. Chen adds that if we were to follow the Buddhists and eliminate emotion, then only "dead" nature would be left.[38] Nature is "live" through being part of the heartmind's continuous responses to the world.

In the next chapter, we explore the conative, cognitive, and perceptual dimensions of the dynamic interactions between nature and emotions that make up the heartmind. To wrap up this discussion of the metaphysics of ZHU Xi's heartmind, we turn now to his development of the terms "Way heartmind" and "human heartmind." Recall from above that CHENG Yi introduced these terms in an effort to explain how his two senses of "heartmind" might interact with one another. The first thing to understand for ZHU Xi is that the "Way heartmind" is not equivalent to Pattern, as it had been for CHENG Yi. Instead, both human heartmind and Way heartmind are "already manifest," which – given what we have just seen about Zhu's understanding of the heartmind – only makes sense if they are both supposed genuinely to be ways of talking about the heartmind, since the heartmind cannot be disconnected from the manifesting of emotion.[39] So what is the difference between these two ways of talking? ZHU Xi explains:

> The heartmind is one. When we speak of it from the perspective of its containing cosmic Pattern and its spontaneous manifestation in each circumstance, we call it "Way heartmind." From the perspective of having goals and conscious motives, we call it "human heartmind." Now having goals and conscious motives is not always bad. We still call it "selfish desire," though, since it is not completely spontaneously manifesting from cosmic Pattern.[40]

Zhu adds that if one can reach the point of no comparison and calculation, such that one's reactions are wholly in accord with the "pervasive circulation of Cosmic Pattern," then this is the "human heartmind with the consciousness of the Way heartmind." In another place, Zhu calls this the "human heartmind being transformed into the Way heartmind."[41] As the contemporary scholar CHEN Lai emphasizes, such a transformation does not mean that one has been purged of emotions. Instead, as ZHU Xi himself puts it, "when the human heartmind and Way heartmind are unified, it is as if that human heartmind had disappeared."[42] One still has emotions, but they do not give oneself any inappropriate weight. More concretely, Zhu puts it this way: "Take the case of food. When one is hungry or thirsty and desires to eat one's fill, that is the human heartmind. However, there must be moral Pattern in it. There are times one should eat and times one should not. ... This is the correctness of the Way heartmind."[43] Whenever one's desires to eat spontaneously match up with Pattern, that is a human heartmind that has been transformed into the Way heartmind.

Throughout this chapter, we have been viewing theories of heartmind via the problem of "accordance": how is one's heartmind – and thus the actual reactions one has to the world – able to accord with Pattern? We saw above that the accordance problem has two basic types of answers: *adapt* the heartmind to norms, which then presents worries about wholeheartedness, or understand the heartmind as the *source* of norms, which then presents worries about independent standards. ZHU Xi's answer leans more in the "adapt" direction than do those Neo-Confucians who assert an equivalence between heartmind and Pattern, so it is fair to ask whether Zhu's approach leaves us unable to wholeheartedly embrace Pattern. Zhu's answer would be to deny that he draws too firm a line between Pattern and the heartmind. Even though it is usually imperfectly realized, the nature of each of our heartminds is, still, cosmic Pattern and, as we have just seen, it is possible for one to transform one's heartmind so that it is the "Way heartmind," perfectly expressing Pattern. Zhu believes that this process of transformation is lengthy and demands that we pay attention to external sources of learning and authority. But he insists that learning can transcend merely superficial adaptations to external standards and attain wholeheartedness, his term for which is "sincerity" (*cheng* 誠), which we discuss in chapter 8.[44]

4 Late Ming and Qing developments: to the extremes

Until now, we have largely focused on leading thinkers in Song and Ming dynasty Daoxue. But beginning in the late Ming and culminating in the mid-Qing, Neo-Confucianism grew increasingly pluralistic and began to experiment with a wider range of views, and this applies especially to their thinking about heartmind. In this section, we will look briefly at some notable views outside the mainstream. The first two come from what has come to be called the Taizhou School of Daoxue, which refers to a group of sixteenth-century thinkers whose intellectual lineage can be traced back to WANG Yangming, but who took Wang's views in more radical directions. For example, major figures in the Taizhou School taught tradespeople and other commoners and (as we will see in chapter 8) defended more equal treatment of women. Two influential Taizhou Neo-Confucians, LUO Rufang and LI Zhi, stand out for proposing that the idea of an "inherent heartmind" be understood as referring to the heartminds that people have before their ideas and emotional dispositions are reshaped by the usual social influences that we take on as we grow up. Like WANG Yangming and others, they embraced the idea that the *benxin*, which we have been translating as "inherent heartmind," is identical to Pattern, but unlike Wang they took the phrase in the somewhat more literal sense of "original heartmind." Luo praised what he called the "infant's heartmind" (*chizi zhi xin* 赤子之心), seen paradigmatically in, for example, the infant's love of nourishment and her parent's affection.[45] Li used somewhat similar language in a famous treatise on the "child's heartmind" (*tongxin* 童心). Li directly identifies Pattern with the inherent heartmind, and then the inherent heartmind with the child's heartmind, emphasizing that the psychological dispositions of children have not yet been changed by external forces:

> From the beginning, aural and visual impressions enter in through the ears and eyes. When one allows them to dominate what is within oneself, then the child's heartmind is lost. As one grows older, one hears and sees what society regards as "moral principles" (*daoli* 道理). When one allows these to dominate what is within oneself, then the child's heartmind is lost. As one grows older, the moral principles that

one hears and sees grow more numerous with each day, thus extending the breadth of what one "knows" and "feels." Thereupon, one realizes that one should covet a good reputation, and endeavor to enhance it. One then loses one's child's heartmind.[46]

Not surprisingly for two philosophers who connected Pattern to youthful minds, both Luo and Li resisted the view, popular in Daoxue and beyond, that one should strive to suppress or contain one's spontaneous emotions, and both explicitly embraced the heartmind's natural tendency to seek pleasure and joy, although Luo sometimes suggested that it should not be something we seek deliberately or self-consciously.[47]

Luo's and Li's accounts again face the problem of identifying an independent standard of assessment but, arguably, in a more forceful way than before because the techniques that other Daoxue Confucians recommend for purging us of our bad desires – e.g., reading the classics, eliminating selfishness – seem harder to apply in a manner consistent with maintaining the spontaneous emotional responses of a child. In certain respects, Li's account poses the greater challenge here. Luo, at least, assumes that the basic emotions of the infant's heartmind are the same across all people, and he thinks those emotions line up neatly with traditional Confucian virtues such as filial piety and parental affection. In contrast, Li, following WANG Yangming, embraces the view that there are no rules of right and wrong that apply across all contexts.[48] He argues that the genuine (*zhen* 真) emotional responses vary from one individual and context to the next, and he is more willing to accept departures from Confucian practices and values when they better reflect what he takes to be the genuine inclinations of the child's heartmind.[49] In the eyes of one contemporary scholar, at least, Li's view provides us with too little by which to judge what appear to be unabashedly selfish emotions and desires, except by appealing to standards set by a phase of the heartmind – the child's one – that is impossible for social creatures like us to reclaim.[50]

At the outset of this chapter, we discussed two sorts of solutions to the accordance problem, one of which makes it the function of the heartmind to adapt to norms given externally and the other of which makes the heartmind a source of norms. It is striking that, up to this point, most of the Daoxue Confucians that we have canvassed attempt to solve the accordance problem by either directly identifying heartmind with Pattern or by proposing that Pattern is a major constituent of the heartmind. In the Qing dynasty, however, major Neo-Confucian philosophers articulate positions closer to the other end of the spectrum. For example, DAI Zhen saw the heartmind as having a natural but still largely undeveloped affinity for Pattern. This is in large part because he thinks it natural for all sentient creatures to love life and life fulfillment – beginning with their own but, for the more intelligent creatures, extending to the life in others as their sphere of awareness expands to include others.[51] In direct opposition to the Daoxue philosophers, Dai also insists that the heartmind is, at bottom, constituted solely by vital stuff and capable of tracking Pattern only insofar as it acquires the virtues and intellectual faculties that enable it to support an orderly process of life-giving generativity. Another unorthodox Neo-Confucian to adopt a more Mencian conception of heartmind is WANG Fuzhi. Like Dai, he sees the heartmind and its constituents as reducible to vital stuff, in his case the most energetic and refined vital stuff.[52] Wang also explicitly contrasts his view with that of mainstream Daoxue philosophers, adopting the by then popular Daoxue distinction between the human heartmind and the Way heartmind, but proposing that the Way heartmind is a more developed variant of the former, rather than something independently grounded in Pattern.[53] Both of these important Neo-Confucians attest to depth and diversity of Neo-Confucian thought on the heartmind.

For further study

Selected primary sources

1. ZHU Xi (CHU Hsi), "The Mind" and "The Mind, The Nature, and The Feelings," in Chan 1963: 628–32.
2. LU Xiangshan, "Second Letter to Senior Official Li," in Ivanhoe 2009: 70–3.
3. LU Xiangshan, *Recorded Sayings*, §6, in Ivanhoe 2009: 77–8.
4. WANG Yangming, selections from *Instructions for Practical Living*, §3 and §10, in Tiwald and Van Norden 2014: #43, 264–6 and 273.
5. LI Zhi, "On the Child-like Mind," in Tiwald and Van Norden 2014: #49: 304–7.

Discussion questions

1. What are the differences between the ways that CHENG Yi and ZHU Xi understand the categories of "human heartmind" and "Way heartmind," and what is the significance of these differences?

2. Which of the philosophers who identify Pattern and heart-mind has the strongest response to the concern about lacking an independent standard of assessment?
3. In what sense is Pattern *dependent* on heartmind, according to WANG Yangming? In what sense is it *independent* of heartmind?
4. LI Zhi takes the view that Pattern is identical with what he calls the "child's heartmind." What are the advantages and disadvantages of this view?

5

Emotions

---

1 Background

Chapter 3 introduced an idea of "nature" that can guide us even though it is formless: according to many Neo-Confucians, at least, we cannot directly experience it. Chapter 4 then explored that faculty which enables us to take nature into account, the heartmind. In this chapter, we meet another of the key ideas describing our basic psychology: the "emotions" (*qing*), which encompass all actual, affective and/or cognitive responses we have to stimuli from the world. While most of our attention here is on this capacious category of "emotion," we will also have occasion to discuss the closely related idea of "intention" (*yi* 意). Intentions are also responses to stimuli from the world. Some Neo-Confucians explicitly say that the two cover much the same territory, even while marking out subtle differences; and some discuss intentions more than emotions, though the issues seem quite similar.[1] Taken as a whole, this chapter examines a series of debates over whether the emotions can be reliable. We will see that over time, Neo-Confucians come to adopt increasingly positive stances toward the emotions.

The word *qing* has a range of senses in early texts, sometimes meaning the essence of a thing and sometimes the basic dispositions, feelings, emotions, or passions that are characteristic of a thing.[2] For Neo-Confucians, *qing* clearly has the latter set of meanings, and among the many classical passages on which they draw to spell out these "emotions," two stand out as particularly important. One of these, from the *Evolution of Rites*, offers a list of the seven emotions that people have without needing to learn them, and which sages must understand and regulate via rituals, if human society is to flourish: "What are human emotions? They are seven: joy, anger, sorrow, fear, love, dislike, and desire."[3] The idea here is clearly that human emotions are natural and unavoidable; they need not be taught and cannot be eliminated, but they can lead us astray and so must be regulated. This same idea appears in a passage we already met in the last chapter. *Centrality and Commonality* tells us: "When joy and anger, sorrow and happiness are not yet manifest, call it 'the center.' When they are already manifest, and yet all are hitting the proper measure, call it 'harmony.'" The four emotions listed here are not explicitly called *qing*, but the general sense is the same: so long as joy, anger, and so on "hit the proper measure," we have harmony. On their own – that is, independent of a context in which they count as either hitting the proper measure or not – it seems that the emotions can only be said to be neutral. Their importance lies in the fact that they motivate or even determine behavior, so it is by shaping one's emotions that we shape our selves and our societies.

The other crucial bit of background we need before looking at the Neo-Confucians themselves is the role played by Buddhism, which helped to popularize the notion that the emotions are fundamentally problematic.[4] Over the centuries, Buddhists employed *qing* in a variety of ways.[5] For our purposes, the most important uses refer to the deluded emotions and thoughts that characterize the interaction of the non-enlightened with the external world. Unlike the thinkers responsible for the classical Chinese discussions of emotion that we examined in the previous paragraph, both Indian and then Chinese Buddhists worried that our emotions and thoughts are systematically problematic. There are countless examples, a few of which will suffice to make the point. According to one sutra that was particularly well known during Neo-Confucian times, only when one's deluded emotions have been "forgotten" does one have the heartmind of a Buddha.[6] Similarly, an influential lay Buddhist from the Tang dynasty announces in his greatest work: "Only the arising of emotions obstructs the wisdom of sentient beings."[7] And an important Chan collection from the tenth century includes this saying: "The moment one produces emotions, one will be bound to the world of suffering for ten thousand kalpas."[8]

It should come as no surprise, therefore, that key participants in the shared Confucian-Daoist–Buddhist discourse of the eighth and ninth centuries also adopt a largely negative view of the emotions. This is perhaps most striking in the famous "Letter on Returning to the Nature," by LI Ao (772–841), who is widely (and correctly) viewed as an important forerunner of the Neo-Confucian revival in general, and of Daoxue in particular.[9] Li's "Letter" begins:

> That whereby a person may be a sage is nature; that whereby a person may be deluded as to this nature is emotion. Joy, anger, sorrow, fear, love, dislike, and desire – these seven are all the workings of emotion. When the emotions are darkened, the nature is hidden, though it is through no shortcoming of the nature: the seven follow one another in constant succession, so that the nature cannot achieve its fullness.[10]

Even more explicitly, later in the text Li speaks of emotions that respond to an external stimulus as follows: "These emotions are a perversion of the nature. Knowing that they are perverse and that perversion has no inherent existence, the heartmind will be absolutely still and not accept them, perverse thoughts will cease on their own, and the nature will shine brightly."[11] Of course, these two quotations do not do justice to the argument and subtlety of Li's essay; indeed, he makes efforts to acknowledge a positive role for something like emotions when he says things like nature must "show its brightness through the emotions" and that the sage, "although he has emotions, he has never had emotions."[12] Various interpretations have been offered for these statements, but, in the context of Li's fairly brief essay, no definitive view is possible. Li's work thus functions best as an expression of the complex state of play in the late Tang dynasty in which the philosophical need for the emotions to play a positive role seems to be straining against widespread worries about their problematic effects.

The overall trajectory of Neo-Confucian views of emotions is easy to summarize. While early Song dynasty thinkers have quite a range of positions – some of which we will see shortly – the stance of early Daoxue philosophers is rather similar to that of LI Ao, and the tensions within Li's position are only partly worked out. Later, ZHU Xi makes major strides toward assigning the emotions a more positive role. On at least one reading, this trend is continued by WANG Yangming and reaches an extreme with thinkers at the end of the Ming dynasty, whom one current scholar describes as engaging in a "soliloquy of emotions."[13] Critics of Daoxue in the Ming and Qing draw attention to some of these extreme views, but they, too, are in general far more affirmative concerning human emotions than was early Song Daoxue. We will discuss some of the philosophical reasons for this below; at the same time, keep in mind that, starting in the sixteenth century, China saw a dramatic acceleration in commercial activity, money economy, literacy, and participation in elite culture by merchants and others. Merchants' status improved and their pursuits were valorized as many Confucian thinkers began to take more seriously claims about the importance of benefit (*li* 利) and desire-satisfaction.[14] There seems little doubt that such social changes help to reinforce the philosophical changes we are considering. In the following sections, we will be able to track this broad trajectory of change through several specific debates, including one over the meaning and value of "desires" (*yu* 欲) and another concerning the relationship between emotions normally regarded as morally neutral or worse (the canonical seven discussed above) and the four emotions widely regarded as the starting points for moral virtue – the four "beginnings" (*duan* 端) identified by Mencius.

2 Emotional dispositions and objectivity in early Neo-Confucianism

Many early Neo-Confucians share the concerns that LI Ao expressed about the emotions, and similarly contrast the subjectively biased emotions with the objectivity of "nature" (*xing*). Here is SHAO Yong, for example: "Using things to contemplate things is nature. Using self to contemplate things is emotions. Nature is impartial and clear; emotions are partial and murky."[15] In a similar vein, in an influential early essay, CHENG Yi declares that:

> When one's emotions become agitated and increasingly numerous, one's nature is injured. This is why one who is awake restrains his emotions so as to conform to centrality, rectify his heartmind, and nourish his nature. This is called "imposing the nature on the emotions." One who is foolish does not know to control the emotions and lets them reach the point of depravity and one-sidedness, and so fetters his nature and loses it. This is called "imposing the emotions on the nature."[16]

Neither passage completely rejects the emotions, but both clearly connect an overreliance on emotions with subjectivity and bias.

Accusations of subjectivity and bias were also made in the other direction, however. Several early Neo-Confucians were suspicious of what they saw as the murky category of "nature" and thought that the basis for objective morality lay in our universally shared "human emotions" (*renqing*). Let us examine each half of this position in turn. SU Shi, an influential early Neo-Confucian who differed in important ways from the founders of Daoxue, worries that philosophers emphasizing the category of nature – as opposed, he says, to the empirical category of one's actual "endowment" (*cai*) – are universalizing certain particular features only possessed by some people, and on this basis criticizing others' failures to live up to the standards of their supposed "nature."[17] Instead of imagining a formless nature independent from our actual endowments, Su argues that we should attend to our actually universal emotional dispositions and build a balanced morality on their foundation. In so saying, Su is drawing on an important strand of Confucian philosophizing about emotions since classical times, which has stressed that the diverse and unavoidable constituents of our emotional makeup are healthy, so long as they are appropriately balanced and limited.[18] The use of the compound term *renqing* – "human emotions" – to refer to unavoidable tendencies in human emotional response also has a long pedigree. When Neo-Confucians use "emotion" alone, they tend to be emphasizing an occurrent emotion and its aptness or inaptness to a particular context. The term "human emotions," in contrast, stresses the ways that certain emotions will reliably occur under conditions characteristic for human beings. For example, another early Song Neo-Confucian, OUYANG Xiu, argues that good public policy must be based on a recognition of our universal emotional dispositions – that is, our human emotions – rather than on fantasies about a self-denying populace always ready to obey. Or, to put this more positively, according to Ouyang, value lies in what people are actually predisposed to find valuable.[19]

As SU Shi makes more explicit than Ouyang does, this does not entail that human emotions should be accepted without qualification. Indeed, SU Shi is willing to talk about "nature" and "Pattern" so long as they are understood as rooted in our actual experiences. He writes:

> There is no person alive who does not feel uncomfortable when hungry or cold, or who has never experienced sexual desire. Would it be acceptable today for someone to say that eating when hungry, drinking when thirsty, or having sexual desires is not part of nature? Everyone knows this is unacceptable. Lacking these emotions, the sage would have no means to be a sage. ... The sage takes his seven emotions ... and harnesses them so that they lead him to humaneness.[20]

Of course, talk of "harnessing" the emotions still leaves key philosophical questions unanswered: what guides our harnessing them in one way rather than another? And is humaneness just a specific combination of the seven emotions, or is it a further and separate achievement? One kind of answer by which Ouyang and Su were tempted is to say that, indeed, there is no further or deeper truth than seeking to fulfill, in a balanced and "centered" way, our human emotions. As SU Shi develops this train of thought, though, he puts significant weight on ideas like Pattern and nature, parting company with Ouyang's more resolute resistance to such abstract concepts. Su sees that the pattern associated with any given activity will be one-sided unless it is connected together with other patterns. He writes: "When the sages order the world ... they connect its joints and arteries with each other to form a unity. ... Thus the world can be made to act as a single human body."[21] SU Shi's final position shares a good deal with the expansive vision of his Daoxue contemporaries. Ouyang, on the other hand, is left feeling disconnected from what he takes to be an unsympathetic and unfeeling natural world; as a contemporary scholar has put it, Ouyang's poetry expresses the idea that "although our emotions might be triggered by external circumstances, their tendency to make us long for what we could not have ... led us eventually to isolation from that world."[22]

OUYANG Xiu and SU Shi are, to varying degrees, critical of the ways that others distinguished nature from human emotions, but they are not the only thinkers of the era to recognize that our emotional responses are patterned: that is, that we tend to respond (or perhaps inevitably respond) in certain ways, which we can call dispositions. Indeed, most Daoxue thinkers also used the concept of "human emotions," although they do not give it the same pride of place that we see in Ouyang or Su. Instead, human emotions tend to be understood in something like the way we might use a neutral, descriptive sense of human nature or human tendencies: they provide a baseline or starting point but cannot, on their own, decree what our best selves and society should be (which depends on our deeper nature). Thus when the Chengs say that the sages "follow human emotions in establishing the rituals," they do not mean that the sages slavishly follow them; rather, that human emotions are taken into account and shaped; without these enduring human dispositions, the rituals would have no way to connect to us.[23]

3 Desire

According to the canonical list of seven, "desire" (*yu*) is one kind of emotion. It is a quite general category, indicating that one is drawn toward a given object or state; when one is hungry, the impulse toward eating that one experiences is a classic desire. As we will see, there is considerable debate about whether desires can sometimes be apt, and those who hold that there are indeed good desires then look for other ways to explain what distinguishes "desire" from other sorts of emotions (for example, some suggest that desires are more dramatic or violent). We will begin by looking at an early, extreme position that appears to argue that we should aim to have no desires at all, very much in keeping with the broader skepticism about emotions that we have already discussed. Within Daoxue, various thinkers criticize the "no desire" position, with ZHU Xi's effort to both endorse and yet qualify it perhaps the most important. We will end this section by evaluating later criticisms of Zhu's stance.

ZHOU Dunyi, a thinker who seems not to have been directly associated with early Daoxue but whom ZHU Xi (among others) insisted should count as a key contributor to the Neo-Confucian revival, famously asserted that sages are without desires.[24] What he means by this, however, isn't immediately apparent. The term "without desires" appears prominently in the early Daoist classic *Daode Jing*, but it is also found in a variety of other early texts and is used in a range of contexts by later thinkers, including Buddhists; as with so many Neo-Confucian terms of art, it is best understood as a polyvalent resource that some Neo-Confucians choose as part of the conceptual, rhetorical, and pedagogical framework they construct. Zhou uses the absence of "desire" to help define a special kind of "tranquillity" (*jing* 靜), in which many aspects of the outer world simply do not matter to one: "The sage settles human affairs using centrality, correctness, humanity, and righteousness. ... He regards tranquillity as fundamental. Having no desire, he will be tranquil."[25] The fundamental kind of "tranquillity" mentioned is a mental state or phase we can achieve not just when at rest but when active as well: "Unity is the essential way. Unity is having no desire. If one has no desire, then one is tenuous while tranquil, straight while active. Being tenuous while tranquil, one becomes intelligent and hence penetrating; being straight while active, one becomes impartial and hence all-embracing.[26] In a final passage, we can see Zhou flesh out these ideas of "tranquillity" and "no desire" in a more concrete context. Zhou cites a description of Confucius' favorite student, Yanzi,[27] and comments:

Wealth and honor are what people love. Yanzi did not love or seek them but instead enjoyed poverty. What does this tell us about his unique heartmind? There are high honors and enormous wealth that one can love and seek after, but Yanzi was unlike others since he could see what was truly great and forget what was really small. He saw the great, so his mind was at peace. His mind was at peace, so there was nothing he lacked. Lacking nothing, he treated wealth, honor, poverty, and humble station in the same way. As he treated them in the same way, he could transform them and equalize them. This is why Yanzi was regarded as second to the sage.[28]

It certainly sounds like some desires that most of us have are ones that the sage should not have at all. If we lack these desires, we will be calm, tranquil, quiescent, and lack for nothing, though we may be desperately hungry and living in filth.

ZHU Xi believed that there was much to learn from ZHOU Dunyi, both from his metaphysical speculations about the "supreme pivot" (discussed already in chapter 2) and from his ideas about the sage. But he felt it was important to qualify or clarify Zhou's statements about desire:

> Zhou said that one should have fewer and fewer desires until one has none, for he was afraid that people thought it enough to have few desires. ... But the task of having no desire depends on one's ability to have few desires. No one but the sage can reach the point of having no desire. Someone then asked: "But what are we to make of this word 'desire'?" Zhu replied: "There are different meanings. This idea of having few desires – that is with respect to those desires that are improper: things like selfish desires. As for being hungry and desiring to eat or being thirsty and desiring to drink, are these desires that one can be without?"[29]

Zhou was right that sages do, in some sense, reach a state of "no desire." But it seems that there are good desires and bad desires. Zhu often refers to bad desires as "human desires" (*renyu*) or "selfish desires" (*siyu*), and it is quite clear that what makes them bad is determined not only by their objects but also by their degree of strength or their priority relative to the situation and to other desires. For example:

> Someone asked: "Were parents to feel boundless love for their children and to desire that the children be brilliant and become established, could that be called the sincere heartmind [i.e. the Way heartmind]?" Zhu responded: "It is proper that parents love their children, but to love without limitation and thus to unquestioningly desire things on their behalf is improper. One must properly distinguish between cosmic Pattern and human desires."[30]

Part of loving is desiring things on behalf of one's loved ones. This can be proper, but when one "unquestioningly desires things on their behalf," one's desires are out of balance. In the same vein, Zhu says that "eating and drinking are the cosmic Pattern, but demanding delicious flavors is human desire."[31] If we read Zhu sympathetically, we must conclude that in most cases it is not the object of a desire that makes it bad, but the strength of that desire at that time and place, in comparison to other desires one might have. Many desires can be acceptable, when felt to the proper degree. It is thus unjust to charge Zhu with advocating wholesale suppression of the desires, and, as we will see in the next section, Zhu has important insights into the role that certain emotions can play in ethically proper motivation. As far as desires are concerned, though, Zhu focuses on their negative effects and has relatively little to teach us about positive roles that desires may play.

The sharpest criticism of Zhu's understanding of desire comes centuries later, from DAI Zhen. Dai succinctly expresses the core of his conception of desire when he writes, "whatever comes from desire is always for the sake of life and nurture."[32] Dai certainly believes that desires can go too far, but in their origins they are good, motivating us to seek things upon whose value all agree. Dai argues:

> There can be no greater affliction in a human life than to lack the means to fulfill one's own life. If, desiring to fulfill one's own life, one also fulfills the lives of others, this is humaneness. If, desiring to fulfill one's own life, one reaches the point even of slaying others and paying no heed, this is inhumaneness. Inhumaneness does indeed begin with the desire to fulfill one's life, and if there were no such desire, necessarily there would be no inhumaneness. But if there were no such desire, then one would also regard the affliction and distress of others in the world with indifference. It is impossible for one to feel that one's own life need not be fulfilled and yet fulfill the life of another.[33]

The last two sentences make the crucial point: we must be motivated by our desires, else we will care neither about ourselves nor about others. Without desires there can be no humaneness. He therefore criticizes Song dynasty Confucians as follows:

> The Song masters said: "If it does not come from Pattern then it comes from desire, and if it does not come from desire, then it comes from Pattern." When they see others crying out from hunger and cold, or experiencing the sorrow and resentment of an unfulfilled love, or hoping for life despite being close to death, it is all just "human desire"; they abstractly designate a sentiment devoid of emotion or desire as the "inherent state of cosmic Pattern," and preserve it in their hearts.[34]

Given all the invective that Song thinkers launched at "human desire," Dai is wondering, what is left for "humaneness"? What, in particular, can it mean to "desire humaneness"? Dai believes that the Song understanding of humaneness is "abstract" or "empty," divorced from the flesh-and-blood desires about which we really care – and which alone can serve to motivate us to do good for our selves and others. At the heart of ethical motivation, according to Dai, are our everyday desires. In the next section, we will return to Zhu and other Daoxue thinkers to see whether they have an answer to Dai's challenge.

4 The four beginnings as morally pure?

In one of the most famous passages from the *Mencius*, the author assigns a special significance to each of four specific moral reactions – reactions that structurally resemble the "emotions" we have just been discussing:

> Suppose someone suddenly saw a child about to fall into a well: anyone in such a situation would have a feeling of alarm and commiseration – not because one sought to get in good with the child's parents, not because one wanted a good reputation among one's neighbors and friends, and not because one would dislike the sounds of the child's cries. From this we can see that if one is without the feeling of alarm and commiseration, one is not human. If one is without the feeling of disdain, one is not human. If one is without the feeling of deference, one is not human. If one is without the feeling of approval and disapproval, one is not human. The feeling of alarm and commiseration is the beginning (*duan*) of humaneness. The feeling of disdain is the beginning of righteousness. The feeling of deference is the beginning of propriety. The feeling of approval and disapproval is the beginning of wisdom. People having these four beginnings is like their having four limbs.[35]

Here, Mencius offers us a thought-experiment for only one of the four feelings, but the passage implies that each of these four feelings is equally automatic. The term we here translate as "feeling" is actually *xin*, "heartmind," but in this context we are to understand it as referring to specific reactions of one's heartmind, thus "feeling." These four feelings are reactions to circumstances, just like the emotions we have been discussing so far. Although the term *qing* is not used, we also see quite explicitly that the possession of these four is partly definitive of what it is to be human, and it also appears that they are natural or innate, rather than learned. In short, they seem to be structurally very similar to the seven emotions listed in the canonical

Evolution of Rites passage cited earlier in this chapter. Two aspects of the passage make things more interesting, however. First is the fact that these four reactions seem not to be neutral, but distinctively ethical, perhaps in their own right and certainly in their connections to the corresponding virtues (of humaneness, righteousness, and so on). Second, the reactions are described as *duan*, a term whose basic meaning is "tip" or "beginning." In the context of the *Mencius*, many scholars today believe that *duan* should be understood as "sprout" – one's nascent ethical character is something that needs to be cultivated and grown from these sprouts – but as we will soon see, Neo-Confucians typically understood the passage somewhat differently.

There are two philosophical problems that the four beginnings have the potential to solve. The first is what we will call the "guidance problem." As we saw in chapter 3, many Daoxue Confucians think we cannot have direct access to nature. Among these, many think that the indirect guide or indicator of nature is the emotions – those that come from nature itself rather than other sources. But this raises a question: which emotions in particular are reliable guides to nature? The theory of the four beginnings offers the hope of answering this question, so long as we can come to identify the four beginnings and learn how to expand on the glimmers of our nature that they afford us. The second is what we will call the "motivation problem." Given that many Daoxue Confucians are suspicious of most emotions, one might criticize their theories as unable to provide some alternative source of motivation sufficient to drive people to do good things. As we just saw, DAI Zhen thinks that the Daoxue Confucians' distaste for self-interested desires deprives them of the very sympathetic capacities necessary to care about the life fulfillment of others. Here, too, the theory of the four beginnings might offer a solution if there is good reason to think that they point to a source of motivation which is both sufficient to drive people to do virtuous things and acceptable in the eyes of the Daoxue Confucians.

We can start by looking at CHENG Yi, who seems to have been the first Neo-Confucian to put particular emphasis on the importance of the four beginnings; the beginnings go unmentioned in the writings of his Confucian contemporaries, both within and without the emerging Daoxue group.[36] In the following passage, we can see CHENG Yi grappling with both of the philosophical problems we have raised: "Alarm and commiseration belong under love, which is an emotion rather than nature. Sympathetic understanding (*shu*) is a means of entry into humaneness, but not humaneness itself. It is on account of our feeling of alarm and commiseration that we know that we have humaneness."[37] CHENG Yi is explicit here that beginnings like "alarm and commiseration" are emotions (or at least aspects of a full-fledged emotion like love), rather than the norm of humaneness itself. However, if we can take the reference to "sympathetic understanding" to relate to the feeling of connectedness with another that "alarm and commiseration" signals, then this beginning might indeed help us understand how we come to feel and be moved by humaneness, thus perhaps solving the motivation problem. In addition, he also claims that it is precisely via this same beginning that we know we have humaneness, which speaks directly to the guidance problem.[38]

CHENG Yi is not entirely consistent in his treatment of the beginnings,[39] nor does he go on to answer questions that arise if one presses at his explanation: for example, do the beginnings always motivate one in the right ways? If so, what makes them different from the standard emotions that we have been discussing throughout the chapter? For exploration of these issues – though not for definitive resolution – we must turn to ZHU Xi. A good place to start is with his famous commentary on the line from the *Mencius* that introduces the idea of "beginnings." Zhu says: "Alarm and commiseration, disdain, deference, approval and disapproval: these are emotions. Humaneness, righteousness, propriety, wisdom: these are nature. The heartmind unites nature and emotion. 'Beginning' refers to a clue: because of the emotion's manifestation, the inherent reality of nature is observable, like when there is an externally visible clue to something hidden inside."[40] One thing this passage suggests is that the beginnings are not "beginnings" in the sense of manifesting the beginning of an immature or incomplete nature.[41] Instead, they render visible the inherent, perfect state of one's nature. They are still only clues or beginnings, though, because they only give us a momentary, bounded glimpse at what is in fact unified, holistic, and all-inclusive.[42] Even a perfect emotional manifestation can only be perfect in its moment, ideally suited to the immediate context.

Are the beginnings always perfect, though? Here, ZHU Xi's recorded sayings provide conflicting evidence. At one point he says that "The four beginnings are the manifestation of Pattern; the seven emotions are the manifestation of vital stuff."[43] But on some interpretations this seems to be at odds with Zhu's broader metaphysical views. For example, the strongest reading of this passage – that the beginnings are *only* Pattern, and the emotions *only* vital stuff – is a complete non-starter since Zhu clearly holds both that any detectable manifestation must be mediated in vital stuff, and that any manifestation of vital stuff must have its Pattern. Even those later interpreters who rest significant weight on this passage still acknowledge these facts.[44]

Another important bit of evidence comes from Zhu's statement that the beginnings are manifestations of emotion in which "the emotion emerges from the nature and is good."[45] This makes it clear that the beginnings are a form of emotion, and it seems to say that they are always good. In a third passage, though, Zhu is explicit that the beginnings are apparently not always good: "As for alarm and commiseration and shame and dislike, there are cases when they hit the proper measure and cases when they do not hit the proper measure. If one feels alarm and commiseration when it is inappropriate ... then it is not hitting the proper measure."[46] Zhu does not say how often a reaction of alarm and commiseration can go awry, but clearly it is a possibility. Recall Zhu's statement quoted above that "to love one's children without limitation and thus to unquestioningly desire things on their behalf is improper." Presumably a reaction of alarm and commiseration can similarly be too strong, perhaps because it is not balanced by other aspects of a situation that also call for one's reaction.

On balance, we should understand Zhu in this way. As we saw in chapter 3, our nature cannot be directly accessed or described – beyond saying (controversially) that it is completely good – but its directionality is revealed through our emotions. As Zhu says at one point: "When one has this nature, one will express these emotions. Via the emotions, one sees the nature. Today there are these emotions, we can then see that inherently there is this nature."[47] The beginnings are special types of emotion because they are paradigmatic cases of the ways in which our emotions can reveal our nature, but they are not infallible. At the same time, any of our emotions can be a perfect expression of our nature, even if the "seven" may be less reliable than the "four." After all, "the sage's joy and anger are supremely impartial and smoothly responsive, the extremity of cosmic Pattern."[48] In short, ZHU Xi assigns the emotions a more active and positive role in human psychology than did many of his predecessors.[49]

Earlier in this section, we introduced the guidance problem and the motivation problem. ZHU Xi's answer to the latter seems to be this: there is no special problem about being motivated to follow Pattern because apt, Pattern-following reactions – whether of the "four beginnings" type or the "seven emotions" type – are all instances of genuine emotions, which are intrinsically motivating. There is no need for a distinctive (and implausible) other type of pure motivation. The guidance problem is trickier. We have suggested that Zhu may find the four beginnings to be more reliable than the seven emotions, but it is hard to see exactly what the basis for this might be, and in any event Zhu clearly holds that even the beginnings can go wrong.

His view, then, is a kind of fallibilism in which we continually strive to put ourselves in positions in which we will respond well, even though we seem to have few ways of guaranteeing that we have succeeded in a given instance.

5 WANG Yangming on emotion and good knowing

The motivation and guidance problems continue to underlie debates about emotions in post-Song dynasty thought, but changes in the socio-political situation help to alter the ways that each of these problems is structured. As discussed in our introduction, Daoxue interpretations of the classics are incorporated into the civil service examination system as orthodoxy under the Mongol emperors of the Yuan dynasty, but it is only in the early Ming dynasty that Daoxue is explicitly embraced by rulers themselves. The result is not, alas, the broad transformation of society toward which Daoxue aspired, but instead a hollowing out of Daoxue discourse. As it becomes mainstream, it becomes superficial: slogans for success in exams rather than for personal ethical commitment. Criticism of this "vulgar learning" is one of the great engines driving Ming Neo-Confucianism, and we will have occasion to discuss it in more than one chapter. Here, we focus on two connections to emotion. First, many Ming thinkers worry about the implication found in Song Daoxue writings that the "nature," the "inherent reality," and the "not yet manifest" are in some sense "tranquil" (*jing*), and thus disconnected from actual motivation. Second, in view of the seemingly limitless ability of Ming emperors to employ Daoxue language to justify their actions, some Ming Neo-Confucians charge that ethical guidance should not rest on abstract and ineffable ideas like "nature," but instead needs to be connected more directly to our actual emotions. For reasons concerned with both motivation and guidance, in short, Ming Neo-Confucians give a strengthened role to the emotions.

These themes can be seen in many of the era's philosophers; in this section, we will concentrate on the most influential of them all, WANG Yangming. We saw in the previous chapter that, according to Wang, Pattern *just is* the heartmind when it is in its proper state, rather than something perceived or grasped by the heartmind. Pattern does not exist ineffably in one's "nature" – or, worse, in the natures of things outside the self – but is the heartmind's proper reactions themselves. Since the heartmind's reactions are, by definition, "emotions," this means that we should expect WANG Yangming to identify Pattern and the emotions. Doing so would answer the questions about motivation and guidance raised in the previous paragraph, although it might simultaneously raise new problems.

Rather than stipulate that some reactions are pure (the beginnings) and others impure (the emotions), Wang introduces the category of *liangzhi*. We will translate this rather literally as "good knowing," but it is as much a kind of emotion as it is a cognitive, judging state.[50] Indeed, Wang says: "When the seven emotions follow their spontaneous (*ziran*) courses of operation, they are all the functioning of good knowing."[51] In other words, any emotion can be an instance of good knowing, so long as it meets two conditions. First, it must be manifested spontaneously, which here means naturally and without interference. Second, as other passages make clear, it must dissipate without lingering influence or attachment. One can love beauty, for example, so long as one is not controlled by it. Wang says that the inherent reality of good knowing is like a perfect mirror: good knowing responds perfectly without leaving anything on the mirror.[52] A closely related idea is articulated here: "Good knowing is simply a place in which one's clear consciousness of cosmic Pattern is spontaneously revealed; its inherent reality is simply a true sincerity and commiseration."[53] The idea, again, is that when one experiences emotions following their natural, non-selfish course of reaction, this revealing of cosmic Pattern is good knowing.

We need to add two, crucial dimensions to the idea that good knowing, as perfect emotion, expresses Pattern: (1) emotions can go wrong, but (2) via good knowing, they are self-correcting. Wang is very aware that our emotions often go wrong. One of his most sensitive treatments of this issue comes in a letter to a student who is experiencing unbearable sorrow upon learning that his son is seriously ill. Wang writes:

> A father's love for his son is of course the noblest emotion. Nevertheless, cosmic Pattern naturally has a point of centeredness and harmony. To be excessive means to have selfish intentions. On such an occasion most people think that according to cosmic Pattern they should be sorrowful. They do not realize that they are already affected by worries and anxieties and their heartminds will not be correct. Generally speaking, the influence of the seven emotions is in the majority of cases excessive, and only in the minority of cases insufficient. As soon as it is excessive, it is not in accord with the inherent reality of the heartmind. It must be adjusted to reach the center before it will be correct.[54]

So the emotions can go wrong: even in a favored case like a father's love for his child, emotions are typically excessive, so we cannot simply be guided by whatever we feel. To use Wang's language, we must not move the center of concern from cosmic Pattern to oneself – which is precisely what he means by "selfish." Still, we must wonder how one can know which emotions are reliable "good knowing" and which are not. Note that this passage does not suggest that we have some sort of independent access to cosmic Pattern outside of our emotions: he says that on occasions like these, "most people think that according to cosmic Pattern they should be sorrowful," but they are wrong. Our thoughts about Pattern are not reliable.

How, then, do we recognize good knowing? Wang begins to face this question squarely in reply to another letter:

> You spoke about following one's emotions and intentions (*yi*), and acting according to these as though they were good knowing, rather than according to the real good knowing. This shows that you have already located the danger. Intentions and good knowing should be clearly distinguished from one another. Intention arises out of response to an object, and can be either good or bad. Good knowing is *that which can distinguish between the good and bad in the intention.* When one follows one's good knowing, all that one does cannot be wrong.[55]

Intentions and good knowing are structurally different from one another since intention depends on some degree of conscious or unconscious interference with the pure, mirror-like expression of emotional reaction. As suggested in this passage, though, the two types of reactions can be difficult or impossible to distinguish at the moment in terms of how they feel. The key, says Wang, is that good knowing "can distinguish between the good and bad in the intention." But how? Statements like this, coupled with the fact that good knowing is called a form of "knowing," might suggest that *liangzhi* is after all not an emotion but a distinct form of cognition, a judgment that we can access somehow independently of our emotions. However, such an interpretation would lead to a variety of new interpretive difficulties, and we believe that Wang in fact has something else in mind.

If good knowing is simply our purest emotional reactions, how can it distinguish between good and bad intentions? By the way that we emotionally react to those intentions. We routinely experience emotional reactions to our emotions, intentions, and behavior. Imagine yourself, tired after a long day of work, feeling exasperated at some foible of your spouse. You may or may not express this feeling out loud, but even if you do not, if you find a moment to reflect – that is, to put yourself in a less selfish frame of mind – you will probably feel embarrassed at your reaction. Such self-correcting or self-reinforcing emotions are commonplace, and important. Of course, you can sometimes anticipate and avoid experiencing the "guilty conscience" by distracting yourself – for example, if instead of giving yourself a moment for reflection, you pile on more reasons for anger, perhaps because in the moment anger feels good (the result of having overly irascible vital stuff). However, Wang insists that good knowing is always there, even in the worst of us, trying to nudge us in the right direction. In one of his letters, Wang writes: "Our inherent heartmind is as bright and clear as the sun in daytime. No one who has faults does not know them himself."[56] In answer to the guidance problem, then, Wang eschews an emphasis on the distinctive "beginnings" in favor of reliance on our ability to experience perfect emotions, as supported by the self-correcting reactions of our heartminds. Wang acknowledges that "reaching good knowing" (*zhi liangzhi* 致良知) (that is, comprehensively experiencing perfect emotions) can be difficult and precarious. He thus puts considerable stress on commitment and focus, as we will see in a later chapter. Self-discipline is important to Wang. In a philosophy that puts so much weight on being guided by one's subjective feeling of aptness, though, there is clearly a potential for self-deception and excess. In the final section of this chapter, we look at how some later thinkers grappled with this problem.

6 A "soliloquy of emotion"?

WANG Yangming's focus on good knowing as perfect emotion and his related identification of the heartmind with Pattern (on which, see the previous chapter) were highly influential, though other philosophers criticized Wang, worrying that the conflation of emotion and Pattern would lead to immorality. For an example of this latter trend, consider the following argument by Wang's contemporary LUO Qinshun. Acknowledging that Mencius had used the term "good knowing," Luo is in no position to reject the concept entirely. However, says Luo:

> Knowing … is a marvelous function of the heartmind, and love …
> is the cosmic Pattern of the human heartmind. On the basis of the
> fact that without need for reflection one spontaneously knows to love
> one's parents, we thus call this "good knowing." But recently there
> are those who take good knowing *to be* cosmic Pattern. But then what
> role is played by love?[57]

In other words, Luo charges that by identifying good knowing – the actual emotional reaction – with Pattern, nothing is left to serve as an independent standard of assessment. In many ways, this resembles earlier debates about whether and how "nature" must be somehow independent from our emotions and heartminds, such that it can serve as a standard for correct emotional responses.

Still, while such criticisms of "good knowing" do not disappear, there is no doubt that the general trend in the Ming was toward endorsing either some version of good knowing[58] or other ways to view emotions in a positive light. The late-Ming Daoxue thinker LIU Zongzhou is a particularly interesting comparison with those – like LUO Qinshun, as just discussed – who insist on a distinction between formless nature and physical emotions. In marked contrast, Liu claims that nature, the virtues, Pattern, and emotion are all fundamentally continuous with one another, making him an excellent example of what we call in the introduction a "heartmind emphasis" Neo-Confucian. Some of his arguments for this position are textual. He cites passages from the *Book of Changes* in which nature and emotion look to be connected rather than distinct. Liu also maintains that when Mencius said that the four beginnings are the "beginnings" of their corresponding virtues, he means that they are literally the initial stages of the virtues, rather than "clues" to the separate (formless) existence of the virtues, Pattern, and nature, as ZHU Xi had said. Liu writes: "Emotions are just nature; it is not that the already manifest is emotion, standing in contrast to the word 'nature.'"[59] Liu does recognize that there are emotions which can go awry; he uses the conventional "seven emotions" to label these. He interchangeably uses Mencius's four beginnings and the four emotions mentioned in *Centrality and Commonality* (namely, joy, anger, sorrow, and happiness) to refer to special forms of emotion that are apparently infallible, saying that these "are used to speak particularly of the four virtues."[60] This approach does solve both the guidance and motivation problems, but at the cost of a marked implausibility.[61]

LIU Zongzhou is far from the only, or most extreme, case of a late-Ming dynasty thinker putting tremendous theoretical weight on the emotions. Another famous instance is LI Zhi, but since we have discussed him in a related context in chapter 4, we end this chapter by looking at the fascinating views of the writer and thinker FENG Menglong, who is somewhat less well-known among historians of philosophy. Feng sees emphasis on Pattern and emphasis on emotion as opposed to one another when it comes to the means we should employ to seek sagely rule and social harmony. He writes: "When it comes to being loyal, filial, and well-regulated, if one does them by following moral principles (*daoli*) then they will necessarily be forced, whereas if one does them by following one's fully realized emotions, then they will necessarily be genuine." In other words, only following our genuine emotions will really motivate us reliably. The result of this "doctrine of emotion" (*qingjiao* 情教), according to Feng, will be a successful achievement of Pattern; he says that "conventional Confucians only understand Pattern as a criterion for emotions, not realizing that emotions are the cords that hold Pattern together."[62] Rather than trying to teach the content of Pattern directly, by emphasizing moral principles, Feng therefore argues for an education of people's emotions.[63] As we will see in chapter 7 in some detail, those who emphasize Pattern and nature do not generally argue for inflexibly following specific "moral principles," but we know that this had become a common way of trying to implement the teachings of Zhu and others, so Feng's charge is understandable. To conclude this look at the "soliloquy of emotion," let us note that Feng's argument that emotion alone can be a successful route to Pattern is not the most extreme view to be found in his day: that honor belongs to someone like the playwright TANG Xianzu, who stressed the wild, anti-"reason" side of emotion without any concern for whether it enabled one to match up, in the end, with Pattern.[64] But with Tang, we have gone beyond the bounds of Neo-Confucianism.

For further study

Selected primary sources

1. LI Ao, "The Fu-hsing Shu of Li Ao" (n.b. this is Li's "Letter on Returning to the Nature"), in Barrett 1992: 88–131.
2. ZHU Xi (CHU Hsi), "The Mind, The Nature, and The Feelings," in Chan 1963: 630–2.
3. ZHU Xi, *Collected Commentaries on the* Mengzi (n.b. "Mengzi" is another way of Romanizing the name "Mencius"), 6A6, in Tiwald and Van Norden 2014: 215–17.
4. LUO Qinshun, *Knowledge Painfully Acquired*, §§16–17, in Luo 1987: 67–8.
5. DAI Zhen, Selections from *An Evidential Commentary on the Meanings of Terms in the* Mengzi, §11, in Tiwald and Van Norden 2014: 327–9.
6. T'oegye, Kobong, Yulgok, Ugye, *The Four Seven Debate* (Kalton 1994). Although not discussed in the main text, this famous debate among Korean Neo-Confucians contains the most sustained and sophisticated discussion in the whole East Asian tradition of the "four beginnings" and the "seven

emotions," and it has also been accessibly introduced and translated in Kalton (1994). This reading is an outstanding supplement to the other texts mentioned here. For specific reading suggestions and discussion questions, see the syllabi posted at http://neo-confucianism.com.

Discussion questions

1. Map out the philosophers discussed in the chapter on a spectrum: who is most worried about emotions (or desires, etc.)? Who is most willing to accept our emotions as they are? Is there a middle ground, and is it plausible?
2. Evaluate DAI Zhen's criticisms of ZHU Xi's stance concerning "desire."
3. What are the "guidance problem" and the "motivation problem"? Why are they problems?
4. What might plausibly ground a distinction between the "four beginnings" and the "seven emotions"?
5. Does WANG Yangming's idea of "good knowing" solve the guidance and motivation problems?

6

Knowing

1 Introduction

Over the last two chapters, we have explicated the heartmind, including its role as the seat of the emotions. In the present chapter, we turn to another crucial aspect of the heartmind's functioning, in this case one that corresponds in certain ways to western conceptions of "epistemology." Like western epistemology, our present interest is in a kind of knowing; the Chinese term at the heart of this chapter, *zhi* 知, is typically translated as "know." Unlike western epistemology, though, Neo-Confucians do not focus on the contrast between beliefs that count as knowledge and those that are merely opinion. Instead, the most important kind of knowing is a spontaneous discerning of Pattern that automatically brings with it motivation and thus action; the important contrast, for most Neo-Confucians, is with those forms of knowing that do not satisfactorily connect us up to Pattern. There is some room in this kind of picture for judgment, justification, and reflection, but these activities are not as central as they are in western epistemology. Instead, key debates focus on questions like: Does the cultivation or activation of ideal knowing involve discriminating between subject and object, or not? What is the role of perception, and can one directly perceive Pattern? Is sudden, holistic insight possible, and if so, what is its significance? Finally, how exactly are knowing and acting related, and does the right kind of knowing always guarantee a proper response? Answers to these questions are both important in their own right and set the stage for our examination of self-cultivation and virtue in chapters to come.

As in other areas, in their theories of knowing Neo-Confucians creatively and critically synthesize a variety of earlier ideas, especially those from classical Confucianism and various schools of Chinese Buddhism. As such, it makes sense to begin with a few of these earlier ideas. Chris Fraser summarizes the situation in classical texts as follows:

> Perhaps the most frequent use of the word *zhi* (know) in early Chinese texts is in contexts in which it is best interpreted as "knowing-of" or "knowing-about," a sort of recognition, familiarity, or understanding. A second common use is to mean roughly "know-to" or "know-how-to," referring to a kind of competence or ability. Occasionally, *zhi* is used in contexts in which it is interpretable as "knowing that" and seems to refer to propositional knowledge.[1]

Many famous passages illustrate the first of these uses. For example, the *Analects'* brief spiritual autobiography of Confucius reads: "At fifteen, I committed myself to learning; at thirty, I took my place in society; at forty, I became free of doubts; at fifty, I understood (*zhi*) the cosmic decree; at sixty, my ear was attuned; at seventy, I could follow my heartmind's desires without overstepping the bounds of propriety."[2]

Similarly, in the *Mencius* we read: "To fully fathom one's heart-mind is to understand (*zhi*) one's nature. To understand one's nature is to understand the cosmos."[3] A theme of much scholarship on early Chinese theories of knowing is that these texts understood "knowing"/"understanding" in terms of competence in distinguishing various aspects of what is known from one another, which is often then linked to appropriate, skilled responses.[4] It is easy to see how this kind of knowing would be closely connected to the virtue of wisdom, which precisely has to do with deeply understanding things and their interconnections, leading to fluid responses even to complex situations. Indeed, early texts often use the very same character for "knowing" and "wisdom."[5] Although there certainly are cases in classical texts where the object of the verb "to know" is a proposition, the general model of knowing was based on competence and distinctions rather than representation.[6]

The central goal of all forms of Buddhism is soteriological, not epistemic: that is, rather than learning something or knowing something, what we need is to awaken, be enlightened, transform. Nonetheless, Buddhist schools engage in considerable discussion of knowing, understanding, perception, and the like. It is helpful to think about these uses of epistemic language as falling into three

types: the problematic, the useful, and the genuine. Regular, empirical, conceptually articulated knowing is often seen as a problem. Such
forms of knowing assume a mistaken view of our reality that must
be overcome for enlightenment to be possible. Second, the idea that
various kinds of knowing or understanding can be useful, expedient
means (*upāya*) on the road to enlightenment is quite common. Finally,
many theorists use one or more terms to express ideas of genuine,
unproblematic knowing. Special terms are sometimes used to mark
these modes of knowing. For example, in the *Platform Sutra* we are
told that, when there are "no objects that one knows [conceptually;
i.e., as a thing distinct from other things], that is called 'genuine
knowing.'"[7] The earliest use of "genuine knowing" (*zhenzhi*) in
fact dates back to the Daoist classic *Zhuangzi*. As we will soon see,
Neo-Confucians take a range of positions on the value of empirical
knowing, some coming closer to Buddhist views than others, and
some Neo-Confucians also adopt the term "genuine knowing," albeit
to mean something rather different than their Daoist and Buddhist
predecessors.

2 Sensory knowing versus virtuous nature's knowing in the Northern Song

We begin with debates among Neo-Confucians over whether there
is one or more than one basic type of knowing and, if more than
one, how they are related. Many Neo-Confucians discuss "sensory
knowing" (*wenjian zhi zhi* 聞見之知) as opposed to "virtuous nature's
knowing" (*dexing zhi zhi* 德性之知), but the meanings and relations
of these terms vary. Both forms of knowing also become intertwined
with the most famous category of Neo-Confucian epistemic cultivation, namely "getting a handle on things" (*gewu* 格物). Without too
much distortion, we can summarize the positions that we will consider
as follows. ZHANG Zai believes that the two types of knowing are
distinct but that sensory knowing is necessary for virtuous nature's
knowing. CHENG Yi thoroughly distinguishes sensory and virtuous
nature's knowing, arguing that the latter does not in fact depend on
the former. This, in turn, leads to difficulties that will encourage ZHU
Xi to deny the usefulness of the distinction altogether, as we will see
in the following section.

Let us start with ZHANG Zai, for whom the meaning of "sensory
knowing" is rather clear: literally "hearing and seeing's knowing,"
it encompasses all knowing activity that involves the senses (including reading), insofar as the thing that is known is understood to

be external to oneself. A distinction between knowing subject and known object is fundamental to sensory knowing. Sensory knowing is not accomplished by the senses alone; it is ultimately one's heartmind that "joins together inner and outer" so that one knows. As ZHANG Zai puts it: "When people say they have knowledge, it comes from the sensations of the sense organs. Human perception comes from the joining of the inner and the outer."[8] Knowing, on this picture, is something that happens as a result of our actual interactions, rather than something that could be innate. We will return to this important point below. We should also note that the known object is conceptualized as a "thing" (*wu*). "Thing" is a broad category that refers to anything that we can individuate or distinguish from something else, including affairs or events.[9]

The term "virtuous nature's knowing" is a bit peculiar. It seems to have been coined by Northern Song Neo-Confucians to refer to the special kind of knowing that they sought.[10] It does not refer to knowledge that we have naturally or innately, but instead to knowing that fully matches with or realizes our nature, in the special sense of "nature" discussed in chapter 3. According to ZHANG Zai, the key difference with sensory knowing is that although virtuous nature's knowing also involves the joining together of differences, these differences are not conceived of in terms of "inner" and "outer," or "self" and "other." Instead, Zhang says that when the heartmind has been expanded to embody (*ti* 體) all things – that is, all things are perceived as interrelated parts of oneself – then we have virtuous nature's knowing.[11] In a sense that we will explain below, the sage "views all-under-heaven as having no things that are not himself (or herself)."[12]

How are sensory knowing and virtuous nature's knowing related? On the one hand, Zhang is very clear that "virtuous nature's knowing does not sprout from seeing or hearing."[13] Zhang complains about those who see ideal knowing as a matter of "exhaustively investigating Pattern" and thus "fully fathoming things." This is to think that by doing sensory knowing – attending to things external to us – evermore carefully, we will eventually succeed in attaining virtuous nature's knowing. But the problem lies in our making a distinction between ourselves (as knowing subject) and the things (as objects of knowing) in the first place. So virtuous nature's knowing cannot just be a highly advanced form of sensory knowing. On the other hand, Zhang also tells us that while "hearing and seeing are not sufficient to exhaust things, yet they are also necessary. If we have no ears or eyes, then we would be as wood or stone. If we have ears and eyes, we have a way of joining together the inner and the outer. If one does not hear or see, what experience can there be?"[14] The senses are required for virtuous nature's knowing, but we only have virtuous nature's knowing when the knowing subject has expanded to encompass all of reality. There is no "other," no external "object." It is for this reason, presumably, that Zhang goes so far as to say that the ultimate state is "without knowing" (*wuzhi* 無知): being without the subject–object distinction that is essential to sensory knowing, virtuous nature's knowing is uniquely all-inclusive.

This is not to say that there are no distinctions of any kind in virtuous nature's knowing. The joining together of distinct things (inner and outer) that we do in sensory knowing is analogous to the joining together of opposites that we do in virtuous nature's knowing. For ZHANG Zai, reality is always in a dynamic process of change, a joining and then separating of the distinct poles of *yin* and *yang*. The object or content of virtuous nature's knowing is not a frozen set of ideal truths, but a dynamic state whereby our heartminds are able to perfectly follow the changing distinctions of reality, perfectly responding to the stimulations and changes in the world. Because all things are viewed as aspects of the self – although they need not all be seen as equally important or valuable parts – virtuous nature's knowing is simply the unimpeded awareness of and response to one's own needs. Unlike Buddhists (as Zhang understands them), Zhang does not hold that this changing world is unreal: it is completely real, which is precisely the reason that actual experience and the actual use of our ears and eyes are necessary for even ideal knowing. Finally, note that to act in accord with virtuous nature's knowing is to act perfectly. For this reason, some scholars translate *dexing zhi zhi*, which we render as "virtuous nature's knowing," as "moral knowing." We agree that virtuous nature's knowing has a normative or ethical dimension to it, but the all-inclusive character of virtuous nature's knowing leads us to resist viewing it as only "moral." Virtuous nature's knowing is not just about moral injunctions, but about interacting well with the world in every way, and includes knowing things with no obvious moral import, such as "thunder follows lightning." Sensory knowing, in contrast, seems not to have direct implications for action, moral or otherwise. We will return to this important point below.

The Cheng brothers take a different tack from ZHANG Zai: they distinguish sensory from virtuous nature's knowing quite sharply, and put little value on sensory knowing. Here is CHENG Yi: "Sensory knowing is not virtuous nature's knowing. In the former, things interact with things and thus one knows them; it is not internal. Today's so-called renaissance men have this kind of knowing. Virtuous nature's knowing does not depend on sensory experience."[15]

One thing we can glean from this is that virtuous nature's knowing is "internal," in some sense, but beyond that it leaves things somewhat vague. In particular, it is not clear what sorts of things we can understand through virtuous nature's knowing alone. At the very least, it must include moral knowing and an understanding of life and growth: we have seen that, for the Cheng brothers, our inherent nature has a kind of direct access to the life-giving generativity of the cosmos. But does it also include knowledge of things that seems to depend largely on empirical evidence – for example, the location in space or time of specific events? CHENG Yi, in an exchange with another Daoxue philosopher, suggests that he indeed "already knows" such things. But, when pressed, Cheng seems to conceive knowing of these sorts of facts as constrained by pragmatic and ethical considerations. Cheng says that thunder "arises in the place it arises," suggesting that this is all we need to know about the subject.[16]

When CHENG Yi says that he "already knows," this raises a significant problem for anyone who believes that what we need to know is already within us: how, then, to explain why so many of us seem ignorant and misguided? One side of the Chengs' answer has to do with distinguishing two kinds of "nature," on which see chapter 4. The other part of their answer draws on a key phrase from the short classic text *Greater Learning*: "Reaching understanding [or knowing: *zhi*] lies in getting a handle on things (*gewu*)."[17] Unfortunately, the classic does not explain what "getting a handle on things" means. CHENG Yi offers the following:

> The word *ge* means "to reach" (*zhi* 至). ... Every single thing has a Pattern, and one must exhaustively investigate it so as to reach its Pattern. There are many ways to do this. One is to read books and elucidate the moral principles (*yili* 義理) in them. Another is to discuss people and events of the past and present and to distinguish which are right and which are wrong. Still another is to encounter things and affairs and deal with them in the proper way. These are all exhaustively investigating Pattern.[18]

In other words, even though Pattern is already within one as one's nature, for it to be part of one's active knowing one must consciously engage with Pattern in any of its multitudinous manifestations in the world, thereby "reaching" Pattern. As CHENG Yi puts it, "Although knowing is something that I innately have, without 'reaching' Pattern one cannot attain it [actively]."[19] The Chengs say relatively little to explain what we are calling "active" knowing, other than to connect it to spontaneously apt action and to label it "genuine knowing" (*zhenzhi*).[20] Later in this chapter, we will see that ZHU Xi offers more of an explanation for why and how active knowing has the effects it does, via the category of "discernment."

The examples of "getting a handle on things" that CHENG Yi lists – reflecting on book learning, dealing with things and affairs, and so on – all sound like external matters that would follow from sensory knowing. That is, the activity that Cheng is calling for would seem to rely on a discrimination between external object and knowing, reflecting subject. And yet if we look further at what the two Chengs say, we will see that things are not so straightforward in two distinct ways.[21] First, the Chengs sometimes assert that one must investigate multiple instances of Pattern and sometimes say that the Pattern of one single thing or event will suffice.[22] Second, and even more consequentially, it is ambiguous whether getting a handle on things is primarily focused on "things" that are external or internal to the self. At one point, one of the Chengs is asked, "Does getting a handle on things refer to external things or to things in the nature?" He replies: "It makes no difference. Whatever is before the eye is a thing, and all things have Pattern. For example, that by which fire is hot, that by which water is cold, and even including the relations between ruler and minister or between father and son: all are Pattern."[23] Although the examples here look like external things or affairs, Cheng's remark that "it makes no difference" makes room for a very different kind of inward-oriented investigation, focused on either specific Patterns within our nature or the one single Pattern that is our nature.[24]

If the Chengs are ambiguous about whether external, sensory knowing must be part of getting a handle on things, several of their most influential followers are not. For YANG Shi and ZHANG Jiucheng, the only kind of knowing that really matters is strictly internal (even though they both emphasize active engagement with the outside world). Yang particularly emphasizes the role of "quiet sitting" in helping one to "embody with the heartmind the state before the emotions ... are aroused; then the meaning of centeredness will appear of itself."[25] ZHANG Jiucheng, who was Yang's student and also a close correspondent with the leading Chan Buddhist teacher of the era, adjusts Yang's teachings by removing the emphasis on "quiet sitting," but he is equally explicit about the internal focus of knowing. For Zhang, the key is to be ever vigilant and watchful over one's "unseen and unheard" inner nature; he repeatedly uses the classical phrase "cautious and apprehensive" to express this idea. For example:

> If a superior person wishes to seek the centeredness common to all, he must get the taste of it through being cautious over what is unseen and apprehensive over what is unheard. This is the basis for knowing

centeredness. If one cannot hold to this method ... it is as if one were to eat and drink all day yet never know the taste. Oh, the taste of it! You will know it when you have become thoroughly immersed and drenched in what is unseen and unheard.[26]

Elsewhere, he says that the important types of knowing all come down to "being cautious over what is unseen and apprehensive over what is unheard. ... If one does not practice this, it will be like duckweed adrift on the water, drifting with the wind to the north or south; where will one anchor oneself?"[27] A contemporary scholar nicely sums up Zhang's exclusive focus on inner "virtuous nature's knowing": "Within Zhang's framework, neither moral judgments nor practical knowing belong to the realm of ordinary human knowing, but must arise as the spontaneous manifestation of one's nature."[28]

3 Sensory knowing versus virtuous nature's knowing: later developments

To sum up so far, we have three influential positions on the role of sensory knowing. ZHANG Zai sees the necessity of sensory knowing but also distinguishes it from the type of knowing he most values, virtuous nature's knowing. Despite the fact that the Cheng brothers are responsible for bringing "getting a handle on things" to the forefront of Daoxue discourse, they are curiously ambiguous on whether sense-based attention to external things needs to be part of our efforts to improve our knowing. Cheng students like YANG Shi and ZHANG Jiucheng, finally, place exclusive emphasis on an inward-focused practice that aims to know our nature directly.

By the mid-twelfth century, when ZHU Xi is coming of age, the mainstream view within Daoxue is that learning is centrally an inward affair aimed at virtuous nature's knowing (though the term "virtuous nature's knowing" is not always used explicitly). Zhu initially shares this view, but comes to see it as philosophically problematic and rejects the possibility of directly accessing nature, as we will discuss in chapter 7. Here, we look at one key consequence of Zhu's mature view: his rejection of the distinction between sensory knowing and virtuous nature's knowing. Asked whether there is such a thing as sensory knowing, Zhu is unambiguous: "There is only one kind of knowing! The only issue is whether it is genuine or not. This is the only difference at issue; it is definitely not the case that after we have sensory knowing we later have another instance of knowing."[29] Discussing an assertion by ZHANG Zai that we must avoid allowing sensory knowing to "handcuff" our heartminds, Zhu argues:

> In order to be able to learn, we must possess senses of seeing and hearing.
> How can we possibly do without them? We work hard with our senses
> until we freely arrive at an interconnected understanding. Ordinarily,
> when we study something by relying on senses, a single affair only leads
> us to know a single principle.[30] However, when we reach the stage of an
> interconnected understanding, all Pattern becomes one.[31]

Even though ZHU Xi only mentions ZHANG Zai here by name, he was
well aware that CHENG Yi had insisted on, if anything, a stronger distinction between these two purported types of knowing; Zhu does not
criticize Cheng explicitly out of respect.[32] He shows no such restraint
for those of the Chengs' students who pursued a single-minded focus
on virtuous nature's knowing even further, saying of ZHANG Jiucheng
that his writings are "outwardly Confucian but secretly Buddhist; ...
his purpose is to confuse the world and lull people to sleep so that
they enter the Buddhist school and cannot extricate themselves from
it even if they want to."[33]

Zhu's picture of knowing – that it was a continuous process,
reliant on the senses, that could eventually lead to a kind of break-
through and consequently to "genuine" knowing – is of course quite
consistent with some of what the Chengs said, and indeed bears
resemblances to aspects of views held by other Northern Song Neo-
Confucians. In subsequent sections, we will explore Zhu's conception
of knowing, including what it is that makes knowing "genuine," in
more detail. Before moving on, though, we need to cover three more
issues: the scope of ZHU Xi's idea of knowing, the persistence of views
emphasizing direct, virtuous nature-knowing, and later attention to
why "getting a handle on things" is necessary.

By the "scope" of Zhu's view of knowing, we mean two things.
First of all, as with all the thinkers we have discussed, for ZHU Xi
"knowing" is a process concerned with coming to understand things,
coming to be able to make distinctions (in practice) among things, as
well as coming to have specific items of articulable knowledge. As we
will discuss in subsequent sections, the "deeper" or more "genuine"
the knowing is, the less it has to do with propositional knowledge
(e.g., coming to know that Mill Street is unusually slippery after it
has rained) and the more it has to do with changes to how we discern
and interact with the world. Second, it is quite common to hear
scholars claim that ZHU Xi (among others) is really only concerned
with "moral knowledge."[34] There is a kernel of truth in this idea
since the kind of knowing that ZHU Xi values always has a normative
upshot, but the norms apply extremely broadly. As we saw in chapter
2, Pattern includes much more than just interpersonal norms; and,

as we will explain in more detail in the next section, the best kind of knowing entails discerning and being motivated by the life-affirming coherence of the cosmos in everything one encounters. As Zhu puts it, when this happens, one sees that "in the midst of daily affairs, there is nothing that is not the pervasive circulation of cosmic Pattern."[35]

Next, we should keep in mind that the idea particularly associated with people like ZHANG Jiucheng – that there is a distinct, nonsensory kind of knowing on which we should really focus our efforts – does not go away. Its standard-bearer in Southern Song Daoxue is LU Xiangshan, famous for his debates with ZHU Xi on this and other issues. On our reading, Lu does not make any significantly new epistemological moves in these arguments; his claim that ZHU Xi focuses on "engaging in inquiry and study" rather than on "honoring the virtuous nature" simply begs the question against Zhu, since Zhu holds that these are crucially connected, as we have just seen.[36] A more interesting version of the focus on virtuous nature's knowing comes with CHEN Xianzhang of the early Ming dynasty. Chen says that he tried to make progress by reading books, but "did not acquire anything." He elaborates:

> What I mean by "did not acquire anything" is that this heartmind of mine and this Pattern of the world outside me did not coincide with and match one another. Then I forsook all the complexities of other methods and pursued, through quiet sitting alone, what was essential within myself. In time I was able to see the inherent reality of my own heartmind manifested inscrutably.[37]

For a wide range of thinkers in the Ming, the obsession of their contemporaries with what these thinkers called "vulgar learning" was a major problem in their society.[38] Even though these critics were aware that the rote book learning and other activities that constituted vulgar learning were not what CHENG Yi and ZHU Xi had called for when they spoke of "getting a handle on things," they still had two concerns: first, that Zhu's teachings could too easily be followed in such a way as to lead to mere vulgar learning; and second, some of these thinkers agreed with Chen that external-oriented "getting a handle on things" did not work.[39] Chen's own critique continues as follows:

> Those who learn should seek the Way not only in books but also in the heartmind. They should take note of the incipience (*ji*) of movement and tranquillity and of being and non-being. They should extend and nourish what they have within themselves. They must not be confused by what they see and hear. They must get rid of the fragmented functioning of the senses.[40]

Unlike most of the thinkers canvassed to this point, Chen doubts that there is a way that our sensory perception of things can lead us to the sense of interconnected, coherent unity that he is seeking; at the very least, his own efforts have failed to show how internal and external patterns tallied with one another. He therefore strives for an exclusively inner-oriented kind of knowing.

Did Chen really mean to abandon sensory knowing, at least as any part of the story of seeking the Way? One of his contemporaries worried that he did, indeed, writing that in the end Chen and his followers "fall into a state of emptiness and mysteriousness."[41] The potential problems with an exclusively inward focus are also discussed astutely by LUO Qinshun, an important mid-Ming Daoxue thinker. He writes: "If one's learning is not extensive and one's discussion is not detailed, one's vision will be limited by the confines of one's own heartmind, and however one may wish to be free from error, it will be impossible."[42] Elsewhere, Luo explains that because of the widespread influence of Chan Buddhism, many students back in the Northern Song "no longer directed their thoughts to the Pattern of heaven and earth and the myriad things," and so were "reduced to onesidedness and solely preoccupied with the self." As a result, the Cheng brothers taught the concept of "getting a handle on things" with the intent that students would "achieve corresponding illumination of things and the self, perfect interfusion of inner and outer, and complete integration of subject and object."[43] We believe that this is a fair summary of the Chengs' concerns and goals, although as noted above, their ambiguity about whether external investigation was actually necessary still seemed to leave the door open to what Luo would no doubt count as a "one-sided" approach. What is most interesting in Luo's discussion, though, is his next assertion:

> The way that this Pattern operates in the world is such that out of unity there proceed the myriad things without the intervention of any artificial contrivance. And when the many reconverge into the one, what possibility could there be for selfish manipulation? Thus to "seek within oneself" one must begin with one's own nature and emotions. One then goes on to extend to other things what one has perceived in oneself, and if it is found to be inconsistent, then it is not ultimate Pattern.[44]

So sensory knowing does have a key role: it helps us weed out any biased intuitions because all manifest emotions that actually realize our natures should fit into the broader Pattern of the entire cosmos. By working back and forth between inner and outer knowing, we can gradually approach what earlier thinkers have called virtuous nature's knowing or genuine knowing.[45]

The last view of sensory knowing that we will examine here is Luo's contemporary, the great WANG Yangming. Although Wang sometimes uses "hearing and seeing" to refer to the problematic kind of "vulgar learning" mentioned above, his most balanced view has room for a more positive understanding of sensory knowing.[46] Wang writes:

> Good knowing (*liangzhi*) does not come from the senses (*jianwen*), and yet all the senses are functions of good knowing. Therefore good knowing is not impeded by the senses. Nor is it separated from the senses. ... So outside of good knowing, there is no other knowing. Therefore reaching good knowing is the great basis of learning and the first principle of the teaching of the sage. Now solely to seek in the subsidiary sources of the senses is to lose that basis, thus clearly falling to the secondary level.[47]

Combine this statement of the role within good knowing of the senses with this related idea:

> To know the specifics of caring for the comfort of parents...is a type of knowing but cannot be called reaching understanding. It is necessary to reach the type of knowing that understands the specifics of how to care for one's parents *and realizes this by means of caring*; ... only then can this be called reaching understanding. Caring for the comfort of parents must be carried out entirely according to what the good knowing knows to be the specifics of caring for them, without the least bit undone. ... Only then can things be said to have been handled (*gewu*).[48]

Taken together, these two passages argue that when an individual properly understands that one's sensory knowing is an aspect of good knowing, then far from being a barrier to moral action, sensory knowing is one of the keys to such action. As was discussed in chapter 5, good knowing is perfect emotion that motivates us appropriately and alerts us whenever our responses go awry; here, we learn that the detailed content of good knowing relies in part on our sensory knowing.[49]

One lesson that can be taken from these last two sections is that some version of virtuous nature's knowing – whatever its exact relation to sensory knowing – is central to all Daoxue Neo-Confucians. It is fitting to end this section, therefore, by noting that a common theme in criticisms of Daoxue was the rejection of virtuous nature's knowing. The Ming dynasty thinker WANG Tingxiang is perhaps the most fascinating example of such a position.[50] He argues that Daoxue-style virtuous nature's knowing is dependent on an "active heartmind" (*dongxin* 動心) that draws on a supposedly innate ability to know what things like filial behavior are. To the contrary, Wang maintains that at birth we cannot even distinguish an ox from a horse: our "responsive heartminds" (*yingxin* 應心) depend on teaching and experience in order for us to know how to make any distinctions at all. Wang does acknowledge that sensory knowing can go awry; his solution lies in the power of the heartmind to "reflect" (*silü* 思慮). All knowing, even of the sage, is ultimately on a continuum; he explicitly rejects the possibility of a separate "virtuous nature's knowing." While we should keep in mind that not all the philosophers we have examined in these sections actually held that virtuous nature's knowing is a distinct type of activity from sensory knowing, nonetheless Wang's approach to knowing becomes increasingly common in the Qing dynasty and is related to the rising importance of the "evidential learning" movement.[51]

4 ZHU Xi's three types of knowing

We have now seen the range of Neo-Confucian views about the roles that our senses and external objects (including books) should play in knowing, including the radical stance that senses and objects should play no role at all in the only kind of knowing that really matters. We also saw reasons to resist thinking of virtuous nature's knowing as narrowly "moral," even though it is certainly normative in the broad sense of guiding us in the best ways to be and act in the world. In this section, we will step away from the long, historical survey offered in the prior two sections and focus on the three different types of knowing that ZHU Xi identifies. (To be clear, Zhu never explicitly says that there are "three types" of knowing, but all three types we discuss here are distinguished in Zhu's writings with distinctive terminology and descriptions.) In so doing, we also bring into our discussion two other important epistemic terms, both with significant roots in Chinese Buddhism: *jue* (awakening to) and *zhijue* (discernment). Because the terminology and details can get confusing, let us begin with a schematic overview of Zhu's understanding of knowing:

Type One: One knows a rule to which things should conform.
Type Two: One sees an isolated instance of how things should be and cannot help but follow it.

Type Three: One awakens to the underlying reason or basis why things are as they are, and responds aptly to whatever situation one encounters.

Knowing of any of these types may be sufficient, in a given case, to lead one to act well, but with Types Two and Three one's apt responses are more automatic and their scope increasingly broad. Fully knowing in the Type Three sense is a central characteristic of a sage. As we explain below, both Types One and Two can contribute toward the attainment of Type Three, but they are quite distinct from one another, and there is no specific order (for example, from One to Two to Three) that must be followed in the process of developing the highest type of knowing.

The most basic and shallow kind of knowing is to know a rule for a given type of circumstance. Knowing that one should be filial to one's parents, that one should not eat an extra piece of chocolate cake, or that chairs are for sitting on, are possible examples of such rules. Knowing the rule means that one can say it and know at least generally how to apply it. ZHU Xi calls such rules "rules to which [a thing or affair] should conform." This type of knowing is common but also problematic because all too often one "knows" a rule in this sense but fails to follow it. In a well-known passage, Zhu talks about the ways in which merely "knowing an affair" to be right or wrong is unreliable; one can know it to be wrong, and yet suddenly start thinking about doing it, or even do it without really being aware of doing so.[52] To be sure, someone who knows the rule can sometimes get him or herself to follow it, but Zhu agrees with earlier Daoxue thinkers that this kind of merely conscientious behavior is worrisome.[53]

Type Two is typically expressed as "seeing an instance of how things should be and being unable not to do it." This seems not to depend on antecedent understanding of any rules; it is rather an instance of brute clarity, whereby one sees and responds to a particular situation. Zhu says:

> If someone does not see "how things should be and be unable not to do it," then all he or she can do is rely on some past model as a guide to how to respond. When someone genuinely sees that it is something that "I ought to do," then there will naturally be that which he or she cannot stop doing. For example, a minister must be devoted: so long as one sees this and is not just mouthing the words, then in acting as a minister one cannot avoid being devoted.[54]

Without Type Two knowing, the best one can do is rely on the words or example of someone in the past who has faced a similar situation and try to shape one's reaction to follow the past model. (Presumably this is Type One knowing.) Sometimes, though, one sees a situation in such a way that the reaction is automatic. What is happening in such a case? Consider this exchange:

> Someone asked: "How is it that Pattern is 'unable to stop'?" Master Zhu replied: "The normative force of Pattern is naturally unable to stop. Mencius understood this most clearly, and thus said, 'Among babes in arms, there are none who do not know to love their parents. When they grow older, there are none who do not know to revere their elder brothers.' Naturally these are places at which one cannot stop."[55]

"The normative force of Pattern is naturally unable to stop": the idea is that there is a deep, structured dynamism to the cosmos that generates all life in unending fashion.[56] Type Two knowing takes place when we are able to get a glimpse of this, but it falls short of Type Three knowing because it does not flow from a broadly inclusive grasp of Pattern's interconnections. Certain situations are ripe for these brief and bounded experiences of Pattern; Zhu insists that they are open to anyone, at any level of cultivation. In addition to the few we have already cited, a final passage that often comes up is Mencius's famous claim that anyone, upon suddenly seeing a child about to fall into a well, would respond with alarm and commiseration.[57] We speculate – although Zhu does not make this clear – that the situations in which Type Two knowing happen most readily are those in which distracting, potentially biasing factors are simply not present. After all, the Pattern is always there to be seen and to motivate response, so what is at issue here is under what circumstances – short of the full, sagely sensitivity that characterizes Type Three – one is able to see and respond fluidly.

There are two strands within ZHU Xi's writings that lead to the conclusion that, in addition to knowing of Types One and Two, there is also a third, most valuable type. The first revolves around the verb *jue*, which means, "awaken to" or "be sensitive to." For Chinese Buddhists, *jue* is a central term that refers to the awakening that the Buddha experienced and which Buddhists seek for all sentient beings. ZHANG Zai and early Daoxue Confucians like the Cheng brothers use *jue* repeatedly to mean "awaken," both when speaking critically of Buddhist ideas of "awakening" and to refer to a Confucian kind of "awakening." As they note, there is a passage in the *Mencius* that speaks of awakening; the Chengs are insistent, therefore, that "awakening" is a legitimate Confucian notion and refers to something different than the Buddhist idea.[58] CHENG Yi also explains the difference between "knowing" and "awakening" as follows: "Knowing is to know this affair; awakening is to awaken to this Pattern."[59] CHENG Yi himself does not offer more explanation of the difference, but ZHU Xi approvingly invokes the further gloss of one of CHENG Yi's students. According to this explanation, when one knows the respect of a minister or the filiality of a son, then this is "knowing this affair." When one knows that by which ministers are respectful or sons filial, though, that is "awakening to this Pattern."[60] In a related context, Zhu himself says that "at first one is simply devoted or filial, and then later one comes to know that by which one is filial and that by which one is devoted, and one cannot be budged."[61] It is an interesting question whether merely "knowing this affair" refers to Type One or Type Two knowing. On one hand, the use of "this," connecting it to a particular situation, suggests that it is Type Two; on the other hand, the statement that only when one has moved to the "awakening" level is one invulnerable to being "budged" suggests that the contrast is with the unreliable Type One. In either case, "awakening to this Pattern" offers a different and deeper kind of understanding.

Both of the last passages connect awakening to the rather cryptic idea of grasping "that *by which* [one is filial, devoted, and so on]." Pursuing this clue will help us better understand how Type Three knowing works. In what is probably his best-known statement on the meaning of Pattern, Zhu says, "As far as things in the cosmos go, we can be certain that each has a reason by which it is as it is, and a rule to which it should conform. This is what is meant by Pattern."[62] We have already seen that when one only knows the relevant rule, this is mere Type One knowing. As Zhu develops the idea of understanding the "reason *by which* it is as it is" – which uses the same terms as the "that *by which*" mentioned above – we will see that it is significantly more important. In a key passage, Zhu explains as follows:

> [Compared with the rule to which it should conform,] the "reason *by which* it is as it is" takes it up one level. For example, that *by which* a lord is humane: the lord is the ruler while the people and territory are his concern. He naturally employs humane love. If we think about this relationship without humane love, it just does not work. This is not to say that a lord cannot help but use humane love; it is rather that to do so matches with Pattern.[63]

There are bad rulers who are governed by their selfish desires and fail to employ humane love, but Zhu is saying that reflection on the organic, structural relationship between a ruler and his people reveals that the relationship works only when the ruler is motivated by humane love. Zhu adds several more examples in the passage, all of which make the point that, no matter whether one is talking about human relations or patterns in nature, it is the affirmation of birth and life that leads to things fitting together in meaningful fashion, each aspect playing its role. When Zhu talks of going up a level, he is saying that one needs to put a given matter into the special context provided by Pattern. When one learns to do that – to view each individual thing as fitting together thanks to the value we accord to life – then one has the flexible Type Three knowing that can make sense of and respond aptly to any stimulus. This is to grasp the "reason *by which*" things are as they are.[64]

In light of our understanding of the three types of knowing, it makes sense that Zhu repurposes the Buddhist term *zhijue* – a compound of "know" and "awaken" that just means perceptual awareness in a Buddhist context – as a general term for the various kinds of knowing activity of our heartmind.[65] Just as "know" (*zhi*) itself can refer to any of the three types, so can *zhijue*. The English verb "discern" does a good job of capturing the meaning of *zhijue* because of the way that "discern" foregrounds the process of making distinctions and connections among things. For ZHU Xi, knowing and discerning are active processes, not inactive states. He says that "knowing is our heartmind being stimulated by something."[66] In a crucial passage, Zhu tells us it is through the actual process of discerning that we come to possess Pattern in its local specificity and activate our specific emotions: "The heartmind's discerning is that whereby we possess this Pattern and activate this emotion."[67] In other words, the world becomes intelligible, normative, and motivational for us precisely through our discerning of it.[68] As we have explained in chapter 3, nature is a kind of metaphysical structuring; because it is metaphysical and only implicitly or potentially sensible, ZHU Xi says that the heartmind can metaphorically be thought of as having empty space within it. If heartmind is really a process whereby emotions emerge from nature – as we discussed in chapter 4 – though, then we should not take the metaphor of "space" too literally.[69] After all, Zhu is quite explicitly metaphorical in passages like this: "Nature is like the heartmind's field, filling all the emptiness, all is simply Pattern."[70] Nature is a metaphorical field, poised to blossom with sprouts of emotion when the time is right. Returning again to the role of knowing, ZHU Xi holds that actual discerning is what leads to the most full-blooded "possession" of specific aspects of Pattern.

5 Deliberation, holistic insight, and the unity of knowing and acting

In the previous section, we showed that ZHU Xi recognizes three distinct types of knowing, and that knowing is a kind of active discernment whereby the Pattern with which all things are implicitly equipped comes to be specifically present to us and motivating. Earlier sections revealed other ways in which Neo-Confucian philosophers distinguish between types of knowing, usually emphasizing the importance of "virtuous nature's knowing," which may or may not have a tie to "sensory knowing." For some of these thinkers, a structured, careful process of deliberation is necessary in order to arrive at the genuine knowing that they seek, while others deny the need for such deliberation. Most agree, however, that genuine knowing is a holistic state in a sense that we will explain below. Most agree, in addition, that genuine knowing is an intrinsically motivational state, though few go as far as WANG Yangming and say that knowing and acting are actually unified. Explaining the various interconnections among deliberation, holism, and motivation is the task of this final section of the chapter.

Let us begin by focusing on Zhu's picture. His core contention is that one begins with whatever Type One knowing of rules one has acquired, as well as with the Type Two moments of brute clarity that one has experienced, and then engages in a process of learning that systematically relates these dimensions of knowing to classic texts, exemplary models, and other dimensions of one's experience. ZHU Xi refers to this process via the classically derived terms "getting a handle on things" (*gewu*) and "reaching understanding" (*zhi zhi*). (We discuss getting a handle on things here in a fairly abstract way, emphasizing its connections to knowing; in the next chapter, on methods of self-cultivation, we look at some of types of "handling" in more concrete detail.) According to Zhu, the process of "getting a handle on things" and thus "reaching understanding" depends on distinguishing among things and distinguishing between self and other, as well as on coming to see connections among things and thus softening the self–other boundary. One of the key tools we are to employ is "analogical extension" (*tui* 推). Zhu says that analogical extension will help us arrive at "that by which" things are as they are, and recall from above that comprehending "that by which" (i.e., Pattern) is the goal of Type Three knowing.[71] These types of deliberative activity are important in the extended transition from a Type One and Type Two knower to a Type Three knower. Insofar as one is already a Type Three knower, then deliberation is not generally necessary.[72]

Two examples will help us to make clear what Zhu has in mind. The first comes in one of Zhu's many discussions of the child-and-the-well thought-experiment from the *Mencius* 2A:6. He writes: "As for a child falling into a well, this is something that all people can perceive; when one is able to analogically extend to clarity this 'beginning' that has manifested to one, then that is [genuine] clarity."[73] In other words, employing techniques like analogical extension on raw materials like the Type Two knowing experienced upon seeing a child about to fall into a well, we can hope to reach full-blown Type Three knowing. We tend to easily experience the intuitive wrongness of letting an innocent child tumble down a well, such that it seems obvious and makes us want to stop the tragedy (at least when there are not powerful countervailing forces to discourage us). We strive to reach genuine Type Three knowing by reflecting on the resonance between the Pattern in saving the child and the Pattern in some proximate matter – say, allowing one's personal rival to fall down a well (rather than a child) or allowing a child to starve (rather than fall to her death).[74] As one reaches toward more capacious knowing, one will see the wrongness of these other situations with the same immediacy and motivational power as the former. Here is a second passage in which Zhu offers a powerful metaphor for this sort of deliberative work:

> For cosmic Pattern is never in all the ages extinguished in any human being; no matter how it is covered over or confined, cosmic Pattern is always constantly there just as ever, emerging from within selfish desire at every moment without cease – it is just that human beings are not aware of it. It is exactly like a bright pearl or a large shell partly covered in sand and gravel, successively flashing forth here and there. Just recognize and gather these successive flashes of the Way and its principles (*daoli*) right where they appear, joining them together until they gradually become an integral whole.[75]

Perhaps the most important thing to note here is that Type Three is not just a generalization of the brute experiences of Type Two. Type Three is not having Type Two experiences all the time, but is the distinctive, holistic result of patient, connective work.

We have already seen two important terms that ZHU Xi uses to describe Type Three knowing, namely "awakening" (*jue*) and "genuine knowing" (*zhen zhi*). With a third term for the same state, he makes more explicit the holism that characterizes this type of knowing: "unimpeded interconnection" (*huoran guantong* 豁然貫通).[76] A crucial point about these holistic states of awakening and unimpeded interconnection, which distinguishes Zhu and the other Neo-Confucians from virtually all Buddhist descriptions of holistic states of enlightenment, is that for the Neo-Confucians, "unimpeded interconnection" is still structured or centered in ways that we can at least partly articulate. This, after all, is what Zhu emphasizes when he talks about having a good nature as being akin to being in the center of a room, oriented toward the possible exits (see chapter 3). Knowing as unimpeded interconnection means that one is not restricted to a single principle – which Zhu analogizes to being stuck in one corner of a room – but instead, having "seen that the myriad Patterns come together, one can choose and follow that which is perfectly apt."[77]

It should be clear that ZHU Xi does not think that the way to Type Three knowing is simply the spontaneous, untutored discernment of the whole: a lengthy process of reflection and deliberation is needed before one can reach unimpeded interconnection. We have already seen some examples of Neo-Confucians who deny that anything like Zhu's process of analogical extension is necessary – think of ZHANG Jiucheng or CHEN Xianzhang discussed above – and even more radical cases can be found in the late Ming dynasty, such as WANG Yangming's follower ZHOU Rudeng, who condemns "deliberation" (*niyi* 擬義) and advocates that one simply awaken one's internal sage and follow one's own path.[78] On the other hand, those Neo-Confucians who reject the "inherent nature" naturally put great emphasis on the role of deliberation, analogical extension, and the like, though they, too, often hold that something like Zhu's understanding of unimpeded interconnection is ultimately achievable.

As mentioned at the outset of this section, most Neo-Confucians hold that genuine knowing is intrinsically motivational. That is, when one knows in the right way, proper motivation and proper action are automatically sparked. CHENG Yi has a particularly famous way of discussing this connection:

> There is a difference between genuine knowing and everyday knowing. I once saw a peasant who had been wounded by a tiger. When someone said that a tiger was attacking people, everyone was startled, but the peasant reacted differently from the rest. Even a child knows that tigers are dangerous, but it is not genuine knowing; it is only genuine knowing if it is like the peasant's. So when people know bad but still do it, this also is not genuine knowing; if it were, decidedly they would not do it.[79]

Cheng implies that the peasant who has personally experienced a tiger would not put on false bravado: genuine, personal knowing leads to apt emotional response and therefore, as Cheng says at the end of the passage, to action. In another discussion of this topic, he puts it this way: the person who has been wounded by a tiger "has completely sincere fear of it, based on having truly perceived the Pattern. This attainment in one's heartmind we call 'having virtue,' and so the person has no need to force himself to act."[80]

This last quotation is particularly helpful because it allows us to see what is at stake in Cheng's emphasis on personal experience. His point is not that the knowledge of the peasant who has experienced the tiger has a different feel or different content from the merely abstract knowing of a child: this is not about what some contemporary philosophers call "qualia." Rather, the personal experience has facilitated a transformation such that the peasant's natural fear of tigers has become an unimpeded disposition, a "virtue," which requires no "forcing" in order to spark action. All this is really just an easily comprehensible example, of course, that is intended to help us understand what it is to genuinely know and thus possess the more important virtues – humaneness, wisdom, and so on – with which the Neo-Confucians are mainly concerned. We will discuss this further in the next two chapters on self-cultivation and ethics.

Subsequent Neo-Confucians generally agree with CHENG Yi and often cite his tiger example, but they do have some important disagreements with one another. Many agree with ZHU Xi that knowing and acting are "mutually dependent" – in that knowing without acting is superficial, while acting without knowing is unreliable – and also that "As for their order, knowing comes first; as for their significance, action comes first."[81] Zhu goes on to explain that while CHENG Yi was sometimes unclear on the need for knowing to come first and only then be followed by acting, to do otherwise risks confusion.[82] WANG Yangming, in contrast, thinks it is a mistake to view genuine knowing as somehow temporally prior to action. He famously argued for the "unity of knowing and acting," writing that:

> But people today instead separate knowing and acting into two distinct tasks to perform and think that one must first know and only then can one act. They say, "Now I will perform the task of knowing by studying and learning. Once I have attained real knowledge, I then will pursue the tasks of acting." And so, till the end of their days, they never act, and till the end of their days, they never know. This is not a minor malady, nor did it arrive just yesterday. My current teaching regarding the unity of knowing and acting is a medicine directed precisely at this disease.[83]

To explain what he means by the unity of knowing and acting, Wang says that "knowing is the intent of acting, and acting is the effort of knowing"; that "knowing is the beginning of acting, and acting is the completion of knowing",[84] and that "where the knowing is honest and genuine, it is acting; where acting is discerning and finely observing, it is knowing."[85] It may seem that the differences between Wang's position and that of Cheng and Zhu are small – perhaps only rhetorical? – but Wang's contemporaries clearly did not see it this way. His many followers eagerly embraced his ideas, while many others criticized him for conflating two activities that need to be kept distinct.[86] Modern readers might also think that at most Wang has shown that genuine knowing and actually being motivated are unified, rather than the more ambitious claim that knowing and "acting" are one and the same. In response to this objection, Wang would argue that the difference that matters is whether or not one is motivated, not whether or not one makes an external action. As he says, "knowing is like water; that our heartmind is never without good knowing is like the fact that water is never without an impulse to go down."[87] All we have to do is realize this about ourselves and remove selfish obstructions to the functioning of this genuine knowing, and external action will follow without any further effort.

How should we understand the difference between Wang and his critics on the relation between knowing and acting? If one just focuses on the things that Zhu and Wang say specifically on this topic, it is hard to avoid the conclusion that they really agree. After all, in response to a question about whether "exhaustively investigating Pattern" (*qiongli* 窮理) (i.e., knowing) or "accumulating appropriate actions" (*ji yi* 集義) (i.e., acting) comes first, Zhu replies, "exhaustively investigating Pattern comes first, but it is not that they are strictly divided into stages of before and after."[88] Together with other things that we have seen from Zhu, this sounds like Wang's "knowing is the beginning of acting, and acting is the completion of knowing." However, we cannot forget the broader philosophical context. As we have seen in other chapters, where Zhu speaks of nature and Pattern, Wang speaks of the heartmind and of our actual, particular experiences of "good knowing." Even if Zhu believes that genuine knowing cannot be separated in practice from acting, Wang's language makes the equivalence between knowing and acting even tighter. It may be that Zhu would agree that what we call Type Two and Type Three knowing are indeed united with acting in WANG Yangming's sense, but this is clearly not the case for Type One.[89]

For further study

Selected primary sources

1. CHENG Yi, "Selected Sayings," §§3–5, in Tiwald and Van Norden 2014: #31, 159.
2. ZHU Xi and Lü Zuqian (eds), "The Investigation of Things ..." (n.b. "investigation of things" is an alternative translation for "getting a handle on things"), in Zhu and Lü 1967: 88–122.
3. ZHU Xi (CHU Hsi), "Discussion of Knowledge and Action," in Zhu 1990: 116–27.
4. WANG Yangming, *Record for Practice*, §§1–8, in Tiwald and Van Norden 2014: #43, 261–72.

Discussion questions

1. Is "virtuous nature's knowing" really a kind of "knowing," as you use the term? Whose account of it do you believe makes the most sense?
2. What makes ZHU Xi's Type Two knowing different from Types One and Three, and why is it important?
3. Neo-Confucians disagree about whether deliberation and inference are helpful toward achieving the kind of knowing that many characterize as "unimpeded interconnection." Why? What, in particular, are the reasons for thinking that deliberation and inference might undermine one's ability to achieve unimpeded interconnection?
4. Are you convinced that knowing – or at least genuine knowing, as that is understood by someone like WANG Yangming – is the same as acting?
5. What is distinctive about "good knowing"? How can we identify real instances of good knowing in ourselves, as opposed to lesser kinds of knowing or outright errors? (See also the discussion of good knowing in chapter 5.)

7

Self-Cultivation

1 Introduction

The heart of Neo-Confucian thought consists in its theories and practices of self-cultivation.[1] Broadly speaking, the theoretical justifications for these practices cover most of the issues that have occupied
us throughout this book. In this chapter, we focus on famous debates
at the intersection of these more general theories and the specific
practices promoted by the Neo-Confucians. To see what was most
important to Neo-Confucian philosophers – what motivated their
theoretical interests – one must imagine (or be) someone who is both
philosophically inclined and deeply committed to self-improvement,
such that one puts virtue even before one's personal and career
ambitions.[2] A key test of any systematic view about cultivation is its
success in helping us to improve ourselves, such that we have access
to rarified states of heartmind and sagely facility in handling the
complex world of human relations. Because of this crucial practical
dimension of cultivation, we find it useful to rely here not just on
standard Neo-Confucian theoretical writings, but also on an autobio-
graphical account that shows us some of the challenges and successes
of Neo-Confucian practice.

To most Neo-Confucian thinkers, being a sage is a live possibility.
Neo-Confucians understand sages to have an extremely rare combination of character traits and aptitudes, giving them penetrating
insights that they can deploy deftly in instructing others, and an
almost effortless ability to respond appropriately to all manner of
demands put upon them. Nonetheless, coming closer to sagehood

is eminently possible, and even the full achievement of sagehood is achievable and therefore worth striving for.[3] A notable manifestation of this belief is the widespread interest in the life and character of Confucius' student YAN Hui (sometimes called Yanzi or "Master Yan"). According to the tradition, YAN Hui was the most talented of Confucius' students, hard working, humble, and showing much promise for sagehood in spite of dire poverty. What prevented him from realizing sagehood was only his premature death.[4]

Given the accessibility of self-improvement and even sagehood, Neo-Confucians feel that all too many of their contemporaries pursue Confucian education merely as a means to self-interested ends like a career or social recognition. For the vast majority of men[5] who live in the Neo-Confucian period, Confucian scholarship offers the only path to a career with widespread public esteem and a generous salary, for it offers the only path to an office in the civil service. Family fortunes rise and fall depending on their success at securing offices for their male members, and competition is intense.[6] Because of the difficulty of setting aside career ambitions, many Neo-Confucians address the proper division of labor between civil service exam preparation, on the one hand, and more authentic study and reflection aimed at moral self-improvement, on the other. One significant shift to keep in mind is that, with the Ming emperors' explicit endorsement of Song Daoxue as orthodoxy, when Ming Neo-Confucians criticize the "vulgar learning" of their day, their targets are often aspiring exam-takers engaged in rote memorization of the works of Song Neo-Confucians like ZHU Xi, notwithstanding the fact that Zhu had warned against such practices three centuries earlier.[7]

A ubiquitous expression of these worries is a widely quoted remark from the *Analects*, in which Confucius contrasts his contemporaries' merely instrumental interest in learning with that of the more noble motives of the ancients: "People of ancient times learned for their own sake. People nowadays learn for the sake of others."[8] The *Analects* and other classical texts are in fact replete with endorsements of the right kind of learning, as well as succinct descriptions of what one should do. *Analects* 2:4 tells of Confucius' own process of development, beginning from making a "commitment to learning at age fifteen," through several more steps, until, at seventy, he can "follow his heartmind's desire without overstepping the bounds."[9] Among other means that the text suggests to this end is introspective reflection, as when we are told that the Master's disciple Zengzi said, "I daily examine myself in three ways. In planning on behalf of others, have I lacked devotion? In associating with friends, have I been unfaithful? That which has been passed on to me, have I failed to practice?"[10] Later in this chapter we also look at the famous steps of moral progress described in *Greater Learning*, the interpretation of which proves to be a rich source of Neo-Confucian argument.

In addition to classical sources of inspiration, Neo-Confucian views concerning cultivation develop in a context where Buddhist ideas about teaching, texts, and meditation serve as significant points of reference. To at least some degree, the Chan Buddhist model of direct master–disciple interaction and its success in stimulating literati interest serve as models for Neo-Confucians, though only a minority of Neo-Confucians are attracted to Chan views about the dispensability of texts (as we will see below).[11] Later in the chapter, we also take up "mental discipline" and note the role played there by Buddhist meditative practices. As in other aspects of Neo-Confucian thought, the distinctive identity of their philosophy of self-cultivation emerges through both adaptation and criticism of existing ideas.

2 Frameworks of cultivation

We can divide Neo-Confucian models of cultivation into three types. The first two, both of which are prevalent among Daoxue thinkers, we call Direct Discovery and Indirect Discovery. According to the Direct Discovery model, by using the correct techniques one can discover the Pattern within one, whether this is understood as one's good nature or simply as one's pure heartmind. That is, one can see into oneself and grasp the contents of Pattern directly. Advocates of the Indirect Discovery model argue that, while we can discover that we have a good nature, we cannot directly access the contents of that nature. This difference will ramify into different conceptions of what the work of cultivation needs to accomplish, although many of the specific techniques overlap. The third model is advocated by several key critics of Daoxue, who for one reason or another deny that our pre-existing nature or heartmind is sufficient to guide us. We refer to this family of views as sharing a Formation model. These philosophers hold that at least some of the resources that we need to be good people must be developed from the ground up, though they disagree about how and where we can find guidance for this development.[12]

To better understand the Direct Discovery model, first recall the distinction that we introduced in chapter 3 between the not yet manifest (*weifa* 未發) and the already manifest (*yifa* 已發). This comes from a key line in *Centrality and Commonality*, which runs: "When joy and anger, sorrow and happiness are not yet manifest (*weifa*), call it 'the center.' When they are already manifest (*yifa*), and yet all are hitting the proper measure, call it 'harmony.'" As we discussed in earlier chapters, once emotions like joy or anger are sparked – that is, manifest – in response to a stimulation of some kind, they often misfire. For example, a selfish perception of some situation might lead one to be overly angry. Prior to manifestation, though, nature itself is balanced, quiet, whole, and "centered." The core idea behind Direct Discovery is that cultivation should have two objectives: find a way to perceive this perfect state, and find a way to carry that perfect balance into one's active life, so that one's actual reactions achieve what *Centrality and Commonality* calls "harmony."[13]

The most important proponents of Indirect Discovery are CHENG Yi and ZHU Xi. Zhu's teacher LI Tong advocated Direct Discovery, but at a crucial moment in Zhu's intellectual development, he came to see Direct Discovery as incoherent: it seemed to him to require that we experience something that is by definition pre-experiential.[14] As he puts it, "The state when the emotions are not yet manifest cannot be sought, and the state after they are manifest permits no manipulation."[15] He is exaggerating when he says that the already manifest "permits no manipulation": after all, one can try to suppress bad reactions, and indeed Zhu (like almost all Neo-Confucians) argues that we should do just this. But the key point is that if one has already had a bad reaction, it is too late to do anything but try to force oneself not to act too badly.[16] One has already fallen short of the ideal, which is to have one's spontaneous responses perfectly accord with the situation, just like a sage would. As we have seen in earlier chapters, though, CHENG Yi, ZHU Xi, and their followers do not abandon the idea that our natures are good and can guide us. In this case, "discovery" is actually indirect in two different senses. First, our reasons for confidence that our natures are good are indirect, as discussed in chapter 3. Second, our means to access the goodness in our nature are also indirect. Rather than striving for direct insight into nature, one employs practices like "getting a handle on things" (*gewu* 格物) and "reverential attention" (*jing* 敬) – both of which we will discuss below – in order to gradually come to fully know Pattern (that is, to achieve what in the previous chapter we called Type Three knowing).

All Daoxue philosophers are committed to one or other of the Discovery models, but many of their key critics part company with them precisely on this issue. We group these Neo-Confucians together under the rubric of a Formation model of cultivation. Notwithstanding many differences among them, they agree that Daoxue thinkers have too much faith in a fully formed nature, arguing that Discovery models underestimate the need for ground-level development of one's innate faculties and character, and give rise to moral agents who have too much confidence in what are essentially unexamined personal opinions.[17] Instead, individuals engaging in self-cultivation should rely on external models to gradually form a robust, moral character. According to the Ming dynasty Neo-Confucian WANG Tingxiang, this means to base oneself on the laws and institutions of one's day; he is explicit that these institutions will need to change as the times change. As a contemporary scholar puts it, for Wang, "morality becomes a part of the institutional framework, rather than its counterpart."[18] Another possible basis for Formation is the rules of ritual. Many Qing dynasty Neo-Confucians embraced this solution. LING Tingkan, for example, argues that human nature is simply vital stuff – he has nothing but disdain for the idea of Pattern – and that in order to keep our vital stuff in balance, we must submit to the rituals long ago established by the sages.[19] Finally, DAI Zhen emphasizes the importance of internalizing the lessons found in the study of the Confucian classics, as we discuss in more detail below.

Although the Direct and Indirect Discovery models disagree on our relationship to the goodness within us, they agree that the reason our nature does not flawlessly manifest itself in the world is because problems with our vital stuff cause each of us to be selfish (*si* 私). Selfishness infects our intentions (*yi* 意) and our desires (*yu* 欲), each serving to prop up the other.[20] Another way to think about cultivation, therefore, is to see it as the process of removing these selfish intentions and desires.[21] Here, we encounter another key distinction, though: should we attack selfishness simply by removing or suppressing selfish desires (a "subtractive" approach) or by "positively" doing something to embrace impartiality (*gong* 公), which will have the result of reducing or even eliminating selfishness? Imagine a tennis player whose game suffers because he regularly gets angry at (and thus distracted by) what he perceives to be bad calls. A subtractive approach to this problem would seek to remove the anger directly, noting whenever it begins and taking immediate steps (deep breaths?) to tamp it down. A positive approach might be to spend time around players with exemplary on-court behavior or to practice focusing on what really matters, like playing well. Success in either approach, according to the Discovery theorists, is tantamount to purifying the bad vital stuff in our contingent constitution (*qizhi*) or embodied nature (*qizhi zhi xing*), variously described as "dark," "turbid," "muddy," or "coarse."[22] The more that one's vital stuff is purified, the more one's functioning in the world should be able to perfectly reflect one's underlying inherent nature. Advocates of the Formation model generally agree that selfishness is a problem, but not (or at least not only) because it interferes with the expression of our inherent nature: rather, it interferes with the development and manifestation of those dispositions that – they argue – need to be more fully formed within us.

Neo-Confucians themselves do not use the language of "subtractive" and "positive" approaches to cultivation. They do talk about a partly related distinction, though, between "honoring the virtuous nature" (*zundexing* 尊德性) and "engaging in inquiry and study" (*daowenxue* 道問學).[23] The former is meant to capture all types of reflection and self-monitoring, while the latter refers to broad learning centered on things outside the self. It is tempting to think that Direct Discovery, the subtractive approach, and honoring the virtuous nature all form a package, with Indirect Discovery, the positive approach, and engaging in inquiry and study forming a contrasting package. In fact, things do not fall out in this neat way. For one thing, many direct, inward-focused activities are positive, not subtractive: a key to the Direct Discovery model is that one can actively embrace one's nature, and thereby make it a more powerful force in one's life, such that one is less likely to be misled by selfishness. In addition, the large majority of Daoxue philosophers see subtractive and positive approaches as complementary rather than contradictory. This is enabled by the fact that a great array of activities can be seen as means to the end of eliminating selfishness. For example, study can help one to imagine the world from other points of view, and rituals can structure one's environment so that one is more likely to encounter and take advantage of opportunities to notice and attend to the subtle expressions of one's inherent nature, as when a rite of ancestral worship provides regular occasions to reflect on how much our welfare is due to our ancestors.[24] In addition, some tasks may serve not as means to the state of being without selfishness, but rather as constituent parts of that state, much as being alert and vigilant are constituent parts of being quick on one's feet. In this way the Daoxue Confucians can justify the practical commitments that make one ever attentive to one's part in a larger whole, and simultaneously be on the lookout for subtle, nascent appearances of selfish thinking in one's own heartmind.[25]

Furthermore, it is arguable that the Daoxue thinkers saw some acquired traits as playing a self-standing role in full and proper moral agency: not as means to the elimination of selfishness nor as a constituent of that end-state, but as a kind of supplement to the guidance provided by one's inherent nature. In one recorded conversation between WANG Yangming and a disciple, the disciple presses Wang on the claim that one can find the "Pattern" in any given affair in one's own heartmind, without engaging in any outward investigation (*cha* 察) to determine the best course of action. The student takes as examples the ways that filial children go about warming their parents' beds in the winter and cooling them in the summer – surely, the student suggests, people cannot simply know how to do these things innately. Wang answers that a virtuous person would indeed have to do some investigation in order to warm and cool a parent's bed in the proper way and at the proper time, but that this arises from an inborn interest in one's parents' comfort. The general inclination to look after his parents' sleeping comfort comes from his heartmind; it is just that certain detailed ramifications of these filial acts are discovered through investigation, presumably referring to facts about the best methods by which to cool a bed, at what time the process should begin, and so on. Wang suggests that this knowledge, although acquired through investigation, nevertheless belongs to one's heartmind in two senses: first, the more general goal of seeking one's parents' comfort continues to govern one's search for the right detailed expressions, perhaps by setting limits to the range of specific methods worth investigating; second, one is inspired to undertake the investigation in the first place because the Pattern that is one's heartmind prompts it. Understood in this way, Wang says, we can liken the relationship between Pattern and its detailed expressions to the relationship between a tree's root and its branches.[26]

No matter what one's model of self-cultivation, an important final question is from where one gets the motivation to engage in cultivation. Why would a selfish person want to become less selfish and better mesh with Pattern? Neo-Confucians repeatedly emphasize the importance of "establishing a commitment" (*lizhi* 立志), but how do we do this, and what does it really mean? How do we maintain such a commitment over time, in the face of temptations to quit? For anyone who has ever made, and then abandoned, a New Year's resolution, these have to be live questions. The Neo-Confucians offer three types of answers. First, some types of cultivation are largely outside of one's control. Children have little choice but to engage in the rituals and other forms of "lesser learning" (see below) that their elders demand of them. Social norms keep the pressure on adults as well. So insofar as rituals are part of (self-)cultivation, this can take place at least in part without any commitment at all. The second answer is to highlight the fact – already hinted at in the prior sentence – that cultivation is often not a solo endeavor. Families, groups of friends, Neo-Confucian academies: all are contexts in which people can encourage one another to try harder and help each other out when they are struggling. Third, our individual experiences can push us along. ZHU Xi writes eloquently about this as a twofold process. On the one hand, it does not take much attention to one's world to experience unease at the disharmony all around one. And on the other hand, Zhu points to experiences that show us the nascent possibility of unobstructed harmony: of everything fitting together, everything making sense.[27] Other thinkers, even those with a different model of cultivation from Zhu's own, make similar reference to the "push" of unpleasant experiences and the "pull" of inspiring ones.

We will end this section with a look at what motivated the early Ming Daoxue scholar WU Yubi in his lifelong practice of self-cultivation. Wu left behind a remarkable journal that describes his efforts – and his doubts and self-criticisms – at making progress toward the ultimate Confucian goal of sagehood.[28] It begins when he is thirty-three, having abandoned studying for the civil service exams and returned to his family home in the countryside. Many of the ideas and practices that we examine throughout the present chapter are explicit parts of Wu's practice. He makes his "commitment" explicit, writing out his goals in a notebook and plastering the walls of his study with reminders of specific objectives, such as "FIRMLY MAINTAIN MY INTEGRITY EVEN IN POVERTY!"[29] Wu clearly experiences both pushes and pulls: he writes of anxiety and shame, but also regularly makes remarks like "How lovely it is today to behold the vital impulse of all the various plants!"[30] He also recognizes the benefits of having what we might call a training partner: after ten days, in which he felt his efforts flagging, he writes, "Now where can I find a good friend to help me realize this ambition of mine to reach sagehood?"[31] He continues the journal for the rest of his life (he passes away at age seventy-seven), and provides a unique window on the way that ongoing self-cultivation requires ongoing motivation, even if it seems to get easier as Wu makes progress over the years.

3 Ritual and physical disciplines

A concern for ritual has been central to the thought and practice of virtually all Confucians, and Neo-Confucians are no exceptions. "Ritual" here does not just mean formal ceremony but covers an enormous range of social norms governing how we interact with one another. Some of these are codified in classic texts; some are spelled out in manuals composed by Neo-Confucians themselves; and some are uncodified but widely followed practices. Rituals operate on many levels. Some are supported by the state and aimed at all individuals; others are quite local. Obeying a ritual has a clear and direct effect upon one's behavior. Less obvious but perhaps even more important, rituals can shape and direct our emotions. At least when we engage in them with the proper spirit, rituals can "nurture" or transform our emotions in a lasting fashion.[32] Because rituals operate simultaneously in multiple ways, we will need to discuss them not just in this chapter – where we focus on their role in cultivation – but also in the following two chapters, where we will emphasize their ethical and political import.

Neo-Confucian philosophers differ on the degree of theoretical centrality that rituals hold. Some believe that explicit rituals are of the first importance. Alan Wood explains that for someone like the early Song dynasty writer SUN Fu, "These 'rituals' were thought to be the outward manifestations of certain absolute moral principles … [and therefore] violations of ritual are violations not only of the human order but of the universal order as well."[33] The same can be said for many Qing dynasty thinkers, who both feel that Daoxue Neo-Confucians had promoted an overly subjectivist reading of the tradition, and that this subjectivism was responsible for the fall of the Ming dynasty to the invading Manchus. A notable exponent of this movement toward ritual purism was LING Tingkan (mentioned above as a supporter of the Formation model) who announces: "The way of the sages is only ritual propriety."[34] Ling strongly distrusts the ability of average people to perceive propriety without the guidance of explicit rituals, and even worries about the ability of sages to avoid mistakes. However, major early Neo-Confucians, such as ZHANG Zai and the Cheng brothers, tend to distinguish between rituals and the underlying Pattern that the rituals are designed to elicit. For example, ZHANG Zai asserts that "Ritual is Pattern. You must first learn to exhaustively investigate Pattern; ritual is then the means by which you put into practice what is right according to Pattern. … Rituals come after Pattern."[35] For his part, ZHU Xi in fact criticizes ZHANG Zai for overemphasizing ritual, and argues that, while ritual offers one route toward personal transformation, it is not the only possible means. Still, Zhu saw ritual as a very useful and broadly applicable educational mechanism and authored the most important ritual manual of the later imperial period, *Master Zhu's Family Rituals.*[36]

A useful way to understand Zhu's perspective on ritual – which was largely shared by many Neo-Confucians – is provided by an ancient distinction, which Zhu helped to revive in his day, between two kinds of learning: lesser learning (*xiaoxue* 小學) and greater learning (*daxue* 大學). This pair of terms names both two short texts and their corresponding approaches to learning. Zhu says that, in antiquity, lesser learning meant instruction in "the chores of cleaning and sweeping, in the formalities of polite conversation and good manners, and in the refinements of ritual, music, archery, charioteering, calligraphy, and mathematics." When they turned fifteen, the children of the elite (as well as, Zhu says, gifted commoners) entered the school of greater learning, in which they were taught to "exhaustively investigate Pattern, correct their heartminds, cultivate themselves, and govern others."[37] He explains the difference more abstractly as follows: "Lesser learning is the study of affairs – such as serving one's ruler, serving one's father, serving one's brother, and dealing with one's friends. It teaches one to behave according to certain rules. Greater learning illuminates the Pattern behind these affairs."[38] In other words, as one first begins to learn the proper way to perform rituals, to engage in polite conversation, to clean and sweep, one follows explicit instructions. Often one is awkward and rigid, only knowing to follow the precise instructions one has been given and unsure how to proceed if one finds oneself in a slightly novel situation. In the terms we developed in the last chapter, this is Type One knowing: not only is it rigid, but it also lacks the built-in motivation that comes from a holistic appreciation of the "Pattern behind the affairs." Greater learning aims to cultivate precisely this appreciation, as we will see in the following sections.

Participating in rituals and lesser learning do not just teach us rules for interpersonal behavior. Importantly, they also help to solidify our motivation to continue to grow as moral beings, and to develop the focused attention that will enable us to do so. Here, for example, is WANG Yangming:

> The ways to raise and cultivate young boys are to lure them to singing so their intentions (*zhiyi*) will be roused, to direct them to practice ritual so their demeanor will be dignified, and to urge them to read and recite in order to open their perception. … Singing is also to release through singing their energy as expressed in jumping around and shouting, and to free them through rhythm from depression and repression.[39]

Wang's discussion of what a lesser learning school should be like is also replete with references to the serious, respectful, concentrated demeanor with which students shall be taught to carry themselves.[40] Similarly, Zhu asserts that in these benighted days without explicit instruction in lesser learning, "only if students are taught to regard reverential attention as central and to discipline their bodies and minds will they be capable of making the proper effort."[41] In short, all forms of lesser learning help to develop habits that can be justified both as means to and constituents of a state of heartmind without selfishness.[42]

4 *Greater Learning* and "getting a handle on things"

Just as there was an ancient text called *Lesser Learning* which provided at least some of the content for Neo-Confucian ritual and physical practices of self-cultivation, so there was the even more famous *Greater Learning* (*Daxue* 大學), a short work embedded in the *Record of Rituals*. Emphasis on *Greater Learning* unites many strands of Neo-Confucianism, well beyond the Daoxue philosophers that formed its core. It is promoted as a definitive statement on the topic even by the early forerunner to Neo-Confucianism, the Tang dynasty philosopher HAN Yu, and after ZHU Xi, disputes about proper interpretation of *Greater Learning* often serve as a proxy for larger debates about the nature and structure of proper learning itself. The text offers a complex account of moral cultivation and its social and political consequences, but the heart of the text is a sequence of eight steps meant to clarify the appropriate order and priority of various tasks in both improvement of character and effective governance, probably because it was originally intended for rulers and for scholars who aspired to high office.

> Wanting to light up the bright virtue of all-under-heaven, the ancients first put their states in order. Those who wanted to put their states in order first regulated their families. Those who wanted to regulate their families first cultivated their selves. Those who wanted to cultivate their selves first rectified their heartminds. Those who wanted to rectify their heartminds first made their intentions sincere. Those who wanted to make their intentions sincere first reached understanding (*zhi*). Reaching understanding lies in getting a handle on things.[43]

The sequence begins with two crucial steps: "getting a handle on things" (*gewu* 格物) and "reaching understanding" (*zhizhi* 致知).[44] Since sincerity and the underlying political theories are important components of chapters 8 (on ethics) and 9 (on governance), and knowing or understanding (*zhi*) was the topic of chapter 6, we focus here on the first step in the sequence, which has great implications for self-cultivation.

Perhaps the most contested term in Neo-Confucianism is "getting a handle on things" (*gewu*). Of the range of plausible interpretations of the phrase, one of the most literal is "reaching things," but there are good arguments for reading it as "rectifying things," and the context of the term suggests that it should be interpreted metaphorically. Due largely to the influence of the Cheng brothers, the most popular interpretation is that it refers to the process by which one comes to thoroughly grasp the Pattern in things, whether those "things" be books, historical accounts, a person's character, one's ordinary affairs, or, less often, non-human life (like plants or animals) or natural phenomena (like fire or thunder).[45] But as we saw in the previous chapter, the Cheng brothers' comments are open-ended enough to make the phrase compatible with an array of interpretations – most notably, with respect to whether getting a handle on things is largely an activity directed toward the (external) things themselves or more toward one's own nature. Most Daoxue philosophers agree that the Pattern in things and the Pattern in oneself are manifestations of the same underlying cosmic Pattern, so one can give either the outward or inward interpretation of getting a handle on things without going too far afoul of the recorded remarks by the Cheng brothers.

Historically speaking, the two most influential rival interpretations of getting a handle on things are ZHU Xi's and WANG Yangming's. For Zhu, getting a handle on things consists in discovering in other things an expression of Pattern that resonates with the Pattern in oneself. A simple example of this sort of activity is the exercise of reading about mourning rites in the *Analects*, such that we see why one should mourn one's parents in a certain way and for a certain period of time. Another example is investigating the general features of the cosmos, so as to learn why heaven is high and earth is low (presumably this has something to do with the active nature of *yang* vital stuff and the passive or inert nature of *yin* vital stuff). Zhu rarely speaks about investigations of the latter sort, but the textual evidence suggests that he did see them as continuous in key respects with the kind of investigation more directly tied to moral virtue and behavior.[46] The goal of all types of investigation is, as *Greater Learning* says, reaching understanding; for details on Zhu's interpretation of that process, and for more on why he sees as crucial the encounter with aspects of Pattern outside the self, see chapter 6.

WANG Yangming famously became frustrated with his youthful efforts to "get a handle on" the Pattern of a stand of bamboo, falling ill after seven days of concentrated effort.[47] As he develops his own philosophical views, one key element is therefore to challenge ZHU Xi's understanding of *gewu*. Part of his argument is philological: Wang provides plausible evidence that the phrase understood by Zhu as investigating things is better read as rectifying one's intentions (*yi* 意) in response to things.[48] Wang holds that the "things" in question are really the objects of one's own understanding and concern, such as serving one's parents or caring for others. Rectifying them is a matter of identifying and rooting out selfish intentions, for selfish intentions distort one's moral judgment in pernicious ways.[49] The other, more philosophical side of his objection concerns cognitive bias and rationalization. Wang believes that the most formidable obstacle to good judgment about a particular affair is not that one is lacking a nuanced understanding of the affair at hand but one's tendency to misconstrue an affair to one's own advantage. Think of the student who condemns cheating as unfair and undignified, but somehow manages to justify it in his own case: a deeper understanding of unfairness and dignity is not likely to cure him of this problem. The problem is that he tends to construe the matter in a self-serving way, perhaps downplaying the consequences of his action or exaggerating the differences between his case and that of others. In Wang's view, this is a kind of self-deception, for one's true heartmind, the locus of good knowing (*liangzhi*), understands intuitively the wrongness of this behavior, but the lesser parts of one's self pretend otherwise. According to Wang, this situation arises because people allow selfish intentions to take hold.[50] The solution, accordingly, is not to investigate cheating in greater depth but to resist or root out one's bad intentions. In the terms that we introduced above, there are therefore both "subtractive" and "positive" aspects to getting a handle on things as Wang understands it; we discuss this further below.[51]

5 Mental discipline

Introduction and self-monitoring

The steps of self-cultivation spelled out in *Greater Learning* – getting a handle on things, reaching understanding, making intentions sincere, and so on – are quite abstract and, as we have just seen, there was disagreement both about what they meant, and how to go about accomplishing them. For ZHU Xi and many others, reading books was the most common way to "get a handle on things," and we will look at reading as a practice of self-cultivation in this chapter's final section. Here, we look at a variety of mental disciplines. By "mental discipline," we mean any form of effort (*gongfu*) focused primarily on what we feel or think, on maintaining the right intentions or suppressing the wrong ones, or on detecting and then influencing what is going on in our heartminds. We can usefully divide the various approaches to mental discipline into three categories: (1) self-monitoring; (2) tranquillity and insight; and (3) reverential attention. Exactly how these forms of self-cultivation relate to the *Greater Learning* schema depends on which thinker you ask. For example, WANG Yangming argues that getting a handle on things, reaching understanding, and making intentions sincere are all aspects of the same process, at the heart of which is the form of "insight" that we discuss below. For his part, Zhu certainly sees connections between the various steps but places particular emphasis on "reverential attention" as a means to achieving sincerity; in his perspective, reverential attention and getting a handle on things are distinct from one another, but mutually supporting as one's understanding or knowing reaches toward the holistic, Type Three mastery of the sage. And these are only two of the more prominent positions that we examine.

Almost all Neo-Confucians think that some forms of self-monitoring should be part of one's cultivation toolkit. Building on classical injunctions like "subdue the self so as to return to propriety" and "be watchful over the self even when alone,"[52] Neo-Confucians explain that we need to guard against allowing selfish intentions or desires to flourish and grow. One particularly interesting approach is to focus on the liminal moment of emotional incipience (*ji* 機), just as emotions are beginning to be expressed (or enter into one's consciousness). Incipience appears to many thinkers to be a particularly opportune moment to suppress problematic intentions or emotions.[53] If one fails to note a bad intention at the moment of incipience, though, it will often be possible to suppress it later on. WANG Yangming mirrors many when he speaks of the thoroughness with which one must remove selfishness: "In trying to subdue the self, every selfish intention must be thoroughly and completely wiped out without leaving even an iota."[54] However much self-monitoring may assist one, though, Neo-Confucians do not believe that it is adequate on its own. According to Wang, the "subtractive" effort of self-monitoring is complemented by attending directly to the pure goodness of which one's heartmind is capable. ZHU Xi writes that if one has sufficiently nurtured oneself and practices reverential attention (on which see below), there will be no need for subduing the self – just as when one is rested and strong, there is no need for medicine because one will have no illness.[55]

Embodying tranquillity

By the time Neo-Confucianism began to flourish in the Song dynasty, one of the most popular techniques of mental discipline was Buddhist meditation, something of which many self-identified Confucian philosophers had experience. There were numerous techniques of meditation associated with a variety of schools, but the form of greatest interest to the Neo-Confucians was called "quiet sitting" (*jing zuo* 靜坐), used to describe an array of practices which, done rightly, were supposed to bring about a state of quietude or tranquillity (*jing* 靜). To be sure, many Buddhists also advocated more active and contemplative types of meditative practice.[56] But it was quiet sitting that most interested the Neo-Confucians, seeing it as a relatively promising technique for achieving mental stability and self-control. For some of the Neo-Confucians who advocated the Direct Discovery approach to cultivation, in fact, quiet sitting was the key element of their teaching. YANG Shi, a student of the Cheng brothers, provides a good example of this kind of practice.[57] Yang taught that by relying on quiet sitting, "students should embody (*ti*) with the heartmind the state when the emotions are not yet manifest, then the meaning of centeredness (*zhong*) will appear of itself. Hold onto it and do not let go so that no selfish desires remain; then, when the emotions are aroused, they will be all certain to attain due measure and degree."[58]

The tranquillity of quiet sitting, according to someone like Yang, is precisely what allows one to avoid sensory distractions and then "embody" the tranquil, stable, not yet manifest inherent reality of the heartmind. Holding onto such tranquillity would lead to perfectly apt actions. Many other thinkers saw problems with too much tranquillity, however. First of all, it is arguable that meditation only prepares us to maintain our mental discipline while relatively passive, but Neo-Confucians are also concerned with the moral side of personal cultivation, which requires that we actively engage with the world. The Neo-Confucians thus need some ability to ensure the heartmind's proper responsiveness to the world even when engaged in activities that are prone to disturb our peace of mind and activate emotional responses.[59] Second, we might also worry that whatever insights we might gain through meditation-induced tranquillity have no connection to the larger world. The goal of meditation is to quiet the heartmind, not necessarily to make ourselves more responsive to the interests of others or to the demands of a larger-scale social or cosmic order. Many Neo-Confucians charged that meditation only won control over the heartmind so that it could serve our own more deeply entrenched subjective aims or inclinations.

A common result of these concerns was to downplay the significance of quiet sitting, even though many prominent thinkers (like ZHU Xi himself) continued to advocate its use as a supportive practice. It is important to realize, though, that quiet sitting was not the only means of cultivation employed by supporters of the Direct Discovery approach. YANG Shi's student ZHANG Jiucheng rejected his teacher's focus on quiet sitting, for example, but still felt that the path to sagehood lay with directly experiencing the deeper kind of tranquillity at our core, which we can again think of as a kind of embodiment. He emphasizes activity rather than quietude, but feels that one can "be cautious over what is unseen and apprehensive over what is unheard" even in the midst of activity. This is the way to "get the taste" of the not-yet-manifest centeredness. He continues: "This is the basis for knowing centeredness. If one cannot hold to this method ... it is as if one were to eat and drink all day yet never know the taste. Oh, the taste of it! You will know it when you have become thoroughly immersed and drenched in what is unseen and unheard."[60] Zhang believes that if one can get used to the "taste" of the perfectly balanced "center," then one can learn to maintain that feeling throughout all one's activities.

Something of the same approach is adopted by the most famous advocate of Direct Discovery, WANG Yangming.[61] Like Zhang, he is no fan of passive reflection or quiet sitting: Wang wants us to be thoroughly, actively engaged in our world. But, also like Zhang, he believes that, with the right kind of attention, we can experience not-yet-manifest centeredness and gradually make it the complete master of our heartminds. Wang writes that you must "Embody the inherent reality of your own heartmind at all times and see to it that it is as clear as a mirror and as even as a balance. Then you will find the not-yet-manifest centeredness."[62] Wang borrows but redefines a term from ZHU Xi to refer to this special kind of introspective experiencing of centeredness, referring to it as "private knowing" (*duzhi* 獨知).[63] Rather than speak of a particular "taste" of centeredness, though, Wang explains that what we are experiencing is our "good knowing" (*liangzhi*). Recall from chapter 5 that good knowing is pure, perfect emotional response; it does not have a distinctive "feel," but it is always there, motivating us in the right direction and nudging us to feel badly about selfish reactions when we have gone awry. If good knowing is emotion, though, how can this be the same as "not-yet-manifest centeredness" – as Wang says that it is?[64] Isn't emotion precisely the "already manifest" (*yifa*)? Wang's answer is that we must not think of the not yet manifest as somehow existing separately from the already manifest. As we discussed in chapter 3's account of "heartmind is Pattern," Pattern and centeredness have no reality apart from a given, situationally perfect reaction of one's heartmind. Wang opposes all dualisms that might lead to an abstract, rigid, reified moral standard.[65] For similar reasons, he rejects the usefulness of "activity" and "tranquillity" as applied to good knowing: "Activity and tranquillity may refer to the heartmind's engaging in something or nothing, but good knowing makes no distinction between doing something and doing nothing."[66] He thus denies that there is any kind of difference, in practice, between the not-yet-manifest and the already-manifest good knowing. The positive work of "reaching good knowing" is to experience it as much as possible: this is Direct Discovery – though, as mentioned earlier, it must also be paired with the subtractive effort of suppressing selfish reactions.

Reverential attention

All the approaches to mental discipline that we have just canvassed depend on the premise that one can directly apprehend one's good nature, either in its tranquil, not-yet-manifest state, or else in the process of activity itself. As we noted in section 2, CHENG Yi and ZHU Xi are among the thinkers who deny this premise and thus fall into the Indirect Discovery camp. They still hold that our natures are good and that we have ample reason to trust our genuinely natural functioning, but argue that cultivation can only indirectly get us to the point of such natural, sage-like spontaneity. Rather than pursuing "tranquillity" (*jing* 靜), they teach their students to engage in "reverential attention" (*jing* 敬) (the two terms are homonyms in Chinese). As a method of maintaining mental discipline while in active states, reverential attention is supposed do two things at once: first, we are to concentrate on a task or object of inquiry with a certain kind of respect, which – second – undercuts selfish intentions, including ones that are easy to overlook or misapprehend. This might seem strange at first blush: isn't one task a matter of directing one's attention outward and the other inward? Recall, though, the distinction between subtractive and positive cultivation. "Subtractive" means to directly pare away selfishness, while "positive" means to actively focus one's efforts and thus become more impartial (and less selfish). Reverential attention is a classic case of positive cultivation.

One way that Neo-Confucians explain reverential attention is by comparing it to the mental posture one adopts when engaged in a ritual – and, after all, rituals and ritual prescriptions pervade their daily lives, from meals to greetings to cleaning the home. ZHU Xi finds it helpful to invoke the most profound kind of reverence that his students understood to be required of them in important ceremonies: "'Sit as though you were impersonating an ancestor. Stand as though you were performing a sacrifice.' The head should be upright, the eyes looking straight ahead, the feet steady, the hands respectful, the mouth quiet and composed, the bearing solemn – these are all aspects of reverential attention."[67] The remarks that Zhu quotes (taken from the *Record of Rituals*) describe what would be familiar physiological aspects of ritual performance and indicate the more elusive psychological phenomena that they induce. We can think of this as a way in which lesser learning contributes to greater learning: the learned physical postures and habits serve as a bridge to the more pervasive attitude that Zhu is trying to teach.

For twenty-first-century people with less regular experience of rituals, this connection may be less helpful, but most of us can at least extrapolate from some relevant experiences. For example, imagine a sixteen-year-old high-school student being asked to read in a history book about model relationships between political authorities and their advisers. How easy would it be for her to get distracted by a detail that reminds her of some drama in her own life? Can we imagine, though, a sense of respect – for her teacher, her education, her history, even for her (and the world's) future – that would enable her to focus on the incidents described in her reading with genuine interest, despite their seeming irrelevance to her life? The idea of reverential attention is that, by seeing her history assignment in this way, she automatically remains focused on its meaning; her thoughts and concern naturally remain on the content. It is not that she has an additional task, of guarding against selfishness; if reverential attention works, it is supposed to eliminate the possibility of external things enticing us or distracting us. Reverential attention combines two key aspects – attentiveness and a sense of perspective about what is truly important – and its effect is twofold: one's attention is engaged in an activity (not passive), but one is also less prone to have the biases that arise from selfish intentions.

The kind of distraction that Zhu is worried about is not the kind where one's attention moves from one object to the next, but the distraction in which shifts of one's attention are not directed by the importance or significance of those objects, so that one ends up paying attention to trivial things.[68] Zhu makes this explicit in the following intriguing set of remarks:

> As for reverential attention, don't think of it as some matter outside yourself. It is simply to collect your own mental energy and focus it here and now. Now it seems to me the reason none of you are making progress is that you only know how to talk about "getting a handle on things" but are lacking in the fundamentals. Unconcentrated as your mental energy and your intentions are, your effort is unpenetrating. It is not that certain matters in particular distract your thinking; just

enjoying the scenery leads your heartmind far astray. How can this compare to maintaining it within at all times? To have absolutely no interest in the inconsequential matters of the world may seem unfeeling at first, but in fact, it is best if this is the case.[69]

Another way to put this is to say that Zhu worries not about allowing one's attention to *move* but rather about allowing it to *wander*. In Zhu's terms, a heartmind that is reverentially attentive has a "master." The mastery in question, though, is not like a slave's master, directing the slave where and when to move. Rather, as a later Neo-Confucian explains it, the heartmind's having a master is like when the master of the house is at home. When the master is at home, chaotic outsiders are prevented from entering the house even without the master's actively warding them away. Similarly, when one is attuned to the broad significance of any given affair, then "chaos" – that is, selfish concerns – cannot enter one's heartmind. The result will be the Indirect Discovery of one's inherent nature, whose issuances track the cosmic Way.[70]

6 Studying the Confucian canon

If one were to attempt to identify some of the core philosophical commitments that run through both classical Confucianism and Neo-Confucianism, high on the list would be a shared belief in the importance of reading the texts they took to represent the wisdom of the ancient sages, who were models of ritual propriety, filial piety, and humaneness. One might be tempted to say that any so-called Confucian who believed in cultivation without studying the Confucian canon was a Confucian only in name.

But in fact, some of the distinctive commitments of the Neo-Confucians, particularly the Daoxue Neo-Confucians, raise the possibility of moral cultivation without textual study. To see why, consider the tremendous "epistemological optimism"[71] expressed in some of the views that we have seen: the Daoxue philosophers tend to believe that our nature provides us with remarkable moral faculties right from the start, faculties that would issue in reliably good emotions and understanding if it were not for certain weaknesses that arise because this good nature cannot exist apart from vital stuff. For a Daoxue philosopher, this leaves open one obvious way of demonstrating why textual study is necessary: by showing that it corrects some of the problems that result from our inherent nature's embodiment in vital stuff. The difficulty is that most of the problems that they trace to vital stuff do not strike the casual observer as requiring textual study of any kind (not to mention of Confucian classics) to resolve them. The Daoxue thinkers tend to stress failures of commitment and most of all the interference of selfish desires. Why should reading the *Analects* and the *Book of Odes* help us get traction on problems like these? Answering this question takes us into some of the most interesting territory in Neo-Confucian thought.

Let us begin with a summary of changing views on reading among the Neo-Confucians.[72] Early thinkers like ZHANG Zai and the Cheng brothers saw reading as an important technique of cultivation and put forward general views about both what should be read (e.g., history and literature were of minimal value, according to ZHANG Zai, while the *Analects* and *Mencius* were well suited to beginners) and how one should read: namely, use the words as pointers toward the meaning and truth behind the text, rather than getting bogged down in detailed exegesis.[73] In this regard, keep in mind that reading is probably the most common form of "getting a handle on things." The potential downside to any stress on reading, of course, is that, in practice, admonitions to look for meaning can be ignored as students focus on memorization for its own sake – especially given the role played in Song dynasty society by success in the civil service exams. LU Xiangshan's famous statement that "The Six Classics are all my footnotes,"[74] emphasizing that the classics are not an authority independent of one's own cultivated judgment, is surely a reaction against overly wooden approaches to reading that were common in his society. ZHU Xi's reaction was different. He sought to make more explicit through his writing, teaching, and commentarial work how and what one should actually read. The tension between the ideal of reading-as-cultivational-practice and the all-too-common reality of reading-as-means-to-success remained, however. WANG Yangming gives us yet another effort at articulating the proper role of reading. As we will see, he continues to see it as playing an important function, and even agrees with Zhu that preparation for the exams is not automatically a problem. The point of reading, though, must be its role in helping one to perceive the Pattern that unites events, past and present, with the judgments of one's own good knowing.

Since ZHU Xi's view of reading is particularly detailed and widely influential, it makes sense to explore it in more detail.[75] We can best understand Zhu's teaching if we break it down into four stages – recitation, reflection, mastery, and going beyond the text – which we will discuss in order. Zhu repeatedly emphasizes the importance of reciting texts over and over again, becoming "intimately familiar" with what one reads; it is better to read less, but truly "personally experience" it, than to read widely yet shallowly.[76] This level of familiarity is necessary because, as we will see, the goal of book reading is not just the acquisition of information. To be sure, it is useful to learn that sages can grasp Pattern and act with ease. But one needs to do more than learn to say these words. One needs to discover their personal relevance, which is much more than merely "knowing" these teachings. Zhu offers many pieces of concrete advice on how best to carry out recitation: "concentrate fully, without thought of gain"; "make a truly fierce effort" on the short passages you choose; do not do too much at once, and rest as needed; avoid skipping around as you read; and so on.[77] Perhaps most importantly, Zhu says to "keep your mind glued on the text": we can approach the text with an "open mind" (*xuxin* 虚心) so long as we "keep it focused on the text."[78] This sort of focus is directly related to the reverential attention we discussed in the prior section.

As a second step toward accomplishing the aims of reading, one moves from recitation to reflection. Zhu says we need to "never stop thinking, turning over and over in our heartminds what has already become clear to us." In a similar vein, "Once our intimate reading of it and careful reflection on it have led to a clear understanding of it, we must continue to raise doubts. Then there might be additional progress. If we cease questioning, in the end there will be no additional progress."[79] Zhu stresses the importance of "doubts": we should both cultivate them and then seek to remove them. We should, in particular, doubt our own views and not just those of others.[80] The goal of ongoing reflection is to fit things together: to discover the coherence between the text, our own reactions to the situations described, and our own sense of our contemporary situations. All these must ultimately fit together as part of the whole that is Pattern.

The third stage is marked by reaching the point in one's reading that understanding comes more easily. Zhu sometimes calls this "mastery." At this stage, we understand with the same felicity as someone highly skilled in a craft. Zhu compares the person who has attained mastery to an expert gardener, who adeptly adjusts the amount of water given to each plant according to its type, and does so effortlessly. Reading then becomes considerably more fluid.[81] This description of mastery suggests that it represents a more significant change in the reader, akin to acquiring a new skill. But Zhu tends to characterize it as something more profound than a skill, more like a realization or fuller expression of a capacity already inside oneself.[82] As we will see next, this paves the way for an understanding of the texts that is more self-reliant.

Finally, we come to the fourth step, in which we go beyond the texts. Zhu says that our goal was never limited to the surface meaning of a given text.[83] The texts are a vehicle through which we can encounter and be shaped by the intentions (*yi*) of the sages. This will ultimately lead us to see the possibilities for Pattern wherever we look, and at this point we no longer need to rely on the texts. Zhu in fact begins his two-chapter discussion of reading with the statement that "Book learning is a secondary matter,"[84] and later adds that "When we read the Six Classics, it should be as if there were no Six Classics. We are simply seeking the Pattern of the Way within ourselves."[85] He concludes his discussion of reading thus: "Because we have commentaries to the Classics, we understand the Classics. Once we have understood the Classics, there is no need for the commentaries. We rely on the Classics simply to understand Pattern. Once we have grasped Pattern, there is no need for the Classics."[86] These passages help us to put Zhu's lifelong devotion to commentary into perspective. The texts are never ends in themselves but means toward personal self-improvement and transformation.[87]

WANG Yangming's views on the controversy between Zhu and LU Xiangshan about book reading are nuanced and relatively charitable to Zhu. In both his letters and his famous *Record for Practice*, he approves of the external investigations (especially book learning) championed by Zhu, so long as they are balanced by more introspective "honoring the virtuous nature" (*zun de xing* 尊德性).[88] Book learning is fine, says Wang, so long as one approaches it with a firm commitment toward personal improvement, rather than as a means to worldly success.[89] Wang favors repeated recitation for many of the same reasons Zhu discusses: as part of lesser learning, such work "steeps one in centeredness and harmony without knowing why."[90] Like Zhu, Wang believes that "In reading, the value does not lie in the amount but in learning the material well."[91] He also stresses that in terms of our ultimate aim of illuminating Pattern, the classics fall away just as would Histories.[92]

We would not want to leave the impression that there are no differences between Zhu and Wang on reading. Zhu promotes a specific curriculum, feels that reading in a particular order is essential to progress, and puts forth extraordinary labor over his long lifetime to provide a consistent commentarial approach to the classics that will enable students to get to the point at which they no longer need its support. Wang has a different temperament, lives at a different time, and devotes his energies to different goals. (Unlike Zhu, he held many high civil and military offices over his career.) Especially in his late writings, he comes across as having little patience with lengthy, systematic approaches to cultivation that dwell overmuch on the classics, focusing increasingly narrowly on his teaching of "reaching good knowing." In addition, he makes explicit that the context-specific nature of standards of right and wrong action – which we have already noted applies to his understanding of ethical judgment in general – also applies to ethical teaching and to self-cultivation. He draws on the practice of medicine to explain: "Sages and worthies teach in the same way that physicians prescribe medicine. They always match the treatment to the ailment, taking into consideration the various symptoms and, whenever appropriate, adjusting the dosage. Their sole aim is to eliminate the ailment. They have no predetermined course of action."[93] Be all this as it may, his own classical erudition continues to shine through in his writings and comments to students, and one can only assume he expected his students to thoroughly understand the sources of his allusions.

One position with which to contrast these views on the benefits of reading the classics comes from DAI Zhen, a major critic of Daoxue. Dai takes issue with the Daoxue idea that we have well-formed moral faculties right from the start, which we referred to earlier as the epistemological optimism of the tradition. For Dai, it is important to recognize that there are certain things that we learn from the classics that are both indispensable for moral understanding and yet not available to us by our very natures. When we study the classics carefully and reflectively, we *add* to our capacity to make sound moral judgments; we do not simply unearth or uncover a pre-existing capacity to do so. Dai also calls attention to the fact that we rely on the classics to know the proper methods of moral cultivation themselves, both the details of the methods and the account of ethical norms and human nature on which they are based. Can we know which methods are viable without some confidence that we are taking them on good grounds and from a reliable authority?[94]

Dai's criticisms raise questions that are both important and wide ranging. The critique that seems to go straight to the foundations of Daoxue thought, however, is the suggestion that they lean too heavily on the notion of a well-formed moral capacity right from the start, without acknowledging the importance of adding to that faculty. Perhaps this charge seems unfair. As we saw earlier in this chapter, the methods that Zhu and Wang endorse are not exclusively subtractive. Study supports our efforts to pare away some selfish desires by allowing us to see the world from other points of view and helps to cultivate some of the very habits of thought and forms of attention that make us astute discerners of moral situations. Still, there is something about Dai's criticism which, when properly understood, does seem to pose a major challenge to Daoxue views. However much Daoxue Confucians may be able to use the subtractive goal of paring away selfish desires to justify positive methods of moral cultivation, they are still committed to saying, at the end of the day, that well-formed moral faculties are already in us. So while the positive methods might help clear the ground for the moral faculties in various ways, they cannot be parts of the moral faculties themselves. It is arguable, at the very least, that the skills and insights acquired by reading are, for the likes of Zhu and Wang, akin to the tools needed for weeding a flower garden, whereas for Dai they are nutrients that become part of the flowers themselves. In short, it seems that Zhu and Wang do see the transformative effects of reading as less far reaching or thoroughgoing than DAI Zhen.

No doubt there is more to say on all sides of this debate, but this should be enough to help us appreciate both the breadth and depth of philosophical resources available from quite divergent strands of the Neo-Confucian tradition. Theories of cultivation and their philosophical underpinnings lie at the very center of Neo-Confucian discourse, so it should come as little surprise that nearly every facet of cultivation is explored over the many centuries of Neo-Confucian thought. What we have tried to do here is highlight the facets that were most important or most contested. To this end, we have discussed both the nature and the function of such techiques as practicing rituals, developing reverential attention, and learning to identify the powerful self-serving thoughts and biases that plague us. In the next chapter, we will look at the most important of the intended fruits of these practices: the chief virtues of Confucianism.

For further study

Selected primary sources

1. ZHU Xi (CHU Hsi), "On Reading," parts I and II, in Zhu 1990: 128–62.
2. ZHU Xi, *Collected Commentaries on the* Great Learning, in Tiwald and Van Norden 2014: #33.
3. WU Yubi, *The Journal of Wu Yubi*, in Wu 2013: xx–xxxix and 3–73.
4. WANG Yangming, "Instructions for Liu Po-sung and Others on Fundamental Ideas for Elementary Education" (n.b. "Elementary Education" is an alternative translation for "Lesser Learning"), in Wang 1963: 182–6.

5. WANG Yangming, "Letter to Ku Tung-ch'iao" in Wang 1963: 91–117.
6. WANG Yangming, *Record for Practice* §7, in Tiwald and Van Norden 2014: #43, 271 only.
7. LUO Qinshun, "Two Letters to Wang Yangming," in Luo 1987: 175–88.

Discussion questions

1. Are the kinds of learning that ZHU Xi promotes entirely alien to you? What relation, if any, do they have to the kinds of learning that you have experienced?
2. How consequential do you think selfish intentions and desires are for us? Do they play a major role in our moral failures, as many Neo-Confucian suggest? If so, does this justify self-monitoring for these intentions and desires?
3. How does reverential attention contrast with seeking tranquillity?
4. Have you ever read a text in the way that Zhu recommends? What comes closest?
5. Do you see significant differences between ZHU Xi's and WANG Yangming's views on the importance of reading the classics for cultivation? If so, what are they?
6. In what respects do ZHU Xi and WANG Yangming envision cultivation as subtractive? In what ways do they see them as positive?

8

Virtues

1 Background

Some shared ethical commitments

We turn now to Neo-Confucian ethics. Although there is much that the Neo-Confucians found contentious in this area of inquiry, it is here that we can best see what unites Neo-Confucians, even bringing together Daoxue Confucians and their critics. Part of what it means to be a Confucian, in the eyes of our thinkers, is to have the ethical commitments that characterize the Confucian way of life (and are largely incompatible with Daoist and Buddhist ways of life). The chief among these commitments is giving ethical priority to one's family. To be a Confucian is to see members of one's family as having a stronger ethical claim on oneself than strangers, mere acquaintances, or even good friends. Historically, there have been many ways of spelling out the concrete implications of this position. In a well-known passage in the *Analects*, Confucius declares that an upright son would sooner cover up the thievery of his father than reveal the crime to the authorities, a claim that many have taken to suggest that the interests of one's family come before the interests of one's state.[1] When asked whether a sage-king would execute his own father for committing murder, Mencius suggests that the sage would instead abdicate the throne and flee with his father to the hinterlands, presumably depriving the kingdom of the benefits of his sagely rule.[2] WANG Yangming says that most people, when forced to choose between saving a stranger or a parent from starvation, would readily choose their parent, and rightly so.[3]

Giving ethical priority to the family is of a piece with other shared features of Confucian ethics. Far back in the classical period of Chinese philosophy, a rival school of thinkers known as the Mohists argued that everyone has an equal moral claim on us in some important sense, collapsing ethical distinctions between family and strangers.[4] The Mohists called this the doctrine of "impartial care" (*jian ai* 兼愛); the Neo-Confucians often called it "care without distinctions," and contrasted it with the sort of care that they promoted, care *with* distinctions. The most important virtue in Neo-Confucianism, as we will see, is humaneness (*ren* 仁), which is a form of care that ultimately includes everyone (and in many cases every *thing*) in its scope, but which preserves the notion of special attachments and relationships by caring about some more than others, in different ways than others. So the humane person cares about strangers, but not as much (nor in the same way) as acquaintances, friends, or neighbors, and none of those so much as family. Mohism disappeared long before the rise of Neo-Confucianism, but not, the Neo-Confucians think, the doctrine of care without distinctions, which survives and is embraced by Buddhists, whose idea of "great compassion" takes all of sentient life as an object and makes no distinctions among them.[5] For the Neo-Confucians, ethics is essentially concerned with relationships. One of the terms that is often translated as "ethics" (*lunli* 倫理), literally means "the Pattern of human relationships." For them, any ethical form of care had to preserve relationships, and for relationships to exist there must be distinctions or gradations in care. So the virtue of humaneness, as the chief virtue, must necessarily make such distinctions.

Another shared point of agreement is that filial piety – love of and devotion to one's parents – is among the most important virtues. It is not the chief virtue in the same way that humaneness is, as it does not describe what it means to be virtuous more generally, but it is crucial in at least two respects. First, filial piety is the "root" or "foundation" (*ben* 本) for virtuous character more generally. Developing filial piety is necessary to develop other virtues, including humaneness; these other virtues build on the sort of love and deference that we can only learn through our relationships with our parents.[6] Second, filial piety is also important because it provides a behavioral principle which comes as close as any to being inviolable. There may be some circumstances in which one can neglect close friends or violate basic duties, but there are very few – perhaps no – cases in which one can neglect one's parents.[7] Neo-Confucians see this as a fundamental point of contention with Buddhists as well.

The final shared commitment is to virtue more generally: not just to the idea that virtue is good and should be cultivated, but also to the more basic idea that virtue gives us our ultimate aims. This is contrasted with the idea that our ultimate aims have something to do with salvation, transcending this world, entering nirvana – all goals that they suspected Buddhist and Daoists of prioritizing over developing virtues and living virtuously. For the Neo-Confucians, ethics, not salvation, provides our ultimate ends, and the locus of those ends is in this world and this life, not beyond this world or in another life.[8]

Since so much of Neo-Confucian ethics is concerned with virtue and specific virtues, these will be the focus of the present chapter. We will discuss the cardinal Neo-Confucian virtues, review various views on humaneness and the senses in which it is inclusive of others, highlight an important quality of all virtues that the Neo-Confucians call "sincerity," and conclude with a close look at some positions on women and virtue. Some of these discussions will primarily be a matter of explicating shared assumptions. There is not a great deal of debate about the nature and psychological structure of virtues like righteousness and wisdom, for example, although the Neo-Confucians often explore their nuances and build on one another's analysis of these virtues. However, there is considerable controversy regarding the nature and significance of humaneness and sincerity, and the similarity or dissimilarity of women's virtues to men's. We will examine these controversies in depth.

2 Virtues and their interrelations

Five cardinal virtues

Neo-Confucians of all stripes agree in treating four virtues as basic and central: humaneness (*ren* 仁, also translated as "benevolence"), righteousness (*yi* 義), ritual propriety (*li* 禮), and wisdom (*zhi* 智). Most Daoxue Confucians also add a fifth virtue, trustworthiness (*xin* 信). One cannot talk about these virtues without quickly entering a thicket of observations in which these virtues overlap and combine, but as a point of entry it is helpful to consider what we might call paradigm cases of each virtue. For speakers of Chinese in the Neo-Confucian era, paradigm cases of humaneness (*ren*) are those in which one acts out of love or care to promote the interests of others, as when helping someone in need of food or looking after a child or sibling. Paradigm cases of righteousness (*yi*) are those in which someone refuses to violate moral prohibitions in ways that would rightly be regarded as degrading or shameful, even when doing so is difficult and appears to come at great personal cost. So, for example, it is righteous to refuse a large bribe in return for special political favors.[9] But being righteous is not always so difficult. Sometimes it just refers to doing what is expected in a way that is fair, without any internal resistance arising from selfish motives, as when a public official distributes goods or when hosts decide which of their own food and drink to share with guests.

Model examples of ritual propriety (*li*) are those in which one performs a ritual properly (e.g., performing all the right steps) with a sense of reverence. But here we must be careful because "ritual" has a much broader scope than the English translation suggests. "Rituals" in the sense of *li* can apply to any protocol of social interaction; simple examples include bowing, offering drinks to guests, and taking care not to touch people of the opposite sex with whom one is not intimate. Those who are advanced in ritual propriety are able to do these things not just consistently and respectfully, but in the right manner. Often *how* one does something matters as much as *what* one does: think of someone who is skillful at making guests feel welcome, or showing that the guests are not burdening or imposing on their hosts.[10]

There are many potential paradigm cases of wisdom (*zhi*), but perhaps the most illustrative are those in which one astutely discerns the character of others, realizing which are truly humane or righteous, as when considering whether a candidate should be appointed to a demanding and consequential administrative position. Most often, wisdom is described as understanding the other virtues, including not just their characteristic behaviors but also their characteristic motives. This understanding both aids in developing the virtues in ourselves and helps us to recognize virtues (or the lack of virtues) in others. Other instances of wisdom include the recognition of what is truly valuable in life (as when one realizes that the family or relationships are more important than wealth) and knowing the best means to achieve a virtuous end.[11]

The fifth of the cardinal virtues is trustworthiness, best understood as the virtue of being committed to being guided by reality in a consistent and reliable way.[12] Unlike for the other cardinal virtues, Neo-Confucians are careful to say that trustworthiness does not have its own characteristic domains of thought and action.[13] Rather, it is a virtue that helps to ensure that other virtues are brought to fruition. Whether we aim to be humane, righteous, ritually proper, or wise, our success depends on seeing things as they are and being committed to see things as they are, without self-serving illusions that get us off the hook. To be sure, there is a narrower sense of "trustworthiness" that refers to things like honesty and being a reliable friend, but this is not the sense that the Neo-Confucians tend to have in mind when they characterize it as one of the five cardinal virtues.[14]

One of the most comprehensive Neo-Confucian accounts of the five virtues is found in a text known as CHEN *Chun's Meanings of Terms*, authored by one of ZHU Xi's closest students and meant as an overview of Daoxue philosophical vocabulary.[15] At one point in the text, Chen offers an example of hosting visitors:

> As soon as we hear that the guests will be coming, naturally there is a feeling of cordiality calmly aroused in our heartminds. That is humaneness. This feeling having been calmly aroused in the heartmind, we solemnly go to receive them with respect. That is ritual propriety. Having received them, we then must discuss together what to provide for them, perhaps tea or perhaps wine. When the matter of how much to offer and how far to go has been settled in the right way, this is righteousness. To understand definitely how much to offer and how far to go is wisdom. Trustworthiness is being genuine from the beginning to the end.[16]

This example illustrates several of the salient features of the virtues described above, each in accordance with its own domain of thought and action, and it also highlights the distinctive nature of trustworthiness as a virtue without a particular domain, one that supports and helps to complete the others.

A final note about humaneness. There is a longstanding view in the Confucian tradition that one of the cardinal virtues, humaneness, is in some sense the chief virtue, and that calling someone "humane" is tantamount to saying that he is virtuous overall or has all of the virtues working in concert with one another.[17] This is a view that most Neo-Confucians adopt as well. So while most Neo-Confucians suggest that humaneness is the virtue of appropriate care for others, they also propose that there is a more basic and encompassing sense according to which humaneness is just the virtue of ceaseless life-generativity.[18] More specifically, it is the virtue of participating in and contributing to regular processes of life-generativity, which one can do in many ways not limited to caring for others. All virtues can thus be part of humaneness. For example, being ritually proper can contribute to life-generativity by helping to reinforce social structures like families and governments that both protect and nurture people and other living things. Many Daoxue philosophers characterize this as an important part of what they call "forming one body with the myriad things," at minimum by participating in sustained life-generating processes that take all life – including plant and non-human animal life – into account.[19] Below, we will discuss in greater depth the ways that the cardinal virtues can overlap, and that will give us an opportunity to explore this more encompassing sense of humaneness in greater depth.

Virtues as deep-rooted character traits

Virtues are more than appropriate emotions and behaviors. If those were all it took to have a virtue, then one could be ritually proper on a fluke, or with only a superficial commitment to performing a particular ritual at a particular time. Someone who respectfully bows only when in a good mood is not ritually proper. Some of her actions might be ritually proper, but she, her person, is not. What is needed to make ritual propriety a true virtue are some durable emotions, aptitudes, and dispositions that can be counted on to produce ritually proper behavior when needed, so that her behavior arises from lasting qualities. "Character trait" is a convenient term to refer to these durable emotions, aptitudes, and dispositions. As ZHU Xi puts the point, "If one is dutiful today, but not tomorrow, then one has not attained dutifulness in oneself, and this cannot be called virtue (*de* 德)."[20]

Most philosophical accounts of virtues assume that virtues must be traits of character in the general sense, but there is room for disagreement about how deep those character traits must go, and what sorts of dispositions and aptitudes will comprise them. Someone might set the bar relatively low and say that the virtuous character traits should be capable of resisting some temptations to vice, but not all temptations, and say that they should be embedded in durable parts of one's psychology, but not permanent parts. Alternatively, someone might set the bar very high and insist that virtuous character traits must reliably produce good behavior, no matter what the circumstances, and insist that they be embedded in permanent parts of the self. It might help to think of the high-bar setters as holding that virtuous character traits should be "deep-rooted" – that is, they should be deep in the unchanging core of the self, and they should hold up no matter what assails them, like a deep-rooted plant resisting wind and rain.

Nearly all Neo-Confucians think that full virtues should be deep-rooted in the sense that they can hold up under great adversity. Superior people, because they have full virtues, can be expected to give up their lives or undertake great suffering for their parents.[21] But there is less agreement about the degree to which they must be embedded in permanent parts of the self. In chapter 3, we noted that, for DAI Zhen, virtues can be made by nurturing and expanding natural predispositions. These predispositions, which are evident in our natural responses to things like seeing a child in danger, are considered by most Neo-Confucians to be essential parts of our humanity, but for Dai they can fail to develop, or even be wiped out, and so are not permanent parts of the self. They are only durable once they have been developed into full-blown virtues.

In contrast, Daoxue Confucians are adamant that the foundational dispositions of the virtues are in some sense features of our inherent nature (*benxing*), which is permanent and present from start to finish. In fact, all things have an inherent nature and the foundational dispositions of the five cardinal virtues are thus in all. To the extent that they are not manifest in our everyday behavior, this shows that we do not have perfect access to our natures, and the bad vital stuff in us must be purified before the virtues are expressed. We need to distinguish, therefore, between the "foundational dispositions" of our nature and what we can call our "manifest dispositions," which are the ways in which a particular person with his or her current quality of vital stuff is in fact disposed to react. As we saw in chapters 2 and 3, Daoxue accounts of what we are now calling foundational dispositions differ, depending on whether the theory is nature-focused or heartmind-focused, though they all hold that these foundational dispositions are permanent features of us. Daoxue thinkers agree, however, that "virtue" (*de* 德) depends on also having manifest dispositions. That is, one's nature is made up, in part, by the Pattern that is humaneness but, until one has transformed one's vital stuff appropriately, one cannot be said to have the "virtue" of humaneness. The Daoxue philosophers typically put this in terms of needing to "attain" (*de* 得) something. ZHU Xi says that, while the Way is general and shared Pattern, virtue is "attaining this Way in one's self."[22] Similarly, WANG Yangming says that "One calls the cosmic mandate within me my nature; when I attain this nature, one calls it virtue."[23] We discuss the mechanics of "attaining" one's inherent nature and its foundational dispositions at length in chapter 7, on self-cultivation.

How virtues overlap

For philosophers interested in the interrelationships among specific virtues, Neo-Confucian ethics offers a philosophical garden of delights. There are numerous ways in which a given event can instantiate two or more virtues. When one admonishes one's parents not to bribe or steal, that act is both humane (it is done out of a sense of love and care) and righteous (it is meant to reinforce right behavior). In fact, CHEN Chun gets more specific than this. He says that admonishing one's parents to do the right thing is in the first instance humane, but it also contains a quality of righteousness that belongs to the humane act, or what he calls the "righteousness of humaneness."[24] This suggests that one sort of virtuous feeling or behavior (righteousness: encouraging people to do the right thing) is for the sake of the other (humaneness: caring about one's parents). This is to be distinguished from another way of instantiating multiple virtues in the same act, which Chen describes as cases where one virtue "carries the other along" (*han dai* 含帶). Here, the idea is that one virtuous response necessarily elicits another virtuous response, as when one's sympathy for a victim of grievous mistreatment (a humane response) necessarily elicits an indignant feeling, understood as a desire to see some justice for the agent and the victim of the mistreatment (a righteous response).[25]

We have just been considering cases in which virtues reinforce one another, but what about situations in which virtues seem to pull us in different directions? In the opening paragraph of this chapter, we briefly mentioned some famous cases in which Confucians believe that care for one's parents should win out over care for others but notice that such conflicts also often involve seemingly competing virtues. Consider the *Analects* passage in which an "upright" son is said to be one who will cover up the thievery of his father: certainly the virtue of humaneness is active here, but what about righteousness? We would normally expect righteousness to motivate one to avoid the shameful violation of public norms, but condoning theft seems like just such a violation. Here, there appears to be two ways of understanding this sort of scenario: either it could turn out that the conflict is only apparent, and the solution does not, in fact, require that we take sides with one virtue against another, or perhaps the conflict is very real, so that even in the best case we must favor one virtue (say, filial piety or humaneness) at the expense of another (say, righteousness). Generally speaking, the Neo-Confucians tend to favor the former approach: for those with sufficient moral acuity and imagination, most conflicts are only apparent. The *Mencius* tells of the sage-king Shun and his wicked brother Xiang. Shun loves his brother and wants to see him treated well, so he sets Xiang up as ruler of a fiefdom within Shun's domain. Shun also knows that the people of this fiefdom must be treated appropriately, so he deprives Xiang of any actual power; a virtuous subordinate has actual say over the treatment of the local people. Faced with a potential conflict between loving his brother and owing fair treatment to his people, Shun has found a path forward in which both virtues are realized. In fact, ZHU Xi comments that this solution represents the "extremity of humaneness and the utmost of righteousness," in contrast to other, less-than-sagely rulers' efforts to resolve similar dilemmas, which fail to realize one or more virtues.[26] The implication is that opportunities exist, at least for those sufficiently attuned to Pattern, to fully realize virtue.[27]

Finally, many Neo-Confucians see humaneness as the chief and all-encompassing virtue, which suggests that it overlaps in some way or another with *all* the other virtues. The clearest but perhaps least informative way of describing this relationship is to say that one cannot have humaneness without having all of the other virtues. So, if someone is humane, he is necessarily righteous, wise, and so on. But this is not sufficient to identify the privileged status of humaneness because it turns out that one cannot be wise without also being humane as well (each draws on and informs the other).[28] A better way of accounting for the special status of humaneness is to invoke what we described above as the broader and more basic sense of humaneness as ceaseless life-generativity. Many Neo-Confucians take "life-generativity" to be the most general description of the good which virtuous people contribute to by developing themselves, contributing in turn to the development of others and to the continuity of living things. Insofar as righteous and ritually proper behavior are virtuous at all, they must contribute to an orderly process of life-generativity.

However, by endorsing this more basic and broader sense of "humaneness," the Neo-Confucians are compelled to take up an interesting conceptual and interpretive challenge. On the one hand, they want to say that humaneness is one virtue alongside others, characterized by caring for others in the right way, as opposed to, say, knowing certain things or performing rituals reverentially. But, on the other hand, they want to say it encompasses the others. Can both of these things be true? Different Neo-Confucians respond to this challenge differently. DAI Zhen, looking at the classical Confucian texts that later Confucians took as canon, ultimately concludes that humaneness cannot just be a stand-in for virtue more generally – there is too much evidence that the ancient sages regarded the virtues as distinct, marking different sorts of achievements. The more enlightened and better informed view, he implies, is to accept that humaneness is the virtue of promoting life-generativity but also acknowledge that life-generativity is a salient but not exhaustive description of the good that virtuous people promote. That more complete description is something like *orderly* life-generativity, and order is provided by the virtues of righteousness and ritual propriety.[29]

By contrast, most Daoxue Confucians propose that "humaneness" can be used in both senses. In its most encompassing sense, it refers to a state in which we "form one body" with others, joining them in ceaseless life-generativity. ZHU XI suggests that humaneness, as life-generativity, provides both impetus and functional meaning to the other virtues. To make this point, he likens the relationship of humaneness to the other virtues to the relationship of spring to the other seasons:

> It is like the four seasons. One must see the divisions between the four seasons but also see how the spring embraces the other three seasons. The vital stuff of the four seasons varies from warm, to cool, to hot, to cold. When the vital stuff is cool or cold then life is not produced. When the vital stuff is hot in the summer, this too is not a time for producing life. The vital stuff is warm and rich only in the spring, and only then can one witness the life-producing heartmind of heaven and earth. ... If the spring did not have the intention to produce living things then the subsequent three seasons would not exist. This is the sense in which humaneness can embrace righteousness, ritual propriety and wisdom.[30]

At times, though, we want to speak about virtues in more specific terms in order to describe which specific intentions and emotions are motivating behavior, rather than just referring to its overarching contribution to life-generativity. At this level of specificity, some behavior will be motivated by care or love, and thus the result of humaneness in its narrow sense. But some behavior will be motivated by a sense of shame or deference, which are characteristic of righteous and ritually proper behavior; and so on for the other specific virtues.[31]

This completes our overview of Neo-Confucian virtues and the ways in which they can intersect with, require, and encompass one another. Next, we turn to another crucial attribute of virtues in the full and complete sense: sincerity.

3 Sincerity and wholeheartedness

One feature of virtues that we have not yet discussed has to do with the comprehensiveness of one's psychological commitment to them. Intuitively, it seems odd or even paradoxical to say that someone is fully humane and yet has intentions, emotions, or desires that resist humane behavior, like a loving parent who cares for his children reluctantly. Historically, most Confucians thought that full virtue required a wholehearted devotion to virtuous ends, and they set the bar of wholeheartedness rather high.[32] The *Analects* famously describes Confucius as being able to "follow his heartmind's desires

without overstepping the bounds of propriety," which is one important indication of wholeheartedness.[33] But even desiring seems not to
be enough. In another memorable passage, he declares that neither
understanding nor loving the Way are adequate: one should take
joy in the way.[34] He also seems to indicate that someone who really
understands the Way and humaneness would be so enthused that
he could not help but want to instruct others in them.[35] Mencius is
similarly adamant that virtuous behavior is characteristically joyful
for the virtuous agent, and he also stresses the effortless, almost
involuntary quality of it, likening it to tapping one's foot in time with
music.[36] In what follows we will see how the Neo-Confucians build
on this longstanding interest in wholeheartedness, exploring both the
significance of wholeheartedness for virtue and its implications for
moral deliberation and behavior more generally.[37]

In Daoxue Confucianism, the term that comes to be used to mark
wholeheartedness of virtue is *cheng* 誠, which we translate as "sincerity."[38] The Daoxue Confucians have a great deal to say about the
meaning of *cheng*, and at first glance they might be taken to suggest
that the term has numerous meanings, including genuineness, being
true, being without folly or error (*wuwang* 無妄), and even forming a
whole or triad with heaven and earth.[39] We use "sincerity" because it
comes closest to the core meaning of the term for Daoxue Confucians,
but it is useful to see why they sometimes try to capture it in these
other expressions, particularly when they say that those who are
sincere are without error and form a triad with heaven and earth.[40]
The main thing to bear in mind is that, for the Daoxue Confucians,
our inherent natures (*benxing*) are good and, furthermore, are an
ineradicable link to the life-generative processes of the cosmos. We
have certain inclinations to produce and nourish life that can be suppressed with some effort, but cannot be destroyed.[41] If sincere (*cheng*)
behavior is necessarily wholehearted and wholeheartedness rules out
internal psychological conflict, then sincere behavior will necessarily
be consistent with our good nature and thus harmonize with the life-
generative processes of the cosmos. So on this view, to say that being
sincere is to be without folly is to say not what it means so much
as what it entails: one who is sincere must necessarily be without
mistake or errors with respect to the virtues. And to say that those
who are sincere form a triad with heaven and earth is to describe a
natural consequence of sincerity.[42]

Like Confucius and Mencius, many Neo-Confucians highlight
the fact that wholehearted virtue comes naturally or spontaneously,
without being forced, and they express corresponding worries about
forced or merely conscientious ethical behavior.[43] One key reason for

this is that natural processes continue endlessly, adjusting to any new circumstances whereas, even if one is successful at forcing oneself to follow a set of rules, one may come upon circumstances unanticipated by the rule makers and not know how to respond. ZHANG Zai explicitly compares the endlessness of cosmic functioning to the ceaselessness of humaneness and filial piety of a "sincere" person.[44] CHENG Yi tends to put the point in terms of the superior person's ability to "act joyously" (*lexing* 樂行) instead of needing to force himself.[45] In addition to potentially facing gaps, those who are forcing themselves to follow rules are also unavoidably rigid, which we saw in chapters 3 and 4 was one of WANG Yangming's chief reasons for basing ethical evaluations on the context-sensitive "good knowing."

A final issue raised by the desirability of wholehearted virtue concerns the role of deliberation in decision making. Oftentimes, some Daoxue philosophers suspect, when we act on the urge to deliberate about what to do, we are in fact indulging or creating opportunities for more selfish intentions and desires to lead us to conclusions that run counter to virtuous ends. If one must ponder whether to accept a bribe in return for political favors, that likely indicates that there is a part of oneself that wants to accept the bribe, which casts doubt on the sincerity of one's virtue (even if one ultimately refuses the bribe). But this might strike some people as absurd: does it imply that people should not stop to ponder pros and cons before making decisions?

There are several responses to this. One comes from DAI Zhen, who is careful to distinguish between the effortlessness of one's *decision making* and the effortlessness of the *resultant actions*. Just because someone takes a while to arrive at a conclusion about what to do, it does not necessarily follow that she is less than wholehearted about it. In fact, it can often be the case that thinking about pros and cons helps any lingering doubts or reluctance to fall away and thus strengthens her resolve. Dai thinks there are certain advantages in quick and easy decision making, which works well enough for many everyday purposes (we do not really need to stop and ponder whether to accept a bribe or steal a horse), but there will be special cases which are unusual enough to warrant what he calls "weighing" (*quan* 權, also translated as "discretion"), and it would be a grave mistake to think that we could arrive at a sound conclusion without it.[46]

However, Dai is a critic of Daoxue Confucianism, in part because of what he perceives as its infatuation with spontaneity. Perhaps the more interesting question is what the supposedly spontaneity-infatuated Confucians themselves think about deliberative decision making. It is true that ZHU Xi and WANG Yangming (among many others) see deliberation as an opportunity for self-serving biases to take hold, especially when one's own perceived welfare and interests are at stake. Zhu suggests that righteousness (*yi*) is manifest in cases where people make decisions without hesitation or ambivalence.[47] But, like Dai, Zhu makes allowances for special cases, when circumstances deviate enough from standard ones (perhaps when deciding whether one may steal some life-saving medicine for someone who cannot afford it) or when the issues are so complicated and consequential that one cannot afford to make a mistake (as when weighing difficult matters of public policy).[48] Furthermore, it is possible that when Zhu condemns ambivalence and hesitation as unrighteous, he has in mind the kind of ambivalence that arises from conflicts between one's own interests and virtuous ends, not conflicts between different outcomes in which one's own interests are largely irrelevant. So there may be little harm in taking time to consider the advantages and disadvantages of two different methods of punishment or tax policies when it makes no difference to the decision maker.

As we have seen thus far, the Neo-Confucians have a great deal to say about specific virtues, their interrelations, and the nature of virtue itself. On this last issue, we noted that wholeheartedness and deep-rooted character traits are essentials feature of virtue of all kinds, and that, at least in the eyes of most Neo-Confucians, humaneness in the broadest sense – referring to ceaseless life-generativity – is an apt description of the most complete and well-rounded virtue. All of these issues are front and center in much of the Neo-Confucian discourse on ethics and character, but it is notable that a great deal of the discourse applies primarily or even exclusively to men. This is particularly the case for our discussion of the cardinal virtues: the Neo-Confucians largely have men in mind both when they describe which virtues are cardinal (humaneness, righteousness, ritual propriety, wisdom, and trustworthiness) and when they attribute specific content to those virtues. A theory of the virtues that applies primarily to men tells us far too little. In this chapter's final section, we turn to examine how their views about virtue change when applied to women.

4 Women and virtue

Background

If the major works of Daoxue philosophers are any indication, the most influential Neo-Confucian philosophers are far more interested in the ethical virtues of men than of women. In fact, it is likely that philosophers like CHENG Yi and ZHU Xi simply fail to think very

systematically about women and virtue, endorsing edu〈
scriptions and ideals of chastity that appear to be at odd
of their own views about women's social roles.[49] But, ou
mainstream, there are some Neo-Confucians who do
carefully and consistently about women and virtue, and where such
philosophers appear they also tend to adopt some decidedly unorthodox views on the matter. In this section, we describe what we take
to be the more mainstream Neo-Confucian views on women, virtue,
and education – warts and all – and then canvass some of the arguments taken up by critics.

For the vast majority of Neo-Confucians, there is little question
about the status of women in the social hierarchy. Virtually none
of the administrative positions in the civil service are available to
women, leaving women with vanishingly few opportunities to become
authorities in public life. Nor is there much room for authority in
domestic life. In the family structures that most Neo-Confucians
envision, every configuration that includes adult males has women
in subordinate positions. Even when the male head of household
dies, his widow is expected to obey her oldest adult son, although
the history and literature of the Neo-Confucian period are rich with
examples of powerful family matriarchs (and deferential sons) who
defy this convention.[50]

Arguably, the lines of obedience were not always so clearly drawn.
In BAN Zhao's *Lessons for Women*, a Han dynasty text widely recommended by mainstream Neo-Confucians, Ban encourages married
women to do everything they can to win the love of their husbands,
but also suggests that a wife's first and greatest allegiance is to her
parents-in-law.[51] Another popular instructional text, the *Book of
Filial Piety for Women*, hints that the ideal married woman can deftly
navigate potential conflicts between husband and parents-in-law by
modeling filial behavior for her husband to emulate, thereby reinforc-
ing the centralized authority of the parents-in-law while retaining the
love and respect of her husband.[52] Many texts that are influential
in the Neo-Confucian period make it relatively clear that a married
woman's first loyalty is to the larger family unit into which she
marries – including not just her own husband and her children, but
nieces, nephews, and the children of her husband's other marriage
partners (wives or concubines).[53]

When Neo-Confucian philosophers do mention women, it is often
to assign women blame for discord within families. ZHOU Dunyi
writes that "it is difficult to govern the family whereas it is easy to
govern the world, for the family is near while the world is distant.
If members of the family are divided, the cause surely lies with

women."[54] By the start of the Neo-Confucian era, Chinese histories had long depicted scheming wives and concubines as sowers of dissension within families, usually by taking advantage of the love and devotion of their husbands to serve their own private interests. For this reason, Neo-Confucians and the didactic treatises they endorse tend to recommend that husbands and wives keep a certain respectful distance from one another so as to curtail the sort of intimacy that makes them more loyal to one another than to the larger family unit. ZHU Xi stands out, however, in recognizing the importance of the distinctive sort of intimacy between husband and wife:

> To live as a man and woman is the most intimate affair, and the exercise of the Way is found therein. This is why the Way of the gentleman is so widespread, and yet secret. It lies within darkness and obscurity, where it cannot be seen atop the sleeping mat, and people may look on it with contempt. But this is not the way of our natural endowment. The Way of the gentleman begins its rise in the confidential moments between husband and wife.[55]

In this passage, we employ the older translation of "gentleman" for *junzi*, instead of our usual "superior person," to emphasize the gendering of that status that Zhu is assuming. Still, Zhu's recognition that the transformation to becoming a superior person – or even a sage – begins with the most subtle, intimate of relationships fits well with his other views about personal cultivation, even if he himself notes this connection only rarely.

Women's virtues: different but equal?

Turning now to philosophical issues concerning women and the virtues that Neo-Confucians address more explicitly, two points of contention are particularly important. First, what sorts of virtue do the Neo-Confucian philosophers regard as valuable for women? Second, are these virtues equal to men's virtues? We will examine three different positions on these two issues, succinctly captured by the terms "different" and "equal." The first position, which is endorsed by most mainstream Confucians, is that women have separate and *un*equal (inferior) virtues: what counts as a virtue for women is significantly different from what counts as a virtue for men, and these distinctive virtues do not bring women as close to the moral ideal as do men's virtues. The second position, defended by LUO Rufang, agrees that women have different virtues than men but rejects the claim that this makes them unequal in virtue. As we will see, in fact, Luo might even be read to suggest that women are morally superior in crucial respects. Finally, a third position is defended by the iconoclastic Neo-Confucian LI Zhi, who views roughly the same virtues as valuable in both men and women, and contends that women are as capable of sagehood as men. Each of these positions has implications for the kind of education that girls and women should receive.

It is the consensus among most Neo-Confucians that the constellation of character traits that qualify as virtues for women is quite different from that of men, although there is little consensus about what those virtues are.[56] BAN Zhao uses the term "virtue" (*de*) in both broad and narrow senses. In the narrow sense, "womanly virtues" (*fude* 婦德) have to do with maintaining chastity, modesty, and self-control. The "great virtues" which qualify a woman as good in a more well-rounded sense include the narrower ones just mentioned, plus the reliable and consistent performance of "womanly words" (*fuyan* 婦言), "womanly bearing" (*furong* 婦容), and "womanly work" (*fugong* 婦功), which are characterized by such things as avoiding vulgar language, staying clean, avoiding gossip, and serving guests.[57] By using the modifier "womanly," she strongly implies that there is something different in kind about these virtues. SIMA Guang, a Song dynasty Confucian whose *Precepts for Family Life* was endorsed by ZHU Xi and widely read, identifies several virtues as indispensable for women in their capacity as wives and mothers, including frugality, purity, and compliance.[58] ZHU Xi also emphasizes frugality as well as character traits like generosity and harmony.[59] To be sure, mainstream views do see some virtues as shared by both men and women, most notably filial piety, dutifulness, and ritual propriety.[60] But on the whole the mainstream tends to treat virtues like chastity and compliance as being the primary characteristics of exemplary women, while making little of the contribution these traits might make to the moral achievement of men.[61]

Just because two different groups of people have different sorts of virtues, it does not follow that one group's virtues necessarily compare unfavorably to the other's. Women might have virtues that are distinctive but can be just as admirable and valuable. Is this a view embraced by mainstream Neo-Confucians? In most respects it was not. Few take seriously the proposal that women could be sages. There is a sense in which both social and ethical inferiority is required by the very nature of women's virtues. Compliance is arguably only a virtue that a social subordinate could have, and perhaps no virtue can achieve sagely heights without a sophisticated grasp of deep truths and worldly affairs that are inconsistent with the modesty and humility expected of women – not to mention being inconsistent with the more parochial sort of education that mainstream Neo-Confucians tend to recommend for women and girls.[62]

The second, minority position we find within Neo-Confucian discourse on women and virtue is that women's virtues are different but nevertheless at least equal. Here, it is useful to distinguish between two different respects in which gendered virtues might be compared. The first has been mentioned already: men's or women's virtues might be equal in potential – for example, both could allow their possessors to achieve sagehood. But another idea is that women's virtues may tend, as a matter of fact, to make women as good as (or even better than) men's virtues make men. The latter claim is not about the ultimate potential of each set of virtues, which after all only matter for those who achieve great heights, but rather about the sort of character that men and women will have on average or under normal circumstances. We look here at the views of LUO Rufang, first mentioned in chapter 4, who appears to hold that women's virtues are equal (or perhaps superior) in at least one of these two senses.

Luo is associated with the Taizhou School, a Ming dynasty group of Daoxue thinkers most notable for entertaining radical ideas and for their commitment to bringing Confucian teachings to ordinary people. Luo does not set forth his thoughts on women and virtue in comprehensive essays devoted explicitly to the topic, but his letters and other writings strongly suggest that he has a considered and distinctive view. Luo aims to highlight and elucidate underappreciated features of maternal affection.[63] By Luo's time, as we saw in section 1 of this chapter, the Confucian tradition had long seen filial piety (*xiao*) as a "foundational" virtue. Acquiring it is necessary for acquiring the other major virtues (especially humaneness), and other virtues are natural extensions or outgrowths of filial piety, drawing on aptitudes and emotional dispositions formed by loving, serving, and showing deference to one's parents. But Luo observes that the affection and care of mothers for their children plays an even more fundamental role than filial piety, as it elicits filial piety of the best and most important kind. He highlights this role in a tribute to one exemplary mother:

> Reading about the maternal affection and lifelong chastity of his mother as recorded on the tablet, the son is easily moved within his heartmind; reading the tablet inscribed in her memory, he also easily expresses his heartmind outwardly. And is this not just as it should be, when filial piety responds to maternal affection … and love is aroused spontaneously, without restraint?[64]

On Luo's reading, filial piety arises out of a sense of gratitude and appreciation for the unsolicited love and sacrifices of the parents.[65]

The son recognizes these and experiences a sense of love and devotion like no other. For Luo, the filial response to parental care is an unparalleled instance of natural virtue, distinctive because it is fully *sincere* in the senses discussed in the previous section – it is a wholehearted and authentic expression of one's true nature, arising spontaneously, effortlessly, and without internal resistance.[66] Children can surely be filial without great parental affection, but it is extremely rare that the filial feelings be fully sincere without it.

For heartmind-focused philosophers like Luo, accessing sincere feelings plays a crucial part in moral cultivation because it helps us to recognize a distinctive faculty and source of reliable moral behavior. Luo (as mentioned in chapter 4) thinks virtue in its proper sense is always an expression of what he called the "infant's heartmind" (*chizi zhi xin* 赤子之心), which is authentic in the sense that it is stripped of conventional beliefs and values that we normally acquire from our social environment.[67] One who has achieved true sincerity in this domain, Luo suggests, will be consistently filial and dutiful.[68]

As we have seen, then, Luo promotes a virtue that he takes to be most characteristic of women and mothers. He also reveres some exemplary women for maintaining lifelong chastity and, in general, understands women's virtues to be tailored to their distinctive roles in childrearing and household management. Thus he shares the mainstream view that women's virtues differ from men's. Does he think that women are men's equals in virtue? Here, we should look again at the two different ways in which their virtue could be compared: the first concerns the potential equality or superiority of the virtues of each sex. For example, one who thinks that both men and women can be sages is likely to endorse the view that men and women are equal in virtue in this respect. Luo's view on this issue is subtle. For him, "sage" is a masculine term that is apt only when applied to men, but Luo strongly suggests that "sage" is not the only term for a moral paragon. Exemplary women are in certain respects the superiors even of sages. The contemporary scholar who has written most extensively about Luo, Yu-Yin CHENG, suggests that, in fact, he saw exemplary women as meeting greater moral demands, and thus as achieving greater moral distinction, than sages. Sages are not asked, as exemplary mothers are, to have the fortitude and strength of character to maintain lifelong chastity to deceased husbands, even when this leaves them destitute, while nevertheless maintaining wholehearted and loving care for their children without regret or resentment.[69] The second way of comparing the virtues of men and women is to ask whether women tend, on average or under normal circumstances, to be as virtuous as men, which would contradict assumptions made by mainstream Neo-Confucians like ZHOU Dunyi and ZHU Xi. Although Luo does not address this question directly, his lifelong preoccupation with the distinctive advantages of maternal affection and his countless tributes to accomplished mothers suggest that women tend to be at least the equals if not superiors to men in virtue. No virtue comes as naturally to men as maternal affection comes to women. Furthermore, his tributes appear to suggest that women more consistently recognize what matters most for living a life according to the Way, putting people's actual interests and welfare before superficial goods like wealth and social status.[70] Finally, Luo notes that women have a certain consistency of virtue unmatched by men in any moral domain, for no mother, he says, has ever failed to rear her children.[71]

The issue of equality in virtue sometimes comes up in Neo-Confucian discussions of another major issue, women's education. Neo-Confucians sometimes discuss the question of whether it is appropriate for women to "learn the Way" (*xuedao* 學道) insofar as a great deal of reading and reflection is required for a deep understanding of human nature, the sources of virtue, and our place in the larger world. Many mainstream Neo-Confucians think women unsuited for this sort of learning, in part because they think it adds little to women's primary responsibilities in the inner chambers. Without a major role in public life, they suggest, there is little justification for using the tremendous pedagogical resources required to master the classics and engage in public debates about issues of ethics and governance, and furthermore encouraging women to undertake such studies might promote an independence of mind that could threaten the family structure.[72] But this view is in tension with a longstanding tradition in Confucianism that lionizes mothers who played a major, often decisive, role in cultivating virtues in their sons, a tradition that stretches back to stories about Mencius' mother, and is evident in CHENG Yi's accounts of his own mother. Cheng, for example, lauds his mother for teaching him to respect the basic humanity in people, no matter what their class or station, and for deft management of their large household, among many other things.[73] Many Neo-Confucians saw that this sort of teaching required a strong grasp of philosophical fundamentals, and the Neo-Confucian era was replete with texts and instruction manuals that promoted the idea of the "learned instructress," mothers and wives who, like Mencius' own, knew enough about the Way to impart lessons to their children during their formative years and to set their husbands aright when the husbands sank into vice.

Few mainstream Neo-Confucians even acknowledge the tension between these two views, and even fewer address it squarely. For Luo, by contrast, the fact that women play so important a role in their children's education – and, for that matter, are often needed to serve as models of virtue to both men and women their own age – makes it abundantly clear that they can and should learn the Way.[74] Although Luo presupposes that virtues like maternal affection and chastity are more appropriate for women than men, he nevertheless thinks that women and men share a need for wisdom and philosophical insight, and Luo is particularly interested in women who exceed all of the men around them in these two respects, citing in particular two women (one of them his own mother) who loved philosophical discussion and reflection and by all appearances achieved perfect tranquillity through a deep understanding of Daoism.[75] On his view, it does not matter that they achieved their enlightenment by means of Daoist rather than Confucian sources. It is a grasp of the Way all the same.[76]

Women's virtues as similar and equal to men's

The topic of women and education brings us to the third and final position in this debate. This is the stance that women and men are moral equals and further proposes that, for the most part, moral achievement in both is characterized by the same virtues. To illustrate this position, we turn to LI Zhi, another Taizhou thinker and the Neo-Confucian tradition's renowned iconoclast.[77] In his "A Letter in Response to the Claim that Women Cannot Learn the Way Because They are Shortsighted," Li describes his view elegantly by drawing an analogy between people's capacity for learning the Way and the faculty of vision (*jian* 見).[78] That faculty is shared by men and women and is essentially the same. Insofar as we do find variants in people's ability to see, their sex itself has little to do with it: "It is fine to say that there are male and female people, but how could one say that there is male and female vision? It is fine to say that there is shortsightedness and farsightedness, but how could one say that men's vision is wholly farsighted and women's vision wholly shortsighted?"[79] As evidence, Li points to numerous accounts of enlightened and capable women in history. Insofar as women of his time seem to have a more parochial understanding of the world, then, it cannot be due to their sex. The better explanation is that their experiences and education have been confined to domestic matters, to life in the inner chambers, giving them too little opportunity to see the world beyond.[80] As Li develops the metaphor, he can be seen as downplaying the outsized importance of biological gender, which he regards essentially as a difference in bodily form and not in "vision" or understanding. He asks whether a person should be any less humbled by a woman with profound understanding simply because she happens to have a woman's body, and he suggests (shockingly, for his time) that the historical Confucius may have been wandering the world in part to find a sage with the body of a woman. On Li Zhi's view, then, history shows that women are as capable of being moral paragons as men, thus establishing moral equality in the first of our two senses. And, furthermore, Li thinks actual inequalities in enlightenment between actual men and women are better explained by the scope of women's and men's experiences than by sex, which strongly suggests a moral equality in the second sense, understood as equality of character under circumstances not distorted by social conventions.[81]

It is a further question whether Li holds that morally accomplished men and women are characterized by the same virtues. Here, the evidence is mixed, and the challenge of understanding Li's views as a whole makes it difficult to give a definitive answer. On the one hand, he joins most traditional Confucians in celebrating certain meritorious women for their chastity, and like most Neo-Confucians he speaks in abstract terms about the benefits of gender complementarity – harmonizing male and female like harmonizing *yin* and *yang* principles.[82] On the other hand, Li thinks that the husband–wife relationship is the supreme expression of the traditional five virtues, in both women and in men, which is one reason why he sees it as the most important of the traditional Confucian relationships.[83] Furthermore, the question is complicated by the fact that, for Li, there is a more fundamental guideline for moral behavior than virtue, which has to do with expressing one's genuine emotions or one's "child's heart-mind." Our genuine emotions can vary a great deal, which could be taken to suggest that some are more genuine in being filial or ritually proper than others. Moreover, the content of one's genuine emotions will vary between members of the same sex, not just between the sexes, so that it would be hard to generalize about either men's or women's virtues as such. In the end, there is a certain coordination of life-generating tendencies built into our genuine emotions, so that each person living in her or his own authentic way will, without intending it, contribute to harmonious life-generativity overall.[84] This suggests that the real similarity between women's and men's virtues is no more nor less than the similarity between the virtues of any individuals, whatever their sex or gender, or at least not different in kind. That already is sufficient to show how dramatically Li departs from other Neo-Confucians on this issue.

Li Zhi thus carves out a position on women and virtue that is, by almost any standard, unusual in Neo-Confucianism. But it should be said that, in spite of the strong stance that Li takes in this essay, there is mixed evidence about the impact that this had on his own thinking and behavior more generally. Li himself lived in a relatively traditional marriage. His essays and letters suggest that his views varied widely and perhaps changed over the course of his life. Sometimes he praised women for observing the principles of lifelong chastity, which traditionally prohibited women from remarrying after their husband's death. At other times, he defended widows' right to remarry.[85] Whatever his true or most heartfelt position on these issues, he did not make major strides in changing the views of his Confucian contemporaries. It is not until much later, in the modern era, that some Confucians look to see how far they can take moral equality in both theory and practice.

For further study

Selected primary sources

1. CHEN Chun, "Humanity, Righteousness, Propriety, Wisdom, and Faithfulness," in Chen 1986: 69–85.
2. ZHU Xi, *Collected Commentaries on the* Mean (n.b. the *Mean* is an alternate translation for *Centrality and Commonality*), in Tiwald and Van Norden 2014: #36, 225–30 only.
3. CHENG Yi, "Biographies of My Parents," in Tiwald and Van Norden 2014: #45.
4. ZHU Xi, "The Way of the Family," in Tiwald and Van Norden 2014: #46.
5. LUO Rufang, "Essay on the Hall of Motherly Affection and Chaste Widowhood," in Tiwald and Van Norden 2014: #47.
6. LI Zhi, "Letter in Response to the Claim that Women Cannot Understand the Way because They are Shortsighted," in Tiwald and Van Norden 2014: #48.

Discussion questions

1. What are some examples of righteousness or ritual propriety, above and beyond those mentioned in this chapter?
2. According to most Neo-Confucians, doing ritually appropriate things, like showing proper courtesy to others, is only virtuous if it is deep-rooted. If you found yourself doing certain ritually proper things on a regular basis, how could you determine whether this is indeed deep-rooted, as opposed to a more superficial characteristic?

3. In what ways does humaneness "encompass" the other virtues?
4. How would you describe wholehearted virtue? How can it be distinguished from mere conscientiousness or inauthentic virtue?
5. What might it mean to say that the virtues of men and women are different but equal?

9

Governance and Institutions

1 Introduction

In the last two chapters, we have looked closely at Neo-Confucian views on the cultivation of virtues and on the virtues themselves. As we noted, there is a real sense in which these topics provide unity and purpose for much Neo-Confucian discourse, as it is widely understood that the ultimate fruits of other areas of thought and debate (e.g., knowing, heartmind) lie in providing us with theoretical models that undergird the more practical goals of self-cultivation and ethics. In this chapter, we turn to a final set of topics which also motivates the broader project of Neo-Confucian philosophy, namely, governance of the state and related institutions. To start, we look at two considerations that made Neo-Confucian theories of governance so crucial: the fact that most people who assumed positions in government were steeped in Confucian ideas, and a general tendency to see Confucian theories of governance as continuous in key respects with Confucian theories of virtue and ethical cultivation.

Throughout most of the Neo-Confucian era, training in the Confucian tradition was necessary for political office. Aspiring officials usually attained their positions by testing well on the civil service exams, major components of which were based on the Confucian classics. By the Song dynasty, it was simply assumed that people in the governing class – up to and including the emperors themselves – were conversant in Confucian ideas and texts. Accordingly, most of the literati involved in governance tended to identify with the Confucian tradition. As authorities on the tradition, many Confucian literati saw it as their role not just to execute the responsibilities of their offices, but also to provide enlightened guidance to the ruling family. Although the dynastic rulers often agreed with this idea in principle, some were more averse than others to such guidance, and the leverage available to the Confucian literati varied a great deal. Consequently, the power of the literati relative to that of the emperor waxed and waned over the centuries; the changes were often connected to major political events. We summarize the major trends in Table 9.1.

Despite these vicissitudes, ministerial and literati power remain significant throughout the period, and the Neo-Confucians remain politically engaged. The nature of the political engagement does change, however. Beginning in the Southern Song, Neo-Confucians often favor a localist, decentralized approach to governance. As we discuss below, they come to see non-state spaces as extremely

Table 9.1 Political trends

Date	Period or event	Ministers/literati vis-à-vis emperor
960	Founding of the (Northern) Song dynasty	Emperors seek to distance themselves from ministers and establish dynastic legitimacy; but leading literati/ministers have great power in practice
1069–85	WANG Anshi's "New Policies" and their eventual failure	In response to resistance from other ministers, Vice Grand Councilor Wang seeks to justify greater authority for the emperor
1127–1279	Song dynasty loses the north to Jurchens: Southern Song	Literati generally favor more local solutions, partly independent from state authority, but this is still in the context of a broad imperial/civilizational project
1279–1368	Mongols conquer all of China: Yuan dynasty	With their culture and identity threatened under foreign rule, ministers seek to preserve traditional Chinese culture
1368–	Early decades of the Ming dynasty	Strong emperors who at least superficially embrace the Neo-Confucian ideal – claiming to be sage-rulers – challenge the independence of literati/ministers
1540s–1644	Later Ming	Localism and comparative independence from state and imperial center revives
1644–1911	Qing dynasty	Strong emperors again embrace the Neo-Confucian ideal, once again challenging the independence of literati/ministers

important to successful change at wider levels of the state. This is not to say that Neo-Confucians abandon efforts to educate, direct, and serve the emperor, and strong emperors early in the Ming and Qing dynasties manage to bring the focus back to themselves for periods of time. Overall, though, the emphasis of Neo-Confucian theories of governance is nicely captured in the modern slogan "think globally, act locally."

According to Neo-Confucians, institutions of governance operate on two levels simultaneously, one socio-political and the other personal. At the socio-political level, they are concerned with the practicalities of keeping order in a large state filled with imperfect people. At the personal level, they are concerned with an individual's moral character. Someone might think that operations on these two levels work at cross-purposes because crafting good institutions and policies requires that we take human imperfections into account, and yet a full commitment to improving one's character requires that we rise above these imperfections. Neo-Confucians disagree. For them, the continuity of the socio-political with the personal received its canonical expression in a passage from the classical *Greater Learning* that we have already had opportunity to discuss:

> Wanting to light up the bright virtue of all in the world, the ancients first put their states in order. Those who wanted to put their states in order first regulated their families. Those who wanted to regulate their families first cultivated their selves. Those who wanted to cultivate their selves first rectified their heartminds. Those who wanted to rectify their heartminds first made their intentions sincere. Those who wanted to make their intentions sincere first reached understanding. Reaching understanding lies in getting a handle on things.[1]

We could understand the continuity described in this passage as a temporally connected set of steps: first get a handle on things, then reach understanding, then make one's intentions sincere, and so on, eventually putting one's state in order. But in fact the Neo-Confucians tend to see the steps as mutually constitutive: getting a handle on things just is reaching understanding, families are regulated through the very act of personal cultivation, and having orderly families is part of what it means for a state to be in order. The implicit relationship between personal cultivation and socio-political order is captured in the frequently used slogan "inner sage–outer king": ethics and governance are two sides of the same coin. In other words, socio-political order entails the ethical transformation of people in the state, as well as their leaders; in the language of the text, this is to "light up the bright virtue of all in the world."

No matter whether we are concerned with practical matters of policy or the transformation of people's character, the continuity from intimate and personal to public and official makes it difficult to delineate some activities or spaces as "political" and others as not. For this reason we will largely avoid use of the word "political," endeavoring instead to use more specific terms. Neo-Confucians have much to say about what we can call the "state" – the hereditary emperors and their families and attendants, plus the ministers of the official bureaucracy – vis-à-vis "the people." Many questions concerning governance and institutions directly relate to the responsibilities and policies of the state, as well as the corresponding responsibilities of the people, but much that is concerned with both order and transformation takes place outside of state confines in what we can call "non-state spaces." Examples of non-state spaces are academies and other places of textual interpretation and teaching, local clan-based charities, and community compacts. As we see below, both state and non-state spaces are implicated in the major Neo-Confucian debates over the role of institutions in ensuring order.

With virtually no exceptions, Neo-Confucians accepted hereditary monarchy as their form of government. This does not mean that all monarchs automatically enjoyed full legitimacy, however. Already in the latter half of the Tang dynasty, Confucian and Buddhist scholars had begun to claim that the proper moral or spiritual teaching was passed on in a genealogical fashion.[2] HAN Yu famously asserted that this transmission of the Confucian "Way" had been lost for many centuries; Northern Song progenitors of Daoxue argued that it was only in their generation that the Way had been recovered. In other words, legitimate succession from one monarch to another did not assure that individual rulers – or even their dynasty as a whole – were following the Way. ZHU Xi gives this idea its most influential formulation when he says that the "succession of the Way" (*daotong* 道統) comes to those who are able to grasp the deep truths embedded in the classics by the early sages.[3] According to this view, the earliest sages both grasped the Way and ruled, but over time rulers lost this tie to the moral Way. A few great teachers like Confucius and Mencius understood the Way and tried to steer their societies in the right direction, even though they were not rulers, but eventually the succession of the Way was lost until it was recovered, says ZHU Xi, by the Cheng brothers.

The idea that the succession of the Way can come apart from the more superficial succession of monarchy has a number of important implications, especially when combined with the view of governance operating at two levels (maintaining social order and achieving moral transformation). Borrowing a term from classical antiquity, Neo-Confucians can argue that a ruler who is successful at keeping order but who falls short of achieving broader transformation is a mere "hegemon" rather than a true "king." It is better to be a hegemon than a cruel tyrant, to be sure, but even the successful hegemon still needs to aspire to something greater. The gatekeepers to these greater achievements, meanwhile, are those scholars who have attained the succession of the Way. According to this manner of thinking, there-fore, monarchs must accept that leaders of the literati should be their teachers or even co-rulers, or that the monarch's central authority should be reined in so that morally cultivated literati can hold sway over local affairs. As our historical summary above suggests – and as we will see in more detail below – over the Neo-Confucian period literati had varying degrees of success in asserting authority derived from the succession of the Way.

2 Loyalty and faction

William de Bary, one of the most influential western scholars of Neo-Confucianism, has said an important "trouble with Confucianism" is that it imposed tremendous moral demands on the Confucian superior person (*junzi*) without providing the political power to fulfill them. The superior person shoulders the responsibility of cultivating humane monarchs and fashioning social and political institutions that work for the public weal, but Confucians are also committed to a system that gives superior people very little leverage with which to accomplish these Herculean tasks. They deprive themselves of this leverage in various ways, some of them obvious (Confucianism embraces powerful and largely unchecked monarchical government) and some of them subtle. One of the ways of undermining Confucians' own power is by refusing to pander to specific constituencies or fac-tions, standing on the side of the right and the public good rather than with allies or friends of convenience. Their weakness, de Bary argues, is "in their indisposition or inability to establish any power base of their own. ... [E]xcept on rare, momentary occasions, they faced the state, and whoever controlled it in the imperial court, as individual scholars unsupported by an organized party or active con-stituency."[4] Indeed, there is no question that the role of the Confucian minister is complex and often vexed. In this section, we highlight two of its dimensions, loyalty and faction, both of which illustrate the ways in which literati ministers both accept monarchy and yet resist absolutism.

The century between the collapse of the Tang and the establishment of the Song was chaotic. As short-lived states flickered in and out of existence, individuals often justified their choices via a "reciprocal" model of loyalty – in which loyalty to a political master was roughly contractual and could be changed under the right circumstances – that was one prominent aspect of classical models of loyalty. Early on in the Song, however, Neo-Confucians help to articulate a new understanding of loyalty, focusing on the idea of "revering the emperor" (*zunwang* 尊王).[5] Tenth-century heroes were now excoriated as turncoats or traitors. An influential eleventh-century literatus declared: "In the home there are husbands and wives, outside in the world there are rulers and ministers. Wives should follow their husbands, and not change throughout their whole lives; ministers should serve their rulers and should not change their allegiance even if it means their deaths; these are cardinal principles of human morality."[6] We discussed Neo-Confucian views of gender relations in the previous chapter. Here, we note that the reasons for the narrowed understanding of loyalty include the consciousness of a unified Han Chinese state beset with foreign threats and the shift from an earlier model of government, dominated by aristocratic families, to a new model, dominated by literati families who owe their status more directly to the state apparatus (via the civil service exam system).

However, it is crucial to see that in the eyes of Daoxue Neo-Confucians, at least, revering the emperor meant both ritual respect for the role of the emperor and obedience to the legitimate authority of the emperor, but not unthinking loyalty to the ruler no matter what he might do or say. Most Neo-Confucians lived in a public culture in which it was expected, at least in principle, that ministers show their loyalty by courageously pointing out flaws and remonstrating with their rulers.[7] And many Neo-Confucians, including ZHU Xi, quietly or reluctantly acknowledged that there are cases when one should not obey one's emperor, presumably after all attempts to dissuade the misguided ruler had been exhausted.[8] This crucial caveat comes out, for example, in the influential commentaries that Daoxue thinkers wrote on the *Spring and Autumn Annals*. This text is a succinct record of events pertaining to the state of Lu, Confucius' home state, from 722 BCE to 481 BCE. It was widely held that Confucius himself had authored the *Annals*, and that through careful word choices he encoded an evaluation of the events that he recorded.[9] Neo-Confucian commentaries on this text articulate various political principles, finding bases for the principles in Confucius' own political judgments. In particular, the commentators argue that only Pattern demands our absolute, unwavering commitment. CHENG Yi writes, in the introduction to his own commentary, that: "Confucius wrote the *Spring and Autumn Annals* because at the end of the Zhou dynasty no sages had reappeared and because there was no one to follow the cosmic Way in managing contemporary affairs. Therefore he wrote the *Annals* in order to provide a great and unchanging norm for a hundred kings."[10] Although CHENG Yi does say that "the way of preserving the people lies in putting the principle of 'revere the emperor' first," his emphasis throughout the commentary is not on the ruler's power but on the ruler's obligation to make his actions conform to Pattern.[11]

In addition to discourse about loyalty, another context in which we see the complex position of a Confucian minister is in debates about factions. Let us start with some context. From late-classical times down into the early Song, the term "faction" (*pengdang* 朋黨) was invariably derogatory, referring to associations of "petty people" who aimed to use their roles in government to further their own ends. There is a certain degree of support for this understanding of "faction" in the earliest texts, but it is significant for our purposes that some passages in early texts like Confucius' *Analects* also suggest that superior people (*junzi*) can form associations, so long as they do not act in partisan ways.[12] A key question that emerges in the midst of the political and intellectual wrangling of the Northern Song is whether horizontal affiliations among equals are in any way appropriate, or whether the only axis of loyalty is the vertical one, from individuals upward to the ruler (and beyond, to the Way or to cosmic Pattern).

We can identify three different positions on this question. The most common is the long-held view that factions and factionalism are the exclusive domains of the selfish; superior people, in contrast, are individually loyal.[13] The radical alternative to this was the claim, made most forcefully by OUYANG Xiu, that genuine factions – which he understands as long-lasting associations organized collectively to pursue the common good – are only formed by superior people. The affiliations of petty people are only temporary, for personal gain.[14] Crucially, Ouyang adds that genuinely superior people will unite around a shared Way (*tongdao*), so disputatiousness at the ruler's court is inevitably seen as a sign of selfishness. Finally, a third position agrees with the first in using "faction" as a term for selfish associations that ignore the common good but agrees with the second view that superior people can and should collaborate with one another for their mutual edification: "When superior people cultivate themselves and regulate their heartminds, their Way is one of collaboration with others."[15] So, according to this third position, while superior people should not engage in factional wrangling at court, they should work together to cultivate themselves and pursue the common good.

What, then, should be done about factions in practice and about ministerial disagreement more generally? Again, there are three main positions. Those who believe that superior people should be individually loyal tend to argue that the ruler should try to wipe out all factions. One strong argument for this view maintains that, even if there is a faction of superior people, they will be outnumbered by factions of the selfish; factionalism itself is destructive, so should be rooted out.[16] OUYANG Xiu's radical view holds that the true faction of superior people can be identified as such, and their one voice – which, after all, is unified around pursuit of the common good – should be heeded. False factions of petty people should be suppressed. The third view, finally, acknowledges that factionalism seems inevitable and calls for a strong and wise ruler who is able to encourage vertical loyalty and to judge among the competing ministerial arguments.[17] By relying on the ruler in this way, this third view is able consistently to maintain that superior people need not themselves form ministerial factions, even though they should collaborate to encourage mutual ethical development.

In his own day, OUYANG Xiu's radical view fails to win out, but over time the idea that there is one genuine faction becomes widespread within Neo-Confucianism. ZHU Xi encourages his contemporaries to support the formation of such a "faction of superior people," to join it themselves, and even to see that the emperor himself becomes part of this faction. For Zhu, it is this faction of superior people – those who have grasped the "succession of the Way" – who have the ultimate legitimacy in society, thus even the emperor needs to be properly educated so that he can strive to join this group. Zhu is also explicit that it is crucial to maintain the ethical purity of those in the faction: "if there are those who are wicked and evil, then you ought to expel them completely."[18] Similar views can be found among the leaders of Neo-Confucianism's most famous faction, the Donglin. This late-Ming dynasty movement is multifaceted, including a broad ethical revitalization movement, a national Confucian "moral fellowship," and a ministerial faction in Beijing; the whole movement takes its name from its institutional base in the privately funded Donglin Academy in southern China.[19] The Donglin faction goes to extreme lengths to promote its cause, driven by its members' conviction that theirs is a battle of the good and the public-spirited against the evil and selfish. Donglin partisans contribute to a toxic political atmosphere in which each side demonizes its opponents. The crucial moment in the struggle comes when a Donglin figure issues a public document explicitly accusing a leading palace figure of gross immorality. In a modern scholar's words, this document is written in the "language of moral terrorism": language that is uncompromising, "heated to the highest possible degree of emotional incandescence."[20] Not long after this comes a violent backlash in which key Donglin figures are arrested, tortured, and killed, the academy is razed, and the movement crushed.

Reflecting on Neo-Confucian ideas of loyalty and faction, we believe that three observations are in order. First, returning to de Bary's conception of the "trouble with Confucianism" with which we began this section, Neo-Confucian principles make it difficult for proper Confucian ministers to establish a power base of their own, in part because they are not supposed to have special commitments or loyalties to groups. Second, even if the primary axis of loyalty is vertical (to the emperor, public good, and more abstract notions like the Way), horizontal solidarity fits very well with key aspects of Neo-Confucian views of self-cultivation, such as the part that one's community plays in developing a "commitment" that we discussed in chapter 7. In this light, and given the excesses to which the "one true faction" view can lead, it is tempting to conclude that the third view of factions described above is most attractive. Finally, recent scholars have disagreed about the significance of Neo-Confucian views of faction. One opines that "had Confucian gentry been able to transmit their local influence to the provincial and national levels through legitimized factional organizations such as the Donglin academy, it is interesting to speculate what sorts of political forces would have been released into Confucian political culture"; he goes on to suggest a parallel to "the trend against absolutist monarchy and toward parliamentary rule in the West."[21] In contrast, another scholar argues that "the Donglin affair was no harbinger of some possible future parliamentarian democracy. Donglin Confucian thought was monarchical and authoritarian to its core."[22] We agree with the latter view that the denial of any space for pluralism, based on the Donglin partisans' assurance of having grasped the Way, is indeed a problem, though we see some truth in the former position as well, insofar as the commitment to literati authority does, partly, mitigate monarchical authoritarianism.[23]

3 Institutional versus character-centered theories of governance

Basically, China's governmental structure in the Neo-Confucian era has four parts: (1) the emperor, imperial family, and inner-court attendants like eunuchs; (2) the outer-court ministers, bureaucracy, and the literati families who staff them; (3) the common people; and (4) the institutions that help to shape the ways in which (1)–(3) interact. One of the great debates of the Neo-Confucian era is about the relative importance or priority of institutions. This debate takes on many guises but at bottom is the sense that there is a tension between two ways of understanding the structure that undergirds a well-ordered society. One sees institutions and their component parts (traditions, rules, and regulations, etc.) as more fundamental. The other sees the people who direct and belong to the institutions, and particularly the character of such people (understood as a combination of talents and ethical dispositions), as more fundamental. Where philosophers stand on this issue can help to explain how they align on other critical issues in matters of governance. Those who tend to see institutions as more fundamental are more inclined to see legal and regulatory reform as the primary way of addressing large-scale problems. Those who see the character of people as more fundamental often think the solution to such problems lies in moral cultivation and transformation. To a certain extent, the former think that institutions should be designed to take human flaws and shortcomings into account, so that the state does not require large numbers of people to be virtuous in order to create social order, while the latter tend to worry that institutions designed for flawed people will, at least at certain levels, inhibit or discourage the kind of self-improvement that makes government truly transformative and successful. For ease of reference, let us use the term "character-centered" and "institutionalist" to refer to these two positions. To be clear, most of the philosophers we discuss have more nuanced or mixed views than this simple outline suggests, but the outline helps to show how ideas about governance and other commitments tend to work in tandem.

By "institutions," we mean structures whose decision-making processes are at least partly independent of personal judgment. Take, for example, a place of learning. Learning can occur in many different contexts, only some of which are strongly or significantly institutional. If one learns to read just by perusing books before bedtime or examining street signs while wandering around one's neighborhood, the home and neighborhood are places of learning, but this does not make them institutions of learning. Schools are more recognizably institutional, and this is largely because they are governed by customs, traditions, and policies that cannot be easily changed. Even the most authoritarian university president would face serious challenges overcoming some of the customs that are taken for granted in higher education, as she would quickly discover if she tried unilaterally to move classes to 3:00 a.m. or turn all undergraduate degrees into fifteen-year programs. And of course most schools are governed by an overlay of laws, codes of professional ethics, and administrative procedures. In all these respects, schools are institutions, and the decision-making processes that comprise them are institutional ones.

On one somewhat simplistic historical account, most Neo-Confucians advocate a character-centered theory of politics, holding that ethical cultivation of people and not institutional reform is the most plausible means of restoring social order. This, supposedly, explains why Neo-Confucians abandon the traditional Confucian interest in state governance and focus instead on their own moral self-improvement. This version of history is not entirely misleading. Neo-Confucians of the Southern Song frequently blame the fall of the Northern Song on its failed experiments in institutional reform, especially those of the institutionalist thinker and statesman WANG Anshi.[24] And the most famous Neo-Confucian philosophers tend to make pronouncements more consistent with the character-centered theory, including the Cheng brothers, ZHU Xi, and WANG Yangming.[25]

But the truth is quite a bit more complicated and more philosophically interesting. From the Song dynasty all the way through the Qing, the Neo-Confucians count among their ranks many thinkers interested in "statecraft" (*jingshi* 經世). By the late Ming dynasty and thereafter, "statecraft" comes to describe almost any technique that can be used for the practical operations of the state, construed so expansively as to include mathematics and history.[26] But in the narrower sense common among earlier Neo-Confucians, it refers to a philosophical orientation that aims to address social problems through institutional reform, changes that do not require dramatic transformations of character in order to succeed. Scholars sometimes describe these thinkers as belonging to a "statecraft school" which includes Song philosophers like CHEN Liang and YE Shi, and the Ming Neo-Confucian WANG Tingxiang.[27] It also includes reform-minded Neo-Confucians who lived through the downfall of the Ming and the rise of the Qing dynasty, such as GU Yanwu and HUANG Zongxi.[28] Even for more character-centered Confucians, what it means to say that people's character is more fundamental than institutions is open to debate. To understand the nuances of the resulting debates, it helps to begin with the classical Confucian philosopher Xunzi, famous as a defender of the character-centered view.[29]

The *locus classicus* of Xunzi's position is found in a chapter titled "The Way of the Ruler," in which Xunzi sums up his own character-centered view with the memorable line, "There are people who create order; there are no rules that create order" (*you zhi ren, wu zhi fa* 有治人, 無治法)."[30] The Chinese character that we have translated as "rules" is *fa* 法, a versatile term that can also be translated as "laws," "regulations," or "standards." In the context of the present debate, it is used to refer to the formal standards or rules establishing and regulating institutions of various kinds, such as legal proceedings, schools, academies, and rituals, including both those directly instituted by the state and those taking place in what we above called non-state spaces. A major theme in Xunzi's writings is that the rules and regulations are necessarily vague, so that the proper implementation of them is under-determined. To see why, consider the laws and regulations that establish and govern public schools – there is a great abundance of decisions to be made that are not spelled out explicitly by the relevant laws and regulations, from when to schedule specific classes to how assiduously one should pursue accusations of cheating. Another point of Xunzi's is that proper implementation of the rules requires a great deal of skill and technique, which itself can only be credited to the talents of the person who applies the rules skillfully. Xunzi draws an analogy to the legendary archer Yi, who presumably had the same formal standards of successful archery as everyone else (e.g., hit the bullseye) but was unique in having the aptitude to meet them perfectly.[31] Furthermore, even if we were to stipulate (for the sake of argument) that the rules and regulations were sufficiently clear and specific, their directives fall well short of explaining how to make them a coherent and systematic whole. Rules and regulations sometimes appear to conflict with one another, and it requires wisdom and experience to know how to balance such competing considerations, for which it is necessary to have some background understanding of the aims and purposes of the rules. Finally, there is no fixed way of systematizing the rules. Changes in circumstance require that the priority of rules will sometimes need to be revised, and this too requires good judgment.[32]

This series of arguments by Xunzi is often invoked by Neo-Confucians interested in governance. Discoursing on Xunzi's claim that order is created by "people" but not "rules" gives them opportunities to explore and develop new ways of explaining how the character of people can be prior to institutions. One helpful elaboration is made by HU HONG, a scholar deeply influenced by the Cheng brothers and later of great interest to ZHU XI. On Hu's view, people enter into the explanatory order of governance at two levels: first, they are the ones who implement the rules and regulations. At this level, Hu's analysis closely follows Xunzi's, stressing the necessary vagueness of law and the need to have skillful magistrates who understand individual laws in a systematic way.[33] But, secondly, we humans are also the ones who fix the rules whenever the rules are not suited to the circumstances. That is, humans govern not just as executives but as originators too:

> Xunzi said, "There are people who create order; there are no rules that create order." I humbly submit that we illustrate this by drawing an analogy between wanting to restore order after a period of chaos, and trying to cross a river or lake [by boat]. The rules are like the boat and the people [i.e. the ruler and his officials] are like the steersman. If the boat is damaged and the rudder is broken, then even if the steersman has seemingly divine technique everyone nevertheless understands that the boat cannot get across. So whenever there is a period of great disorder it is necessary to reform the rules. There has never been a case where one could successfully restore order without reforming the rules.[34]

In short, for Hu, people bear credit for successful governance not just by guiding the institution correctly, but also by creating and modifying the very rules on which governance is founded. Credit goes not just to the steersmen but to the shipwrights as well. In fact, as we will see later in this chapter, Hu ultimately thinks the shipwrights do the most consequential work.

The philosophers we have examined so far have stressed the role of human discretion in creating social order, which in turn led them to think of human beings as the primary agents of successful governance. But there is another way of thinking about human discretion that puts institutions and the rules that govern them back at the center of one's theory. Although discretion may allow people of talent and good character to update rules or apply them differently in different contexts, it also allows people who lack talent and good character to misuse them. In these cases, it helps to set limits to abuses of authority and leadership by requiring that leaders adhere to rules. The philosopher who argues for this view most forcefully is HUANG Zongxi, who lived in the late Ming and early Qing. In a remarkable essay titled "On Rules" (*Yuanfa* 原法), Huang argues that people should distinguish between legitimate and illegitimate rules, where the illegitimate ones are marked by the fact that they are created or modified primarily to serve the interests of rulers. Huang maintains that what gives rules legitimacy is the purpose for which they are fashioned, not just tradition or the duty to respect the ancestors who fashioned them. The rules of China's most successful dynasties, Huang argues, were created to help the people to flourish rather than to enrich and preserve the ruling class.[35]

As we have seen, thinkers like HU Hong would be quick to point out that rules and regulations require a great deal of skill and uncodifiable know-how to implement effectively, which suggests that people still play a large role in creating social order. Huang turns this line of argument on its head. When rules are designed with the interests of the people in mind, they tend to be loose and open-ended, for their purpose is not just to control human behavior but also to cultivate virtues. People are more likely to develop good judgment and virtuous character traits if their orderly conduct is done willingly rather than under threat,[36] and they are more likely to act willingly if they are brought up under a regime of rules that protects their interests. Ironically, it is the rules of self-serving authorities that require greater and greater stringency. Because such rulers rely heavily on coercion and work against the welfare of ordinary people, they must create one layer of rules that governs human conduct, then a second layer of rules establishing institutions to enforce the first, then a third layer of rules to enforce those in the second, and so on. The result is a regime with considerably less flexibility and room for human discretion than the proponents of the Xunzian principle envision:

> When [the authorities] employ a person they suspect him of selfishness and hire yet another person to keep his selfishness in check. When they implement a policy they worry that it will be easy for people to cheat and establish another policy to guard against cheating. ... Consequently, the laws have to be made tight. The tighter the laws, the more disorder that springs up in their midst. These could be called "unruly rules." ... Some pundits say, "There are people who create order; there are no rules that create order." To this I say, "Only if there are rules that create order can there be people that create order."[37]

Huang's argument is notable for being institutionalist without favoring robust, heavily interventionist institutions. As we see here, he affirms that institutions bear a great deal of credit for success in governance – essentially, there will not be people of good character when the institutional rules are poorly designed. So well-designed institutions are a necessary condition both for effective governance and good character. But Huang also proposes that the institutions that govern most successfully are those that give much discretion to the people to make decisions for themselves.

Here, it would be helpful to note an ambiguity in the debate about institutions and character in governance. Neither party to this debate proposes that one can govern without institutions and people of good character. Character-centered theorists do not think that a ruler can govern, as though by magic, without policies and procedures of state (penal codes, tax codes, mechanisms of enforcement, etc.). And institutionalists do not think that the empire can be in good order without virtuous officials and subjects. The debate as Hu and Huang frame it is about which of these two components bears credit *for the other*. Hu's analogy to the shipwright is meant to show that one cannot have adequate institutional rules without virtuous rule makers, suggesting that virtue comes first. And Huang's argument is meant to show that something like the reverse is true. Institutional rules are necessary for a populace and officialdom that are able to exercise sufficient judgment and self-control to make for an orderly empire. Each maintains that we must have an adequate version of one before we can have an adequate version of the other.

It also helps to identify some of the concrete implications of these more abstract debates about the priority of character versus institutions. For all of the Neo-Confucians mentioned in this chapter, the debate was motivated by immediate and pressing questions about how to help the empire restore and maintain order. Probably the most identifiable form of the character-centered view suggests that the empire will never be well ordered until it is ruled by an emperor of extraordinary virtue – someone who, for example, is wise in assessing the character of his appointees, who has profound humaneness and compassion for his subjects, and who weighs competing policies on their merits rather than on the basis of personal interests. In practice, most Neo-Confucians of a character-centered bent recognize that virtuous formal and informal advisers are able to make up for some of the shortcomings in an emperor, but the emperor still must be concerned enough with the empire's well-being to identify and listen to good advisers. Therefore, educating the heartmind of the ruler through the "Learning of the Emperors" (*dixue* 帝學) emerges as an important means to good governance and a nexus where the Neo-Confucian teachings on self-cultivation and governance coincide. ZHU Xi sums up this train of thought when he announces that the "great basis of the cosmos ... is Your Majesty's heartmind," since "when the ruler's heartmind is correct, not a single affair of the realm will fail to proceed from rectitude."[38] Several well-known Daoxue thinkers – including CHENG Yi – serve as personal instructors to an emperor, and various curricula for the "Learning of the Emperors" are published and debated. As we have pointed out, even strong character-centered views acknowledge some role for institutions; in the context of teaching the emperor, the office of the "classics mat lecturer" is a good example.[39]

The "Learning of the Emperors," which involves lecturing and directed reading, is designed to directly cultivate the imperial heartmind. In chapter 7 we discussed the important role that rituals have in ethical cultivation, and now we can add that rituals are a second point at which theories of self-cultivation and governance overlap. As we saw in chapter 7, rituals can both discipline behavior and help to develop one's character. In the present context, it is important to notice that whether or not one follows a ritual can also be quite obvious, whereas whether or not one learns a "classics mat" lesson may not be obvious at all. For this reason, disputes over rituals often served as flash points between emperors and their Neo-Confucian advisers (or, in some cases, would-be advisers). Let one example serve to explain how serious these disputes could be. During the Southern Song, Emperor Guangzong refused to perform even the minimal ritual visitations due to his father, who had abdicated as emperor. Here was an obvious case of failing to follow the prescribed rituals, and we know from chapters 7 and 8 that proper familial rituals and the cultivation of filial piety are central to Neo-Confucian views of ethical growth. Neo-Confucian contemporaries of this wayward emperor were therefore strongly critical of his actions, ultimately succeeding in forcing Guangzong to abdicate the throne.[40] Disagreements between emperors and Neo-Confucians over ritual matters did not always end so well for the critics; recall the bloody end to the Donglin faction, discussed earlier in this chapter, which was at least in part a dispute about rituals. In any event, we see here another type of institution that character-centered theorists endorse as useful toward their end of order within the empire and, ultimately, harmony in the cosmos.

We will leave the debate here, having clarified what is at stake between what we are calling character-centered and institutionalist theories of governance. Let us now turn to look more closely at the crucial institutions of laws and law making.

4 Law and authority

In modern times, when we think of laws as such, we tend to think of punishments. It would be uncharacteristic or even incoherent to pass a law without presupposing some mechanism to enforce it, and punishment is typically that mechanism. In pre-modern China, however, it was also thought that laws could help to shape the dispositions of the people, inculcating good habits and inclinations. One way in which Confucianism stood out from other views about governance was in insisting that there is a tension between the punishment function of laws and their character-shaping function. Already in the *Analects*, Confucians recognized that governments will be more successful when people's characters can be shaped in positive ways, as opposed to simply manipulating their actions by prodding them with rewards and punishments:

> The Master said, "If you try to guide the people with coercive regulations and keep them in line with punishments, the common people will be evasive and will have no sense of shame. If, however, you guide them with virtue and keep them in line by means of ritual, the people will have a sense of shame and will rectify themselves."[41]

In other words, although laws can influence people through external coercion, such processes are unreliable because people only acquire motives to avoid the punishment, not to act properly. Given an opportunity to act badly without being caught, they will do so shamelessly. When people's dispositions are transformed, however, they will come to see bad behavior as shameful and therefore avoid it themselves. The *Analects* passage advocates virtue and ritual as means to such transformation, but it also follows that, insofar as laws are capable of promoting the transformation of character, they will be more successful in the long term.

The best-known Neo-Confucians express mixed feelings about the law. ZHU Xi says that penal statutes (*lü* 律) "are, after all, of some help in teaching and transforming people. But fundamentally they are deficient to some extent."[42] When CHENG Hao served as a magistrate, he sometimes took official actions that appeared to ordinary people to be slight violations of the law; his younger brother CHENG Yi reports this fact as evidence of the elder Cheng's wisdom.[43] A comment in one of WANG Yangming's letters can help us to see how legal adjudication might be a context for "teaching and transforming people": Wang writes that the magistrate

> has to see why the party in the wrong might have done something because he could not help it, while the party in the right may also have shown some faults. In this way, [the magistrate] would allow the persecuted party to state his situation, while the party receiving redress also must not escape responsibility. This would be to exhaust to the utmost the impartiality (*gong*) of Pattern.[44]

That is, for both ZHU Xi and WANG Yangming, at least, law can be a valuable site for moral transformation.

Laws and law making form an important part of the institutionalist conception of effective governance, and thus give us another significant point of contention between the institutionalists and character-centered theorists. To make the case for institutionalism, its defenders tend to defend two general claims. The first is that well-designed laws can be valuable tools for realizing successful rule – that is, instruments for helping the ruler bring about conditions like social stability and securing the basic needs and interests of the people. The second claim is that these laws are in fact more fundamental than good character in securing good order because they play an essential part in shaping the very people who govern, including the people (to speak in a somewhat circular fashion) who shape other institutions. As it happens, it is really the second of these claims that is necessary to substantiate institutionalist theories. As we noted earlier, *both* parties to this debate think that laws and institutions play an important role in effective governance; it is just that they disagree about whether character or laws and institutions are more fundamental. Accordingly, it should come as no surprise that Neo-Confucians of many kinds – including those who seem to lean more toward character-centered theories – are willing to endorse the first claim.

Mainstream Daoxue Confucians like the Cheng brothers, ZHU Xi and WANG Yangming urge that rulers not lean too heavily on laws as instruments of rule. Outside of mainstream Daoxue, however, there were many Neo-Confucians who took a keen interest in refining laws and the legal regime for instrumental purposes, and furthermore tended to see well-tailored laws as accounting for much of a government's success. The Ming dynasty critic of Daoxue, WANG Tingxiang, provides an excellent example. In chapter 2, we mentioned that Wang denied the idea at the core of Daoxue metaphysics that there is a deep unity to the cosmos (which is ultimately characterized as Pattern or grounded in Pattern). Instead, as a modern scholar puts it, Wang holds that "since man is unable to rely upon the cosmos or human nature to provide the human world with a basis for unity, he will have to depend on the government to create a unified order and to ensure that the society be kept intact despite its inherent diversity."[45] As a result, Wang concludes that the top-down imposition of institutional structure – very much including law – is the only source of order in our fragmented world; he writes: "The way of the sages simultaneously uses the Way, virtue, ritual, music, and the penal law."[46]

Another way to credit the use of laws as instruments of successful governance is to confront more directly the mainstream Daoxue assumption that legal incentives are necessarily in tension with the development of virtuous character traits. Not all Neo-Confucians see the options in these terms. Both CHEN Liang and YE Shi promote the idea that self-interest, even the crude interest in accumulating wealth, can be harnessed in such a way that the desire for personal benefit is itself righteous. They propose to align the drive to accumulate wealth with the public good, proposing policies of taxation and land distribution that strengthen the central government (thus promoting unity) and encourage productivity. Chen and Ye actually see the convergence of righteousness and personal benefit in slightly different ways. Chen thinks that any amount of self-interested desire is fine so long as it is aligned with the public good, whereas Ye holds that righteousness sets independent limits to self-interested pursuits. At some point, Ye believes, seeking one's own good (even if it happens to align with the public good) lacks righteousness, such that the two sorts of motives need to be balanced against one another. But both figures, who loom large among the literati of ZHU Xi's day, serve as vivid reminders of the diversity of Neo-Confucian political and ethical thought.[47]

Let us now turn to the second and crucial claim for institutionalists: namely, that laws are more fundamental than character in securing good order. One way they might go about this is by proposing that laws should have a certain authority over government itself, even the emperor (a vision akin to what modern day scholars and political commentators call the "rule of law"). If this argument is to work, it must be the case that the certain constraints be set on the emperor's ability to issue laws, and one familiar way of accomplishing this is to propose that law derive some of its authority directly from the institutional procedures and rules that determine which laws are ratified, much as laws in modern constitutional republics derive their authority directly from electoral and legislative procedures. This is not a route available to Neo-Confucian defenders of institutionalism because it presupposes a view of authority that few were ready to embrace. The overwhelming consensus among Neo-Confucians was that law derives its authority from the dictates of the emperor. As one modern scholar explains, "All officially enacted law, as opposed to socially enforced custom, derived its force from the emperor, even if it had not been handed down directly by him."[48] Although Song dynasty statutory law was roughly based on the statutes of the Tang dynasty before it, any law could be changed or abrogated through the expression of imperial will. And since social and economic conditions had changed mightily in the hundreds of years since the founding of the Tang, Song emperors issued edicts that revised or established new laws at a furious pace.[49] To be sure, rulers have an interest in presenting themselves as continuing, and in some sense being constrained by, the laws of their predecessors.[50] However, whatever deference they might show to those laws in word or deed, any revision of rules is seen as legitimate so long as it is sanctioned by the emperor.

Nevertheless, there is a subtler and more circuitous route by which institutions might be more fundamental than character for laws and law making. This view concedes the widely shared position that monarchical rulers themselves – and not institutional procedures – are the sole direct source of a law's authority. However, it nevertheless requires that the rulers participate in processes that are likely to shape the sorts of laws that they make. Here, these processes play a role analogous to requiring that a professor get formal training in course design before creating assignments. The assignments that a professor ultimately chooses are binding by virtue of the fact that she chose them, so her direct authority as assignment maker remains unchallenged, but if she ends up producing better assignments, some of the credit would go to the required formal training in course design. Similarly, the monarch is the author of laws, but certain institutions provide something akin to required formal training in skills necessary for virtue and good governance, so that those institutions play a more fundamental role in shaping his character.

In general, institutionalist Neo-Confucians are more inclined to follow this second and more circuitous route. A notable example of how institutional procedures can take indirect credit for shaping laws comes, once again, from the reform-minded statecraft thinker HUANG Zongxi. Among the many dramatic political reforms that Huang advances, probably the most striking are his ideas about the proper role and governance of academies. Huang's vision is to create a well-funded system of universal education, financed and supported by the state but nevertheless given a great deal of autonomy. He proposes that there be a nominal center of education in the Imperial College, whose director is to be appointed by the emperor. But directors of the local schools would be appointed by the local communities, and they would be given the freedom to run the schools as they see fit. Huang also proposes that political leaders, including the emperor, be compelled periodically to visit the academies to observe open discussion of social and political issues.[51] And perhaps the most remarkable requirement is that the crown prince (that is, the designated successor to the throne) be educated at the Imperial College along with other young scholars, with the aim of giving the emperor-to-be a great deal of exposure to the views and experiences of people outside the palace walls: "They should be informed of real conditions among the people and be given some experience of difficult labor and hardship. They must not be shut off in the palace, where everything they learn comes from the eunuchs who serve them and palace women alone, so that they get false notions of their own greatness."[52] Of course, measures such as these are no guarantee that a ruler will be a good law maker, but it is easy to see how exposure to a wider range of human experience could have a positive impact on his deliberations, opening up possibilities that would otherwise be out of reach to rulers insulated from public life and the opinions of an informed public.

Huang's proposed reforms, as well as the discussions of law, non-state institutions, and ritual mentioned above, help to spell out some of the concrete implications of the more abstract or theoretical positions that some Neo-Confucians adopted. In our final section, we turn to their implications for one of the most high-profile debates about institutional structures of the day.

5 State structure: commanderies versus fiefdoms

Two competing systems

In this section, we will explore how sophisticated and influential character-centered approaches inform Neo-Confucian views on a critical, long-running debate over state structure and regional governance. By the start of the Neo-Confucian era, emperors had long maintained control over the many districts of China through a system of direct appointments that we will call the "commandery system."[53] A guiding aim of this system is to help to centralize power and thereby shore up the imperial court's control over regional affairs. Under this system, regional governors are appointed directly by the central government for a finite period of time (usually just a few years) and only to districts of which they are not native. Regional governors hold office at the pleasure of the central government and are meant to have no pre-existing loyalties to the people in that region; whatever ties they develop in the course of their work are to be severed when the governor is moved to his next post. A different way of assigning regional authority is the "enfeoffment system,"[54] according to which governorships are inherited rather than granted by appointment. The Neo-Confucians generally believed that this was the system that prevailed in the ancient golden age, and many saw it as responsible for the sustained period of peace and prosperity in that era. In this section, we identify the major arguments for each side of the debate and examine the philosophical issues at stake, including the importance of centralized authority and the role of special attachments in character formation. We will also see that subtle differences between variants of character-centered theories of governance can lead to quite different conclusions about the competing state structures.

Defenders of the commandery system identify several advantages. First, the system enables the emperor (or the imperial court) to maintain a great deal more control over the various localities. Since regional governors are appointed by the court and moved from one position to another on a regular basis, they largely owe their desirable position to the emperor, and they do not develop the sort of local ties that might lead them to prize the interests of their charges over and above the aims of the central government. All of this is meant both to ensure greater harmony between regions and greater deference to the interests of the empire as a whole. Second, this system is also meant to be more meritocratic. In principle, at least, the emperor can hire and dismiss officials depending on their competence and character, whereas replacing an incompetent or vicious feudal lord would be much more difficult.[55] Finally, by the time of the Song dynasty and thereafter, some form of the commandery system had been in place for several centuries, making it difficult to replace without a radical break from longstanding customs and practices, something not easily accomplished without doing damage to the conventions and social fabric that hold a state together.[56]

These arguments are advanced most forcefully by some Tang and Northern Song Confucians who played prominent roles in Confucian debates about governance, including LIU Zongyuan, SU Shi, and WANG Anshi, the aforementioned architect of the "New Policies" which became a focal point of so much political conflict in the Northern Song. In fact, both of the major political factions in the final years of the Northern Song – the reformists and the conservatives – advocate one variant or another of the commandery system. In that time, the most notable and unequivocal defender of enfeoffment is ZHANG Zai, whose views later become influential among major Neo-Confucians in the Southern Song, including HU Hong and ZHU Xi (although Zhu ultimately adopts a position that opens the door to either system, as we shall see). While pro-enfeoffment arguments and ideas gain a great deal more currency in the Southern Song, there are assuredly many Southern Song Neo-Confucians who remain steadfast defenders of commanderies, including the institutionalist thinker CHEN Liang, whom we discussed earlier.[57]

The case for reinstating the enfeoffment system is varied and wide ranging. Many Southern Song proponents of enfeoffment see the decentralization of political power as a strength rather than a weakness.[58] Central authorities tend to be less intimately acquainted with conditions on the ground in their various districts, leaving them with a weaker grasp of the needs of their subjects and without versatility to adjust their directives to local circumstances.[59] These philosophers also note that centralization makes the state as a whole more vulnerable. For example, HU Hong argues that commanderies, while quite successful under ideal circumstances, lack the resilience to endure real tests of the state's authority and control: "By making commanderies in the empire one can maintain a sustained period of peace [under normal circumstances] but cannot hold up in the face of extraordinary circumstances. By enfeoffing regional governors one can maintain a sustained period of peace [under normal circumstances] and can also hold up in the face of extraordinary circumstances."[60]

Another major line of argument emphasizes the role of special attachments – the sort of attachments that develop out of close proximity and regular interaction with a community. As we saw in chapter 8, most Neo-Confucians follow Mencius in seeing special attachments as a central and basic feature of their ethics, being both necessary for proper moral development and an indispensable feature of a full and virtuous life, without which one couldn't function as parent, child, friend, or neighbor. But while nearly all of the Neo-Confucians agree that special attachments are necessary for virtue, they are somewhat more divided about the importance of special attachments in governance. The commandery system is supposed to undercut special attachments by ensuring a regular rotation of regional governors and prohibiting the appointment of locals.[61] But to defenders of enfeoffment, the power of special attachments is useful and valuable in regional governance, just as it is valuable and useful in village and family life. By working with rather than against the natural tendency to care more about one's near and dear, a state official can become a more thoughtful and conscientious administrator.[62] All of this is part of a larger set of assumptions about the continuities between families and larger socio-political units. ZHANG Zai insists that in governance we should treat larger social units as analogous to families in significant ways – as families writ large.[63] In this respect, Zhang is probably more faithful than are his pro-commandery opponents to the vision of politics described at the outset of this chapter and in the famous passage from *Greater Learning* that we have frequently quoted, which suggests that success in governance builds on and closely resembles success in regulating one's family.

Let us now return to the larger philosophical issue that we discussed earlier, regarding the character-centered understanding of governance. In sections 3 and 4, we looked in some detail at the views of two character-centered thinkers, HU Hong and ZHU Xi, both of whom maintain that in some respect it is the people, or more specifically their virtue or lack thereof, that bear credit for successful governance. How, then, would thinkers such as these argue for one system of regional governance (enfeoffment or commandery) over another? As we will show, both Hu and Zhu largely stay true to this way of explaining the sources of social order but, as often happens in complex matters of political thought, the same general theory can lead to quite different conclusions. Hu is an unabashed proponent of the enfeoffment system and makes explicit use of character-centered arguments to justify it. By contrast, Zhu seems to take more seriously the idea that institutions are interchangeable so long as the people who run them have the right talents and moral fiber.

Hu Hong's defense of the enfeoffment system is not just an idle expression of political ideals. It is the cornerstone of the extensive system of thought about socio-political institutions, about which he wrote prolifically.[64] Perhaps this seems to be at odds with the character-centered theory of governance that he articulated so forcefully: if one thinks it is really the character of people that makes the difference between good and bad governance, should it not be the case that government can prosper under a wide array of institutional systems? As we will see, that is an idea that Zhu would later find attractive, but Hu does not draw this conclusion. To see why, consider again how Hu makes the case for his general theory of governance. Hu argues that people's character is fundamental because it explains how the apparatus of government is set aright when it becomes broken. To use his lucid analogy, people not rules create order, just as shipwrights not steersmen repair boats: when the rules are broken, the state needs people of great talent and virtue to reform them; no amount of proficiency and moral rectitude in using the broken laws will make it possible to restore order, just as no amount of skillful steering is going to get a broken boat across a body of water.[65] So on Hu's variant of the character-centered theory of governance, the principal credit-bearer is the talent and virtue of those who establish and reform institutions, not that of the people who operate within its parameters. If this is right, then it is quite consistent with character-centered theories to say that some institutions are better than others because some institutions are more likely to be chosen by people of good character than others.

Indeed, that is precisely the sort of argument that Hu highlights in his defense of the enfeoffment system. On Hu's telling of ancient history, the first iteration of the commandery system was instituted by the vicious, Legalist rulers of the short-lived Qin dynasty. For Hu, the Qin's rules were largely unsuccessful, and Hu thinks we can identify the particular features of those rules that made them so unsuccessful, but that does not yet address the primary question for him, which is to explain how these broken rules came about in the first place. And for that, Hu argues, we have to look at the character of their originators:

> The feudal lords are the mainstay of humane government. The Qin people were obsessed with profit; they abolished the enfeoffment system and set up the commandery system for all in the world. After the way of the sages was abandoned, sovereigns all nurtured the idea of conquering all in the world. Therefore, they repeatedly used the commandery system, and could not reform it. Alas! The moment one develops the idea to take over all in the world, the basis of the Kingly Way has already been destroyed. Under these institutions, they might cultivate virtue and employ the wise, and practice humane government, but it would not prevent great chaos.[66]

Put differently, Hu's point is that bad institutions make all the difference between successful and unsuccessful governance, between order and disorder, but institutions go bad because of the vices of those who design the rules and standards of those institutions. Thus, as Hu says, poor institutions could be populated with virtuous and wise people but produce disorder nonetheless. Elsewhere, Hu suggests that something similar is true for good institutions: the enfeoffment system is designed to minimize the harm in making bad appointments or poor judgments, so that order prevails in the state overall and the state endures even when the ruler makes occasional mistakes.[67]

As we saw earlier, however, a character-centered theorist might well think that much success in governance is due not just to the designers of institutions but also to the people who execute the rules and procedures in specific circumstances. So long as the boat is reasonably sound, so to speak, adroit and worthy steersmen can guide it well. This is how we understand ZHU Xi's view. Although Zhu was a strong proponent of the enfeoffment system in his early years, his mature view, in a nutshell, is that both the enfeoffment and the commandery systems are good enough to work.

> Master Zhu's students were discussing the defects of the commandery and enfeoffment systems. The Master said, "In general established laws (*fa*) invariably have defects and no laws are without them. What is really important is to get the right person for the job. If the person is right then even if the laws are not good he will still amply make up the difference in score. If the person is not right and yet the laws are good, how could this improve anything?"[68]

Given that both systems are viable, Zhu proposes that his contemporaries should take account of some of the more contingent social, economic, and historical factors to determine which system is better suited for the present moment. Doing so, he proposes, favors the current commandery system. By Zhu's time, the Chinese state has expanded significantly compared to the time of the ancient sage-kings, requiring a greater degree of control by the central government than was necessary in ancient times.[69] Most importantly, reestablishing the enfeoffment system would upend the social and political order, exacting too great a cost to justify such measures. As Zhu says when asked about HU Hong's position,

> The enfeoffment system ... is an institution of the sages and offers rules for all the world inclusively and impartially. How could I dare deny this? But in the present day I fear it would be difficult to implement. Even if one were able to establish it through great effort I fear that it would produce unintended maladies.[70]

In this matter, as in many other issues of governance in his day, Zhu's specific views are deeply informed by his broader philosophical position on the significance of institutions and character, evident not just in his conclusions about the two systems but in his arguments as well. Both Hu and Zhu demonstrate a degree of consistency and philosophical care evident in a great number of Neo-Confucians who take a philosophical interest in governance.

Much of this volume has been concerned with Confucian accounts of virtue and moral cultivation, and the philosophical concepts and frameworks that help to justify those accounts. At first glance it might seem that their views on governance are somewhat tangential to such concerns. As we have seen in this chapter, however, this is hardly the case. Virtue and cultivation provide one of the central aims and purposes of government, and for nearly all Neo-Confucians – including the institutionalists – success in restoring and maintaining order depends on having people of good character. Furthermore, both state and non-state institutions play important roles in helping to develop good character in both public officials and ordinary subjects. No examination of the core philosophical commitments of the competing strands of Neo-Confucianism would be complete without taking account of their views on governance.

For further study

Selected primary sources

1. ZHANG Zai, "Land Equalization and the Enfeoffment System," in deBary and Bloom 1999: 605–6.

2. ZHU Xi and LÜ Zuqian (eds), "On the Principles of Governing the State" and "Systems and Institutions," in Zhu and Lü 1967: 202–37.
3. ZHU Xi, "Governing the State" and "Laws and Regulations," in Zhu 1991b: 129–40.
4. HUANG Zongxi, "On Law," in Tiwald and Van Norden 2014: #50.

Discussion questions

1. How might Neo-Confucian worries about factions be compared with present-day worries about political parties and partisanship?
2. Using your own words, explain the difference between character-centered and institutionalist theories of effective governance.
3. Which of the two theories of governance do you think is more accurate, and why?
4. How does modern government affect our opportunities to develop good character? Do any of the Neo-Confucian concerns about the government's effect on character apply today?
5. We have seen that the debate about the advantages and disadvantages of the enfoeffment system, as compared with the commandery system, was tremendously important to many Neo-Confucians. Can you think of reasons why, over and above those mentioned in the chapter?

10

The Enduring Significance of Neo-Confucianism

This book has introduced the key ideas debated by Chinese Neo-Confucians from the eleventh to the eighteenth centuries. For nearly a millennium, this revival of Confucianism was at the center of Chinese – and broader East Asian – intellectual and spiritual life. By the nineteenth century, though, dramatic changes were taking place that marked the waning of Neo-Confucianism as a vital philosophical tradition and set the scene for the collapse of China's entire imperial system. In this final chapter, we will briefly narrate these changes before turning to our final question: in the new world of the twenty-first century – what enduring significance might Neo-Confucianism possess?

1 The historical fate of Neo-Confucianism

The collapse of the imperial system

The Manchus complete their conquest of Ming China in 1644 and found the Qing, which proves to be China's last imperial dynasty. Early Manchu emperors endorse many aspects of Chinese culture and values, including embracing Daoxue Neo-Confucianism and presenting themselves as sage-kings. In the latter part of the seventeenth century and throughout the eighteenth, recognizably Neo-Confucian philosophical activity continues, though the distinctive and influential voices are increasingly found among critics of Daoxue. Original thinking that is focused on the nature or heartmind becomes rather rare. The Qing thinkers we have discussed in this book – such as

WANG Fuzhi and DAI Zhen – have generally been more focused on vital stuff, though all the major Neo-Confucian categories play roles in their thought.

With other thinkers in the eighteenth and especially the nineteenth centuries, there is much less continuity with Neo-Confucianism. To be sure, the civil service examination system and its connection to ZHU Xi's commentaries continues right into the twentieth century, but Confucian intellectual vitality is elsewhere, with three notable trends characterizing the period. First, there is rising interest in evidence-based, philological approaches to ancient texts, which is seen as conducive to empirical problem solving. Second, another side of the renewed attention to ancient texts (as opposed to the narrower canon on which Daoxue educators focused) was a "purist" demand to recover the norms and language of original or pure Confucianism. This developed into a socially conservative emphasis on ritual as "the most effective method for cultivating Confucian virtues." Finally, another side of the classicist movement had a more activist and reformist political dimension: certain scholars critical of the Qing emperors emphasized those ancient texts that could justify political changes, and this strand of thinking ultimately culminated in the dramatic reform movements of the late nineteenth century (which even has heirs in present-day China).[1]

Over and above these new intellectual trends, the nineteenth-century witnesses dramatic challenges to the basic socio-cultural-political order of late imperial China that had developed hand in hand with Neo-Confucianism. Millenarian religious movements lead to large-scale rebellions, the most dramatic of which nearly brings down the empire. Beginning with the First Opium War of 1839–42, Europeans and Americans use military force to compel the Qing government to open markets to their products and comply with other demands. Chinese scholars and foreign missionaries begin translating a range of works into Chinese and, especially in the last decades of the century, opportunities for education in "western learning" grow rapidly. Literati leaders and Qing officials collaborate on a series of evermore radical efforts to improve the plight of the dynasty, from the explicitly Confucian Tongzhi Restoration of the 1860s, to the more technology-oriented and institution-building Self-Strengthening Movement that continues into the 1890s, to the "Hundred Days' Reform" of 1895.[2] Neo-Confucian ideas are not entirely absent from the discourse around these various movements, but they definitely have ceded any kind of intellectual leadership to new or different strains of thought. The last straw for Neo-Confucianism comes when the imperial government decides to abandon the civil service examination system in 1905 as part of a last-gasp effort to preserve the dynasty while accepting certain kinds of institutional change. Overnight, years or even decades of training in the Neo-Confucian interpretation of the classics is rendered useless, at least for the purpose of obtaining a position in government. Even this dramatic step comes too late for the Qing regime, however, as the dynasty collapses in 1911, ending two thousand years of imperial rule.

A difficult century

The twentieth century proves to be even more difficult for Neo-Confucianism – and for Confucianism more broadly – than the nineteenth century was. Beginning in 1915, Chinese intellectuals who are frustrated with China's floundering in the years since the 1912 establishment of the Republic of China declare the need for a "New Culture Movement": China's problems run deeper than political institutions, they say, and need to be addressed at the fundamental level of norms, values, and even language. Various forms of Confucianism continue to have their supporters and, indeed, strands of "New Confucianism" emerge in the 1920s and thereafter, as we will discuss shortly. The dominant schools of thought throughout the twentieth century, though, are various "isms" that are appropriated and adapted from the West, such as liberalism, pragmatism, anarchism, nationalism, socialism, and communism. The People's Republic of China, founded in 1949, is generally unfriendly to any form of Confucianism over its first several decades, especially during the Great Proletarian Cultural Revolution of 1966–1976, which includes a mass campaign specifically targeting Confucius. Confucian scholarship continues to be promoted by some in Hong Kong and Taiwan (which after 1949 is the sole territory occupied by the Republic of China), and Confucianism gradually starts to make a comeback in mainland China in the 1980s, but, on the whole, historian YU Ying-shih's characterization of Confucianism as a "wandering soul," bereft of any institutional "body," aptly characterizes Confucianism throughout this period.[3]

If we look for evidence of Confucianism as a live concern in the twentieth century – as a step toward understanding where and whether Neo-Confucianism has continued significance today – we believe that three contexts are worth our attention. First of all, daily life practices that are closely related to Confucianism have never disappeared from any part of East Asia, although the details vary from China to Taiwan, Hong Kong, Japan, and Korea. To one degree or other, all of the following continue throughout the century: reverence for and ceremonies in honor of ancestors; respect for and obedience to one's parents; emphasis on personal moral self-cultivation; and even, in some cases, reading and recitation of classic texts. How much these practices matter today for any kind of "Confucianism" is disputed, but it may be that the continued existence of "Confucian public culture" in a place like South Korea makes desirable a distinctive Confucian form of democracy.[4]

The other two contexts are more immediately relevant to our concerns here. First, the middle decades of the twentieth century gradually give birth to new forms of Confucian thinking that are sometimes called "New Confucianism." Unlike "Neo-Confucianism," which does not correspond to any single Chinese term (as discussed in the book's Introduction), "New Confucianism" is a direct translation of a newly coined Chinese term, *xin rujia* 新儒家. From the earliest uses of this term to refer to a new kind of Confucianism, it was understood that part of what is distinctive about "New Confucianism" is that its practitioners were knowledgeable about, and engaged in dialogue with, western philosophy.[5] For example, the most famous "New Confucian," MOU Zongsan (1909–1995), took Kantian philosophy particularly seriously, translating all three of Kant's *Critiques* and arguing that New Confucianism improved on Kantian philosophy in certain important ways.[6] Mou and other New Confucians drew widely on Confucian and other Chinese traditions but, like many of his peers, Mou takes certain Neo-Confucian thinkers as representing the acme of Confucian thinking. The scholarship of Mou and others is critical to our modern understanding of Neo-Confucianism, and Neo-Confucianism also plays vital roles in the continued development of New Confucian philosophy – on which more in a moment.

The final context we want to emphasize is the explicit articulation of Neo-Confucianism as a kind of "philosophy." As we mentioned briefly in the book's introduction, an explicit category of philosophy (and the corresponding Chinese term, *zhexue*) begins to be adopted in China in the late nineteenth century as part of a broad reimagination of forms of knowledge and educational institutions. Another category adopted around this time is "religion" (*zongjiao*), and indeed, early in the twentieth century, some intellectuals argue that Confucianism should be institutionalized as the state religion.[7] There are also moments when Chinese governments endeavor to use Confucian-derived ideas as explicit ideological support.[8] For the most part, though, Confucianism comes to be seen as philosophy and properly taught within the confines of philosophy departments in China's new, modern-style universities. MOU Zongsan and the other advocates of "New Confucianism" are all philosophy professors who teach ZHU Xi, WANG Yangming, and the other Neo-Confucians in their classes.[9]

Fast-forward to today, early in the twenty-first century. Neo-Confucianism plays a major role in some current approaches to Confucianism, and much less in others. In China and other Sinophone communities, many philosophers are continuing the New Confucian project which has Neo-Confucian ideas very much in the foreground. The best known is probably Taiwanese philosopher LEE Ming-huei, who studied in Germany and has focused particularly on the ways in which Neo-Confucianism and Kantian philosophy can support one another. The Beijing-based philosopher CHEN Lai is another good example of a contemporary thinker strongly influenced by Neo-Confucianism; his recent *The Ontology of Humaneness*, for example, aims to build an original philosophy on the foundation of Neo-Confucianism.[10]

A contrasting trend, particularly within the People's Republic, is toward viewing Confucianism less through the lens of philosophy and more as "national learning" (*guoxue* 国学), national culture, religion, or political institution. One thing that these various approaches have in common is to downplay Neo-Confucianism, which is viewed as overly concerned with individual moral development, in favor of other strands of Confucianism, which proponents see as more amenable to the institutional changes that they seek. Intellectuals interested in these latter trends are often more politically and culturally conservative than those promoting New Confucianism or Neo-Confucianism.

Finally, in European and especially North American scholarly communities, there is a real bifurcation: historians of China's last millennium pay careful attention to Neo-Confucianism, just as their peers studying early China attend to classical Confucianism; but philosophers interested in China have been attending much more extensively to classical Confucians (and Daoists and others) than to later thinkers like the Neo-Confucians. As we turn to this conclusion's final section, we will reflect a bit on why Neo-Confucianism has received less attention from philosophers, and whether – perhaps with the help of this book? – the future might be brighter.

2 Neo-Confucianism and comparative philosophy

With the historical account of Neo-Confucianism up to date, we turn now to the future. How will philosophers engage with Neo-Confucianism, and what enduring significance might it have? As we look ahead, we envision three, mutually complementary approaches: intellectual and cultural history; history of philosophy; and various styles of comparative philosophy.

To date, the most common mode of scholarly engagement with Neo-Confucianism has been within the closely allied fields of intellectual and cultural history, and we see no reason to expect this scholarship to abate. Such investigations into the lives, political concerns, and socio-cultural worlds of Neo-Confucian thinkers make possible a deeper understanding of what and why they wrote, argued, and acted as they did. In writing this book, we have learned a great deal from this kind of historical work.

We see our book as contributing to the second mode of engagement with Neo-Confucianism: the history of philosophy. History of philosophy is usually undertaken by contemporary philosophers – as in the present case – and it is focused on the ideas, problems, and debates with which the historical philosophers were concerned. An important feature of the history of philosophy is that its practitioners do not simply report the ideas of their subjects but engage with them. That is, practitioners do not only describe the historical ideas, as one might describe an object on a museum shelf, but they also seek to understand them and challenge the reasoning that lies behind them. It is thus possible for one writing the history of philosophy to argue that some ideas are more plausible than others, some arguments more convincing, and that sometimes a historical philosopher may have erred in giving one answer rather than another. All of this, though, is based on an effort to understand what is at stake within the philosophical context under study, and any assessment is relative to the concepts and problems of their day.

Philosophers have come a long way in recent decades in our understanding of Neo-Confucianism, and we hope that this book will help to solidify this progress and to catalyze new work in the history of Neo-Confucian philosophy. There is much more to do, including working to expand the instances in which Neo-Confucianism is taught as philosophy within universities in both East and West. Research and teaching on the history of Neo-Confucian philosophy is all the more important, furthermore, because only with some level of understanding of Neo-Confucianism can one go on to use it to do one or another variety of productive work following our third approach, comparative philosophy.

We suggest that "comparative philosophy" be broadly understood as doing philosophy by drawing on at least two significantly different traditions.[11] There are a variety of things that this can mean, and some good instances of recent philosophers employing

Neo-Confucianism in the service of these different types of compara-tive philosophy. In some cases, the primary audience is philosophers trained in western traditions, and Neo-Confucianism is being used primarily as a spur to new thinking within those traditions; in other cases, the goal is the further development of Neo-Confucian think-ing by drawing on modern or western ideas – or, in other words, the articulating of a novel kind of "new Confucianism." In fact, this distinction is somewhat artificial since, often enough, works of comparative philosophy operate in both of these modes, but distin-guishing between them is still helpful for clarity. Spending a bit of time with these recent works is a good way to understand both the ways in which Neo-Confucianism can continue to have significance for philosophers today, and what some of the pitfalls may be along that road.

Looking first at examples of books drawing on Neo-Confucianism in order to make progress within a primarily western framework, let us start with an early instance, Warren Frisina's *The Unity of Knowledge and Action: Toward a Nonrepresentational Theory of Knowledge.* (The fact that Frisina's 2002 book counts as an "early instance" of a western philosopher engaging with Neo-Confucianism in this way says something about how recent a trend this is.) Frisina's overall goal in the book is to build on the pragmatist and process traditions within western philosophy to further articulate an under-standing of knowledge that is "active, aesthetic, and hypothetical," rather than static and representational, but in order to do this he finds WANG Yangming's philosophy to be an inspirational point of depar-ture.[12] Frisina says that, according to Wang, knowing something is "equivalent to reconstructing our relationship to it" – an interpreta-tion that will make sense to readers of chapter 6 of the present book.[13] It may be that Frisina does not make as much use of Wang as he might have,[14] but the resonances that Frisina detects between Wang's con-ceptualization of knowing and the ideas in Frisina's western sources are real and are good grounds for constructive dialogue.

ZHU Xi features prominently in two books published in 2015, Catherine Hudak Klancer's *Embracing Our Complexity* and Asher Walden's *The Metaphysics of Kindness.* Klancer relies on both Zhu and Thomas Aquinas to articulate a vision of humans as creatures inhabiting – not creating – a moral order and developing their moral potential "in human and cosmic community," in which context human authority should be "humble."[15] Walden's book employs Zhu alongside several other thinkers (from India, Europe, and Japan) to explore ways in which theories of ethics that take compassion as central can explain how ethics is sufficiently objective and yet also knowable and achievable (which he calls the "problem of the standard").[16] As we have seen throughout the present book, both the way in which Pattern exerts itself as moral order and the balance between objectivity and accessibility that Walden discusses are indeed central problems for Zhu and other Neo-Confucians, and so it is plausible to think that they might serve as resources for present-day thinkers in the West grappling with these same issues.[17]

Yong HUANG's 2014 *Why Be Moral? Learning from the Neo-Confucian Cheng Brothers*, finally, is an explicit and sustained argument that contemporary western philosophers can learn from the ways that Neo-Confucians provide answers to some of the main questions with which western thinkers are currently engaged. Huang selects topics that he feels meet three criteria: (1) they are problems that have vexed both historical and current western philosophers; (2) these same problems (or a sufficiently close correlate) have also been addressed by the Cheng brothers; and (3) the Cheng brothers' solution is better than the best of the western thinkers. Huang is quite explicit that he is taking the Chengs' theorizing as he finds it, rather than speculatively developing it to make it better fit with the western problems that organize his book. And, indeed, readers of his book and our present book will find quite compatible accounts of topics like humaneness, (human) nature, knowing, and the role of context sensitivity and difference in ethical judgments.[18]

Let those books stand as examples of the ways that Neo-Confucianism is being used to spur new thinking within a more inclusive but still primarily western-focused approach to philosophy. We have already mentioned some philosophers who write mainly in Chinese and are using Neo-Confucianism to further develop "New Confucianism." Among anglophone philosophers, we can also find some efforts along these lines, addressed as much to those already interested in Confucianism as to thinkers with a primarily western background. Several of the chapters of Stephen Angle's 2009 book *Sagehood: The Contemporary Significance of Neo-Confucian Philosophy* offer challenges to Neo-Confucian teachings and then explore possible ways for Neo-Confucianism to respond and grow. For example, after a chapter that introduces Neo-Confucian ideas of self-cultivation (somewhat along the lines of the present book's chapter 7), the following chapter then raises questions about the roles that imagination and dialogue can play in moral growth. These are not issues that historical Neo-Confucians confronted, and the cultural context out of which they emerge is very different from the world of ZHU Xi and his brethren. Still, Angle argues that it is possible to take Neo-Confucianism seriously today, and from that perspective think about how modern Neo-Confucians should include imagination and dialogue in their practices of self-cultivation.[19]

Michael Kalton is another philosopher who treats Neo-Confucianism as a live philosophy, something that we can critique, develop, and learn from today. In a series of essays, Kalton has argued that recent advances in western understanding (mostly within the natural and life sciences, as well as in computer science and information theory) of self-organizing, complex, holistic systems enables a productive interface with Neo-Confucianism, with each side able to learn from the other.[20] As Kalton puts it, insofar as Neo-Confucianism is taken up in our contemporary world, "it will surely be transformed, graced with a renewed conceptual vocabulary related to streams of thought and understanding unknown to the past." After all, "refusal to rethink Neo-Confucian concepts seriously in the light of the best contemporary information would amount to consigning them to the museum of intellectual history." Still, his goal is to think as a modern or postmodern Neo-Confucian would, not to domesticate Neo-Confucianism so that it fits into pre-existing categories. Indeed, he argues that concepts like Pattern, vital stuff, and heartmind can "enter the contemporary world without too much difficulty," leading to new ideas and new connections.[21]

In all of the comparative philosophical work we have just canvassed, there are varying goals, varying degrees of creativity, varying degrees of concern with abiding by all of the Neo-Confucians' premises. We believe that we moderns learn best from the Neo-Confucians by starting with an effort to understand them in their own terms, as we have done here. As another contemporary scholar puts it, such an approach "safeguards the strangeness of the text," and only by preserving the "strangeness" of Neo-Confucianism can we best be challenged and learn from it.[22] We can hope to learn from Neo-Confucianism in many ways. Perhaps it will help us answer questions that we already have. Perhaps we will discover, among the many issues that the Neo-Confucians debated, new and different problems that modern philosophers should take seriously. And perhaps we will find that what is most striking about Neo-Confucianism is the difference of its central premises from our orientations today. In fact, we, the authors of this book, expect that all three of these reactions are likely to make sense, given the diversity of views that Neo-Confucians held on the many topics they explored. Our central goal has been to open up Neo-Confucianism in such a way that readers today can work out for themselves what to make of it.

Appendix 1

Teaching Neo-Confucianism Topically

Almost every course that has been taught about Neo-Confucianism has been arranged chronologically by thinker – and this includes courses taught by the two authors of this book, prior to our beginning this project together. The primary sources that one might assign, whether in Chinese or in translation, are inevitably organized by author, which makes it natural to treat one thinker after another. It is also attractive to ask how one part of a given writer's thought fits with another, and much of the secondary literature on Neo-Confucianism is conceived historically or even biographically. For all these reasons, it is not surprising that this approach to the material has dominated our pedagogy.

Still, there are reasons to think a different pedagogy might have distinctive advantages. For Neo-Confucians themselves, there were two distinctive ways of writing about their tradition. Historians seeking to narrate the development of the tradition did so chronologically. But the anthology that ZHU Xi and LÜ Zuqian themselves compiled to teach the ideas of their Neo-Confucian predecessors, *Reflections on Things at Hand*, is organized into a series of fourteen topical chapters. Like our book, *Reflections* begins with abstract topics (its first chapter is "The Inherent Reality of the Way" [*daoti* 道體]) and moves toward more concrete issues like techniques of personal cultivation and institutions of governance.[1] Throughout the Neo-Confucian period, this topical approach continued to dominate texts aimed at teaching the basic ideas of Neo-Confucianism. In similar fashion, we have found that by examining the views of a number of thinkers on a given topic together, students can better discern what is at stake. Where do the philosophers agree (and why?), and – perhaps more importantly – where do they disagree (and why?)? By focusing on debates and on problems that the thinkers are trying to solve, we have sought to emphasize such questions in our own presentations.

There is a further, more practical, reason for teaching Neo-Confucianism topically. Because most of the thinkers use similar terminology to discuss similar issues, treating the same questions over and over in slightly different contexts, as chronology often requires, can lead to several undesirable results, including declining student interest or efforts to exaggerate the differences among thinkers. In our earlier experiences teaching chronologically, in fact, we found a good way to avoid such boring repetition is to focus on different issues when discussing different thinkers. Once an instructor has decided to take this step, it becomes natural to want to make connections to other thinkers' views on the currently highlighted issue, and it is only a short further step to a full-fledged topical presentation.

There are of course some challenges that come with teaching Neo-Confucianism topically. The most obvious difficulty concerns how to enable students to keep track of different Neo-Confucian thinkers, especially at the beginning of the course when everything is new. For many students, not only will the ideas and philosophers be unfamiliar, but so will the basic history of the era, and these difficulties will be exacerbated by the need to keep straight a slew of Chinese names and terms. To some degree, the only solution to these problems is to encourage students to put extra effort into learning the basics (for example, with quizzes), but course design can also help out. Beginning with an overview of the history, some key ideas, and the most important few thinkers can be extremely productive; chapter 1 of this book is intended to provide some direction. As we note there, even though we do not endorse the common practice of dividing Neo-Confucians into two (or more) schools, we do think it is useful to track the "focus" of each individual's philosophy. By starting with just a few thinkers, roughly divided by dynasty and focus, students should be able to orient themselves sufficiently to get going.

The details of how, exactly, to implement topic-based instruction of Neo-Confucian philosophy will depend on the nature of the course. We have tended to teach full-semester courses on Neo-Confucianism, but others may be interested in semester-long courses on Buddhism and Neo-Confucianism or on the full Confucian tradition, or a shorter section on Neo-Confucianism within a course on Chinese (or East Asian) culture, or a section on the Neo-Confucian treatment of a given problem or topic within a broader course in comparative philosophy. All of these can work, and in addition to the suggested primary texts and discussion questions after each chapter, we offer sample syllabi and other teaching ideas at http:// neo-confucianism.com. We begin our full-semester courses with rapid reviews of classical Confucianism and of Chinese Buddhism; in other contexts, other approaches may be better. Finally, the website also allows us to post helpful ideas that others share with us, as well as to try to answer questions that arise both in the interpretation and the teaching of Neo-Confucianism. We welcome suggestions!

Appendix 2

Table of Neo-Confucians (by Date and Philosophical Emphasis)

Dynasty	Vital Stuff Emphasis or Other	Nature Emphasis	Heartmind Emphasis
Northern Song (960–1127)	OUYANG Xiu 歐陽修 (1007–1072)		
	SHAO Yong 邵雍 (1011–1077)		
	ZHOU Dunyi 周敦頤 (1017–1073)		
	SIMA GUANG 司馬光 (1019–1086)		
	ZHANG Zai 張載 (1020–1077)		
	WANG Anshi 王安石 (1021–1086)		
	CHENG Hao 程顥 (1032–1085)		
		CHENG Yi 程頤 (1033–1107)	
			SU Shi 蘇軾 (1037–1101)
Southern Song (1127–1279)			YANG Shi 楊時 (1053–1135)
			ZHANG Jiucheng 張九成 (1092–1159)
		HU Hong 胡宏 (1106–1161)	

Dynasty	Vital Stuff Emphasis or Other	Nature Emphasis	Heartmind Emphasis
Southern Song (1127–1279)		ZHU Xi 朱熹 (1130–1200)	
			LU Xiangshan 陸象山 (1139–1193)
	CHEN Liang 陳亮 (1143–1194)		
	YE Shi 葉適 (1150–1223)		
		CHEN Chun 陳淳 (1159–1223)	
Ming (1368–1644)		WU Yubi 吳與弼 (1392–1469)	
			CHEN Xianzhang 陳憲章 (1428–1500)
	LUO Qinshun 羅欽順 (1465–1547)		
			WANG Yangming 王陽明 (1472–1529)
	WANG Tingxiang 王廷相 (1474–1544)		
			WANG Ji 王畿 (1498–1583)
			LUO Rufang 羅汝芳 (1515–1588)
			LI Zhi 李贄 (1527–1602)
Qing (1644–1911)		HUANG Zongxi 黃宗羲 (1610–1695)	
	WANG Fuzhi 王夫之 (1619–1692)		
	DAI Zhen 戴震 (1724–1777)		
	LING Tingkan 凌廷堪 (1757–1809)		

Appendix 3

Abbreviations of Primary Sources

This appendix lists all the Chinese language primary sources we have used in this book, together with the specific modern edition of each source that we use when citing the text. The exact method of citation varies by text, depending on the organization of the edition we have chosen; whenever possible, we cite both the *juan* 卷 (roughly the same as a chapter) number and a page number.

BXZY – Chen Chun 陳淳, *Beixi Ziyi* 北溪子義 (*Neo-Confucian Terms Explained*). Cited as: *juan* number / page number from Chen 1983.

CXL – Wang Yangming 王陽明, *Chuanxi Lu* 傳習録 (*Record for Practice*). Cited as: passage number / page number in Wang 1992.

CY – Cheng Hao 程顥 and Cheng Yi 程頤, *Er Cheng Cuiyan* 二程粹言 (*The Pure Words of the Two Chengs*). Cited as: *juan* / page number from Cheng and Cheng 1981.

DX – *Da Xue* 大學 (*Greater Learning*). Cited as: passage number.

DXHW – Zhu Xi 朱熹, *Daxue Huowen* 大學或問 (*Questions on the Greater Learning*). Cited as: section number from *Greater Learning* / page number from Zhu 2002, vol. 6.

DXW – Wang Yangming 王陽明, *Daxue Wen* 大學問 (*Inquiries on the Great Learning*). Cited as: page number in Wang 1992.

DXZJ – Zhu Xi 朱熹, *Daxue Zhangju* 大學章句 (*Greater Learning in Chapters and Sentences*). Cited as: section number from *Greater Learning*.

FXS – Li Ao 李翱, *Fuxing Shu* 復性書 (*Letter on Returning to the Nature*). Cited as: *juan* / section number.

GW – Shao Yong 邵雍, *Huangji Jingshi Guanwu Waipian Yanyi* 皇極經世觀物外篇衍義 (*Extended Meanings of the Outer Chapter "On the Observation of Things," in the* Book of the August Ultimate through the Ages). Cited as: section number in Shao 1999.

HJYS – Zhang Zai 張載, *Hengju Yi Shuo* 横渠易說 (*Zhang Zai's Explanation of the Changes*). Cited as: page number from Zhang 1978.

HWDJ – Hu Hong 胡宏, *Huang Wang Daji* 皇王大紀 (*The Greater Chronicles of Emperors and Kings*). Cited as: page number in Hu 1987.

JSL – Zhu Xi 朱熹 and Lü Zuqian 呂祖謙 (eds), *Jinsi Lu* 近思錄 (*Reflections on Things at Hand*). Cited as: *juan* number. passage number from Zhu and Lü 2008.

JXLK – Zhang Zai 張載, *Jingxue Li Ku* 經學理窟 (*The Profundities of the Classics*). Cited as: page number from Zhang 1978.

KZJ – Luo Qinshun 羅欽順, *Kun Zhi Ji* 困知記 (*Knowledge Painfully Acquired*). Cited as: *juan* number / page number from Luo 1990.

LJ – *Li Ji* 禮記 (*Record of Rituals*). Cited as: chapter.

LY – *Lunyu* 論語 (*Analects* of Confucius). Cited as: book . passage.

LYJZ – Zhu Xi 朱熹, *Lunyu Jizhu* 論語集註 (*Collected Commentaries on the Analects*). Cited as: section number from *Analects*.

LZFS – Li Zhi 李贄, *Fenshu* 焚書 (*A Book to Burn*). Cited as: page number in Li 2009.

Mao – *Shi Jing* 詩經 (*Book of Odes*). Cited as: Mao number.

MC – *Mengzi* 孟子 (*Mencius*). Cited as: *juan* number A/B: section number.

MRXA – Huang Zongxi 黃宗羲 (ed.), *Mingru Xuean* 明儒學案 (*The Records of Ming Scholars*). Cited as: *juan* number / page number from Huang 1965.

MYDFL – Huang Zongxi 黃宗羲, *Mingyi Daifang Lu* 明夷待訪錄 (*Waiting for the Dawn*). Cited as: page number from Huang 2011.

MZHW – Zhu Xi 朱熹, *Mengzi Huowen* 孟子或問 (*Questions on the Mencius*). Cited as: *juan* / page number from Zhu 2002, vol. 6.

MZJZ – Zhu Xi 朱熹, *Mengzi Jizhu* 論語集註 (*Collected Commentaries on the Mencius*). Cited as: section number from *Mencius*.

MZZ – Zhang Jiucheng 張九成, *Mengzi Zhuan* 孟子傳 (*Commentaries on the Mencius*). Cited as: *juan* / page number in *Sibu congkan* 四部叢刊.

MZZYSZ – Dai Zhen 戴震, *Mengzi Ziyi Shuzheng* 孟子字義疏證 (*Evidential Analysis of the Meanings of Terms in the Mencius*). Cited as: *bian* . section number / page number from Dai 2009.

NJ – Ban Zhao 班昭, *Nüjie* 女誡 (*Lessons for Women*). Cited as: *ji* 輯 (anthologized chapter number) . page number a/b in Ban n.d.

NXJ – Zheng鄭 [personal name unknown], *Nü Xiaojing* 女孝經 (*Book of Filial Piety for Women*). Cited as *ji* 輯 (anthologized chapter number). page number a/b in Zheng n.d.

RL – Wu Yubi 吳與弼, *Rilu* 日錄 (*Journal*). Cited as: passage number / page number from Wu 2013.

SGSHDS – Hu Hong 胡宏, *Shang Guang Shun Huangdi Shu* 上光舜皇帝書 (*A Book that Brings Out the Luster of Emperors Shun and Huang*). Cited as: page number in Hu 1987.

T – *Taishō shinshū dai zōkyō* 大正新脩大藏經 (*Taishō Tripiṭaka*). Cited according to Taishō numbers in http://cbeta.org.

TJTS – Zhou Dunyi 周敦頤, *Taiji Tushuo* 太極圖說 (*Explanation of the Diagram of the Supreme Pivot*). Cited as: page number from Zhou 1990.

TS – Zhou Dunyi 周敦頤, *Tongshu* 通書 (*Penetrating the Book of Changes*). Cited as: section number / page number from Zhou 1990.

WJ – Zhu Xi 朱熹, *Zhu Wengong Wenji* 朱文公文集 (*Collected Writings of Zhu Xi*). Cited as: *juan* number / page number from Zhu 2002.

WL – Wang Yangming 王陽明, *Wenlu* 文錄 (*Collected Writings*). Cited as: *juan* number / page number in Wang 1992.

WWJ – Wang Yangming 王陽明, *Waiji* 外集 (*Additional Writings*). Cited as: *juan* number / page number in Wang 1992.

XJSL – Zhu Xi 朱熹, *Xu Jinsi Lu* 續近思錄 (*Further Reflections on Things at Hand*). Cited as: *juan* . passage number from Zhu 1991 / page number from Zhu 1974.

XSYL – Lu Xiangshan 陸象山, *Xiangshan Yulu* 象山語錄 (*Lu Xiangshan's Recorded Sayings*). Cited as: *juan* / page number from Lu 1980.

XZ – *Xunzi* 荀子. Cited as: *pian* number / page number in Xunzi 1979.

YJXC – *Xici Zhuan* 繫辭傳 (*Great Commentary to the Book of Changes*). Cited as: passage number.

YL – Zhu Xi 朱熹, *Zhuzi Yulei* 朱子語類 (*Classified Conversations of Master Zhu*). Cited as: *juan* number / page number from Zhu 2002.

YS – Cheng Hao 程顥 and Cheng Yi 程頤, *Henan Chengshi Yishu* 河南程氏遺書 (*The Extant Works of the Chengs of Henan*). Cited as *juan* number / page number from Cheng and Cheng 1981.

YSDZ – Dai Zhen 戴震, *Yuanshan* 原善 (*On Goodness*). Cited as: part . section number / page number from Dai 2009.

ZM – Zhang Zai 張載, *Zheng Meng* 正蒙 (*Correcting the Unenlightened*). Cited as: *juan* number / page number from Zhang 1978.

ZY – *Zhong Yong* 中庸 (*Centrality and Commonality*). Cited as: passage number.

ZYHH – Hu Hong 胡宏, *Zhiyan* 知言 (*Understanding Words*). Cited as: passage number / page number from Hu 1987.

ZYHW – Zhu Xi 朱熹, *Zhongyong Huowen* 中庸或問 (*Questions on Centrality and Commonality*). Cited as: *juan* / page number from Zhu 2002, vol. 6.

ZYS – Zhang Jiucheng 張九成, *Zhong Yong Shuo* 中庸說 (*Explaining Centrality and Commonality*). Cited as: *juan* / page number from *Sibu congkan* 四部叢刊.

ZYZJ – Zhu Xi 朱熹, *Zhongyong Zhangju* 大學章句 (*Centrality and Commonality in Chapters and Sentences*). Cited as: section number from *Centrality and Commonality*.

ZZYL – Zhang Zai 張載, *Zhangzi Yulu* 張子語錄 (*Recorded Sayings of Master Zhang*). Cited as: page number from Zhang 1978.

Notes

Chapter 1   Introduction

1   In a series of essays beginning with Tillman 1992, Tillman has argued
    against the use of "Neo-Confucianism" and for the use of terms that are
    more historically precise. As others have pointed out, though, Tillman
    himself recognizes that in order to speak broadly across multiple dynas-
    ties, no single native term will suffice. See de Bary 1993 and Makeham
    2010: xii.

2   The leading anglophone historians of Song dynasty Daoxue include
    Hoyt Tillman and Peter Bol. Tillman 2015 is a good summary of the
    development of Daoxue, and see also the other scholarship cited there.
    Bol 1992, Bol 2015, and especially Bol 2008 offer broader narratives
    explaining the emergence of Neo-Confucianism in general, and Daoxue
    in particular (as we use those terms).

3   Ditmanson 1998, Kim 2001, and Bol 2008 provide complementary
    perspectives on the question of Daoxue in the Ming. See CXL 257/104
    for Wang's rejection of Daoxue.

4   In particular, we include ZHANG Zai within Daoxue, although this is
    strictly speaking an anachronism. See Ong 2005 and the "Appendix on
    Zhang and the Cheng brothers" in Kasoff 1984.

5   For an illustrative study emphasizing the role of genealogy, see Dit-
    manson 1998.

6   The two-way division into Cheng–Zhu and Lu–Wang schools is most
    common, but scholars have employed others divisions as well. One
    popular option is to add a third school, "vital stuff learning" (*qixue*),
    which is made up of Neo-Confucians who emphasize the idea of *qi* (the
    "vital stuff" that makes up the cosmos; see chapter 2). We agree that
    calling attention to the philosophers who stress vital stuff can be useful

(and say more about this later in this chapter) but deny that there was such a "school." Another well-known tripartite distinction derives from the work of the modern Confucian MOU Zongsan (1909–1995). Mou challenges the formulation of Daoxue genealogy championed by ZHU Xi and his later followers and puts in its place an alternative understanding of Daoxue orthodoxy. We are sympathetic to Mou's resistance to the standard view – recall that we ourselves prefer a looser version of "Daoxue" than the narrow orthodoxy of the thirteenth century and thereafter – but we find Mou's alternative to be unconvincing. For helpful discussion, see Chan 2011: 221–3.

7   Lu was one of ZHU Xi's rivals, and near the end of WANG Yangming's (much later) life, he came to see some resemblances between his teachings and those of Lu. But this never led to a "Lu–Wang" school. In a narrow sense it is possible to talk about ZHU Xi and LU Xiangshan schools since each man had students (who in turn taught more students). For Lu's students and influences, see Walton 2010, Lo 1974, and Huang 1995. In their day, Zhu and Lu sought to take Daoxue in somewhat different directions, as can be seen from Lu's remark that if Zhu's circle continues to use "Daoxue" as they were, "those who use the expression *daoxue* will be profoundly rejected and vigorously censured" (Tillman 2015: 761). However, the differences between Lu and Zhu should not be exaggerated and, in any event, Lu's "school" did not carry on into later dynasties. The lengths to which LI Fu (1675–1750) went to invent a Lu school lineage testify to its nonexistence. See Huang 1995. In addition, it is problematic to associate "heartmind learning" too narrowly with Lu, Wang, and their various followers, both because an emphasis on the heartmind antedates Lu and because the heartmind is an important idea in the thought of both Chengs, ZHU Xi, and many others. For a strong statement of the latter position, see de Bary 1989. Starting in the seventeenth century, there are occasional mentions of "Lu–Wang" (based on the influence of WANG Yangming, and on his recognition of similarities with Lu), but according to de Bary 1989: 223, the earliest division of Neo-Confucianism into the two schools of "Cheng–Zhu Pattern learning" and "Lu–Wang heartmind learning" seems to have been volume two of FENG Youlan's seminal work on the history of Chinese philosophy (Fung 1953).

8   This is not to say that there were no related distinctions. We mention below the divide between *wen* (culture) and *dao* (Way), and Neo-Confucians also distinguished "the learning of norms and Patterns (*yili zhi xue* 義理之學)" from philological or empirical studies (Elman 2001: 46, 56–62).

9   The best work on the emergence of the category of "Chinese philosophy" is Makeham 2012.

10 Admittedly, as Fabien Heubel has stressed to us in conversation, there are no purely pre-existing, unchanging categories. Terms like "autonomy" (and its Chinese correlate, *zilü* 自律) were adopted and adapted by modern Chinese thinkers for their own purposes, based on their own

discourse contexts, rather than simply being straitjacketed by earlier meanings. We entirely agree with this point – indeed, Angle argues for a similar approach to understanding Chinese rights discourse in Angle 2002 – but we must distinguish between understanding what the modern thinkers are saying in their own right, and the interpretive claims that the modern thinkers are making about Neo-Confucianism. That is, we can agree that FENG Youlan or MOU Zongsan can creatively adapt "rationalism" or "autonomy" to develop their own ideas in their own context, but still disagree that it is fruitful to ask, of a given Neo-Confucian thinker, whether his view is autonomous or heteronomous. To ask such a question is to assume that such a distinction is important and meaningful in the context of Neo-Confucianism.

11 The classic book on this subject is Hadot 1995. Books that explicitly emphasize this dimension of Chinese philosophy include Stalnaker 2006 and Angle 2009.

12 Theories about language are not a major part of Neo-Confucian thinking, but this is not to say that they had nothing to say on the subject. For some stimulating preliminary work on the topic, see Van Zoeren 1991.

13 See Wilson 1995.

14 See Taylor 1990. Most modern scholars are more skeptical about what role, if any, Confucius may have played in the formulation of the classics. Even the extent of his authorship of the *Analects* has been questioned (Brooks and Brooks 1998).

15 So argue Taylor 1990 and Adler 2004, and see Streng 1985. In her "Introduction" to the two-volume collection *Confucian Spirituality*, Mary Evelyn Tucker is somewhat coy about whether Confucianism is a religion, seeing this question as too often distracting us from the real issue of the nature of Confucian religiosity or spirituality, but she adds in a footnote that Streng's definition does indeed apply (Tucker 2003: 27n4). Another important scholarly perspective on Confucian religiosity is that of theologian and philosopher Robert Neville; he sets out three criteria for a religious tradition – it must have a cosmology, a body of rituals, and a path of spiritual perfection – and argues that Confucianism has all three (Neville 1990).

16 Adler 2004: 141; emphasis in original.

17 See Makeham unpublished.

18 See Bol 2008: ch. 1.

19 See Hartman 1986 and Barrett 1992.

20 See Bol 2008: 31–9.

21 We take the term "conventional Confucians" (for *shi ru* 世儒) from Tillman 2015.

22 For more on the "Daoxue style," see Borrell (unpublished).

23 See Bol 2008: 15f. on the north versus south distinction. Khee Heong KOH 2011 examines the neglected topic of Neo-Confucianism in the north, focusing on an important northern thinker from the Ming dynasty.

24 See, in particular, Tillman 1992.

25 See Ditmanson 1998 and Tillman 2015.
26 See de Bary 1981: 20–7, on the religious zeal of the Daoxue group to save China and restore the Way, which led them to work with (and try to educate) the Mongol rulers.
27 Ditmanson 1998: 10–11.
28 See Dardess 1983.
29 See Bol 2008: 145–9.
30 See, among other works in English, Kalton et al. 1994 and de Bary and Haboush 1985.
31 An excellent place to start on Japanese Neo-Confucianism is Huang and Tucker 2014.
32 These issues are explored in Woodside 2002 and Taylor 2002.
33 See Huang 1995: 160.
34 For some exceptions to this generalization, see Ng 2001.

Chapter 2   Pattern and Vital Stuff

1 Other translations include "ether," "material force," "matter energy," and "psycho-physical stuff."
2 Other translations include "principle" and "coherence."
3 All three passages come from YJXC A.
4 This is not to imply that early China had no creation myths. There were some, but they were not central to the widespread way of thinking that we are sketching here. See Goldin 2008.
5 "Concrete object" is our translation of *qi* 器, a homonym with the word *qi* 氣 ("vital stuff") that we mentioned above.
6 Other good examples of stage one include the ideas of "nature" in the *Mencius* (on which see our next chapter), "nonbeing" (*wu* 無) in the *Daode Jing*, and "pattern," "order," or "coherence" (*li* 理) in texts like the *Xunzi* and *Record of Music*.
7 For examples, see the discussion of WANG Bi and GUO Xiang in Ziporyn 2013, and of WANG Bi in Makeham 2003b: 45–6.
8 See Gregory 2002.
9 For a concise history of the development of theories of vital stuff, see Wang and Ding 2010: 42–5.
10 *Huainanzi* 3; cf. Zhang 2002: 50.
11 See Needham et al. 2000.
12 For other discussions of Zhang's "supreme void" that we have found helpful, see Kasoff 1984, Wang and Ding 2010, and Ziporyn 2015.
13 Zhang argues that the void cannot be a boundless nothingness separate from vital stuff: "If we say that the void can produce vital stuff, then the void is infinite while vital stuff is limited, inherent reality and function are split apart, and you fall into Laozi's doctrine of spontaneity, which says that being is produced from non-being" ZM 1/8; cf. Kasoff 1984: 39.

14 ZM 1/7; cf. Kasoff 1984: 37.
15 ZM 1/7; cf. Kasoff 1984: 37.
16 ZM 1/8; cf. Kasoff, 1984: 40.
17 ZM 1/7.
18 ZM 17/63; cf. Ziporyn 2015.
19 ZM 17/63; cf. Ziporyn 2015. Zhang also often uses the first two hexa-grams of the *Book of Changes*, *qian* (乾) and *kun* (坤), to symbolize the same polarity.
20 See Kim 2015 for a sustained argument that Zhang's idea of *qi* (which Kim translates as "vital energy") must be understood through categories like polarity and organic unity, rather than as a "substance monism." We believe our understanding to be quite compatible with Kim's.
21 See MC 2A:2, and *Huangdi Neijing*.
22 ZM 1/9.
23 The same goes for the pair of "bright" (*ming* 明) and "dark" (*hun* 昏): we can find passages that are somewhat ambiguous, but dark vital stuff is not a definite source of human badness.
24 YS 22/291–2.
25 Other influential Neo-Confucian theorists of vital stuff include Luo Qinshun (Luo 1987) and Wang Fuzhi (JeeLoo Liu 2010), and, in Japan, Kaibara Ekken (Kaibara 2007).
26 Ziporyn 2013: 21.
27 See Angle 2009: 34 and Ziporyn 2013: 27–8.
28 See Ziporyn 2013: 50.
29 The related verbal use continues as well: the Explanation of Trigrams (*Shuo Gua*) essay attached to the *Book of Changes* uses it twice in the sense of "clarify" or "discriminate," which sense we can still see in modern Chinese words like *lijie* (to understand).
30 See Gregory 2002: 6–7n8.
31 In fact, the Buddhist position was more complicated than this cursory description suggests. Many Buddhists proposed that the phenomenal side of human experience should carry ontological weight as well, so long as it was understood in the right way. Often Buddhists depicted the reality of a thing's Pattern and the reality of its phenomena as two sides of the same coin. For example, Huayan Buddhists tended to say that phenomena were real insofar as they were unified into a larger whole, and it was Pattern that accounted for their unity.
32 YL 62/2024.
33 Fuji 2011: 159.
34 YL 18/607.
35 YL 6/237.
36 YL 6/237.
37 YL 18/619.
38 CY 1/1202–03. The word we translate as "particularizations" is "*fèn* 分" in Chinese; its range of meaning includes allotment, part (of a whole), role, and allocated duty. It has a homonym written with the same character ("*fēn* 分") which means things like division or to divide.

Wing-tsit CHAN has emphasized that in the present context, the character must be read in the former way, as *fèn*, rather than in the latter way, because CHENG Yi does not mean to say that Pattern is divided, but only that it is particularized or manifested in different ways in different contexts (Chan 1989: 299). In contrast, each of the three passages quoted in our prior paragraph use this same character, but in its latter sense (*"fēn* 分"), which we translate as "distinguish" and "divide." The point here is not that Pattern itself is divided, but that we humans can analytically divide it up in various ways as suits different contexts, which in fact helps us to understand that it is actually unified.

39   Wood 1995 has a useful comparison between Pattern and medieval European ideas of natural law.

40   See Ziporyn 2013: 259.

41   For example, CHENG Yi says, "There is nothing in the world more substantial than Pattern" YS 3/66.

42   YS 1/3; cf. Graham 1992: 89.

43   YJXC A.

44   This idea explains why the Neo-Confucians thought it a special problem to determine whether and how dead things ("dry and withered things") could have their own Pattern; see YL 4/189.

45   For example, CHENG Yi writes that "The Way spontaneously generates life without end" (YS 15/149). Although most human behavior lacks the quality of effortlessness and spontaneity that we witness in the cosmos, ease and spontaneity are often treated by Neo-Confucians as markers of superb moral character or sagehood; see chapter 8 and Angle 2009.

46   Mao #192.

47   For example, see CHENG Yi's comment: YS 3/59.

48   Kim 2008: 116. See also Ong 2006: 482.

49   YSDZ A.1/156–7; cf. Dai 1971: 67.

50   Graham 1992: 29.

51   See Ziporyn 2000: 30–41. Ziporyn is particularly interested in Tiantai Buddhist holisms which deny that there is any one, privileged center, but his insights are still quite relevant, and see also Ziporyn 2013: 321–44.

52   There may well be specific situations in which it is the Pattern of a specific boat to sink even from an impartial, life-embracing perspective: perhaps some cargo on board has become infected with a terrible virus, and the only safe way to end the threat is by sinking the boat.

53   ZM 2/12; and see also LUO Qinshun's invocation of this passage, KZJ B/38; cf. Luo 1987: 128–9.

54   JeeLoo LIU 2010: 359.

55   HJYS 206; cf. Kasoff 1984: 141. The eighteenth-century Neo-Confucian DAI Zhen supported a similar position when he argued that the expression "formless" was better understood as something like "prior to forming" stable and distinct entities, thus describing vital stuff in

an amorphous and ethereal state. MZZYSZ B.17/287–8; cf. Dai 1990: 212–16.

56 YS 15/160.
57 See Wong 2010.
58 KZJ C 68; KJZ A 5; cf. Luo 1987: 173, 59.
59 JeeLoo Liu 2010: 361–2.
60 MZZYSZ A.15/282–6; cf. Dai 1990: 190–203.
61 Kim 2000: 37.
62 Van Norden helpfully describes these functions as "speciation" and "individuation" in Tiwald and Van Norden 2014: 174.
63 YL 1/115–16; cf. Zhu 1990: 92.
64 YL 1/115.
65 See the various positions of Krummel 2010: 424, Adler 2015: 53, and Kim 2000: 37–8.
66 YL 17/585.
67 Modern interpreters of Neo-Confucianism have extensively debated the best way to characterize the kind of priority that Pattern has to vital stuff, according to Zhu Xi. Our view bears relations to those of scholars arguing for "logical priority," such as Feng Youlan (Fung 1953: 545) and Chen Lai (Chen 2000: ch. 3). The kind of inference picked out by Zhu's choice of word, *tui* 推, refers especially to inferences that (a) trace the basis or foundations (*ben* 本) of things, and (b) appeal to similarities between things (as when he shows how benevolent love is analogous to the season of spring in certain respects). Most likely, Zhu has in mind a sense of inference that combines both (a) and (b), where we use analogical similarities to explain how some important notion or thing is based in something more fundamental. Zhu sometimes characterizes Pattern as prior when talking about things (and presumably explaining them) in terms of their basis (*ben*) or origins (*yuan* 原) (YL 1/115–16). This again affirms that it is not just any sort of inference that makes it prior, but the sort of inference that reveals the grounds or basis of things. For more on analogical inference, as well as the similar ideas at play in Zhu's conception of Type Three knowing, see chapter 6.
68 On Pattern manifesting the "four beginnings," see chapter 5. We thank Shen Hsiang-min for suggesting "pervasively circulates" as a translation of *liuxing*.
69 YL 1/112. There is a tradition in Chinese philosophy of using of the expression "master" (*zhuzai* 主宰, also "host" or "ruler") to describe something important that stands behind the cosmic order. This tradition often treats the mastery as having a problematic causal status. For the early Daoists, the Dao itself was considered to have a kind of agency that was difficult to characterize, seen from one side as though there were some power or person orchestrating things, but from another side as a bunch of individuals that happen to work in concord. In a memorable passage in the *Zhuangzi*, the author extends this puzzlement to the agency of the self, which "seems to have a master" (*zai*) even though we can only find an array of organs, senses, and desires. See

Zhuangzi 2. As we will see below, ZHU Xi also describes the operations of Pattern as like the pivot, which doesn't budge and yet regulates the movements of the wheel to which it is attached. This too recalls the *Zhuangzi*'s description of the Way.

70   For example, at YL 94/3128–9.
71   Most famously in the "Four-Seven Debate" in Korean Neo-Confucianism. See Kalton 1994 and Lee 2005.
72   YL 1/114.
73   YL 4/200.
74   For a thought-provoking look at the way that the cosmos can constrain or nudge us, see the pendulum model in Ziporyn 2013: 7–15.
75   See Graham 1992: 12 (speaking here of CHENG Yi).
76   *Tianming* is often translated as "mandate of Heaven."
77   For example, "*tiandi* 天地" is "heaven-and-earth"; and "*tianxia* 天下" is "all-under-heaven."
78   BXZY A/1; cf. Chen 1986: 37.
79   Graham 1992: 23–4.
80   JSL 7.23–4/286–7; cf. Zhu and Lü 1967: 192–3.
81   A. C. Graham traces this way of conceiving *tian*'s decree to the Cheng brothers: "The great innovation of the [Chengs] ... is the elevation of [Pattern] to the place formerly occupied by heaven; and this involves treating 'heaven' and its 'decree,' as well as the 'Way,' as merely names for different aspects of [Pattern]. One of the main functions of the terms 'heaven' and 'decree' had been to indicate what is objectively given, independent of human action and desire" (Graham 1992: 23). And see Berthrong 2010: 167–8.
82   The Neo-Confucians occasionally invoke the binome "decreed allotment" (*mingfen* 命分) to spell out this sense of "decree." See BXZY A/1–2; cf. Chen 1986: 37–8. John Berthrong discusses the tension between the two senses of decree (Pattern-based and vital stuff-based) in an essay on ZHU Xi's cosmology, showing that Zhu was aware of the tension and found it a useful way to instruct students on the peculiar relationship between Pattern and vital stuff (Berthrong 2010: 166–8).
83   An older translation of *taiji* is "great ultimate," and it has also been translated as "supreme polarity."
84   TJTS; cf. Adler 2015: 52–3.
85   Although this is the only diagram that we will examine in this book, it is worth noting that Neo-Confucians often employed diagrams as they sought to explain and systematize their more abstract ideas. For a number of fascinating examples from Korean Neo-Confucianism, see Kalton 1988.
86   Adler 2015 argues persuasively and at length for this understanding. Zhou's conception of the supreme pivot bears comparison to ZHANG Zai's supreme void: both are intended to explain the possibility of change.
87   Adler 2015. Adler himself translates *wuji* as "Non-polar," which makes sense if one renders *taiji* as "supreme polarity," as he does. However,

as we explain in the main text, *ji* ("pivot") is itself singular, even though as changeability it enables duality. "Supreme pivot" captures this meaning nicely. We feel that "pivotless" (as in "Pivotless, yet the Supreme pivot") is too cryptic, though, so we render *wuji* a bit more loosely as "nondual."

88 Adler 2015: 61 provides helpful discussion and several relevant quotations.

89 For an early and influential statement of this interpretation, see Chan 1987.

90 Ong 2006: 468–9. This view bears comparison to LUO Qinshun's somewhat deflationary view of Pattern, discussed above, according to which Pattern is only the "pattern of vital stuff," and cannot be discussed independently.

91 MZZYSZ B.18/288–9; cf. Dai 1990: 219–21.

92 We thank John Makeham for the point that *ti* is simply shorthand for *benti*. Another common translation of *ti* is "substance," but we feel that this suggests too strongly that *ti* is the stuff out of which something is made. Stuff, though, is *qi* (vital stuff), whereas *ti* is *li* (Pattern).

93 ZM 6/21.

Chapter 3 Nature

1 MC 6A:2.

2 MC 2A:6.

3 MC 7A:1. *Centrality and Commonality* opens with these lines: "What the cosmos decrees is called 'the nature'; complying with nature is called 'the Way'; cultivating the Way is called 'teaching.'" (ZY 1). We will discuss these lines further below; see section 2.

4 The rival is Gaozi; see MC 6A:3 and 4.

5 MC 6A:6.

6 The idea of Buddha nature (though not the term "Buddha nature," which seems to be a Chinese invention) has roots in certain Indian Buddhist doctrines, though these ideas were not particularly prominent aspects of Indian Buddhism. As Buddhism gradually adapted to and grew in Chinese soil, the notion of Buddha nature took on increasing importance. Part of the reason for this is undoubtedly the prominence that debates about "nature" already had within Chinese intellectual and spiritual discourse. In the sixth century, a philosophical treatise on the subject was produced in China, allegedly translated from Sanskrit, even though no evidence of a Sanskrit original has been found (*On Buddha Nature* [*Foxing Lun*], on which see King 1991). The same "translator" produced a treatise called *The Awakening of Faith* which is also said to be a translation of an Indian original; again, no Sanskrit version exists, but *Awakening of Faith*, with its central emphasis on Buddha nature and related ideas, went on to be one of the most influential Buddhist texts in China. See Hakeda 2006.

7 Gregory 2002: 251.
8 See Han 1968.
9 ZY 1; cf. Johnston and Wang 2012: 407.
10 ZYZJ 1; cf. Johnston and Wang 2012: 411.
11 Several passages in YL 4 make this point, and see also Fuji's discussion of this metaphor (2011: 73–4).
12 YL 4/192–3, cited and discussed in Fuji 2011: 71–4. As Fuji notes, there is a degree to which one consciously takes up one's role, but the responsibilities are there whether the minister recognizes them or not.
13 ZHU Xi makes the directionality of our nature more explicit than most Daoxue thinkers, but we can see similar ideas in others as well. For example, ZHANG Zai's "nature" has a definite "direction," and Kasoff argues convincingly that it is "good" (Kasoff 1984: 70).
14 Here we focus on Zhu Xi's use of the metaphor of "centered" nature, but many Daoxue thinkers connect nature with being centered, and this connection can even be found in LI Ao, the Tang dynasty anticipator of many Neo-Confucian ideas. See Bol 1992: 137–40.
15 YL 62/2037; cf. Fuji 2011: 76.
16 *Tiaoli* 條理, also translatable as "order" or "organization."
17 WJ 58/2779; cf. Graham 1986: 432.
18 Zhu is contrasting this position with that which he finds in Buddhism, whose doctrine of emptiness he understands as implying that the nature has no structure: it is "homogenous," providing no guidance. As a result, without a distinction between the everyday flow of desires, on the one hand, and the Way, on the other, one "falls into the Buddhists' mistake of seeing all functioning whatsoever as the nature" (ZYHW A/557; cf. Araki 2008: 284). As Ziporyn has emphasized (and as we noted in chapter 2), when operating within a holistic metaphysic of interdependence (as both Buddhists and Neo-Confucians are doing, in their own ways), a center provides the orientation that gives each aspect of the whole a distinct meaning. In the radical holism of at least some Buddhists, the center can be anything, making the identity of any single aspect of the whole indeterminate or, at best, provisional (Ziporyn 2000).
19 MC 2A:6.
20 MZJZ 2A:6; most interpreters believe that Zhu's understanding of *duan* is quite different from that intended by Mencius himself; see Ivanhoe 2002: 105.
21 WJ 58/2779; cf. Graham 1986: 433. Notwithstanding his many differences from Zhu, as we will discuss in time, the Ming dynasty thinker WANG Yangming has a similar view on our ability to infer from – as he puts it – the "function" of our heartminds to their "inherent reality" (see chapter 2 for these categories): WL 4/146–47; cf. Wang 1972: 11–12.
22 In his commentary on the assertion in MC 7A:4 that "The myriad things are complete in me," ZHU Xi says that the heartmind is that "which possesses the myriad Patterns and which responds to the myriad affairs."

23 An examples of an interpretation that leans in the direction of pre-existing, individual Patterns is Fuji 2011: 133n19, where Fuji says that what Zhu means by saying the heartmind possesses the myriad Patterns is that "the heartmind knows *a priori* all of the principles, essences, and truths in the world; in other words, the heartmind possess complete 'knowledge.' "

24 It may be relevant that in a famous discussion of the Tiantai Buddhist idea of "inherent possession in the nature," the monk Guangding explicitly denies that this doctrine – according to which the heartmind includes all dharmas – should be understood on the model of individual grains of sand stored in a sack (Ziporyn 2000: 162).

25 WJ 58/2779; cf. Graham 1986: 432.

26 This is explicitly stated at the beginning of the same letter (WJ 58/2778).

27 See also our discussion in chapter 6 of the way that Pattern becomes live to us through the active knowing process. Also related is Ziporyn's argument that ZHU Xi distinguishes a metaphysical sense in which Pattern pre-exists vital stuff, and a psychological sense in which it does not. See Ziporyn forthcoming.

28 ZHU Xi suggested that HAN Yu confused the good, inherent nature with our actual physical constitutions; and if we are talking about the latter, he says, why just have three types – why not one thousand varieties? (WJ 44; see discussion in Araki 2008: 297). Hartman recognizes this deficiency, although by drawing on sources other than just HAN Yu's "On the Nature," he is able to argue with some plausibility that HAN Yu's considered position may have been closer to his contemporary LI Ao's view, which in several ways anticipates the Daoxue view (Hartman 1986: 205–9).

29 SIMA Guang (1019–1086) is a good example; see Graham 1986: 45.

30 Examples might include SU Xun and SU Shi. See Bol 1992: ch. 8.

31 GW 8; cf. Bol 1992: 279.

32 See *Daode Jing* 1, 2, and 25, among others.

33 According to the "Great Appendix" of the *Book of Changes*, "The alteration of *yin* and *yang* is called 'the Way.' What succeeds it is goodness; what completes it is the nature" (YJXC 7a/147; cf. Graham 1986: 134–5).

34 Araki 2008: 317n105.

35 From Mingjiao Qisong (1007–1072); quoted in Araki 2008: 317n105.

36 HHJ 333; cf. also the discussion and translation of this passage in Van Ess 2010: 114 and in Chen 2003: 118–20.

37 See HHJ 330 and 333, as well as discussion in Tillman 1992: 65–9.

38 YL 101/3395.

39 HHJ 1 and 3.

40 ZYHH 11.5/29.

41 CXL 315/117; cf. Wang 1963: 243 and Shun 2011: 105. "Getting a handle on things" is our translation of *gewu*, which we take from Tiwald and Van Norden 2014. For more on this concept, an older translation for which is "investigation of things," see chapters 6 and 7.

42   CXL 315/117; cf. Wang 1963: 244.
43   CXL 3/2, 4/3, 91/25, 92/25, 318/120. He also says that cosmic Pattern is completely good, which makes sense, given his repeated insistence that "heartmind is Pattern" (CXL 3/2, 4/3), which we discuss in chapter 4.
44   CXL 290/111, 162/66. Araki 2008: 443–4 is outstanding in his analysis of this point.
45   CXL 139/49; see also discussion in Angle 2009: 124–5.
46   We are still left with the question of what to make of WANG Yangming's agreement with WANG Ji that there is a sense in which all four categories can transcend the dichotomy of good and bad. Considerable evidence suggests that for both Yangming and WANG Ji, reference to "intentions" and "knowing" that are "without good and bad" is not meant to indicate morally neutral or morally inert functioning of the heartmind, but instead – very much on the same model as with the discussion in the main text – functioning that is spontaneous and correct, rather than consciously directed or biased (Araki 2008: 442–5). Peng's detailed discussion of WANG Ji's "four withouts" ("the heartmind without a heartmind," "knowing without knowing," "intentions without intending," and "things without things") certainly agrees that these categories are not meant to be morally neutral, but also argues that WANG Ji's discussion of the "four withouts" enables him to bring out more fully than does WANG Yangming a distinct, non-empirical functioning of the heartmind that bears comparison to Kant's notion of "intellectual intuition" (Peng 2005: ch. 4; see esp. 187).
47   Another common term is "endowment" (cai). Zhang and the Chengs use it to speak about our actual raw material, which could be good or bad. Cai can also mean "talent," and while CHENG Yi sometimes uses it this way – as when he says that learning is not about the development of talents of memorization or other skills, but instead about the gradual cultivation of virtuous dispositions – he elsewhere makes it explicit that cai should really be used to refer to one's overall endowment or dispositions (zizhi 資質) (YS 22a/292). In a similar fashion, some of ZHANG Zai's uses of cai focus on its positive dimensions, but his underlying view is clearly that cai or endowment can be problematic. ZHANG Zai's view of the cai as potentially problematic is particularly clear when he says, "The fact that [positive] human emotions are not [firmly] established is not the fault of one's endowment [cai]" (JXLK 267). In other words, the fact that one is weak of character and too often fails to respond with healthy, ethically apt emotions, cannot be blamed on one's endowment: it is the fault of one's lack of commitment to learning, which could ultimately transform one's dispositions.
48   We are influenced here by Moran's extensive analysis in Moran 1983. Here is a relevant passage from ZHANG Zai: "Qizhi is like what people call innate qi. This qi has the varieties of rigid, yielding, slow, fast, pure, and turbid. Zhi is endowment. Qizhi is a single thing, just as the life of plants or trees can also be called qizhi. Only the ability to overcome

oneself can be called the ability to change. Transforming the habitual *qi*-nature and restraining the habitual *qi*: these are how flood-like *qi* is to be nurtured through the accumulation of right [actions]." JXLK 281; cf. Moran 1983: 262–3.

49 See Moran 1983.
50 MZHW 3/934; for discussion, see Fuji 2011: 70.
51 Kim 2000: 194–5.
52 LY 17:2. "Nature" is also mentioned in LY 5:13, but only in the context of being told that the Master's students could not get to hear his views on "nature."
53 MC 6A:3.
54 YS 24/313; cf. Graham 1992: 49.
55 From the classic *Record of Music*, referring to the nature given us by the cosmos. LJ 19/7.
56 "Following [the Way] is good" is from the *Book of Changes* and is followed by "what completes it is the nature." YJ 7/147.
57 For this analogy, see MC 6A2.
58 YS 1/10–11; cf. Graham 1992: 131–2.
59 Luo Qinshun is one example: see KZJ A 7–8; cf. Luo 1987: 65–7.
60 See JXLK 282. Zhang is here alluding to MC 7B:24. See also the discussion at Kasoff 1984: 72–6, although Kasoff accords the "nature of *qizhi*" more weight, relative to *qizhi* itself, than we think appropriate.
61 WJ 61; see also the discussion in Araki 2008: 298.
62 Zhu's view on this issue develops over time; see Moran 1983: 273–5.
63 YL 4/195.
64 YL 4/196. "The nature of heaven and earth," like "the cosmic decree is what is meant by 'nature,'" refers to inherent nature.
65 MC 2:A6, 7:A15.
66 See Ivanhoe 2000a: 17–22.
67 MZZYSZ B.27/302; cf. Dai 1990: 284–5.
68 See Tiwald 2010.
69 MZZYSZ B.27/302–3; cf. Dai 1990: 284–6.
70 See Cheng 1991: 504–36 and JeeLoo Liu 2010: 364–7.

Chapter 4   Heartmind

1 YS 21b/274; YL 126/3939; cf. Chan 1963: 649.
2 XZ 22/527; cf. Xunzi 2014: 22.275–300, pp. 243–44. Van Norden 2000 calls attention to Xunzi's use of *ke* as a technical term for a power of approval that can override (and ultimately reshape) desires, though this interpretation is disputed in Wong 2000. For more on the adaptability of the heartmind for Xunzi, see Ivanhoe 2000b, which compares Xunzi's views on the acquisition of moral knowledge to a language empiricist's views on the acquisition of language.
3 In our view, Confucius himself understood the function of the heartmind in ways that closely resemble Xunzi's account. Like Xunzi, he did

not appear to think of the heartmind as a source of norms, and like Xunzi he nevertheless thought the heartmind was highly adaptable, so that eventually one's every desire could be in step with the Way (LY 1.15, 2.4, 12.1). Most Neo-Confucians disagreed with this reading of Confucius and instead saw his view as consistent with that of Mencius, who, as we will see, thought the heartmind's natural character was more in accord with moral norms.

4 See Makeham 2003b: 287–95 and Tiwald 2016.
5 Tiwald 2016.
6 YL 126/3932.
7 A particularly important view of this type is found in the highly influential (but admittedly terse and thus contested) *Discourse on the Awakening of Faith*. See especially the opening of Part 3: T 32n1666.0576a03; cf. Hakeda 2006: 38.
8 YS 21b/274.
9 YL 126/3939.
10 To adapt a metaphor from DAI Zhen discussed in chapter 3. See MZZYSZ B.27/302 and C.29/307-08; cf. Dai 1990: 284–5 and 304–5.
11 As we saw in our discussion of Mencius on human nature in chapter 3.
12 YS 18/204.
13 YS 5/76. CHENG Yi's statements about the heartmind's identity with nature and Pattern sound strikingly like the famous slogan "heartmind is Pattern (*xin ji li* 心即理)" that historians have long associated with LU Xiangshan and WANG Yangming, and often take to mark a definitive break from the philosophy of CHENG Yi and ZHU Xi. It is indeed true that Lu and Wang hold versions of this view, and that ZHU Xi finds much that is objectionable in Lu's attempts to identify heartmind and Pattern. But the historical Daoxue thinkers do not divide as neatly as the conventional account suggests. As we see here, CHENG Yi embraces a version of the view that heartmind is Pattern, even if it is not entirely clear how he reconciles this with the rest of his thought (see below in the main text). Furthermore, recent scholarship has shown that the slogan "heartmind is Pattern" originated among Buddhist scholars of the early Song, of whom the Chan monk and essayist Qisong was the most influential. To give some context to this contentious position, we will look briefly here at Qisong's account. In light of the dialectic between objectivity and subjectivity that we have been discussing, it is striking that in response to criticisms of Buddhism in his day, Qisong seems to be connecting heartmind to Pattern in order to shore up the objectivity of the (Buddhist understanding of) heartmind (T 52n2115_002.0680c15); cf. Xiang 2011. Still, Qisong's position is importantly different from that of CHENG Yi. Recall that CHENG Yi marked the difference between Buddhism and Confucianism by associating the former with the heartmind and the latter with the cosmos. The cosmos is something of which we humans are just a part, and even if there is one nature and Pattern shared by humans and the cosmos as a whole, CHENG Yi's emphasis on the cosmos implies that to access this Pattern and so transform

ourselves, we should attend to the cosmos and our place in it. We should look outside ourselves as well as within. For Qisong, in contrast, the cosmos plays no significant role. For example, in one of his essays, he rephrases the opening lines of *Centrality and Commonality*, removing the key role played in the original text by the cosmos. Instead of "What the cosmos decrees is called 'the nature,' complying with nature is called 'the Way,' and regulating the Way is called 'teaching,'" Qisong gives us: "The heartmind alone is called 'the Way'; clarification of the Way is called 'teaching'" (T 52n2115_002.0654b24; and see the discussion in Xiang 2011: 179). Instead of a doctrine that calls attention to an order or normativity that lies at least partly outside our own consciousness, Qisong's version places emphasis on clarifying the heartmind itself. This looks to be quite at home with some of the earlier Buddhist teachings about heartmind that we have already mentioned.

14 *Book of Documents* 2.2.15; cf. Legge 1985: 61–2.
15 YS 24/312.
16 For more on the sense of *ben* as "inherent," see the discussion of "inherent reality" in chapter 2. *Benxin* is not commonly used by the founders of Daoxue or their other contemporary Neo-Confucians, with only a few uses in the writings of the Cheng brothers and ZHANG Zai, for example. The late Northern Song figure ZHANG Jiucheng uses it much more often, and we see Southern Song thinkers use it regularly. For example, ZHU Xi's contemporary LU Xiangshan speaks of humaneness as one's inherent heartmind, urging his audience to "manifest" or "return to" this responsive capacity, which for many of us has been "lost" because we are misled by material desires, opinions, and empirical perceptions (Lu 1980: 5; cf. Ivanhoe 2009: 49; and Lu 1980: 149; cf. Ivanhoe 2009: 73). Lu uses the term "lost" because Mencius did, but for Lu this simply means temporarily lost access to, not altogether lost. We can see this even more explicitly in ZHU Xi. Zhu says that when one has managed to unify one's human heartmind and Way heartmind (so that all one's reactions accord with the Way), this is to "preserve the correctness of the inherent heartmind and never depart from it" (ZYZJ Preface; cf. Johnston and Wang 2012: 400). The balance of human heartmind versus Way heartmind can shift, but the standard provided by the inherent heartmind is always present. We discuss ZHU Xi's understanding of human heartmind and Way heartmind in greater detail later in this chapter.
17 In one passage that we can positively assign to CHENG Hao, he says (in slightly different language from the famous slogan) that "heartmind is Pattern, and Pattern is heartmind" (ECJ 13/139).
18 Our discussion of CHENG Yi both here and elsewhere acknowledges some significant ambiguity in his teachings; his emphasis on the cosmos sometimes fails to come through in his statements about the importance of the heartmind, as we have seen above.
19 For "heartmind is Pattern, and Pattern is heartmind," see MZZ 19/6a; cited in Araki 2008: 293. Elsewhere, Zhang writes that "The cosmos is

just me, and I am just the cosmos" and "Heartmind is cosmos! People
have this heartmind, and the heartmind has this cosmos," quoted in
LIU Yumin 2010: 14.

20 For some discussion, see LIU Yumin 2010.

21 Lu 1980: 273; cf. Ivanhoe 2010: 253n16; and Araki 2008: 295. He
also objects to making any hard distinction between "human desires"
and "cosmic Pattern," writing that "if Pattern is cosmic and desires
are human, then this denies the identity of the cosmic and the human"
(LJYJ 34/295; cf. Ivanhoe 2010: 77).

22 For some further discussion of these themes, see Ivanhoe 2010.

23 Lu 1980: 395–6; cf. Ivanhoe 2009: 78.

24 "Earlier insights expressed Pattern in response to particular times and
so what they recommended does not always agree" (Lu 1980: 263; cf.
Ivanhoe 2010: 81).

25 CXL 3/2; cf. Wang 1963: 7.

26 CXL 321/121: cf. Wang 1963: 251.

27 CXL 6/5-6; cf. Wang 1963: 14. For discussion of the claim that "the
inherent reality of intention is knowing" – which is an anticipation of
Wang's idea of "good knowing" – see chapters 5 and 6.

28 CXL 275/107–8; cf. Ivanhoe 2009: 109 and Wang 1963: 222.

29 Invoking this passage, Philip J. Ivanhoe suggests that for Wang the
ontological status of Pattern is somewhat analogous to the ontological
status of color or taste. See Ivanhoe 2009: 109–11.

30 CXL3/2, 5/3–4, 72/22, 96/26–7.

31 WJ 70/3403; see discussion in Araki 2008: 274.

32 ZZYL 338–40.

33 For a short review of the scholars who see heartmind as vital stuff and
for passages from ZHU Xi that are at odds with this view, see Chen
2010: 117–29.

34 In addition to Fuji 2011: ch. 6, we have also benefited from Wu 2009
although we are not persuaded by Wu's ultimate conclusion. Both scholars review the existing literature: QIAN Mu and MOU Zongsan hold that
according to Zhu, the heartmind is that aspect of vital stuff capable of
knowing; CHEN Lai says that it is a kind of perceptual category but is not
vital stuff; and scholars like MENG Peiyuan and JIN Chunfeng maintain
that Zhu's idea of heartmind is actually closer to WANG Yangming's
idea of "inherent heartmind" (Fuji 2011: 151–2 and Wu 2009: 112).

35 YL 5/220; cf. Fuji 2011: 163–4.

36 See Fuji 2011: 156, and YL 98/3305.

37 Fuji 2011: 165. See also the discussion in Wu 2009: 113 of another
passage from Zhu that makes the same point: "The heartmind is mas-
tered by the nature and put into effect by the emotions" (YL 5/230).

38 BXZY A/11; cf. Chen 1986: 56 and Fuji 2011: 156; and BXZY A/15;
cf. Chen 1986: 63 and Fuji 2011: 160.

39 Chen 2000: 229 argues explicitly for this view that both *daoxin* and
renxin are already manifest, contrary not only to CHENG Yi but also to
the Ming Neo-Confucian LUO Qinshun. Other Ming Neo-Confucians

who took themselves to be followers of ZHU Xi also misunderstood Zhu's view and equated *daoxin* and nature: for example, see the discussion of CHEN Jian (1497–1567) in de Bary 1989: 101.

40 WJ 32/1396; cf. Fuji 2011: 60.
41 WJ 51/2381, cited in Chen 2000: 230.
42 YL 78/2666; cf. Chen 2000: 230.
43 YL 62/2014; cf. Chan 1989: 202.
44 For the details of how he thinks this is possible, see both our discussion of Zhu's Type Three knowing in chapter 6, and his account of learning in chapter 7.
45 See Lee 2012: 57. "Infant's heartmind" is a reference to MC 4B:12.
46 FSLZ 98##; cf. Tiwald and Van Norden 2014: 305.
47 See Lee 2012: 57–8 and HUANG Zongxi's account of Luo's evolution in thought in MRXA 34/1–2. See also the similar views we discuss in chapter 5's section on the "soliloquy of emotion."
48 For more discussion of this view in connection with WANG Yangming, see chapter 3, section 3.
49 See FSLZ, 99##; cf. Tiwald and Van Norden 2014: 307 and Lee 2012: 58, 69, 104.
50 Ye 2012: 56.
51 MZZYSZ B.21/295–6; cf. Dai 1990: 244–6.
52 Cheng 1991: 515.
53 LIU Yumin 2010: 367.

Chapter 5   Emotions

1 For example, here is the beginning of a brief exchange between ZHU Xi and a questioner: "[Someone asked]: 'How is the idea that "the intentions are the manifestations of the heartmind" related to emotions and the nature?' [Zhu] replied: 'Intentions are very close to emotions'" (YL 98/3305). Elsewhere, Zhu distinguishes between intentions and emotions as follows: "Intentions are the manifestation of the heartmind, emotions are the movement of the heartmind, and commitment is the direction of the heartmind. Commitment is more important than intention or emotion" (YL 5/232). We discuss the importance of commitment (*zhi* 志) in chapter 8. As we see in section 5, below, WANG Yangming prefers to analyze things in terms of intention rather than emotion. Indeed, "intention" appears 286 times in his *Record for Practice* and 32 times in his short "Questions on the *Greater Learning*," while "emotion" appears only 38 times in the former and not at all in the latter.
2 See Eifring 2004, Harbsmeier 2004, Puett 2004, and Yu 1997: 56–66.
3 LJ 9/430.
4 We note that the contrast between *xing* and *qing* is not simply an invention of Buddhism. See Barrett 1992: 94–8 for anticipations of the distinction in both Zhuangzi and WANG Bi.

5 Already near the beginning of the adaptation and translation of Buddhism into Chinese, *qing* is used to express the idea of a "sense faculty," and it is periodically used in this way thereafter. Somewhat later and more commonly, *qing* comes to be used to correspond to "sentience": a sentient being is one who "has *qing*" (有情). See Anderl 2004: 151-2, 159.

6 The *Sutra of Perfect Enlightenment*; T X09_243_1.c033.

7 From LI Tongxuan (635–730)'s *Xin Lun*, T36.1739.721a6–8; cf. Sunghak KOH 2011: 23.

8 Cited in Anderl 2004: 153.

9 See Barrett 1992: 28.

10 FXS 1.1; cf. Barrett 1992: 94. Barrett argues throughout his commentary for a less-negative view of emotion than has become the conventional interpretation, but we do not find this particularly convincing. Barrett also resists the idea that LI Ao was simply drawing on Buddhism; here he seems to us to be correct, but fighting an old fight. LI Ao was clearly well aware of, drawing on, and even speaking to a context shot through with Buddhist ideas and terminology.

11 FXS 2; cf. Barrett 1992: 114.

12 FXS 1.3 and 2.2; cf. Barrett 1992: 96, 97.

13 Ye 2012: 56-8.

14 See Lufrano 1997 and Brook 1998.

15 GW 8; cf. Bol 1992: 279 and Virág 2007: 71.

16 Cheng and Cheng 1981: 577; cf. Virág 2007: 69. The two quoted phrases ("imposing the nature on the emotions" and "imposing the emotions on the nature") come from WANG Bi. For discussion of "awaken," see chapter 6.

17 See discussion in Bol 1992: 266.

18 For all their disagreement about how best to understand human "nature," both Mencius and Xunzi would agree with the sentiment in the main text. See MC 1B:5 and 7B:24 and *Xunzi* 19.

19 See Virág 2007: 70n43 and Egan 1984: 72-3.

20 Cf. Egan 1994: 9–10.

21 Cf. Bol 1992: 261.

22 Virág 2007: 70. For more on the contrast between OUYANG Xiu and SU Shi as well as certain key similarities between Su and his sometime rival CHENG Yi, see Smith et al. 1990: 207–9.

23 YS 6/87.

24 On the place of ZHOU Dunyi within the Daoxue fellowship, see Tillman 1992: 115–16.

25 ZDYJ 1/6, JSL 1.1/15; cf. Zhu and Lü 1967: 1.

26 ZDYJ 2/29–30; JSL 4./190; cf. Zhu and Lü 1967: 123.

27 Yanzi is described as "having only a single dish of rice, a single gourd of drink, and living in a narrow lane; others could not have endured this distress, but he did not allow his joy to be affected" (LY 6:9).

28 ZDYJ 2/31; cf. Chan 1963: 475. Zhou's reference to "transform and equalize" is an obvious reference to Chapter Two of the Daoist classic *Zhuangzi*.

29   YL 94/3172; cf. Chan 1963: 155.
30   YL 13/398–9.
31   YL 13/389; cf. Chan 1989: 200.
32   MZZYSZ A.10/274; cf. Dai 1990: 149.
33   MZZYSZ A.10/273; cf. Dai 1990: 146–7. For stylistic reasons, we have
     chosen to translate *qing* as "feel" in the final sentence, following Ewell.
     Normally, we translate it as "emotion."
34   MZZYSZ C.40/323; cf. Dai 1990: 387.
35   MC 2A:6.
36   *Duan* is used rarely, and never in its specifically Mencian sense, by
     figures such as ZHANG Zai and ZHOU Dunyi. All the uses of the term
     (in the Mencian sense) in the important Daoxue anthology *Reflec-
     tions on Things at Hand* are by CHENG Yi. The same pattern can be
     observed in uses of *Mencius'* specific terms for the *duan* (like "alarm
     and commiseration").
37   YS 15/168; cf. Bol 1992: 324, and Graham 1992: 54.
38   Bol 1992: 323–6 argues that CHENG Yi uses the four beginnings to
     flesh out his understanding of Pattern as a kind of unified, coherent
     organization. Much of what Bol says here seems right, except that he
     equivocates between the beginnings themselves (as emotions) and their
     corresponding norms (such as humaneness); his discussion is really
     about the latter.
39   At one point, CHENG Yi actually says that "within human nature there
     is only the four beginnings," in much the same way that the nature
     of water is to be "still and tranquil like a mirror," even though when
     stimulated from without water can form waves (YS 18/204; cf. Graham
     1992: 53). This equation of the four beginnings with nature seems to
     us to be a mistake even by CHENG Yi's own lights, perhaps a result of
     the difficulty of explaining answers to the sorts of questions we go on
     to discuss in the main text.
40   MZJZ 2A:6.
41   See here our further discussion of this theme in chapter 3.
42   Such a momentary, bounded glimpse of Pattern is what we call, in
     chapter 6, Type Two knowing.
43   YL 53/1776.
44   For example, the most that the Korean Neo-Confucian YI T'oegye says
     (as part of the famous Four-Seven Debate) is that "although neither [the
     four nor the seven] is separable from Pattern and *qi*, on the basis of
     their point of origin, each points to a predominant factor and emphasis"
     (Kalton 1994: 11, slightly modified).
45   YL 5/228.
46   YL 53/1762.
47   YL 5/224; cf. Virág 2007: 81.
48   WJ 67/3277.
49   Many modern scholars have emphasized this theme in ZHU Xi; see, e.g.,
     Araki 2008, Virág 2007, and Fuji 2011. To be sure, Zhu is not alone in
     holding such a view; it seems to be a rather common feature of Southern

Song Daoxue. For example, Tillman shows that ZHANG Shi held quite similar views – indeed, Zhang seems to have been importantly influential on Zhu in this regard. See Tillman 1992: 47–9.

50   Other popular translations of *liangzhi* include "pure knowing" and "innate knowledge."

51   CXL 290/97; cf. Wang 1963: 229. All of our emotions can be apt, including anger or sorrow, as Wang makes explicit. For example, see WL 27/1012, where he stresses that sorrow can be "harmonious."

52   Loving beautiful women is discussed in Wang's letter to HUANG Mianzhi. Wang is a bit dismissive of Huang's elaborate analysis, but in our view Huang fleshes out Wang's position quite helpfully (CXL 56/19). For the mirror passage, see CXL 167/70. For the idea of emotions not lingering, see CXL 114/32–3.

53   CXL 189/84–5; cf. Wang 1963: 176. "Commiseration" is a translation of *ceda* 惻怛, a slightly different term from the first beginning, *ceyin* or "alarm and commiseration," but the two terms are closely related and, in at least one passage from ZHU Xi, used practically interchangeably; see YL 95/3183.

54   CXL 44/17; cf. Wang 1963: 38.

55   WL 6/217, emphasis added; cf. Wang 1972: 114.

56   WL 4/172; cf. Wang 1972: 49. We discuss Wang's idea of the "inherent heartmind" in the next chapter. For another expression of this same idea, see DXW 1/968; cf. Tiwald and Van Norden 2014: 242. And again: "Whenever [one is attached to an instance of the seven emotions], the emotion becomes selfish desire and an obscuration to good knowing. Nevertheless, as soon as there is any attachment, good knowing is naturally aware of it. As it is aware of it, the obscuration will be gone and its structure will be restored" (CXL 290/111; cf. Wang 1963: 229).

57   KZJ 3A.

58   Debates raged over whether good knowing required cultivation or is "ready made" (*xiancheng* 現成), and whether it requires a period of stillness or is always naturally operative. See Chang 1962: 104 and Peng 2005: 321–43 and 378–94.

59   MRXA 62/33. For Zhu's "clue" interpretation, see section 4 above.

60   MRXA 62/11.

61   Some modern interpreters argue that Liu has articulated a kind of "moral feeling" rather than "emotional feeling"; these moral feelings are said to be "pure consciousness ... pure feeling, and pure willing" (Cheng 2010: 340–2). Such interpretations draw heavily on the theories of modern New Confucians like MOU Zongsan. Without taking a stand on the independent plausibility of New Confucian views, we are not persuaded that they are convincing interpretations of thinkers like Liu in their original contexts.

62   Ye 2012: 57 and, more generally, Huang 1998.

63   Feng is by no means alone in this. Here is another of his contemporaries, the moralist YUAN Huang: "In the ancient times, the sage kept order

under Heaven by setting a good example of self-cultivation. This was nothing more than making full use of the emotions of an individual. Humans are born because of emotion and there is Pattern because of humans. Pattern is something not far away from emotion in the first place. Scholars of later times pursue Pattern while neglecting emotion. They study so much that their heartminds are blocked. The more they understand Pattern the less they know about how to harmonize their own six pulses; when given the reins, they do not know how to control a horse. All they should do is to think back about emotion" (quoted in Huang 1998: 169–70, slightly modified. On Yuan, see also Brokaw 1987).

64 Huang 1998: 171.

Chapter 6 Knowing

1 Fraser 2011: 131n9. For an earlier, similar, analysis, see Harbsmeier 1993.
2 LY 2.4.
3 MC 7A:1.
4 For example, see Hansen 1983 and Geaney 2002 in addition to Fraser 2011; Harbsmeier 1993 also discusses related themes.
5 Gradually a different, though both phonetically and graphically related, character comes to be used for "wisdom." The connection between competence at making distinctions and wisdom is most famously brought out in the *Mencius*, where we read that "The feeling of approval and disapproval is the beginning of wisdom (MC 2A:6).
6 Harbsmeier 1993.
7 T 48n2008.0356b23.
8 ZM 7/25; cf. Ziporyn 2015; see also Birdwhistell 1985: 38–9.
9 Perkins 2015 is an excellent discussion of the relation between *wu* and the discourse of individuation.
10 ZHANG Zai, whose discussion of sensory versus virtuous nature's knowing is the most extensive, uses two closely related phrases to refer to virtuous nature's knowing: "*dexing suo zhi*" 德性所知 and "*dexing zhi zhi*" 德性之知. Although Wang 2011 argues for an important difference in meaning between the two, we are unconvinced.
11 See ZM 7.
12 ZM 7/24. (On the question of whether women can be sages, see chapter 8.)
13 ZM 7/24.
14 ZZYL A/313; cf. Birdwhistell 1985: 52.
15 YS 25/317.
16 YS 21a/269–70. Cheng's interlocutor in this dialogue is SHAO Yong. For considerable discussion of the dialogue, see Smith et al. 1990: 216. For more on Shao's distinctive epistemological view, see Birdwhistell 1989.
17 DX 4. "Reaching understanding" is our translation of *zhizhi* 致知, which has often been rendered "extension of knowledge." However,

zhi 致 means "to cause to reach," rather than the more open-ended idea of "extending," and as we have discussed throughout this chapter, *zhi* 知 usually means understanding rather than just a collection of factual "knowledge." *Zhizhi* means to attain the goal of understanding, not simply to add to one's stock of known facts. The translation of *gewu* is much debated. James Legge pioneered "investigation of things" in the nineteenth century, and he has been followed by many scholars since. In Angle 2009, Angle opted for "apprehending coherence in things"; here, we have decided to use "getting a handle on things" (following Tiwald and Van Norden 2014), though we will see that for CHENG Yi and ZHU Xi, the point of *gewu* is indeed to apprehend Pattern in each thing. The advantage of "getting a handle on things" is twofold: it more closely follows the classical meaning of *ge*, and is ambiguous in a way that will allow us to use it for both the Cheng–Zhu meaning and for WANG Yangming's quite different interpretation, on which see the next chapter.

18 YS 18/188; cf. Borrell 1999: 66.

19 YS 25/316.

20 Though he does not have a word like our "active knowing," CHENG Hao is quite explicit that everyday "knowing" is too narrow a category to capture what happens when one has reached Pattern through exhaustive investigation (YS 2A/15). For a helpful discussion of the Chengs' understanding of "genuine knowing," see Chen 2000: 321–5.

21 We draw here on the insightful analysis of Borrell 1999.

22 Here are two contrasting statements by CHENG Yi: "Even YAN Hui would not have been able to get a handle on only a single thing and thoroughly grasp the myriad Patterns. One must get a handle on one item today and another tomorrow. When one has practiced this extensively, there will freely and naturally occur an interconnective understanding" (YS 18/189; cf. Borrell 1999: 66); and " 'To get a handle on things in order to exhaustively investigate Pattern' does not mean that it is necessary to exhaustively investigate all things in the world. One has only to fully investigate the Pattern in one thing or one event, and the Pattern in other things and events can be then be inferred. ... The reason why one is able to exhaustively investigate in this way is because all things share the same Pattern" (YS 15/156; cf. Borrell 1999: 67).

23 YS 2A/247; cf. Graham 1992: 75.

24 To forestall the possibility that readers will take the inner-oriented kind of investigation of things to be solely associated with CHENG Hao, here is a passage unambiguously identified with CHENG Yi: "To learn them from what is outside, and grasp them within, is called 'understanding.' To grasp them from what is within, and connect them with outside things, is called 'sincerity.' Sincerity and understanding are one" (YS 25/317; cf. Graham 1992: 75).

25 Quoted in Borrell 1999: 68. We discuss inner-oriented self-cultivational practices like this – which Borrell has aptly termed "*weifa* practice" – in chapter 7.

26 ZYS 1:6b–7a; cf. Borrell 1999: 70.
27 ZYS 3:11a–b; cf. Lee 2008: 105.
28 Lee 2008: 104.
29 YL 34/1255, cf. Yu 1986: 242.
30 "Principle" here is *daoli* 道理; in this context, Zhu is referring to a single, codifiable rule or principle. In terms of the distinctions we develop later in the chapter, this is Type One knowing.
31 YL 98/3311; cf. Yu 1986: 242.
32 Yu 1986: 243.
33 Cited in Borrell 1999: 62.
34 For example, Kim says that for ZHU Xi *gewu* rarely refers to the investigation of non-moral objects and phenomena. And even where Zhu does describe the investigation of non-moral things (e.g., the fact that heaven is high and the earth thick), Kim says that Zhu seems to mean it "rhetorically" (Kim 2000: 21).
35 LYZJ 12:1/167.
36 See Yu 1986: 228–9 for some discussion. For more on the distinction between engaging in inquiry and study and honoring the virtuous nature, see chapter 7.
37 CHEN Xianzhang 1987: 145; cf. Kim 2001: 20.
38 KIM Youngmin's description of vulgar learning (*suxue* 俗學) is excellent: it included "such activities as memorization and recitation (*jisong* 記誦), literary composition (*cizhang* 詞章), textual studies (*xungu* 訓詁), and broad learning (*boxue* 博學). They were often considered by Neo-Confucian moral philosophers to be connected to the desire for profit (*gongli* 功利) because they were instrumental in the achievement of worldly success through the civil service examinations. A critical attitude toward this kind of 'vulgar learning' had existed among the earliest Neo-Confucian thinkers. However, what is interesting in the mid-Ming period is that the rampancy of such vulgar learning was seen as linked to the very triumph of Neo-Confucianism in general, and to ZHU Xi's learning in particular" (Kim 2003: 372n15).
39 Further examples of thinkers with these views are discussed in Kim 2001.
40 CHEN Xianzhang 1987: 20; cf. Kim 2001: 23.
41 This is HU Juren, who saw himself as developing the thinking of ZHU Xi; quoted in Kim 2001: 25.
42 KZJ A/22–3; cf. Luo 1987: 106.
43 KZJ, A/3; cf. Luo 1987: 55.
44 KZJ A/3; cf. Luo 1987: 56.
45 For all of the Daoxue Neo-Confucians we discuss, even when sensory knowing is valued, that value is ultimately tied to our ability to achieve some kind of virtuous nature's knowing. Still, a position like Luo's (or ZHU Xi's) allows for a considerable degree of attention to the details of sensory knowing. Perhaps the most extreme case within Neo-Confucianism of emphasis on sensory knowing is the Japanese thinker KAIBARA Ekken. He engaged in extensive taxonomic studies of flowers,

plants, fish, birds, and shells; his 1709 *Plants of Japan* (*Yamato honzō*) has been called "the first systematic botanical text produced in Japan" (Kaibara 2007: 55).

46 Wang is clearly identifying "hearing and seeing" (*wenjian*) with merely vulgar learning – as opposed to the more sophisticated, though still mistaken, views of someone like ZHU Xi – in this passage: "[People of old were all able to learn about virtue because in those days,] there was no pursuit after the knowing of hearing and seeing to confuse them, no memorization and recitation to hinder them, no writing of flowery compositions to indulge in, and no chasing after success and profit" (CXL 142/53–4; cf. Wang 1963: 119). In a second passage, though, Wang seems to be using "hearing and seeing" to correspond to something closer to ZHU Xi's notion of getting a handle on things: "what later scholars called understanding and examination are, after all, narrowly constrained to hearing and seeing and obscured by wrong habits of thought. They follow, grope after, and imitate what is apparent or illusory" (CXL 165/68–9; cf. Wang 1963: 147).

47 CXL 168/71–2; cf. Wang 1963: 150.

48 CXL 138/48–9, emphasis added; cf. Wang 1963: 106.

49 See chapter 7 for our discussion of the role that "outward investigation" (*cha*) plays for WANG Yangming, and also for his redefinition of *gewu* and its role in self-cultivation.

50 Our discussion of Wang here is based on Zhu 2003.

51 Benjamin Elman writes, "an emphasis on experiential knowledge (*wenjian zhi zhi* 聞見之知) was closely linked during the Ming–Qing transition period to the important role of doubt as the starting point for scholarly inquiry. Suspension of judgment and detached scrutiny of beliefs based on empirical criteria were required of *kaozheng* scholars" (Elman 2001: 91).

52 YL 13/394; cf. Zhu 1990: 184.

53 We discuss the contrast between conscientious and sincere behavior in more detail in chapter 8.

54 YL 18/625.

55 YL 18/625; Zhu is quoting MC 7A:15.

56 Here is another passage, also from YL 18/625, in which the connection of "unable to stop" to the whole functioning of the cosmos is made. "Someone asked: 'When you wrote that "The changes of heaven, earth, ghosts, and spirits; the apt responses of birds, beasts, flowers and trees – none can avoid seeing an instance of how things should be and being unable not to do it," what did you mean by "be unable not to do it"?' Zhu replied: 'Spring gives life and autumn kills: this is unavoidable. At the acme of *yin*, *yang* is born. Even if behind your back someone tried to interfere, how could it be avoided!'"

57 We discuss this passage (MC 2A:6) at length in chapter 5.

58 *Jue* does not feature very significantly in classical Confucian epistemic discourse, but there is MC 5A:7: "The cosmos, in giving birth to the people, directs those who first become wise (*zhi*) to awaken (*jue*) those

who will later become wise." In more than one place, the Chengs make explicit this Confucian pedigree for *jue*; for example, YS 14/142.

59 CY 1/1180.
60 YL 17/586.
61 YL 23/813.
62 DXHW A/512; cf. Zhu 1990: 90.
63 YL 17/585.
64 Zhu uses a variety of terms to refer to this type of knowing, including "genuine knowing"; the "discernment of the Way heartmind"; "eventual awakening"; and "knowing the cosmic mandate," among others. The idea of "going up a level" also bears comparison to Zhu's discussion of the role of inference in understanding Pattern's "mastery," on which see chapter 2.
65 Among Zhu's key predecessors, the Cheng brothers do not use *zhijue* in Zhu's capacious way, but instead only in the earlier Buddhist sense (see, for example, CHENG Yi's use of the term in YS 18/201), but in a much-quoted passage, ZHANG Zai anticipates Zhu quite closely: "To the combination of nature and *zhijue*, we give the name 'heartmind'" (ZM 1/9). As for ZHU Xi himself, he says things like "That which has *zhijue* we call the heartmind" (YL 140/4340), and "Our heartmind is our *zhijue*, that which is the master of our body and which responds to things and affairs" (WJ 65/3180).
66 WJ 67/3263; quoted in Fuji 2011: 168.
67 WJ 55/2590, quoted in Fuji 2011: 172.
68 Zhu makes the same point in more concrete fashion when commenting on *Mencius* 1A:7. In this passage, we read that upon seeing an ox being led to a ritual sacrifice, King Xuan felt pity for it, ordered that it be spared, and that a sheep be found and sacrificed in the ox's place. Mencius' conversation with the king about what this incident reveals is complex, but for our purposes the key has to do with why the king was able to bear sending some unseen sheep to be sacrificed, when he could not bear to have the ox sacrificed. ZHU Xi says: "Having seen the ox, this heartmind was already manifest and could not be suppressed, while not yet having seen the sheep, its Pattern had not yet taken form and there were no [emotions] to hinder him" (MZJZ 1A.7/254). As we know from chapters 2 and 3, Pattern never actually "takes form," so what this must mean is that specific configurations of Pattern are "possessed" (*ju* 具) or become live to us only as our heartminds actually respond to a stimulus and produce emotions in reaction. For some relevant discussion of this passage, see Marchal 2013: 209–10, though we do not agree with Marchal that "the limits of the king's perception are the limits of his moral obligation."
69 Although we are drawing here on Virág 2007: esp. 80, we believe that she may be taking the special metaphor somewhat too literally.
70 YL 98/3305.
71 For example: "analogically extend to that by which [something is as it is]" (YL 23/811); and the similar statement at YL 32/1152. Zhu also

instructs us to "explicate" (*lun* 論), as in "explicate that by which [it is as it is]" (YL 18/625).

72 Zhu makes exceptions for "important affairs of state," writing that "in matters of life and death, preservation and destruction, there were times when they couldn't act directly on their [good] impulses but had to weigh things carefully, then act" (YL 13/404; cf. Zhu 1990: 188).

73 YL 14/436.

74 Some notion of proximity is very important for Zhu here. One loses the distinctive gains of extension by "gazing far into the distance" or "skipping steps." This is how Zhu understands the general Confucian mandate (as he sees it) to begin one's reflections with things "near at hand" (YL 49/1660).

75 YL 117/3677. We thank Brook Ziporyn for calling our attention to this passage.

76 Zhu associates these various categories in passages like this one: "The 'awaken' in 'The first awakened awaken the later awakened' is the awakening of self-enlightenment, much like when the *Greater Learning* speaks of 'getting a handle on things and reaching understanding [leading to] unimpeded interpenetration'" (YL 58/1859).

77 YL 75/2544. For the reference to being stuck in a corner, see YL 35/1292.

78 See Eichman 2016.

79 YS 2A/16; cf. Graham 1992: 80.

80 YS 15/147.

81 YL 9/298.

82 YL 9/298; cf. Zhu 1990: 116–17. CHENG Yi is in fact sometimes explicit about the temporal priority of knowledge, as when he claims that "understanding must precede doing. Take an analogy. If one wants to walk, one first needs to have the road brightened" (YS 3/67).

83 CXL 5/4; cf. Ivanhoe 2009: 142.

84 CXL 5/3–4; cf. Ivanhoe 2009: 142.

85 CXL 133/42–3; cf. Wang 1963: 93.

86 See Araki 2008: 381–6 for helpful discussion and, for details of one critic, see Zhu 2003: 10–12.

87 WL 5/277.

88 YL 9/303. For further discussion of the tight relation between knowing and acting in Zhu, see Chen 2000: 321–5.

89 In his study of ZHU Xi, CHEN Lai argues for a similar conclusion (2000: 324–5).

Chapter 7   Self-Cultivation

1 "Self-Cultivation" is a translation of *xiu shen* 修身, a widely used term within Neo-Confucianism that derives from classical texts like *Centrality and Commonality* 21. Another term often used in this regard is "effort" (*gongfu* 功夫).

2　Bol has shown that the elite class of "literati" (*shi* 士) increasingly saw their membership in this class as dependent on their commitment to Confucian moral cultivation, and less dependent on their erudition or success in securing a position in government (Bol 1992: 6–14, 32–75). De Bary argues that the commitment of Yuan dynasty Daoxue scholars amounted to a "religious zeal," such that they were willing to work with, and try to educate, their Mongol overlords (de Bary 1981: 20–7). In the Ming dynasty, the devotion of the Donglin group to their understanding of Neo-Confucianism stands out for its fervor; see our discussion of the Donglin partisans in chapter 9. See also the further discussion of commitment in section 2 of the present chapter.

3　Angle 2009: 16–20.

4　Kasoff 1984: 26–8.

5　We discuss educational and ethical issues related to women in the next chapter.

6　By the year 1500, millions of males were taking the lowest-level civil service examination, which was offered every two years. Success rates were very low. For a review of the anxiety disorders and depression precipitated by the exams and the (commonplace) lifelong failure of many males to succeed in them, see Elman 2000: 295–8.

7　For more on "vulgar learning," see chapter 6 and Kim 2001. We discuss the establishment of Daoxue as official orthodoxy in chapter 1 and further explore the implications of Ming (and Qing) imperial endorsement of Neo-Confucianism in chapter 9.

8　LY 14.24. CHENG Yi explains: "People of ancient times learned for their own sake, wanting that which they achieve to be within themselves. People nowadays learn for the sake of others, wanting their achievement to be seen by others" (JSL 2.14/75–6; cf. Zhu and Lü 1967: 47).

9　LY 2.4.

10　LY 1.4.

11　For one provocative discussion of the attractiveness of Chan's model of social influence, see Araki 2008: 242–3.

12　In describing some of these processes as types of "discovery," we borrow language first introduced by Yearley 1990: 59–61 and then developed and enriched by Ivanhoe 2000a. Van Norden also explores Neo-Confucian "discovery models" of moral cultivation (Van Norden 2007: 44–55). What we call the "formation model" is meant to be neutral with respect to what these other scholars have referred to as "development," "re-formation," "praxis," "realization" and other related categories.

13　Advocates of Direct Discovery include CHENG Hao (at least ambiguously), YANG Shi, ZHANG Jiucheng, LI Tong, LU Xiangshan, CHEN Xianzhang, and WANG Yangming, as well as many of Wang's later followers.

14　Zhu's point is closely anticipated by CHENG Yi. When asked whether one can seek the not-yet-manifest centrality, Cheng replies: "Impossible. As soon as one has thought about seeking that before the [emotions] have been manifested, that is already thought, which is precisely the already manifest. Thinking and [emotions] are the same in this respect" (YS 18/200). For more on Zhu's turn away from Direct Discovery, see Chen 2000: 157–63, Qian 1989: 2.123–182, and Tillman 1992: 59–64.

15 WJ 64/3130–1.

16 For more on this see the discussion of the "unity of knowing and acting" in chapter 6.

17 MZZYSZ A.5/267-69 and C.43/328; cf. Dai 1990: 119–23 and 421–2.

18 Kim 2008: 117; see also Ong 2006.

19 Chow 1994: 192–3.

20 Although the Daoxue philosophers were interested in rooting out both selfish intentions and selfish desires, and developed distinctive techniques for addressing each, in their more general descriptions they tended to characterize the ultimate goal in terms of eliminating the latter. This is probably because they saw eliminating the relevant intentions as a necessary condition for eliminating the relevant desires, so that the former goal was implicit in the latter.

21 As it happens, we are now witnessing a revolution in psychology and the cognitive sciences that bears much of this out, showing that biases (often implicit or hidden ones) pervade our decision making at almost every level. Moreover, the evidence suggests powerfully that these biases cannot be corrected through more careful or more informed thinking. The usual textbook or classroom-style pedagogical techniques have little impact on them. In both respects, the Neo-Confucians were way ahead of western moral psychologists.

22 For more on the "continent constitution" and "embodied nature," see chapter 3.

23 These two terms come from *Centrality and Commonality* 28, where the superior person is said to pursue both of them.

24 Angle 2009: 138–9.

25 Angle 2009: 114–18.

26 CXL 3/2. See also our discussion of Wang's identification of Pattern and the heartmind in chapter 4.

27 See Araki 2008: 369. For more on this, see chapter 6 on both Type Two knowing and the possibility of "unimpeded interconnection" (*huoran guantong* 豁然貫通).

28 Wu 2013 is a marvelous translation of the whole text; for the Chinese original, see RL.

29 RL 17/10. He also repeatedly speaks of his "commitment" (*zhi* 志).

30 RL 145/41.

31 RL 101/31.

32 In his influential discussion of ritual, the classical Confucian Xunzi emphasizes the "nurturance" aspect of ritual, which is also implied in *Analects* 2:3. See *Xunzi* 19.

33 Wood 1995: 103–5.

34 Cited in Chow 1994: 191.

35 ZZYL 3/326–7.

36 For Zhu's criticism of Zhang, see YL 95/3216. There are various other indications that ritual is less important for ZHU Xi. One is his consistent emphasis on the need to adapt old rituals to the changed circumstances of Zhu's day (YL 84–91: passim). This is not to do away with rituals, but it does put into the foreground the values in terms of which the new rituals need to be designed or assessed. Most tellingly, Zhu does not see ritual as providing a distinctive, necessary means toward one's transformation. In a characteristic passage, he cites classical sources that evoke the idea of ritual (e.g., "Go out as if you were seeing an important guest") as one in a list of texts that stress other ideas (e.g., "Preserve your heartmind and nourish your nature"). He then concludes, "There is only a single Pattern in all of these, and we need only put forth our effort in one place and the rest will be included. The way of sages and worthies is like a room: although all the doors are different, you can enter through any one of them" (XJSL 11.19/204–5; cf. Zhu 1991b: 154). Finally, for more on *Master Zhu's Family Rituals*, see Zhu 1991a.
37 WJ 36/3672.
38 YL 7/269; cf. Zhu 1990: 93.
39 CXL 195/87–8.
40 CXL 196–9/88–9.
41 YL 7/269; cf. Zhu 1990: 93.
42 For further discussion of lesser learning, see Angle 2009: 136–40 and Van Norden 2007: 47–8.
43 DX 4.
44 For a discussion of the translation of *zhizhi* and *gewu*, see chapter 6.
45 See YS 18/188.
46 See chapter 6 of this book, and Kim 2000: 21–2.
47 CXL 318/120. For a similar sentiment, see CHEN Xianzhang's frustration with reading, which leads him to employ quiet sitting (seeking Direct Discovery), as discussed above.
48 DXW 6/971–2; cf. Tiwald and Van Norden 2014: 246–50; CXL 6/4–5, 7/6, 318/120.
49 CXL 6/4–5. For more on Wang's philological argument and its implications, see Ivanhoe 2002: 97–9.
50 CXL 62/20; 218/94–5; 297/113–14.
51 We have only scratched the surface of debates over *gewu*. For example, Wang's position is then subject to a wide-ranging critique by his contemporary, LUO Qinshun. One particularly interesting line of argument runs as follows. Wang's vision of "getting a handle on things" seems to assume that the only "thing" to be grasped is the Pattern in the reactions of one's own heartmind to a particular object. But surely there must be something to be gained in seeing the Pattern as others see it, and not just as any one of us sees it when he or she is free of selfish intentions. If we are to make good sense of the idea that we can learn about Pattern from those wiser than us, correcting the reactions of our own heartminds cannot be sufficient. See KZJ C/113; cf. Luo 1987: 187–8.

And advocates of the Formation model of cultivation also have their say about *gewu*. For example, the Qing dynasty scholar YAN Yuan argues that it means "to *ge* 'reach into' *wu* 'thing' by mastering the daily practice of the rites and norms of the Confucian way" (Ivanhoe 2000a: 81).

52 LY 12:1 and ZY 1, respectively.

53 For more on incipience, see Allen 2015: 172 and 187, and Smith et al. 1990: 190–9.

54 CXL 60/20.

55 YL 9/302.

56 A major dispute among Buddhists of the Song dynasty was between advocates of "Silent Illumination Chan," a kind of quiet sitting meditation, and "Gong'an Introspection Chan," which aimed to provide enlightenment through contemplation of Buddhist kōans. See Schlütter 1999.

57 Others who saw quiet sitting as the key to Direct Discovery include LI Tong in the Song and GU Xiancheng in the Ming. See Taylor 1990: 84–5.

58 Cited in Borrell 1999: 68. We see a similar claim in CHEN Xianzhang in the early Ming dynasty, whom we discussed above in chapter 6. Recall that he chose to "forsake all the complexities of other methods and pursue, through quiet sitting alone, what was essential within myself. In time I was able to see the inherent reality of my own heartmind manifested inscrutably."

59 For example, WANG Yangming says that meditation actually cultivates a fondness for tranquillity and a distaste for action, thus making over-zealous meditators reluctant participants in the world (CXL 217/94). For more on this general concern, see Fu 1986: 393–4 and Cai 2009.

60 ZYS 1:6b–7a; cf. Borrell 1999: 70. See also our discussion of Zhang in chapter 6.

61 Araki 2008 writes insightfully about this aspect of Wang's thought; see especially 387–9 and 434.

62 CXL 119/34.

63 CXL 120/34–5, and see Stanchina 2015 for a very helpful discussion of "private knowing."

64 CXL 155/54–5: "Genuine knowing is the not-yet-manifest centeredness." Wang uses "genuine knowing" and "good knowing" interchangeably.

65 See CXL 170/72–3: "In the task of learning, wherever there is single-ness, sincerity will prevail, but wherever there is doubleness, there will be falsehood"; and see also CXL 153/62.

66 CXL 157/62; cf. Wang 1963: 136.

67 YL 12/373. The quotation comes from the *Record of Ritual*.

68 For more on the types of distraction that Zhu can and cannot allow, see Angle 2009: 169.

69 YL 12/378; cf. Zhu 1990: 174.

70 This elucidation of the "master of the house" metaphor comes from the Ming dynasty Daoxue philosopher HU Juren; see Ch'ien 1979: 197.

71 We take this term from Thomas Metzger; see Metzger 2005: 21–5.

72 This and the next few paragraphs are based on similar material in Angle 2009: 147–9.
73 Kasoff 1984: 83–4.
74 XSYL A/395
75 For a thorough discussion of Zhu's theories including a stimulating comparison with Christian hermeneutics, see Peng 2012.
76 YL 10/318; cf. Zhu 1990: 132.
77 YL 10/318; cf. Zhu 1990: 132; YL 11/334; cf. Zhu 1990: 147; and YL 10/319; cf. Zhu 1990: 133.
78 YL 11/332; cf. Zhu 1990: 145; YL 11/333; cf. Zhu 1990: 146.
79 YL 10/319–20; cf. Zhu 1990: 133; and YL 10/322; cf. Zhu 1990: 135.
80 YL 11/343.
81 YL 10/320; cf. Zhu 1990: 134–5.
82 See chapter 8, section 2, where we introduce the distinction between foundational dispositions and manifest dispositions. For Zhu, reading – and particularly this third stage – is a key means to the realization of manifest dispositions.
83 YL 10/315.
84 YL 10/313; cf. Zhu 1990: 128.
85 YL 11/345; cf. Zhu 1990: 152.
86 YL 11/350; cf. Zhu 1990: 157.
87 Earlier in the chapter we introduced WU Yubi, who described his forty-year practice of self-cultivation in his journal. The journal is replete with discussion of reading, reciting, and reflection. Here is just one example: "This evening, slowly walking through the fields, I was silently chanting passages from *Centrality and Commonality*. I took my time, going over each word and phrase, chanting them with great feeling. Realized in my heartmind, verified by my experiences, this book has given me a great deal of insight" (RL 49/18).
88 CXL 14/10; 25/13.
89 WL 1/143; cf. Wang 1972: 43.
90 CXL 195/87–8.
91 CXL 199/89.
92 CXL 13/10, CXL 14/10.
93 See WL 41/1567; cf. Tiwald and Van Norden 2014: 263–4.
94 MZZYSZ, 1.9/272–3 and 1.14/279–81; cf. Dai 1990: 146–53 and 176–84. See also Ivanhoe 2000a: 89–91; and YSDZ, A.preface/330; cf. Dai 1971: 65.

Chapter 8 Virtues

1 LY 13.18.
2 MC 7A:35.
3 CXL 276/108; cf. Wang 1963: 222–3.
4 Our focus here is on the way that Neo-Confucians understood the Mohists, as a means toward understanding Neo-Confucian views; for

a recent, revisionist account of the Mohists views themselves, see Fraser 2016.

5 YL 126/3924–5 and 126/3953.

6 Sometimes they pair this with *ti* 悌, respect for one's elders, as another root virtue (LYJZ 1.2 and CXL 93/25–6; cf. Wang 1963: 56–7). In its genesis, *ti* is modeled on the respect one develops for one's elder brother.

7 MZJZ 7A:35.

8 Many influential Neo-Confucians are reluctant to declare a position on what happens to people after death, in part because they think theories about the afterlife are too difficult to substantiate, and in part because they think it matters little for how one ought to live in the present life. The value of living as a virtuous member of a family, society, etc., does not depend on its consequences for future lives. See, for example, LYJZ 11.12 and YL 126/3955.

9 MZJZ 6A:10. See also Van Norden 2007: 257–70.

10 MZJZ 4A:27.

11 BXZY A/20; cf. Chen 1986: 73. See also Van Norden 2007: 275–7.

12 The *Mencius* only treats the first four as cardinal virtues, omitting trustworthiness, which required some Neo-Confucians – who took themselves to be following Mencius – to go to great lengths to explain why it was omitted. See Fuji 2011: 29.

13 MZJZ 2A:6; cf. Tiwald and Van Norden 2014: 211; BXZY A/18; cf. Chen 1986: 69–70.

14 Fuji 2011: 31.

15 Probably the student closest to Zhu (Chen 1986: 9–11).

16 BXZY A/21; cf. Chen 1986: 74.

17 We think this a quite plausible description of the view attributed to Confucius in major parts of the *Analects*. In the *Mencius*, humaneness seems to be one virtue among others.

18 See BXZY A/18; cf. Chen 1986: 70 and MZZYSZ C.36/316–17; cf. Dai 1990: 351.

19 YS 2A/15 and CXL 89/25; cf. Wang 1963: 55–6. ZHU Xi suggests that "forming one body" with others is a consequence of humaneness but not humaneness itself (YL 6/259). See Ivanhoe 2015 on the significance of "forming one body" with others. This view has significant implications for our commitments to nature and the environment, as described in Chen 2010: 43–5 and Tu 1989: 72–7.

20 YL 34/1218.

21 It might be the case that DAI Zhen thinks that even superior people will allow their personal interests to set limits to what they are willing to do for virtue. Another possibility, however, is that for DAI Zhen, allowing one's own interests to set limits is part of the definition of virtue – virtuous people take some consideration of themselves (MZZYSZ A.10/273 and B.21/293–6; cf. Dai 1990: 146–7 and 240–7).

22 YL 13/397.

23 Wang 1992: 1168.

24 BXZY A/23; cf. Chen 1986: 79.

25   BXZY A/24; cf. Chen 1986: 81. DAI Zhen explores different ways in which one virtue can be dependent on another in MZZYSZ C.36–7/316–19; cf. Dai 1990: 351–61.
26   YL 58/1853.
27   Even in the case of the son's covering up for his father, Zhu says this is the "extremity of cosmic Pattern and human emotion" (LYJZ 13.19). For considerable discussion, see Angle 2009: ch. 6.
28   MZJZ 2A:7; cf. Mengzi 2008: 47–8.
29   MZZYSZ C.36/316–17; cf. Dai 1990: 351–4.
30   YL 20/694.
31   CHEN Chun clarifies this relationship by drawing an analogy to the way people talk about groupings of families. According to the protocol of his era, when we want to refer to a group of families linked together by its brothers (that is, males all born to the same father), we should refer to the title and position of the oldest brother, who stands in for all of the others. But when we want to refer just one "household" (that is, father, wife, concubines and children) within the larger group, we should refer to the father's title and position individually, without reference to his brothers. Humaneness, Chen suggests, is like the oldest brother in this arrangement, and the other virtues are like his younger brothers. A more contemporary analogy might be to English usage of the word "cars." There are times when "car" is used specifically to distinguish one type of motorized vehicle from others, such as trucks and jeeps, but there are other contexts in which "car" stands in for all such motorized vehicles, as when describing a "parking lot full of cars." See BXZY A/18; cf. Chen 1986: 70. See also YL 20/695.
32   Tiwald forthcoming.
33   LY 2.4.
34   LY 6.20.
35   LY 1.1, 7.34.
36   MC 4A:27.
37   In chapter 4, we discussed another important implication of the whole-heartedness criterion for virtue: namely, that it lends some weight to the view that for true virtue to be possible, the heartmind must be a source of Pattern, rather than something external that merely conforms to Pattern. See especially sections 1–3.
38   Other translations include "genuineness" and "integrity."
39   For example, see ZYZJ 22 and CXL 101/29–30; cf. Johnston and Wang 2012: 465 and Wang 1963: 65.
40   Like Fuji, we think the core meaning of *cheng* is ethical rather than cosmic or metaphysical, and its primary function is to specify qualities of people that make them virtuous, marking distinctions between fake or phony virtue and true or sincere virtue, between forced and spontaneous moral behavior, and ultimately between mere worthiness of character and genuine sagehood (Fuji 2011: 9–34).
41   BXZY A/33–4; cf. Chen 1986: 98–9. See also CXL 207/93; cf. Wang 1963: 193–4.

42 ZHU Xi makes these connections more explicit in some comments on an extended gloss of "sincerity" in the classical Confucian text *Centrality and Commonality*, a gloss that Neo-Confucians took to be one of the definitive statements about sincerity: "'The utmost sincerity in the world' refers to the genuineness (*shi*) of a sage's virtue. Nothing in the world can add to it. For those who completely develop their nature, their virtue is entirely genuine. Thus they have none of the selfishness of human desires; they follow the cosmic decree that is within us all, in both the great and the small, the refined and the crude, never falling even a hair's breadth short of fully developing it ... 'Forming a triad with Heaven and Earth' means to join together with Heaven and Earth in establishing a triad. This is what is done by someone who reaches enlightenment through sincerity" (ZYZJ 22; cf. Johnston and Wang 2012: 465 and Tiwald and Van Norden 2014: 229).

43 Worries about merely conscientiousness behavior can be found throughout classical Confucianism; see Angle 2013. As pointed out at Fuji 2011: 17–19, an important nexus of Neo-Confucian discussion of conscientiousness is their interpretation of *Mencius* 7A:30, which contrasts those whose virtue comes naturally, with those for whom it is fully embodied only after a period of cultivation, and finally those who virtue is "feigned" (*jia* 假). It is possible to read the passage as suggesting that the outward appearance of virtue – that is, forced virtuous activity without an inner, virtuous character – is satisfactory, but ZHU Xi and fellow Neo-Confucians reject this interpretation, insisting on full "sincerity."

44 ZM 6/21, and see the discussion at Fuji 2011: 28.

45 CHEN Lai emphasizes this point in Chen 2000: 321–5.

46 See Tiwald 2010: 411 and MZZYSZ C.41/324–5; cf. Dai 1990: 392–7.

47 BXZY A/19; cf. Chen 1986: 71–2.

48 See YL 13/404; cf. Zhu 1990: 188 and YL 37/1379.

49 For example, CHENG Yi holds some women – including his own mother – in high esteem for providing examples and moral insights to their sons that served their sons well in public life, but nevertheless proclaims that women's education should be limited to affairs of the household. In their formal lessons and writings, both CHENG Yi and ZHU Xi maintain that chastity – a particularly important virtue for women – forbids women from remarrying under any condition, even after the death of their husbands or at the risk of dire poverty and starvation. But in life they allowed some women to remarry to avoid destitution. See JSL 6.17/267; cf. Zhu and Lü 1967: 177; cf. Tiwald and Van Norden 2014: 290–2, and Pang-White 2013.

50 One of the most famous examples is "Grandmother Jia" in *The Story of the Stone*, which is among the most important and influential novels in Chinese literature. See Cao 1974.

51 NJ 5.1a–5.9a; cf. Tiwald and Van Norden 2014: 55–63.

52 NXJ; cf. Zheng 2001: 52–4.

53 CHENG Yi praises his mother for "caring for and loving the children of my father's concubines just as she did her own" (JSL 6.17/267;

cf. Tiwald and Van Norden 2014: 291). SIMA Guang, author of the influential *Precepts for Family Life*, celebrates women who save nieces and nephews at the expense of their own children (Ebrey 2003: 28). As Patricia Ebrey explains, "To SIMA Guang and probably most of his contemporaries, marriage was only in part about the joining of two spouses. It was primarily about how families perpetuate themselves through the incorporation of new members" (Ebrey 2003: 32).

54 JSL 8.1/299; cf. Zhu and Lü 1967: 202.
55 XJSL 6.14/119–20; cf. Tiwald and Van Norden 2014: 295. Zhu elaborates on a wife's potential role as a confidante here: "[The relationship between] husbands and wives is the most intimate and the most private of all human relations. We may not want to tell something to a father or brother, but it can all be told one's wife. These are the most intimate of human affairs and the Way is exercised therein" (XJSL 6.15/120; cf. Tiwald and Van Norden 2014: 295).
56 See Du and Mann 2003.
57 NJ 5.5a; cf. Tiwald and Van Norden 2014: 60.
58 Ebrey 2003: 27 and 33–6.
59 Chan 1989: 542.
60 See Ebrey 2003: 27–8.
61 Ann A. Pang-White points out that some Song dynasty Neo-Confucians think men should also be prohibited from remarrying after the death of their spouses (Pang-White 2013: 438). But the consensus among the Neo-Confucians on this issue is not as strong, and certainly not featured as prominently in their discussions of virtue.
62 See Ebrey 2003: 29–31 and Raphals 1998: 254–6. To be sure, Confucians of almost any stripe allow that women will often be more virtuous and even wiser than their husbands, fathers-in-law, or brothers; just because men's virtues make greater ethical achievements available to them, it does not follow that men will take advantage of the opportunity. See NXJ 6.9b–10b; cf. Zheng 2001: 61–3. But this is a different matter, one that we will address in conjunction with the Neo-Confucian position on women and virtue next.
63 "Maternal affection" translates the Chinese character *ci* 慈. In other contexts, it refers to parental affection more generally, but Luo sees it as coming most naturally to mothers, and in what follows he focuses primarily on them.
64 See Luo 2007: 564; cf. Luo 2001: 115.
65 For more on the role of gratitude in developing a sense of filial piety, see Ivanhoe 2007.
66 Luo explains, "Our heartminds and our love are innately endowed by the cosmos. What we sense and what we touch stimulate them and arouse them spontaneously. How could this happen in the absence of sincerity?" (Luo 2007: 564; cf. Luo 2001: 115).
67 See chapter 4, section 4, and Lee 2012: 57.
68 Later in the same essay Luo notes that a mother's extraordinary sacrifices give the son an opportunity to learn about "good knowing"

(*liangzhi*), referring to that crucial form of moral insight promoted by WANG Yangming, whose teachings were central for Luo and other Taizhou thinkers. See Luo 2007: 564; cf. Luo 2001: 115. For our discussion of good knowing in Wang, see chapter 3 and chapter 5.

69   See Luo 2007: 563–4; cf. Luo 2001: 114–15 and Cheng's analysis in Cheng 2001: 107.

70   Luo regarded his own mother as his greatest and most positive influence, and he often cited the fact that his mother encouraged her children to pursue careers that they found most satisfying, even if it meant resigning from a prestigious position in the civil service and accepting a certain degree of poverty, as she encouraged both her husband and her son to do. See Cheng 2001: 104–5. See also his praise for his wife in Luo 2007: 680–1; cf. Luo 2001: 109–10.

71   Luo 2007: 563; cf. Luo 2001: 114. We take Luo to mean that no mother has ever failed due to lack of love and commitment, allowing that sometimes parents lose their children at an early age or are deprived of opportunities to rear them.

72   Raphals 1998: 252–4.

73   JSL 6.17/267–8; cf. Tiwald and Van Norden 2014: 291–2.

74   Two other exceptions in the Neo-Confucian era are the Empress Xu 徐皇后 (1362–1407) of the Ming dynasty, author of "Instructions for the Inner Chambers" and ZHANG Xuecheng, a philosopher-historian in the mid-Qing and author of a treatise called "Women's Learning." See Xu 1999 and Mann 1992.

75   Luo 2007: 629–30 and 638–9; cf. Luo 2001: 108–11.

76   Like some other philosophers in the radical Taizhou school, Luo did not see as many insurmountable obstacles to reconciling Confucian approaches to studying the Way with Daoist and Buddhist ones. He even praised his own wife for pursuing the Way through recitation of Buddhist sutras (Luo 2007: 680–1; cf. Luo 2001: 109).

77   For more discussion of Li's views, see chapter 4, section 4.

78   FSLZ 59–60; cf. Tiwald and Van Norden 2014: 301–4.

79   FSLZ 59; cf. Tiwald and Van Norden 2014: 301.

80   FSLZ 59–60; cf. Tiwald and Van Norden 2014: 301–4.

81   FSLZ 59–60; cf. Tiwald and Van Norden 2014: 302.

82   Lee 2012: 87, 90–1.

83   Lee 2012: 87–91, esp. 89.

84   Lee 2012: 91–4.

85   See Lee 2002: 63–9 and Lee 2012: 32–6, 76–7, and 86–91.

Chapter 9   Governance and Institutions

1   DX 4.

2   Wilson 1995 explains the origin of the genealogical approach to the Way.

3 See the opening of Zhu's Preface to his ZYZJ; cf. Johnston and Wang 2012: 400–1. For related discussion, see Bol 1992: 130–1.
4 De Bary 1991: 49.
5 The term *zunwang* itself is not new; it appeared in the Hong Fan chapter of the ancient *Book of Documents*.
6 SIMA Guang, as quoted in Standen 2007: 60. Standen's book is an excellent work on the shifting contours of "loyalty."
7 As ZHU Xi notes, when people are reluctant to criticize the ruler, then there is no guarantee that people of good judgment and true virtue will be recognized and promoted. Compliance requires little of either (YL 108/3522).
8 See Schirokauer 1986: 141–3.
9 For example, as Wood explains, "if the title of a particular official … is mentioned on one occasion but not on another, this may be interpreted as conveying Confucius' censure of that individual" (Wood 1995: 59).
10 Quoted in Wood 1995: 115.
11 Wood 1995: 117, and see Wood's discussion of both CHENG Yi's and HU Anguo's commentaries for more details. Quotation is from Wood 1995: 115.
12 See Levine 2008: 25–6 and 34–5 and, for example, LY 12:24.
13 Even if the meaning of "individually loyal" had shifted somewhat, on which see above.
14 See Levine 2008: 47–56. Ouyang's essay is translated in de Bary and Lufrano 2001, though Levine takes issue with some aspects of that translation.
15 So writes SIMA Guang; see Levine 2008: 58.
16 So says WANG Yucheng; see Levine 2008: 46–7.
17 The inevitability of factionalism is a common refrain; see Levine 2008: 59f on SIMA Guang and others who hold variations of this position.
18 WJ 28/1244; we have benefited from conversation on this issue with Byounghee MIN.
19 John Dardess is excellent on the details of the factional struggles in Beijing, and sheds important light on the broader goals of the movement. Dardess writes: "The Donglin program for Ming China consisted of three main elements. First was their insistence upon scrutinizing all high-level official appointments with a view to supporting the 'good species' and rejecting the morally unfit. Second was their nationwide effort at Confucian moral rearmament, revolving around the organization of lecture meetings and academies, with the Shoushan academy, which they set up in Beijing in 1622, as the center. And third was their claim to a right on moral grounds to interfere in the affairs of the Ming imperial family and its inner palace staff" (Dardess 2002: 31–2).
20 Dardess 2002: 71.
21 Elman 1989: 389.
22 Dardess 2002: 7.
23 For another valuable perspective on Neo-Confucian thought on factions, see Tze-ki HON's detailed discussion of Neo-Confucian analyses

of the *Book of Changes* to justify more nuanced understandings of factions (Hon 2004).

24 See Bol 1993.

25 On Wang's character-centered politics, see (ZHU Cheng 2008: 106–46). For examples of the Cheng brothers' views, see JSL 9.5/326–7, 10.3/349, and 10.41/368. Later in this chapter, we offer a more qualified picture of ZHU Xi's character-centered politics.

26 See Elman 2001.

27 On YE Shi and the Yongjia School, see Niu 1998: 50–62. On CHEN Liang, see Tillman 1982 and on WANG Tingxiang's politics, see Ong 2006.

28 See Angle 2002: 84–92.

29 Xunzi is best known for his contention that human nature is bad (*xing'e*), a view which put him at odds with nearly all of the Neo-Confucians mentioned in this volume. But while most Neo-Confucians joined in condemning his theory of human nature, there was a surprising (even if grudging) admiration of his views on governance (Tiwald 2016).

30 XZ 12/263; cf. Xunzi 2014: 117.

31 XZ 12/263; cf. Xunzi 2014: 117.

32 Xunzi touches on these facets of the character-centered view in the following set of remarks: "With the superior person present, even if the rules and regulations are sketchy, they are enough to be comprehensive. Without the superior person, even if the rules and regulations are complete, one will fail to apply them in the right order and will be unable to respond to changes in affairs, and thus they can serve to create chaos. One who tries to correct the arrangements of the rules and regulations without understanding their meaning, even if he is broadly learned, is sure to create chaos when engaged in affairs" (XZ 12/263–4; cf. Xunzi 2014: 117).

33 "Those who want to restore order should rectify the general guidelines. Only after understanding the general guidelines can the roots be corrected and the branches stabilized. If the general guidelines are not understood then even if some are good at formulating specific clauses and there is the occasional period of good results, in the end there will invariably be places that do not correctly accord with the general guidelines, which in turn will give rise to great chaos" (ZZHY 8.19/24).

34 ZYHH 8.18/23–4.

35 MYDFL 23–5; cf. Tiwald and Van Norden 2014: 316–17.

36 Following a longstanding view found in Confucian political thought, as we will see in the next section.

37 MYDFL 23–5; cf. Tiwald and Van Norden 2014: 317.

38 WJ 11/590; cf. Schirokauer 1978: 131.

39 De Bary 1981 emphasizes the "Learning of the Emperor" and elaborates in particular on the educational theories of ZHU Xi's follower ZHEN Dexiu. De Bary also discusses the "classics mat" institution at some length.

40 See Schirokauer 1978: 144. For an outstanding evocation of the demands that rituals placed upon emperors, see Huang 1981.

41 LY 2.3.

42 Zhu and Lü 1967: 234.

43 JSL 10.3/349; cf. Zhu and Lü 1967: 239.

44 WJ 3/665; cf. Wang 1972: 70. Overseeing litigation can also be a site for the magistrate's own self-cultivation. Wang says elsewhere: "When you interrogate a litigant, do not become angry because his replies are impolite or glad because his words are smooth; do not punish him because you hate his effort to solicit help from your superiors; ... do not decide the case carelessly on the spur of the moment because you are busy with your own affairs. ... To do any of these is selfish. You need only to follow what you know in yourself. You must carefully examine and control yourself, lest your heartmind become in the least prejudiced and distort who is right and who is wrong" (CXL 218/94–5; cf. Wang 1963: 197–8).

45 Ong 2006: 482; and see also Kim 2008.

46 Wang 1989: 850; cf. Kim 2008: 117.

47 See Tillman 1994 and Niu 1998.

48 McKnight 1987: 113.

49 McKnight 1987. See also Stephens 1992, who argues that traditional Chinese law is similar to the standing orders in a military unit, although we believe he somewhat overstates the case, on which see Angle 2009: 219.

50 Metzger 1977: 187.

51 MYDFL 37–53; cf. Huang 1993: 30–4, 104–10.

52 MYDFL 46; cf. Huang 1993: 107.

53 Our translation of *junxian* 郡縣, more literally, the "prefecture-county system." Other popular translations include "the imperial system" (Brown 2011), "the centralized prefectures and counties system" (de Bary 1991: 64), and "the province-district system" (Schirokauer 1993: 217).

54 *Fengjian* 封建. Modern scholars sometimes render these characters as "feudalism" or "the feudal system."

55 As ZHU Xi explains in YL 108/3513.

56 See Xiao 1982: v.1, 539–40 and YL 108/3516.

57 Song 2011.

58 Xiao 1982: v.1, 539.

59 Hu 1987: 91–3, and YL 108/3516.

60 ZYHH 4.16/12. See also ZYHH 15.15/48 and YL 108/3514–15. This line is adopted by many Southern Song proponents of enfeoffment, who argue that more independent feudal states and their militaries would have been better equipped to resist the Jurchen invaders even while the central government was weak and divided (Song 2011: 311–15).

61 In the treatise "On Enfeoffment," pre-modern China's most influential critique of the enfeoffment system, LIU Zongyuan writes that the ancient sage rulers Yao and Shun separated their special attachments

to their own families from their political obligations, most famously by choosing meritorious administrators rather than their own sons as their successors (Song 2011: 307).

62 Brown 2011: 47.
63 Ong 2005.
64 See SGSHDS 82–103 and HWDJ 187–223.
65 See Hu's discussion of Xunzi in section 3 of this chapter.
66 HWDJ 1141; cf. Song 2011: 317.
67 ZYHH 15.14/47–8.
68 YL 108/3513. For the evolution of Zhu's views on this matter, see Tillman 1994: 51–4.
69 YL 108/3513.
70 YL 108/3514. For a similar argument, see YL 108/3516.

Chapter 10   The Enduring Significance of Neo-Confucianism

1 The classic study of the Qing "evidential learning" movement is Elman 2001. Ritualism and purism are the topic of Chow 1994; we quote Chow 1994: 8. Elman 1990 is a study of the Changzhou school of "New Text" reformist Confucianism, and see Chang 1987 for the late-nineteenth century reformism of KANG Youwei and others. Contemporary Confucian scholar-activists like Jiang 2013 and Gan 2006 both, in their different ways, draw on Kang and New Text Confucianism.
2 Wright 1957 is a classic study of the Tongzhi Restoration. One good starting point for the broader Self-Strengthening Movement and the Hundred Days' Reform is Spence 1990.
3 Yu 2004.
4 So argues Kim 2014.
5 In an important study of the category of "New Confucianism," John Makeham argues that it is not used as a designation for a self-conscious school of or approach to philosophy until the 1970s. Still, Makeham shows that the term *xin rujia* (and, somewhat later, "contemporary New Confucianism," *dangdai xin rujia* 當代新儒家) was in use from considerably earlier. Already in a 1941 essay by HE Lin (1902–1993), the connection with western philosophy was explicit. See Makeham 2003a: 25–7 for details.
6 Chan 2011 is one of several excellent studies of MOU Zongsan.
7 Sun 2013: 42–3.
8 One example is the "New Life" movement promoted by the Nationalist government in the 1930s; another is the partial use of Confucian teachings to explain how communist cadres should cultivate themselves in LIU Shao-chi's *How to be a Good Communist* (Liu 1964) from 1939. Since coming to power in 2012, XI Jinping has increasingly

embraced "traditional Chinese culture," including some classical and Neo-Confucian teachings.

9   Makeham 2012 in an outstanding collection of essays on the emergence of philosophy as a discipline in China.
10 See Lee 1990 and Chen 2014.
11 For considerable discussion, see Angle 2016.
12 Frisina 2002: 144.
13 Frisina 2002: 73.
14 See Ho 2016.
15 Klancer 2015: 10–11.
16 Walden 2015: 33.
17 Admittedly, Walden does more to raise the possibilities suggested by his subjects than he does to synthesize their accounts or solve lingering problems, and as such his argument is quite preliminary; see McGill 2016.
18 Huang 2014. For one early review of Huang's book that raises some challenging questions about its methodology, see Hall 2016.
19 See Angle 2009: ch. 9.
20 Kalton's writing in this area includes both published and unpublished essays, all of which are available at his website: http://faculty.washington.edu/mkalton/21st%20century%20interface.htm. One exemplary instance is Kalton 1998.
21 Kalton 1998: 79 and 100.
22 Ziporyn 2012: 13.

Appendix 1 Teaching Neo-Confucianism Topically

1   See Zhu and Lü 1967.

Bibliography

Adler, Joseph A. 2004. "Varieties of Spiritual Experience: *Shen* in Neo-Confucian Discourse." In Wei-ming Tu and Mary Evelyn Tucker (eds), *Confucian Spirituality, Volume Two*. New York: Crossroad Publishing Co., pp. 120–48.

Adler, Joseph A. 2015. "On Translating *Taiji*." In David Jones and He Jinli (eds), *Emerging Patterns within the Supreme Polarity: Rethinking Zhu Xi*. Albany, NY: SUNY Press.

Allen, Barry. 2015. *Vanishing Into Things: Knowledge in the Chinese Tradition*. Cambridge: Harvard University Press.

Anderl, Christoph. 2004. "The Semantics of *Qing* 情 in Chan Buddhist Chinese." In Halvor Eifring (ed.), *Love and Emotions in Traditional Chinese Literature*. Leiden: Brill, pp. 149–224.

Angle, Stephen C. 2002. *Human Rights and Chinese Thought: A Cross-Cultural Inquiry*. Cambridge: Cambridge University Press.

Angle, Stephen C. 2009. *Sagehood: The Contemporary Significance of Neo-Confucian Philosophy*. New York: Oxford University Press.

Angle, Stephen C. 2013. "Is Conscientiousness a Virtue? Confucian Answers." In Stephen C. Angle and Michael Slote (eds), *Virtue Ethics and Confucianism*. New York: Routledge.

Angle, Stephen C. 2016. "Introduction." In Stephen C. Angle (ed.), *Comparative Philosophy: Reviewing the State of the Art*. Self-published.

Araki, Kengo 荒木見悟. 2008. 佛教與儒教 [*Buddhism and Confucianism*], trans. LIAO Zhaoheng 廖肇亨. Taibei: Lianjing chubanshe.

Ban, Zhao 班昭. (n.d.) "女誡 [Lessons for Women]." *Tingyu Tang Cong Ke, Nüer Shu* 聽雨堂叢刻•女兒書, ed. ZHANG Chengxie 張承燮, 5.1a–9a (輯第五, pp. 1–9).

Ban, Zhao. 2014. "Lessons for Women," trans. Nancy Lee Swann. In Justin Tiwald and Bryan W. Van Norden (eds), *Readings in Later Chinese*

Philosophy: Han Dynasty to the 20th Century. Cambridge: Hackett, pp. 55–63.

Barrett, T. H. 1992. *Li Ao: Buddhist, Taoist, or Neo-Confucian?* Oxford: Oxford University Press.

Berthrong, John. 2010. "ZHU Xi's Cosmology." In John Makeham (ed.), *Dao Companion to Neo-Confucian Philosophy*. Dordrecht: Springer, pp. 153–75.

Birdwhistell, Anne. 1985. "The Concept of Experiential Knowledge in the Thought of Chang Tsai." *Philosophy East & West* 35(1): 37–60.

Birdwhistell, Anne. 1989. *Transition to Neo-Confucianism: Shao Yung on Knowledge and Symbols of Reality*. Stanford: Stanford University Press.

Bol, Peter K. 1992. *"This Culture of Ours": Intellectual Transitions in T'ang and Sung China*. Stanford: Stanford University Press.

Bol, Peter K. 1993. "Government, Society, and State: On the Political Visions of Ssu-Ma Kuang and Wang An-Shih." In Robert P. Hymes and Conrad Schirokauer (eds), *Ordering the World*. Berkeley: University of California Press, pp. 128–92.

Bol, Peter K. 2008. *Neo-Confucianism in History*. Cambridge: Harvard University Asia Center.

Bol, Peter K. 2015. "Reconceptualizing the Order of Things in Northern and Southern Song." In John W. Chaffee and Denis Twitchett (eds), *The Cambridge History of China: Volume 5, Part Two – Sung China, 960–1279*. Cambridge: Cambridge University Press, pp. 665–727.

Bol, Peter K., Adler, Joseph A., Wyatt, Don J., and Smith, Kidder. 1990. *Sung Dynasty Uses of the I Ching*. Princeton: Princeton University Press.

Borrell, Ari. 1999. "*Ko-Wu* or *Kung-an?* Practice, Realization, and Teaching in the Thought of Chang Chiu-Ch'eng." In Peter N. Gregory and Daniel A. Getz, Jr (eds), *Buddhism in the Sung*. Honolulu: University of Hawaii Press, pp. 62–108.

Borrell, Ari. (Unpublished) "The Daoxue Style and Song Political Culture." Conference paper presented Dec. 2, 2011. Copy on file with the authors.

Brokaw, Cynthia. 1987. "Yüan Huang (1533–1606) and the Ledgers of Merit and Demerit." *Harvard Journal of Asiatic Studies* 47(1): 137–95.

Brook, Timothy. 1998. *The Confusions of Pleasure: Commerce and Culture in Ming China*. Berkeley: University of California Press.

Brooks, E. Bruce and Brooks, A. Taeko. 1998. *The Original Analects: Sayings of Confucius and His Successors*. New York: Columbia University Press.

Brown, Miranda. 2011. "Returning the Gaze: An Experiment in Reviving Gu Yanwu (1613–1682)." *Fragments* 1: 41–77.

Cai, Zhenfeng 蔡振豐. 2009. "朱子對佛教的理解及其限制 [Zhu Xi's Understanding of Buddhism and Its Limits]." In Zhenfeng Cai 蔡振豐, 東亞朱子學的詮釋與發展 [*Interpretations and Development of Zhu Xi Learning in East Asia*]. Taibei: Taiwan Daxue Chuban Xin.

Cao, Xueqin. 1974. *The Story of the Stone: The Dream of the Red Chamber*, vol. 1, trans. David Hawkes. London: Penguin.

Ch'ien, Anne Meller. 1979. "Hu Chü-Jen's Self-Cultivation as Ritual and Reverence in Everyday Life." *Journal of Chinese Philosophy* 6: 183–210.

Chan, Nganying S. 2011. *The Thought of Mou Zongsan*. Leiden and Boston: Brill.

Chan, Wing-tsit. 1963. *A Sourcebook in Chinese Philosophy*. Princeton: Princeton University Press.

Chan, Wing-tsit. 1987. "Chu Hsi's Completion of Neo-Confucianism." In *Chu Hsi: Life and Thought*. Hong Kong: Hong Kong University Press, pp. 103–38.

Chan, Wing-tsit. 1989. *Chu Hsi: New Studies*. Honolulu: University of Hawaii Press.

Chang, Carsun. 1962. "A Manifesto for a Re-appraisal of Sinology and Reconstruction of Chinese Culture." In *The Development of Neo-Confucian Thought*. New York: Bookman Associates, pp. 455–83.

Chang, Hao. 1987. *Chinese Intellectuals in Crisis*. Berkeley: University of California Press.

Chen, Chun 陳淳. 1983. 北溪字義 [*Chen Chun's Explanation of the Meanings of Terms*]. Beijing: Zhonghua Shuju.

Chen, Chun (Ch'en, Ch'un). 1986. *Neo-Confucian Terms Explained (the Pei-Hsi Tzu-I)*, trans. Wing-tsit Chan. New York: Columbia University Press.

Chen, Lai 陈来. 1991. 有无之境–王阳明哲学的精神 [*The Border between Being and Nonbeing – the Spirit of Wang Yangming's Philosophy*]. Beijing: Renmin chubanshe.

Chen, Lai 陈来. 2000. 朱熹哲学研究 [*Research into Zhu Xi's Philosophy*]. Shanghai: Huadong Shifan Daxue Chubanshe.

Chen, Lai 陈来. 2003. 宋明理学 [*The School of Li in the Song and Ming Dynasties*], 2nd edn. Huadong Shifan Daxue Chubanshe.

Chen, Lai 陈来. 2010. 中国近世思想史研究 [*Research into the History of Modern Chinese Thought*]. 陈来学术论著集. Beijing: Sanlian Shudian.

Chen, Lai 陈来. 2014. *Ren de Bentilun* 仁学本体论 [*The Ontology of Humaneness*]. Beijing: Sanlian Shudian.

Chen, Xianzhang 陳獻章. 1987. *Chen Xianzhang Ji* 陳獻章集 [*Collected Works of CHEN Xianzhang*]. Beijing: Zhonghua Shuju.

Cheng, Chung-yi 鄭宗義. 2010. "Liu Zongzhou on Self-Cultivation." In John Makeham (ed.), *The Dao Companion to Neo-Confucianism*. Dordrecht: Springer, pp. 337–53.

Cheng, Chung-ying. 1991. "Li-Ch'i and Li-Yü Relationships in Seventeenth-Century Neo-Confucian Philosophy." In Chung-ying Cheng (ed.), *New Dimensions of Confucian and Neo-Confucian Philosophy*. Albany, NY: SUNY Press, pp. 504–36.

Cheng, Hao 程顥, and Cheng Yi 程頤. 1981. *Ercheng Ji* 二程集 [*Collected Works of the Cheng Brothers*]. Beijing: Zhonghua Shuju.

Cheng, Yu-yin. 2001. "Translator's Preface" and "Introduction." In Susan Mann and Yu-yin Cheng (eds), *Under Confucian Eyes: Writings on Gender in Chinese History*. Berkeley and Los Angeles: University of California Press, pp. 104–7.

Chow, Kai-wing. 1994. *The Rise of Confucian Ritualism in Late Imperial China: Ethics, Classics, and Lineage Discourse*. Stanford: Stanford University Press.

Dai, Zhen. 1971. *Tai Chên's Inquiry into Goodness*, trans. Chung-ying Cheng. Honolulu: East-West Center Press.

Dai, Zhen. 1990. *Evidential Commentary on the Meanings of Terms in Mencius*, trans. John Woodruff Ewell, Jr. Ann Arbor: University Microfilm.

Dai, Zhen 戴震. 2009. *Dai Zhen Ji* 戴震集 [*The Collected Works of DAI Zhen*]. Shanghai: Shanghai Guji Chuban She.

Dardess, John W. 1983. *Confucianism and Autocracy: Professional Elites in the Founding of the Ming Dynasty*. Berkeley: University of California Press.

Dardess, John W. 2002. *Blood and History in China: The Donglin Faction and Its Repression, 1620–1627*. Honolulu: University of Hawaii Press.

de Bary, William Theodore. 1981. *Neo-Confucian Orthodoxy and the Learning of the Mind-and-Heart*. New York: Columbia University Press.

de Bary, William Theodore. 1989. *The Message of the Mind in Neo-Confucianism*. New York: Columbia University Press.

de Bary, William Theodore. 1991. *The Trouble with Confucianism*. Cambridge: Harvard University Press.

de Bary, William Theodore. 1993. "The Uses of Neo-Confucianism: A Response to Professor Tillman." *Philosophy East & West* 43(3): 541–55.

de Bary, William Theodore and Bloom, Irene (eds). 1999. *Sources of Chinese Tradition*, Vol. 1. New York: Columbia University Press.

de Bary, William Theodore and Haboush, JaHyun Kim (eds). 1985. *The Rise of Neo-Confucianism in Korea*. New York: Columbia University Press.

de Bary, William Theodore and Lufrano, Richard (eds). 2001. *Sources of Chinese Tradition*, Vol. 2, 2nd edn. New York: Columbia University Press.

Ditmanson, Peter. 1998. "The Yongle Reign and the Transformation of Daoxue." *Ming Studies* 39: 7–31.

Du, Fangqing and Mann, Susan. 2003. "Competing Claims on Women and Virtue in Late Imperial China." In JaHyun Kim Haboush, Dorothy Ko, and Joan Piggott (eds), *Women and Confucian Cultures in Premodern China, Korea, and Japan*. Los Angeles/Berkeley: University of California Press.

Ebrey, Patricia Buckley. 2003. *Women and the Family in Chinese History*. Critical Asian Scholarship. New York: Routledge.

Egan, Ronald C. 1984. *The Literary Works of Ou-Yang Hsiu*. Cambridge: Cambridge University Press.

Egan, Ronald C. 1994. *Word, Image, and Deed in the Life of Su Shi*. Cambridge: Harvard-Yenching Institute Monograph Series.

Eichman, Jennifer. 2016. *A Late Sixteenth-Century Chinese Buddhist Fellowship: Spiritual Ambitions, Intellectual Debates, and Epistolary Connections*. Leiden: Brill.

Eifring, Halvor. 2004. "Introduction: Emotions and the Conceptual History of *Qing* 情." In Halvor Eifring (ed.), *The Semantics of Qing* 情 *in Chan Buddhist Chinese*. Leiden: Brill, pp. 1–36.

Elman, Benjamin A. 1989. "Imperial Politics and Confucian Societies in Late Imperial China: The Hanlin and Donglin Academies." *Modern China* 15(4): 379–418.

Elman, Benjamin A. 1990. *Classicism, Politics, and Kinship: The Ch'ang-Chou School of New Text Confucianism in Late Imperial China*. Berkeley: University of California Press.

Elman, Benjamin A. 2000. *A Cultural History of Civil Examinations in Late Imperial China*. Berkeley: University of California Press.

Elman, Benjamin A. 2001. *From Philosophy to Philology: Intellectual and Social Aspects of Change in Late Imperial China*, rev. edn. Los Angeles: UCLA Asia Pacific Monograph Series.

Fraser, Chris. 2011. "Knowledge and Error in Early Chinese Thought." *Dao: A Journal of Comparative Philosophy* 10(2): 127–48.

Fraser, Chris. 2016. *The Philosophy of the Mòzi: The First Consequentialists*. New York: Columbia University Press.

Frisina, Warren G. 2002. *The Unity of Knowledge and Action: Toward a Nonrepresentational Theory of Knowledge*. Albany, NY: SUNY Press.

Fu, Charles Wei-hsun. 1986. "Chu Hsi on Buddhism." In Wing-tsit Chan (ed.), *Chu Hsi and Neo-Confucianism*. Honolulu: University of Hawaii Press, pp. 377–407.

Fuji, Michiaki 籐井倫明. 2011. 朱熹思想結構探索 [*Research on the Structure of Zhu Xi's Thought*]. Taibei: Taida chuban zhongxin.

Fung, Yu-Lan. 1953. *A History of Chinese Philosophy, Vol. 2: The Period of Classical Learning (From the Second Century BC to the Twentieth Century AD)*, trans. Derk Bodde. Princeton: Princeton University Press.

Gan, Chunsong 干春松. 2006. *Zhidu Ruxue* 制度儒学 [*Institutional Confucianism*]. Shanghai: Shiji chuban jituan.

Geaney, Jane. 2002. *On the Epistemology of the Senses in Early Chinese Thought*. Honolulu: University of Hawaii Press.

Goldin, Paul. 2008. "The Myth That China Has No Creation Myth." *Monumenta Serica* 56: 1–22.

Graham, A. C. 1986. "What Was New in the Ch'eng-Chu Theory of Human Nature?" In *Studies in Chinese Philosophy and Philosophical Literature*. Singapore: Institute of East Asian Philosophies, pp. 412–35.

Graham, A. C. 1992. *Two Chinese Philosophers*. La Salle: Open Court.

Gregory, Peter N. 2002. *Tsung-Mi and the Sinification of Buddhism*. Honolulu: University of Hawaii Press.

Hadot, Pierre. 1995. *Philosophy as a Way of Life: Spiritual Exercises from Socrates to Foucault*, ed. Arnold I. Davidson. Cambridge, MA: Wiley-Blackwell.

Hakeda, Yoshito S. 2006. (trans.). *The Awaking of Faith*. New York: Columbia University Press.

Hall, Erik. 2016. "Metaphysical Modularity – Review of Yong Huang, *Why be Moral? Learning from the Neo-Confucian Cheng Brothers*." In Stephen C. Angle (ed.), *Comparative Philosophy: Reviewing the State of the Art*. Self-published.

Han, Yu 韓愈. 1968. "原性 [On the Nature]." In 昌黎先生集 [*The Collected Works of Mister Changli*]. Taibei: Zhonghua Shuju (*Sibu beiyao* edition), vol. 1, *juan* 11, 5b–8a.

Hansen, Chad. 1983. *Language and Logic in Ancient China*. Ann Arbor: University of Michigan Press.

Harbsmeier, Christoph. 1993. "Conceptions of Knowledge in Ancient China." In Hans Lenk and Gregor Paul (eds), *Epistemological Issues in Classical Chinese Philosophy*. Albany: State University of New York Press, pp. 11–30.

Harbsmeier, Christoph. 2004. "The Semantics of *Qíng* 情 in Pre-Buddhist Chinese." In Halvor Eifring (ed.), *Love and Emotion in Traditional Chinese Literature*. Leiden: Brill, pp. 69–148.

Hartman, Charles. 1986. *Han Yu and the T'ang Search for Unity*. Princeton: Princeton University Press.

Ho, Justin. 2016. "Towards a Unity of Knowledge and Action – A Review of Warren G. Frisina, *The Unity of Knowledge and Action: Toward a Nonrepresentational Theory of Knowledge*." In Stephen C. Angle (ed.), *Comparative Philosophy: Reviewing the State of the Art*. Self-published.

Hon, Tze-ki. 2004. *The Yijing and Chinese Politics: Classical Commentary and Literati Activism in the Northern Song Period, 960–1127*. Albany, NY: SUNY Press.

Hu, Hong 胡宏. 1987. 胡宏集 [*Collected Works of HU Hong*]. Beijing: Zhonghua Shuju.

Huang, Chin-shing. 1995. *Philosophy, Philology, and Politics in Eighteenth-Century China: Li Fu and the Lu–Wang School under the Ch'ing*. Cambridge: Cambridge University Press.

Huang, Chun-chieh and Tucker, John Allen (eds). 2014. *Dao Companion to Japanese Confucian Philosophy*. Dordrecht: Springer.

Huang, Martin W. 1998. "Sentiments of Desire: Thoughts on the Cult of Qing in Ming-Qing Literature." *Chinese Literature: Essays, Articles, Reviews (CLEAR)* 20: 153–84.

Huang, Ray. 1981. *1587: A Year of No Significance*. New Haven: Yale University Press.

Huang, Yong. 2014. *Why Be Moral? Learning from the Neo-Confucian Cheng Brothers*. Albany, NY: SUNY Press.

Huang, Zongxi 黃宗羲. 1965. 明儒學案 [*The Records of the Ming Scholars*], Vols 1–4. Taibei: Zhonghua Shuju.

Huang, Zongxi. 1993. *Waiting for the Dawn*, trans. William Theodore de Bary. New York: Columbia University Press.

Huang, Zongxi 黃宗羲. 2011. 明夷待訪錄 [*Waiting for the Dawn*]. Beijing: Zhonghua Shuju.

Ivanhoe, Philip J. 2000a. *Confucian Moral Self-Cultivation*, 2nd edn. Indianapolis/Cambridge: Hackett.

Ivanhoe, Philip J. 2000b. "Human Nature and Moral Understanding in the *Xunzi*." In T. C. Kline III and Philip J. Ivanhoe (eds), *Virtue, Nature, and Moral Agency in the Xunzi*. Indianapolis/Cambridge: Hackett, pp. 237–50.

Ivanhoe, Philip J. 2002. *Ethics in the Confucian Tradition: The Thought of Mengzi and Wang Yangming*. 2nd edn. Indianapolis/Cambridge: Hackett.

Ivanhoe, Philip J. 2007. "Filial Piety as a Virtue." In Rebecca Walker and Philip J. Ivanhoe (eds), *Working Virtue: Virtue Ethics and Contemporary Moral Problems*. Oxford: Oxford University Press, pp. 297–312.

Ivanhoe, Philip J. 2009. *Readings from the Lu-Wang School of Neo-Confucianism*. Indianapolis: Hackett.

Ivanhoe, Philip J. 2010. "Lu Xiangshan's Ethical Philosophy." In John Makeham (ed.), *Dao Companion to Neo-Confucian Philosophy*. Dordrecht: Springer, pp. 249–66.

Ivanhoe, Philip J. 2015. "Senses and Values of Oneness." In Brian Bruya (ed.), *The Philosophical Challenge From China*. Cambridge: MIT Press, pp. 231–51.

Jiang, Qing. 2013. *A Confucian Constitutional Order: How China's Ancient Past Can Shape Its Political Future*, trans. Edmund Ryden, ed. Daniel A. Bell and Ruiping Fan. Princeton: Princeton University Press.

Johnston, Ian, and Wang, Ping (eds). 2012. *Daxue & Zhongyong*, bilingual edn. Hong Kong: Chinese University of Hong Kong Press.

Kaibara, Ekken. 2007. *The Philosophy of Qi: The Record of Great Doubts*, trans. Mary Evelyn Tucker. New York: Columbia University Press.

Kalton, Michael C. 1988. *To Become a Sage: The Ten Diagrams on Sage Learning by Yi T'oegye*. New York: Columbia University Press.

Kalton, Michael C., with Oaksook, C. Kim, Park, Sung Bae, Ro, Young-chan, Tu, Wei-ming, and Yamashita, Samuel. 1994. *The Four–Seven Debate: An Annotated Translation of the Most Famous Controversy in Korean Neo-Confucian Thought*. Albany, NY: SUNY Press.

Kalton, Michael C. 1998. "Extending the Neo-Confucian Tradition: Questions and Reconceptualization for the Twenty-First Century." In Mary Evelyn Tucker and John Berthrong (eds), *Confucianism and Ecology*. Cambridge: Harvard University Center for the Study of World Religions, pp. 77–101.

Kasoff, Ira E. 1984. *The Thought of Chang Tsai (1020–1077)*. New York: Cambridge University Press.

Kim, Jung-Yeup. 2015. *Zhang Zai's Philosophy of Qi*. Albany: State University of New York Press.

Kim, Sungmoon. 2014. *Confucian Democracy in East Asia: Theory and Practice*. Cambridge and New York: Cambridge University Press.

Kim, Youngmin. 2001. "Rethinking the Self's Relation to the World in Mid-Ming: Four Responses to Cheng–Zhu Learning." *Ming Studies* 44: 13–47.

Kim, Youngmin. 2003. "Luo Qingshun (1465–15–47) and His Intellectual Context." *T'oung Pao* LXXXIX: 367–441.

Kim, Youngmin. 2008. "Cosmogony as Political Philosophy." *Philosophy East & West* 58(1): 108–25.

Kim, Yung Sik. 2000. *The Natural Philosophy of Chu Hsi, 1130–1200*. Philadelphia: Memoirs of the American Philosophic Society.

King, Sallie B. 1991. *Buddha Nature*. Albany: SUNY Press.

Klancer, Catherine Hudak. 2015. *Embracing Our Complexity: Thomas Aquinas and Zhu Xi on Power and the Common Good*. Albany, NY: SUNY Press.

Koh, Khee Heong. 2011. *A Northern Alternative: Xue Xuan (1389–1464) and the Hedong School*. Cambridge, MA: Harvard University Asia Center.

Koh, Sunghak. 2011. "Li Tongxuan's (635–730) Thought and His Place in the Huayan Tradition of Chinese Buddhism." PhD dissertation. Los Angeles: University of California.

Krummel, John W. M. 2010. "Transcendent or Immanent? The Significance and History of *Li* in Confucianism." *Journal of Chinese Philosophy* 37(3): 417–37.

Langlois, John D. 1981. "Political Thought in Chin-Hua Under Mongol Rule." In John D. Langlois (ed.), *China Under Mongol Rule*. Princeton: Princeton University Press.

Lee, Junghwan. 2008. "A Groundwork for Normative Unity: Zhu Xi's Reformulation of the 'Learning of the Way' Tradition." PhD dissertation. Cambridge: Harvard University.

Lee, Ming-huei 李明輝. 1990. 儒家與康德 [*Confucianism and Kant*]. Taibei: Lianjing Press.

Lee, Ming-huei 李明輝. 2005. 四端與七情: 關於道德情感的比較哲學探討 [*The Four Beginnings and the Seven Emotions: Explorations in the Comparative Philosophy of the Moral Emotions*]. Taibei: Guoli Taiwan Daxue Chuban Zhongxin.

Lee, Pauline C. 2002. "Li Zhi (1527–1602): A Confucian Feminist in Late Ming China." PhD dissertation. Palo Alto: Stanford University.

Lee, Pauline C. 2012. *Li Zhi, Confucianism, and the Virtue of Desire*. Albany, NY: SUNY Press.

Legge, James. 1985. *The Shoo King*. Vol. 3, *The Chinese Classics*. Taibei: Southern Materials Center.

Levine, Ari Daniel. 2008. *Divided by a Common Language: Factional Conflict in Late Northern Song China*. Honolulu: University of Hawaii Press.

Liu, JeeLoo. 2010. "Wang Fuzhi's Philosophy of Principle (*Li*) Inherent in *Qi*." In John Makeham (ed.), *Dao Companion to Neo-Confucian Philosophy*. Dordrecht: Springer, pp. 355–79.

Liu, Shao-chi. 1964. *How to be a Good Communist*. Beijing: Foreign Language Press.

Liu, Yumin 刘玉敏. 2010. "心学的肇始–张九成的哲学逻辑结构 [The Origins of Heartmind Learning: The Logical Structure of ZHANG Jiucheng's Philosophy]." 孔子研究 [*Confucius Studies*] 2: 13–18.

Lo, Winston Wan. 1974. *The Life and Thought of Yeh Shih*. Hong Kong: Chinese University of Hong Kong Press.

Lu, Xiangshan 陸象山. 1980. 陸九淵集 [*Collected Works of Lu Xiangshan*]. Beijing: Zhonghua Shuju.

Lufrano, Richard John. 1997. *Honorable Merchants: Commerce and Self-Cultivation in Late Imperial China*. Honolulu: University of Hawaii Press.

Luo, Qinshun. 1987. *Knowledge Painfully Acquired*, trans. Irene Bloom. New York: Columbia University Press.

Luo, Qinshun 羅欽順. 1990. 困知記 [*Knowledge Painfully Acquired*]. Beijing: Zhonghua Shuju.

Luo, Rufang. 2001. "Selected Writings by Luo Rufang (1515–1588)," trans. Yu-yin Cheng. In Susan Mann and Yu-yin Cheng (eds), *Under Confucian Eyes: Writings on Gender in Chinese History*. Berkeley and Los Angeles: University of California Press, pp. 103–17.

Luo, Rufang 羅汝芳. 2007. 羅汝芳集 [*The Collected Works of LUO Rufang*]. Fang Zuyou 方祖猷, Liang Yiqun 梁一群, Li Qinglong 李慶龍, et al. (eds). Nanjing: Fenghuang Chuban She.

Makeham, John. 2003a. "The Retrospective Creation of New Confucianism." In John Makeham (ed.), *New Confucianism: A Critical Examination*. New York: Palgrave, pp. 25–53.

Makeham, John. 2003b. *Transmitters and Creators: Chinese Commentators and Commentaries on the Analects*. Cambridge, MA: Harvard University Asia Center.

Makeham, John (ed.). 2010. *The Dao Companion to Neo-Confucianism*. New York: Springer.

Makeham, John. 2012. *Learning to Emulate the Wise: The Genesis of Chinese Philosophy as an Academic Discipline in Twentieth-Century China*. Hong Kong: Chinese University of Hong Kong Press.

Makeham, John (ed.). Unpublished. *The Buddhist Roots of Zhu Xi's Thought*. Manuscript on file with the authors.

Mann, Susan. 1992. "'Fuxue' (Women's Learning) by Zhang Xuecheng (1738–1801): China's First History of Women's Culture." *Late Imperial China* 13(1): 40–62.

Marchal, Kai. 2013. "Moral Emotions, Awareness, and Spiritual Freedom in the Thought of Zhu Xi (1130–1200)." *Asian Philosophy* 23(3): 199–220.

McGill, Adam. 2016. "The Problem Below – a Review of Asher Walden, *the Metaphysics of Kindness: Comparative Studies in Religious Meta-Ethics*." In Stephen C. Angle (ed.), *Comparative Philosophy: Reviewing the State of the Art*. Self-published.

McKnight, Brian E. 1987. "From Statute to Precedent: An Introduction to Sung Law and Its Transformation." In Brian E. McKnight (ed.), *Law and the State in Traditional East Asia: Six Studies on the Sources of East Asian Law*. Honolulu: University of Hawaii Press, pp. 111–31.

Mengzi (Mencius). 2008. *Mengzi: With Selections from Traditional Commentaries*, trans. Bryan Van Norden. Cambridge: Hackett Publishing.

Metzger, Thomas A. 1977. *Escape from Predicament: Neo-Confucianism and China's Evolving Political Culture*. New York: Columbia University Press.

Metzger, Thomas A. 2005. *A Cloud Across the Pacific: Essays on the Clash Between Chinese and Western Political Theories Today*. Hong Kong: Chinese University of Hong Kong Press.

Moran, Patrick Edwin. 1983. "Explorations of Chinese Metaphysical Concepts: The History of Some Key Terms from the Beginnings to Chu Hsi (1130–1200)." PhD dissertation. Philadelphia: University of Pennsylvania.

Needham, Joseph, Lu, Gwei-Djen, and Sivin, Nathan. 2000. *Science and Civilisation in China: Volume 6, Biology and Biological Technology, Part 6, Medicine.* Cambridge: Cambridge University Press.

Neville, Robert Cummings. 1990. "Foreword." In Rodney L. Taylor (ed.), *The Religious Dimensions of Confucianism.* Albany, NY: SUNY Press, pp. ix–x.

Ng, On-cho. 2001. *Cheng–Zhu Confucianism in the Early Qing: Li Guangdi (1642–1718) and Qing Learning.* Albany, NY: SUNY Press.

Niu, Pu. 1998. "Confucian Statecraft in Song China: Ye Shi and the Yongjia School." Arizona State University.

Ong, Chang Woei. 2005. "We Are One Family: The Vision of 'Guanxue' in the Northern Song." *Journal of Song–Yuan Studies* 35: 29–57.

Ong, Chang Woei. 2006. "The Principles are Many: Wang Tingxiang and Intellectual Transition in Mid-Ming China." *Harvard Journal of Asiatic Studies* 66(2): 461–93.

Pang-White, Ann A. 2013. "Zhu Xi on Family and Women: Challenges and Potentials." *Journal of Chinese Philosophy* 40(3–4): 436–55.

Peng, Guoxiang 彭国翔. 2005. 良知学的展开：王龙溪与中晚明的阳明学 [*Developments in the Learning of Good Knowing: Wang Longxi and Yangming Learning in the Mid- to Late Ming Dynasty*]. Beijing: Sanlian Shudian.

Peng, Guoxiang 彭国翔. 2012. 儒家传统的诠释与思辨 [*Thought and Interpretation of the Confucian Tradition*]. Wuhan: Wuhan Daxue Chuban She.

Perkins, Franklin. 2015. "What is a Thing (*Wu* 物)? The Problem of Individuation in Early Chinese Metaphysics." In Chenyang Li and Franklin Perkins (eds), *Chinese Metaphysics and Its Problems.* Cambridge: Cambridge University Press, pp. 54–68.

Puett, Michael. 2004. "The Ethics of Responding Properly: The Notion of *Qing* 情 in Early Chinese Thought." In Halvor Eifring (ed.), *Love and Emotions in Traditional Chinese Literature.* Leiden: Brill, pp. 37–68.

Qian, Mu 錢穆. 1989. 朱子新學案 [*Master Zhu: New Studies*], 3rd edn, Taibei: Sanmin Shuju.

Raphals, Lisa. 1998. *Sharing the Light: Representations of Women and Virtue in Early China.* Albany: State University of New York Press.

Ruan, Yuan 阮元 (ed.) 1980. 十三经注疏 [*The Thirteen Classics with Commentaries and Subcommentaries*]. Beijing: Zhonghua Shuju.

Schirokauer, Conrad. 1978. "Chu Hsi's Political Thought." *Journal of Chinese Philosophy* 5: 127–48.

Schirokauer, Conrad. 1986. "Chu Hsi and Hu Hong." In *Chu Hsi and Neo-Confucianism*, ed. Wing-tsit Chan. Honolulu: University of Hawaii Press, pp. 480–502.

Schirokauer, Conrad. 1993. "Chu Hsi's Sense of History." In Robert P. Hymes and Conrad Schirokauer (eds), *Ordering the World: Approaches to State and Society in Sung Dynasty China.* Berkeley: University of California Press, pp. 280–309.

Schlütter, Morten. 1999. *How Zen Became Zen: The Dispute Over Enlightenment and the Formation of Chan Buddhism in Song-Dynasty China.* Honolulu: University of Hawaii Press.

Shao, Yong 邵雍. 1999. 皇極經世觀物外篇衍義 [*Extended Meanings of the Outer Chapter "on the Observation of Things." In the Book of the August Ultimate through the Ages*], ed. ZHANG Xingcheng 張行成. Hong Kong: Digital Heritage Publishing.

Shun, Kwong-loi. 2011. "Wang Yang-Ming on Self-Cultivation in the *Daxue*." *Journal of Chinese Philosophy* 38s: 96–113.

Smith, Kidder, Bol, Peter K., Adler, Joseph A., and Wyatt, Don J. 1990. "Sung Literati Thought and the I Ching." In *Sung Dynasty Uses of the I Ching*. Princeton: Princeton University Press, pp. 206–35.

Song, Jaeyoon. 2011. "Redefining Good Government: Shifting Paradigms in Song Dynasty (960–1279) Discourse on 'Fengjian.'" *T'oung Pao* 97: 301–43.

Spence, Jonathan D. 1990. *The Search for Modern China*. New York: W. W. Norton & Co.

Stalnaker, Aaron. 2006. *Overcoming Our Evil: Human Nature and Spiritual Exercises in Xunzi and Augustine*. Washington, DC: Georgetown University Press.

Stanchina, Gabriella. 2015. "*Zhi* 知 as Unceasing Dynamism and Practical Effort: The Common Root of Knowledge and Action in Wang Yangming and Peter Sloterdijk." 学问: 思勉青年学术期刊 [*Inquiry: Simian Youth Academic Journal*] (1): 280–307.

Standen, Naomi. 2007. *Unbounded Loyalty: Frontier Crossing in Liao China*. Honolulu: University of Hawaii Press.

Stephens, Thomas B. 1992. *Order and Discipline in China: The Shanghai Mixed Court 1911–27*. Seattle: University of Washington Press.

Streng, Frederick. 1985. *Understanding Religious Life*. Belmont: Wadsworth.

Sun, Anna. 2013. *Confucianism as a World Religion: Contested Histories and Contemporary Realities*. Princeton: Princeton University Press.

Taylor, K. W. 2002. "Vietnamese Confucian Narratives," ed. Benjamin A. Elman, John B. Duncan, and Herman Ooms. Los Angeles: University of California, pp. 337–69.

Taylor, Rodney L. 1990. *The Religious Dimensions of Confucianism*. Albany, NY: SUNY Press.

Tillman, Hoyt Cleveland. 1982. *Utilitarian Confucianism*. Cambridge, MA: Council on East Asian Studies.

Tillman, Hoyt Cleveland. 1992. *Confucian Discourse and Chu Hsi's Ascendancy*. Honolulu: University of Hawaii Press.

Tillman, Hoyt Cleveland. 1994. *Ch'en Liang on Public Interest and the Law*. Honolulu: University of Hawaii Press.

Tillman, Hoyt Cleveland. 2015. "The Rise of the *Tao-Hsüeh* Confucian Fellowship in Southern Sung." In John W. Chaffee and Denis Twitchett (eds), *Reconceptualizing the Order of Things in Northern and Southern Song*. Cambridge: Cambridge University Press, pp. 727–91.

Tiwald, Justin. 2010. "Dai Zhen on Human Nature and Moral Cultivation." In John Makeham (ed.), *Dao Companion to Neo-Confucian Philosophy*. Dordrecht: Springer, pp. 399–422.

Tiwald, Justin. 2016. "Xunzi among the Chinese Neo-Confucians." In Eric L. Hutton (ed.), *The Dao Companion to the Philosophy of Xunzi*. Dordrecht: Springer.

Tiwald, Justin. Forthcoming. "Confucianism and Neo-Confucianism." In Nancy Snow (ed.), *Oxford Handbook of Virtue*. New York: Oxford University Press.

Tiwald, Justin, and Van Norden, Bryan W. (eds). 2014. *Readings in Later Chinese Philosophy: Han Dynasty to the 20th Century*. Cambridge: Hackett.

Tu, Wei-ming. 1989. "The Continuity of Being: Chinese Visions of Nature," in J. Baird Callicott and Roger T. Ames (eds), *Nature in Asian Traditions of Thought: Essays in Environmental Philosophy*. Albany: SUNY Press, pp. 67–78.

Tucker, Mary Evelyn. 2003. "Introduction." In Wei-ming Tu and Mary Evelyn Tucker (eds), *Confucian Spirituality*, Vol. One. New York: Crossroad Publishing Co., pp. 1–35.

Van Ess, Hans. 2010. "HU Hong's Philosophy." In John Makeham (ed.), *The Dao Companion to Neo-Confucianism*. New York: Springer, pp. 105–23.

Van Norden, Bryan W. 2000. "Mengzi and Xunzi: Two Views of Human Agency." In T. C. Kline III and Philip J. Ivanhoe (eds), *Virtue, Nature, and Moral Agency in the Xunzi*. Indianapolis: Hackett, pp. 103–34.

Van Norden, Bryan W. 2007. *Virtue Ethics and Consequentialism in Early Chinese Philosophy*. Cambridge: Cambridge University Press.

Van Zoeren, Steven. 1991. *Poetry and Personality: Reading, Exegesis, and Hermeneutics in Traditional China*. Stanford: Stanford University Press.

Virág, Curie. 2007. "Emotions and Human Agency in the Thought of Zhu Xi." *Journal of Sung-Yuan Studies* 37: pp. 49–88.

Walden, Asher. 2015. *The Metaphysics of Kindness: Comparative Studies in Religious Meta-Ethics*. Lanham: Lexington Books.

Walton, Linda. 2010. " 'The Four Masters of Mingzhou': Transmission and Innovation among the Disciples of Lu Jiuyuan (Xiangshan)." In John Makeham (ed.), *The Dao Companion to Neo-Confucian Philosophy*. Dordrecht: Springer, pp. 267–93.

Wang, Qianshou 王黔首. 2011. " '德性所知' 与 '德性之知' 之区别及其意义– 张载 《大心篇》 解读兼论其知识论 [The Difference Between and the Meaning of 'That Which the Virtuous Nature Knows' and 'The Virtuous Nature's Knowing']. *Guizhou Daxue Xuebao (Shehui Kexue Ban)* 29(5): 15–19.

Wang, Robin R. and Weixiang, Ding. 2010. "Zhang Zai's Theory of Vital Energy." In John Makeham (ed.), *Dao Companion to Neo-Confucian Philosophy*. Dordrecht: Springer, pp. 39–57.

Wang, Tingxiang 王廷相. 1989. 王廷相集 [*Collected Works of Wang Tingxiang*]. Beijing: Zhonghua Shuju.

Wang, Yangming 1963. *Instructions for Practical Living*, trans. Wing-tsit Chan. New York: Columbia University Press.

Wang, Yangming. 1972. *The Philosophical Letters of Wang Yang-Ming*, trans. Julia Ching. Canberra: Australia National University Press.

Wang, Yangming. 王陽明. 1992. 王陽明全集 [*Complete Works of Wang Yangming*]. Shanghai: Shanghai Guji Chuban She.

Wilson, Thomas A. 1995. *Genealogy of the Way: The Construction and Uses of the Confucian Tradition in Late Imperial China*. Stanford, CA: Stanford University Press.

Wong, David B. 2000. "Xunzi on Moral Motivation." In T. C. Kline III and Philip J. Ivanhoe (eds), *Virtue, Nature, and Moral Agency in the Xunzi*. Indianapolis: Hackett, pp. 135–54.

Wong, Wai-ying. 2010. "The Thesis of Single-Rootedness in the Thought of Cheng Hao." In John Makeham (ed.), *Dao Companion to Neo-Confucian Philosophy*. Dordrecht: Springer, pp. 89–104.

Wood, Alan T. 1995. *Limits to Autocracy: From Sung Neo-Confucianism to a Doctrine of Political Rights*. Honolulu: University of Hawaii Press.

Woodside, Alexander. 2002. "Classical Primordialism and the Historical Agendas of Vietnamese Confucianism." In Benjamin A. Elman, John B. Duncan, and Herman Ooms (eds), *Rethinking "Confucianism" and "Neo-Confucianism" in Modern Chinese History*. Los Angeles: University of California.

Wright, Mary Clabaugh. 1957. *The Last Stand of Chinese Conservatism*. Stanford: Stanford University Press.

Wu, Zhen 吳震. 2009. "'心是做工夫处' – 关于朱子'心论'的几个问题 [" 'The Heartmind is the Locus of Effort' – Some Questions Concerning ZHU Xi's 'Doctrine of Heartmind']." 宋代新儒学的精神世界 [*The Spiritual World of Song Dynasty Neo-Confucianism*], ed. WU Zhen 吳震. Shanghai: Huadong Shifan Daxue Chubanshe, pp. 112–38.

Wu, Yubi. 2013. *The Journal of Wu Yubi: The Path to Sagehood*, trans. Theresa Kelleher. Indianapolis: Hackett.

Xiang, Shiling. 2011. "Between Mind and Trace – A Research into the Theories on Xin 心 (Mind) of Early Song Confucianism and Buddhism." *Frontiers of Philosophy in China* 6(2): 173–92.

Xiao, Gongquan 蕭公權. 1982. 中國政治思想史 [*A History of Chinese Political Thought*]. Vol. 2. Taibei: Lianjing chubanshe.

Xu, Empress. 1999. "Instructions for the Inner Quarters." In William Theodore de Bary and Irene Bloom (eds), *Sources of Chinese Tradition*, Vol. 1. New York: Columbia University Press, pp. 833–6.

Xunzi 荀子. 1979. 荀子集釋 [*Xunzi, with Collected Interpretations*], ed. LI Tisheng 李滌生. Taibei: Xuesheng Shuju.

Xunzi. 2014. *Xunzi: The Complete Text*, trans. Eric L. Hutton. Princeton: Princeton University Press.

Ye, Qingchun 叶青春. 2012. "'性'的失语与'情'的独语：阳明学性情思想及影响考察 [The Lost Voice of 'Nature' and the Soliloquy of 'Emotion': Investigating the Thought and Influence of the Yangming School's Views of Nature and Emotion]." *Journal of Yanbian University (Social Science)* 延边大学学报(社会科学版) 45(4): 53–9.

Yearley, Lee H. 1990. *Mencius and Aquinas: Theories of Virtue and Conceptions of Courage.* Albany: SUNY Press.

Yu, Anthony C. 1997. *Rereading the Stone: Desire and the Making of Fiction in Dream of the Red Chamber.* Princeton: Princeton University Press.

Yu, Yamanoi. 1986. "The Great Ultimate and Heaven in Chu Hsi's Philosophy." In Wing-tsit Chan (ed.), *Chu Hsi and Neo-Confucianism*, Honolulu: University of Hawaii Press, pp. 79–115.

Yu, Ying-shih. 1986. "Morality and Knowledge in Chu Hsi's Philosophical System." In Wing-tsit Chan (ed.), *Chu Hsi and Neo-Confucianism*. Honolulu: University of Hawaii Press, pp. 228–54.

Yu, Ying-shih 余英时. 2004. *Zhu Xi de Lishi Shijie: Song Dai Shi Dafu Zhengzhi Wenhua de Yanjiu* 朱熹的历史世界：宋代士大夫政治文化的研究 [*The Historical World of ZHU Xi: Investigations into the Political Culture of the Song Dynasty Scholar-Officials*]. Beijing: Sanlian Shudian.

Zhang, Dainian. 2002. *Key Concepts in Chinese Philosophy*, trans. Edmund Ryden. New Haven: Yale University Press.

Zhang, Zai 張載. 1978. *Zhang Zai Ji* 張載集 [*Collected Works of ZHANG Zai*]. Beijing: Zhonghua Shuju.

Zheng 鄭. (n.d.). (personal name unknown). "女孝經 [The Book of Filial Piety for Women]." In *Tingyu Tang Congke* 聽雨堂叢刻•女兒書. Zhang Chengxie 張承燮 (ed.). 6.1a–13a (輯第六), pp. 1–13.

Zheng. 2001. (personal name unknown). "The Book of Filial Piety for Women." In Susan Mann and Yu-yin Cheng (eds), *Under Confucian Eyes: Writings on Gender in Chinese History*. Berkeley and Los Angeles: University of California Press, pp. 47–69.

Zhou, Dunyi 周敦頤. 1990. *Zhou Dunyi Ji* 周敦頤集 [*The Collected Works of ZHOU Dunyi*]. Beijing: Zhonghua Shuju.

Zhu, Changche 朱昌彻. 2003. "浅论王廷相的认识论 [On Wang Tingxiang's Theory of Knowledge]." 赣南师范学院学报 [*Journal of Gannan Normal University*] 1: 8–12.

Zhu, Cheng 朱承. 2008. 治心與治世–王陽明哲學的政治向度 [*Governing the Heartmind and Governing the World: The Political Dimensions of WANG Yangming's Philosophy*]. Shanghai: Shanghai Renmin Chuban She.

Zhu, Xi 朱熹. 1974. *Xu Jinsi Lu* 續近思錄 [*Further Reflections on Things at Hand*], ed. ZHANG Boxing. Shijie Shuju.

Zhu, Xi 朱熹. 1987. *Sishu Zhangju Jizhu* 四书章句集注 [*Collected Commentaries on the Four Books*]. Shanghai: Shanghai Shudian.

Zhu, Xi. 1990. *Learning to be a Sage*, trans. Daniel K. Gardner. Berkeley: University of California Press.

Zhu, Xi. 1991a. *Chu Hsi's Family Rituals: A Twelfth-Century Chinese Manual for the Performance of Cappings, Weddings, Funerals, and Ancestral Rites*, trans. Patricia Buckley Ebrey. Princeton: Princeton University Press.

Zhu, Xi. 1991b. *Further Reflections on Things at Hand*, trans. Allen Wittenborn. Lanham: University Press of America.

Zhu, Xi 朱熹. 2002. *Zhuzi Quanshu* 朱子全書 [*Complete Works of Master Zhu*]. Shanghai and Hefei: Shanghai Guji Chuban She and Anhui Jiaoyu Chuban She.

Zhu, Xi, and Lü, Zuqian. 1967. *Reflections on Things at Hand*, trans. Wing-tsit Chan. New York: Columbia University Press.

Zhu, Xi 朱熹, and Lü, Zuqian 呂祖謙. 2008. *Jinsi Lu* 近思錄 [*Reflections on Things at Hand*]. Zhengzhou: Zhongzhou Guji Chuban She.

Zhuangzi 莊子. 2001. *Zhuangzi Jishi* 莊子集釋 [*Collected Explanations of the Zhuangzi*], ed. Guo Qingfan 郭慶藩. Taibei: Dingyuan Wenhua Shiye.

Ziporyn, Brook. 2000. *Evil and/or/as the Good: Omnicentrism, Intersubjectivity, and Value Paradox in Tiantai Buddhist Thought*. Cambridge, MA: Harvard University Asia Center.

Ziporyn, Brook. 2012. *Ironies of Oneness and Difference: Coherence in Early Chinese Thought; Prolegomena to the Study of Li* 理. Albany: State University of New York Press.

Ziporyn, Brook. 2013. *Beyond Oneness and Difference: Li and Coherence in Chinese Buddhist Thought and Its Antecedents*. Albany, NY: State University of New York Press.

Ziporyn, Brook. 2015. "Harmony as Substance: Zhang Zai's Metaphysics of Polar Relations," in Chenyang Li and Franklin Perkins (eds), *Chinese Metaphysics and Its Problems*. Cambridge: Cambridge University Press, pp. 253–82.

Ziporyn, Brook. Forthcoming. "The Ti/Yong Model and Its Discontents: Models of Ambiguous Priority in Chinese Buddhism and Neo-Confucianism." In John Makeham (ed.), *The Buddhist Roots of Zhu Xi's Thought*.

Zongmi. 1995. *Inquiry into the Origin of Humanity*, trans. Peter N. Gregory. Honolulu: University of Hawaii.

Index